Wisdom of the Heart

Wisdom of the Heart

The Teachings of Rabbi Ya'akov of Izbica-Radzyn

Ora Wiskind-Elper

2010 • 5770
The Jewish Publication Society
Philadelphia

JPS is a nonprofit educational association and the oldest and foremost publisher of Judaica in English in North America. The mission of JPS is to enhance Jewish culture by promoting the dissemination of religious and secular works, in the United States and abroad, to all individuals and institutions interested in past and contemporary Jewish life.

The Jewish Publication Society
2100 Arch Street, 2nd floor
Philadelphia, PA 19103
www.jewishpub.org

Design and composition by Desperate Hours Productions
Manufactured in the United States of America

10 11 12 13 10 9 8 7 6 5 4 3 2 1

ISBN: 978-0-8276-0894-8
eISBN: 978-0-8276-0950-1

Library of Congress Cataloging-in-Publication Data:

Wiskind-Elper, Ora, 1960–
Wisdom of the heart : the teachings of Rabbi Ya'akov of Izbica-Radzyn / Ora Wiskind-Elper. — 1st ed.
p. cm.
Includes bibliographical references and index.
ISBN 978-0-8276-0894-8 (alk. paper)
1. Leiner, Ya'akov, 1818–1878—Teachings. 2. Hasidism—Poland—Izbica. 3. Hasidism—Poland—Radzyn Podlaski. I. Title.
BM755.L418W57 2010
296.8'332092--dc22

2009042310

To Eliezer

איש בריתי

Contents

Acknowledgments

"Like mushrooms in the forest," the contents of this book emerged in some unexplainable way amid the leaves, between the trees that fill my days. A debt of gratitude is owed to those who have given me the opportunity to teach—to Rabbis Yehuda Kopperman, Chaim Pollack, Mordecai Kopperman, and Devorah Rosenwasser of Michlalah College, Jerusalem; and to Carmi Horowitz, Nechama Grunhaus, and Joseph Tabory of the Lander Institute of Jewish Studies, Jerusalem. Much in the chapters of this book developed through the interest and searching of my students, who have learned together with me over the years.

The wisdom, spirit, and kindness of my own teachers find expression in every page of this book. In different and important ways, Avivah Gottlieb Zornberg, Erich Heller, Stephane Moses, Jacob Elbaum, Tom Smith, R. Tuvia Rosen, and Jenny Rosen have taught me how to read and write, think, feel, and understand.

Simi Peters, Harvey Belovski, Ellen Sucov, Edna Azriel, and Avivah Zornberg read drafts of these chapters at various stages. The interest and encouragement of these dear friends and colleagues somehow always came at just the right time—directing, focusing, and strengthening my lines of thought. I am especially grateful to Susan Handelman, who not only read and gently but firmly critiqued my work but also introduced me to Ellen Frankel of The Jewish Publication Society. Susie's endless reserves of hope and vision have guided me through many a narrow place. R. Elchanan Reuven Goldhaber generously helped clarify vital biographical and historical details related to Izbica-Radzyn tradition. Special thanks to Rena Potok for her enthusiastic reception of the book from the very beginning. My gratitude, finally, to Karen Schnitker, Janet Liss, Anita Bihovsky and the rest of the staff of The Jewish Publication Society who efficiently and graciously saw the work through to publication.

Expressions of thanks sound most inadequate when it comes to those who are closest. My first teachers are my parents, Edith and Milton Wiskind.

They and my parents-in-law, Larissa and Gregory Elper, have been a warm and wonderful presence and a continual source of support for our family. My husband Eliezer and our children know that blessings (and gratitude) dwell most securely in places that remain concealed from the public eye.

R. Simḥah Bunem of Przysucha is said to have offered these words of advice: "Every person must find oneself a teacher from among the living, and a teacher from among the great ones in the World of Truth." Over the months and years during which this book took form, I've come to see who those two figures are for me. "Among the living"—my deepest gratitude is to Rabbi Daniel Epstein, without whose influence this book would never have been written. May he be blessed with health and length of days, gratification from his children, grandchildren, and students, and continued strength to share his own "wisdom of the heart" with all who can listen. And, "in the World of Truth"—my thanks, far beyond what words can express, to Rabbi Ya'akov of Izbica-Radzyn, of blessed memory. His soul's greatness, audible and tangible in every line of his teachings, has guided, inspired, and formed me immeasurably. May the power and holiness of his words help my own readers find a way "home" in the *Beit Ya'akov.*

Introduction

> Sometimes I was afraid to be alone at night or to go outside by myself. But my grandfather, of blessed memory, tried in many ways to help me become courageous. Once, late at night, when no one but I was in his room, he said, "Would you like to go for a walk with me?" I answered, "If you'll be with me I would." So he took his cane and said, "Come with me." We walked together through the darkness, and he showed me different things, and he talked with me about how one shouldn't fear anything in the world.
>
> —*Dor Yesharim*

These memories, written by R. Ḥayyim Simḥah Leiner, preface the family history he compiled and first published in 1909.[1] The grandfather of his childhood is Rabbi Ya'akov Leiner, whose teachings are the subject of this book.[2] R. Ya'akov (1818–1878) was the rebbe and spiritual leader of a community of Hasidim in Izbica and then in Radzyn, located in the Podalski region of Congress Poland for over 24 years. His quiet, unassuming manner, his incisive scholarship in the revealed and concealed Torah, and his profound understanding of the human soul won the respect and affection of all who knew him. The discourses and insights he shared throughout his life were gathered by his sons and grandson in four large volumes entitled *Beit Ya'akov* (The House of Jacob). They are a powerful testimony to the richness and depth of Hasidic thought and to the authentic spiritual quest that is its driving force.

This book seeks to present the treasure of thought and sensibility voiced in his teachings to the modern reader. Ironically, the quiet greatness of the *Beit Ya'akov*—comprising both the personal figure of R. Ya'akov and the works in his name—has remained nearly invisible to both the wider Jewish community and the scholarly world. One reason for that is surely the dense, highly allusive nature of the texts, with their complex structure and often uncustomary manner of expression. A second, more concealed reason concerns the stormy political climate in which this branch of Hasidic thought developed in the middle decades of the 19th century. Before we turn to a closer consideration of these important factors, I would like to offer some words in explanation of how the book before you is put together.

Overview of Contents

Chapter 1

Chapter 1 introduces some of the groundwork underlying the edifice of R. Ya'akov's thought as a whole. Dualities or countervalences inform human experience and exert a profound psychological and spiritual influence on perceptions of reality. These valences crystallize, for most people, in clear hierarchical relations: light and darkness, right and left, day and night, soul and body, wakefulness and sleep. My suggestion, in this first chapter, is that attention to the "minor modes" or "other side" of human experience is a continual and essential guiding force in R. Ya'akov's worldview. Uncovering the values of forgetting, translation, the back, and other forms often seen as deficient opens new horizons and ways of understanding. This fundamental belief is at the root of many of the themes that will emerge in subsequent chapters. The logic that guides this chapter is admittedly nonlinear. It requires the reader to follow associative and intuitive leaps—to use that very other side of consciousness it seeks to discover. Guiding this approach is an attempt to initiate the reader into the atmosphere of these teachings, rather than merely naming and explaining the themes they discuss.

Chapter 2

The second chapter attempts to understand the notion of the self as it takes form in R. Ya'akov's teachings. It begins with a look at some of the hermeneutical tools developed in the first generations of Hasidic exegetical tradition. These include the fundamental importance of self-knowledge; the search for the personal relevance encoded in every verse of Scripture, with its multiple layers of meaning; and the emotional and psychological responses that must be evoked through engagement with the Torah. The unique approach that took form in Izbica-Radzyn tradition, voiced most explicitly by R. Gershon Ḥanokh Henikh in his "Introduction" to the *Beit Ya'akov*, is considered in that context.

This theoretical and historical preface provides a framework in which the rest of Chapter 2 takes form. It focuses on two biblical figures—Moses and Judah. An attentive reading of many of R. Ya'akov's teachings shows that, in effect, he conceives of both Moses and Judah as evolving "selves" who pass through successive stages of psychic and spiritual development. Moses' individual path toward self-understanding is set against the background of a similar process unfolding within the Jewish nation and leading the people toward a coherent, collective sense of selfhood. The resonances between personal and national realms play an important role in defining Moses' metahistorical identity. An additional, cogent dimension of that identity, however, concerns the potential for growth that exists for every individual, realized through dialogue and humility.

The second portrait of an evolving self is more readily evident in the biblical narrative. The figure of Judah is sketched through the chapters of his life and deeds. In R. Ya'akov's commentary, the thoughts, emotions, and inner worlds of many of the major players in Judah's life are explored with striking directness. These insights chart the spiritual journey Judah personally undergoes. This journey leads to the discovery of some true, previously concealed identities, and toward a unique vision of the historical and metahistorical destiny of the Jewish people. A subtext relating to contemporary figures in Przysucha, Kotsk, and Izbica is considered in this context as well, along with some possible implications in forming the self-image of Izbica-Radzyn Hasidism.

Chapter 3

The third chapter addresses an original and largely unknown aspect of Izbica-Radzyn teaching: the role of figures of the feminine in understanding human experience.[3] It begins by setting out two central concepts developed in Hasidic thought from rabbinic and mystical tradition: *yirah* (symbolizing awe and the property of containment) and *mayyin nukvin* (feminine waters). Then the symbolic five-stage process of "becoming," first introduced in the teachings of his father, R. Mordecai Joseph, is considered through the lens of R. Ya'akov's commentary. These stages reflect fundamentals of Lurianic thought, while augmenting its metaphysical thrust with a thoroughly Hasidic dimension. *Zeri'ah* (the sowing of seed), *'ibbur* (conception/pregnancy), *leidah* (birthing), *yenikah* (nursing), and *moḥin* (consciousness) mirror successive stages in human life, psychological as well as physiological. Reflections on these themes are scattered throughout *Mei ha-Shiloaḥ* and *Beit Ya'akov*. Sometimes they are linked to biblical figures and their stories; in other cases they stem from the metaphors and imagery of biblical verses or from insights voiced in rabbinic literature. This chapter attempts to gather, order, and interpret the underlying sense of these disparate reflections. It brings to light a vital and thought-provoking aspect of Hasidic teaching and marks the contribution of Izbica-Radzyn tradition to understanding gender issues and forms of relatedness.

Chapter 4

Chapter 4 draws together many of the themes and issues raised in the course of the book. The axis of the discussion here consists of two poles, a beginning and an endpoint, two cogent loci of significance evoked frequently in Izbica-Radzyn tradition. The first is the controversial understanding of the biblical story of Adam, Eve, Creation, and sin proposed in *Mei ha-Shiloaḥ* and developed in *Beit Ya'akov*. This innovative and complex alternate reading is considered in detail, with attention to its implicit reevaluation of the feminine and corporeity. The second, opposite pole is a moment beyond time—the resurrection of the dead. Here, as well, the relationship between body and soul is reconsidered; new understandings about doubt, fear, death, and despair emerge. The alternate perspective R. Ya'akov offers, seen from a nearly unimaginable "other side," is a moving one. Refiguring sin and suffering, it gestures toward a way to hope.

To gain a fuller appreciation of the innovative teachings contained in the *Beit Ya'akov*, we must devote some attention to the religious and cultural milieu in which R. Ya'akov's thought took form. A heightened awareness of the circumstances at play during the formative stages of this Hasidic tradition will, in turn, aid us in evaluating some of the prevalent attitudes toward it that guide contemporary scholarship.

Above, I noted that many aspects of Izbica-Radzyn Hasidic tradition have remained largely unrecognized, both in Jewish and in wider intellectual circles. One unfortunate result of this is that accurate elementary information, biographical as well as bibliographical, concerning its central figures is difficult to find. In the following section, I have tried to fill in some needed details to offer a broader framework of understanding.

Izbica-Radzyn Hasidism in Historical Context

R. Yaʿakov was heir to the nascent Hasidic dynasty of Izbica, founded by his father, R. Mordecai Joseph, in 1839. The events that led up to that move are infamous; the personages involved include many of the dominant figures in the contemporary Hasidic milieu. We'll recall them briefly, with the purpose of gaining a more comprehensive appraisal of the historical context in question.

R. Mordecai Joseph (1800–1854) entered the close circle of R. Simḥah Bunem of Przysucha as a young man around 1819. He joined a formidable group of peers and disciples, many of whom would later become famed in their own right by founding influential Hasidic dynasties of the 19th and 20th centuries. Among them were R. Isaac of Warka, R. Meir Yeḥiel of Mogielnica, R. Abraham of Ciechanow, R. Yeḥezkel Taub of Kuzmir, R. Ḥanokh of Alexander, R. Jacob Aryeh of Radzymin, R. Isaac Meir of Ger, and R. Menaḥem Mendel of Kotsk. All of them had been drawn to Przysucha and chose to follow the radical new path that was being forged there.

In the first decade of the 19th century, Przysucha became the focus of controversy and innovation in the Hasidic world under the aegis of R. Jacob Isaac Rabinowitz (1766–1813), the "Holy Jew." The new ideals that Przysucha embodied were spiritual autonomy, extreme personal integrity, intellectual rigor, and the return to serious, traditional study of Talmud as well as medieval and early modern Jewish philosophy. These values galvanized the energies of many Jews in search of an intense and authentic religious life.

Upon the passing of the Holy Jew in 1813, some of his followers transferred their allegiance to his son, R. Yeraḥmiel. The majority placed their loyalty with his disciple R. Simḥah Bunem (1765–1827). A colorful and unusual figure, R. Simḥah Bunem incorporated a variety of influences. His activities in the timber business, his involvement with the secular Jewish and non-Jewish worlds, his Western dress, and his medical education are well known. In his youth, R. Simḥah Bunem received a thorough traditional education as well as exposure to Jewish medieval philosophy and kabbalistic teaching. His masters in the Hasidic world included R. Moses Aryeh Leib of Sassov; R. Israel, the Maggid of Koznience; and R. David of Lalov. According to Izbica-Radzyn tradition, R. Simḥah Bunem enjoyed a close relationship with R. Jacob Isaac, the Seer of Lublin (1745–1815), who "transmitted the mysteries of Torah to him."[4] During the 13 years that R. Simḥah Bunem was rebbe, Przysucha grew into a thriving center of Hasidic life in Central Poland.

These were formative years for R. Mordecai Joseph. Like many of R. Simḥah Bunem's disciples, R. Mordecai Joseph assimilated much in Przysucha that would guide him throughout his life. His grandson recounts that R. Simḥah Bunem foresaw R. Mordecai Joseph's future greatness. "He once said that he is like the waters of Siloam—though they flow slowly, they penetrate to the utmost depths."[5]

When R. Simḥah Bunem died in 1827, his followers split ranks. A small group maintained allegiance with his son, R. Abraham Moses. The majority recognized one of his eminent disciples, R. Menaḥem Mendel Morgenstern-Halperin (1787–1859), as the successor of Przysucha tradition, and subsequently moved with him to Kotsk. Among the many peer/disciples in that group were R. Isaac Meir Rotenberg-Alter, the future founder of the Hasidic dynasty of Ger; R. Ḥanokh of Alexander; and R. Mordecai Joseph.

R. Mordecai Joseph spent the next 13 years in the court of R. Menaḥem Mendel of Kotsk. Izbica-Radzyn tradition portrays this as an intense and difficult period. R. Mordecai Joseph's own path began to take form dialectically, in response and in opposition to the ways of R. Menaḥem Mendel. Following Simḥat Torah in the Hebrew year 5600 (1839–1840), a portentous date in mystical tradition, R. Mordecai Joseph left the circle of R. Menaḥem Mendel. After some months in nearby Tomaszow, his birthplace, he and his family moved to the neighboring town of Izbica, where he began to act as rebbe.[6] Some of the Hasidim who had been followers of R. Menaḥem Mendel, among them R. Leibele Eiger (1816–1888), left Kotsk to join R. Mordecai Joseph in Izbica. Other prominent figures, including R. Zaddok Ha-Kohen (1823–1900), later of Lublin, entered the circle that had gathered in Izbica and recognized R. Mordecai Joseph as their master.

The animosity and, at times, open battle between key figures in Kotsk and Izbica has been amply documented. We'll leave its details to others.[7] The main effect of this tension most relevant to our discussion was that it pushed R. Mordecai Joseph and Izbica off to the margins of the Jewish world. R. Mordecai Joseph himself left no written record of his beliefs and motivations. The dominant voices that would guide historical memory were those inimical to Izbica on personal or ideological grounds. Thus R. Mordecai Joseph is absent from a major bibliography documenting the period, *Shem ha-Gedolim he-Ḥadash* (Warsaw, 1864), written by Aaron Walden, a follower of Kotsk; a second important collection of testimony on contemporary Hasidic life, *Siaḥ Sarfei Kodesh*, compiled by an adherent of Gerer Hasidism, contains but a handful of references to R. Mordecai Joseph, most of them unsympathetic.[8]

R. Mordecai Joseph served as rebbe in Izbica for 13 years. Like most Hasidic masters of the period, his teachings were transmitted orally, most probably in Yiddish. Some of them were written down and at times incorporated by his sons, grandsons, and disciples in various contexts, including their own works.

Six years after his death, the first volume of teachings in his name, gathered from these notes by his grandson, R. Gershon Ḥanokh Henikh, was published under the title *Mei ha-Shiloaḥ*. A second volume of the same title was compiled by his grandson R. Mordecai Joseph of Lublin and published in 1922.[9]

R. Mordecai Joseph and his wife Tobe had two sons. The younger son, R. Samuel Dov Asher (died 1915), served for much of his life as rabbi in the town of Biskovitz. His Torah commentary, *Neot Deshe*, and stories recorded in his name present material concerning Przysucha and R. Mordecai Joseph's teachings. The firstborn son, R. Ya'akov, became rebbe of Izbica as his father's successor upon his passing. Izbica-Radzyn tradition speaks of the years R. Ya'akov served as spiritual leader as a peaceful and prosperous time. His humility and dislike for controversy and sensation neutralized some of the tension that had beset Izbica during his father's lifetime.[10]

In the course of his 13th year in Izbica, R. Ya'akov moved with his followers to Radzyn, a small town 60 kilometers north of Lublin. His son R. Abraham Joshua Heschel reflected on the reason behind this move: "Most leaders tended the flocks of Yeshurun no more than 13 years—so it was for the holy Rebbe [Simḥah Bunem] of Przyshucha and for [R. Mordecai Joseph] the author of *Mei ha-Shiloaḥ*. … And for that reason [R. Ya'akov] served as rebbe in Izbica for 13 years, and then changed his place to Radzyn, where he served another similar period."[11] By the time of R. Ya'akov's passing in 1878, Radzyn had grown into a significant Hasidic community.[12]

Further Publication of Izbica-Radzyn Teachings and Dynastic Successors

R. Ya'akov and his wife Ḥavva had two sons and a daughter. The oldest son, R. Gershon Ḥanokh Henikh, initiated the publication of his father's teachings. The first volume of *Beit Ya'akov* on Genesis (Warsaw, 1891) contains discourses that R. Gershon Ḥanokh recorded personally or collected from notes written by other students. He writes of this process in his "Introduction" to the *Beit Ya'akov* published at the beginning of that volume.[13] R. Ya'akov's second son, R. Abraham Joshua Heschel, took on the responsibility of publishing the second volume of his father's teachings, *Beit Ya'akov* on Exodus (Lublin, 1904), which he recorded and collected in a similar manner. R. Abraham Joshua Heschel and his wife Pesa Riva had four sons. The oldest, R. Ḥayyim Simḥah, authored the family history entitled *Dor Yesharim*. Another son, R. Ḥanina David, gathered and edited the third volume of teachings by his grandfather,

R. Ya'akov. They were published as *Beit Ya'akov* on Leviticus (Lublin, 1937).[14] A fourth volume of R. Ya'akov's teachings was published by R. Yeruḥam, son of R. Abraham Joshua Heschel and his second wife, on the basis of manuscripts written by R. Gershon Ḥanokh Henikh (Lublin, 1906). It included short teachings on all five books of the Torah, the festivals, and other subjects.[15]

After the premature death of his wife Ḥavva in 1854, R. Ya'akov remarried, but divorced soon afterward.[16] Some years later he married again and fathered two sons and two daughters. One son of this marriage in the later years of R. Ya'akov's life was R. Yeruḥam Meir. The other was R. Mordecai Joseph of Lublin. From the handwritten notes of disciples, R. Mordecai Joseph gathered teachings spoken by his grandfather that had not been included in the first volume of *Mei ha-Shiloaḥ* and published them in a second volume (Lublin, 1922).[17]

Many other manuscripts recording R. Ya'akov's teachings were lost in the Holocaust. These include his commentary on Numbers, Deuteronomy, and the festivals; commentary on the *Siddur* and *ta'amei ha-mitzvot*; and commentaries on the kabbalistic works *Zohar, Tikkunei Zohar,* and *'Etz Ḥayyim.* His son, R. Gershon Ḥanokh Henikh, lists these as still-unpublished works; his grandson, R. Yeruḥam, commemorates them in *Ma'amar Zikaron la-Rishonim* as having been consumed in flame along with Polish Jewry.[18]

R. Ya'akov passed away on 15 Av, 5638/1878. After a short period, leadership of the Izbica-Radzyn dynasty was taken up by his elder son, R. Gershon Ḥanokh Henikh. A commanding figure, R. Gershon Ḥanokh's fiery personality and political activism soon returned Radzyn to the focus of controversy.[19] He became known for his innovative publishing activities and his revolutionary claim to have rediscovered the snail known as the *ḥilazon,* said to produce the dye (*tekhelet*) needed for the blue thread of the tzitzit. He was also noted for his extensive halakhic defenses, which aroused the opposition of rabbinic authorities throughout the world.[20]

Unlike his father, R. Ya'akov, who never responded openly to the polemic that was waged against Izbica, R. Gershon Ḥanokh confronted the opposition directly. Similar to his grandfather in temperament, and clearly motivated by his own messianic convictions, R. Gershon Ḥanokh inarguably "captured the headlines." His flamboyant presence and strength of conviction, it seems, have played a notable part in diverting attention from R. Ya'akov's place in Izbica-Radzyn tradition.

When he passed away, leadership of the dynasty was inherited by R. Mordecai Joseph Elazar, the only son of R. Gershon Ḥanokh Henikh and his wife Hadassah. R. Mordecai Joseph Eleazar's Torah commentary, entitled *Tiferet*

Yosef, is based on the teachings developed in Izbica-Radzyn tradition.[21] His son, R. Samuel Solomon, was the last dynastic successor to serve as rebbe of Izbica-Radzyn Hasidism. R. Samuel Solomon's heroic death in 1942, when he was summoned and shot by Nazi gunfire in the cemetery of Wlodawa, is legendary.[22]

Most of the thousands of Radzyn Hasidim in Poland perished in the Holocaust. The few who survived resettled in Israel and the United States. Small groups gathered in Bene-Berak, Tel Aviv, Netanya, Haifa, and Jerusalem; others joined the Radzyn Hasidim already in Borough Park, Brooklyn.[23] In 1953, the community in Israel named as rebbe R. Abraham Issakhar Englard, brother of R. Samuel Solomon's wife, Shifra Mirel. He actively served as head of the community in Bene-Berak from 1971 until his death in 2005.[24] His successor has not yet been named definitively.

Academic Discourse on Izbica-Radzyn Tradition

The teachings attributed to R. Mordecai Joseph of Izbica, recorded in *Mei ha-Shiloaḥ*, are considered to be the most radical of all branches of Hasidic thought. Terms associated with these teachings include "anarchism," "religious determinism," "freedom of the spirit," "idiosyncratic interpretation of divine will," "antinomianism," and "heresy." Academic discussion has focused almost exclusively on the nonconformist aspect of Izbica-Radzyn tradition.

R. Ya'akov's presence in that tradition has been overlooked (at best) by every scholar who has studied it. For example, Morris Faierstein states: "The pivotal figure in the history of the Radzyn period was Mordecai Joseph's grandson, Gershon Henoch … The writings of Mordecai Joseph's son, Jacob Leiner of Izbica-Radzyn, which elaborate some of the less controversial strains in Mordecai Joseph's thought, offer little that illuminates Mordecai Joseph's more radical ideas."[25] Joseph Weiss wrote: "The works of Jacob Leiner (d. 1878), son of Mordecai Joseph, already show a marked departure from the radical ideas of his father. The briefly formulated, keen lines of thought of the father are elaborated and embedded in endless quotations from the *Zohar* and related literature. There is, in general, a noticeable tendency to tone down the more radical expressions to make them more acceptable."[26] In Shaul Magid's estimation: "The real ideological architect behind the Izbica/Radzin dynasty is Rabbi Gershon Henokh Lainer of Radzin. The opaque and sketchy comments in R. Mordecai Joseph's *Mei Ha-shiloah* are not conducive to careful scholarly analysis without reference to R. Gershon Henoch's more voluminous writings on the Torah and the Zohar."[27] Jerome Gellman says: "The son of Mordecai Joseph, Jacob

Leiner, beginning with the language of his father, proceeds to moderate the father's radicality by interpreting the latter's words in a more prosaic sense than that suggested by the wording."[28]

While identifying provocative, even iconoclastic thought is an important scholarly pursuit, in this case it risks obscuring a larger picture. Issues of free choice, responsibility and sin, unequivocal truth and illusion are indeed vital aspects of this Hasidic school of thought. I would suggest, though, that placing them as the sole element of value is misguided. Moreover, to analyze by isolating and abstracting those subjects does an injustice to the living tradition from which they stem. An insider to that tradition, R. Elḥanan Goldhaber, sees things somewhat differently: "Without the *Beit Ya'akov* we wouldn't have Izbica." That is, R. Ya'akov's teachings are an essential, integral means of understanding the ideology first voiced by his father, R. Mordecai Joseph, and recorded in brief, often cryptic form in *Mei ha-Shiloaḥ*.[29] This is the guiding force in my own reading. It seeks, among other interests, to reconsider the "radical" aspects of Izbica-Radzyn tradition and to formulate an understanding of their meaning in the broadest possible textual framework.

Methodology

The teachings recorded in R. Ya'akov of Radzyn's name belong to the genre known as homilies, or *derashot*. Like R. Mordecai Joseph's teachings, and like nearly all written Hasidic works of the 18th and 19th centuries, they were originally spoken in Yiddish and recorded later from memory, in Hebrew, by his students.[30] Formally, they are arranged following the order of the weekly Torah portions and the cycle of the Jewish festivals. Their language is recondite, often enigmatic, and charged with intertextual allusions. At the same time, the sense of their immediate, personal address is evident, a direct appeal to the listener/reader to contemplate and internalize their larger message. The content of this commentary goes far beyond interpretative exegesis of the Bible in its overtly present narratives and verses. For all Hasidic masters, R. Ya'akov included, the overarching concerns are questions of the highest order—metaphysical truth, religious faith, the nature of the self. The biblical text offers a familiar matrix in which these issues can be addressed. That basic text is then refracted through the prism of traditional Jewish exegesis—including midrash, medieval commentary, Kabbalah, and Hasidic thought. In addition to the layers of sources, the hermeneutical tools developed in earlier generations of Hasidic interpretative tradition play a vital role in R. Ya'akov's unique project of reading.

The challenges involved in opening this remarkable work to a modern, English-speaking audience are formidable. To recast its ideas into understandable form goes far beyond the linguistic struggles every translator confronts. These powerful teachings, written in Hebrew, engage the reader on many levels—intellectually, emotionally, and psychologically. At the same time, the length of the teachings, their formulation, and their highly unsystematic nature resist facile generalization and comfortable, ready-made conclusions. Traditional Hasidic style is discursive; important concepts and central themes emerge associatively, in varied and often unexpected contexts. Identifying and gathering these separate pieces into some kind of coherent unity, relating one unit to another, demands patience, memory, and a good measure of trust that an integral worldview really does stand behind it all.

Undeniably, R. Ya'akov's teaching is rooted in the original ideas engendered by his father, R. Mordecai Joseph, in the light of central innovations of the Przysucha Hasidic school. An attentive, sustained reading of many pages of the *Beit Ya'akov* makes clear that one of R. Ya'akov's goals is to set out those innovations, recorded in *Mei ha-Shiloaḥ* in laconic, coded form, in a manner he believed was loyal to R. Mordecai Joseph's intent.

At the same time, R. Ya'akov must be seen as an original and impressive thinker in his own right. His teachings are deeply informed by his own sensibility, intellectual acumen, and personal experience. For these reasons, the *Beit Ya'akov* forms an integral part of Izbica-Radzyn tradition. I have tried to portray this composite ideological entity with awareness of the multiple, distinct elements within it.

The perspective offered here is informed by modern sensibilities. It seeks to bring these Hasidic teachings into dialogue with current modes of literary and philosophical criticism. At the same time, it retains the greatest respect for the integrity, depth, and inherent reserve of the text. These teachings resist rigorous analysis. Their power cannot be unlocked with objective, analytical tools alone. While taking historical context into account, the focus here is not a comparison with other schools of Hasidism, influences, and effects. Nor does it engage in academic polemics with other interpretations of Izbica-Radzyn tradition.

My approach integrates close readings of R. Ya'akov's teachings with consideration of the interpretative principles at work in them. Care is taken to note the dynamics among layers of meaning and between one context and another. I believe that presenting and distinguishing these layers is an essential factor in preserving the authenticity of classic Jewish text study. Thus, I've tried to set out the primary sources—biblical verses, midrashic interpretations, Talmudic statements, citations of and allusions to kabbalistic works—interwoven in his commentary. At times, I have cited a few additional words to clarify the context of the teachings and appreciate their original meaning more clearly.[31] Determining that original meaning, of course, involves a second textual substructure—the classical commentaries on the Bible, midrash, and Talmud, and the library of Jewish thought potentially relevant to a Hasidic thinker in 19th-century Poland.[32] This second layer often proves to be an interface between the prooftexts chosen and the Hasidic teaching that emerges from them. My discussion seeks to be attentive to this interplay of voices and the role of each of them in conveying meaning.

As for conventions of style: whenever possible, I used the New Jewish Publication Society translation of the Bible (NJPS). This, however, was often not possible, as these Hasidic homilies frequently part ways from conventional understanding of the biblical verses. In such cases, I offer a translation that reflects or cooperates with R. Ya'akov's reading of the verse.[33] Translations of all other texts are my own, unless noted otherwise, for the same reasons. Transliteration of names and *parshiyot* follows JPS guidelines and/or the *Encyclopedia Judaica*. The obvious exception, of course, is the name of R. Ya'akov.[34]

References to the volumes of *Beit Ya'akov* include note of the volume (1 corresponds to Genesis; 2 corresponds to Exodus; 3 corresponds to Leviticus; and 4 corresponds to *Beit Ya'akov ha-Kollel* and *Likkutim*), the name of the *parashah*, and the teachings as they are numbered in the standard Jerusalem (1997–1998) editions. In the case of exceptionally long teachings, I noted the page number(s) as well, according to the Arabic numeration of the standard edition. References to *Mei ha-Shiloaḥ* note the volume, the *parashah*, and the page number in the Bene-Berak 1995 edition. References to *Sod Yesharim al-ha-Torah* (*Tinyana*) are to the Brooklyn 1982 edition; references to *Sod Yesharim* on the festivals are to the Brooklyn 1992 editions.

Finally, it has been said that no one writes without a personal agenda. Some time would probably be saved, then, by putting mine on paper right here at the outset. I've tried to give the *Beit Ya'akov* a fair reading, without getting in the way too much. I wanted to open R. Ya'akov's teachings to a wide reading audience, with or without knowledge of Hebrew, with or without a solid background in Jewish texts. I tried to be as loyal as possible to the letter and spirit of those teachings while pouring them from one cultural-linguistic vessel to another. I hope that I have struck some form of balance between academic rigor and human authenticity, at least most times, in the pages and notes of this book.

R. Ya'akov's son, R. Abraham Joshua Heschel, closes his redaction of *Beit Ya'akov* on Exodus with these verses:

> Just as the rain and snow drops from heaven and returns not there, but soaks the earth and makes it bring forth vegetation, yielding seed for sowing and bread for eating—So is the word that issues from My mouth: It does not come back to Me unfulfilled, but performs what I purpose and achieves what I sent it to do. (Isa. 56:10–11)[35]

That, it seems, was R. Yaʿakov's agenda—to plant the words he had understood in the hearts of those who heard him, trusting and knowing they will someday bear fruit.

Chapter 1

A World of Opposites

Introduction: The "Two" and the "One"

> Lift your eyes on high and behold: *Who* has created these things, *Who* brings out their host by numbers; He calls them all by name. Because of the greatness of His might, and His strong power, not one is missing. (Isa. 40:26)

> שְׂאוּ מָרוֹם עֵינֵיכֶם וּרְאוּ מִי בָרָא אֵלֶּה הַמּוֹצִיא בְמִסְפָּר צְבָאָם לְכֻלָּם בְּשֵׁם יִקְרָא מֵרֹב אוֹנִים וְאַמִּיץ כֹּחַ אִישׁ לֹא נֶעְדָּר.

"'Who,'" says Rabbi Ya'akov, "is there to be questioned." The teaching that follows, it seems to me, is seminal to our understanding of the Izbica-Radzyn Hasidic worldview. I would like to read it closely and draw from it some key concepts that will accompany us throughout the chapters to come.[1]

By basing his teaching on the same prophetic call evoked on the *Zohar*'s first page (fol. 1b), R. Ya'akov reawakens the sense of mystery shrouding the primordial act of Creation. The passage in the *Zohar* reads: "R. Elazar began: 'Lift up your eyes on high'—to that place on which all eyes depend, where all eyes are opened. There you will recognize that the Hidden Ancient One, who exists in order to be sought, has created all these. His Name is 'Who.'"

> ותמן תדעון דהאי סתים עתיקא דקיימא לשאלה ברא אלה ומאן איהו מ״י.

These lines are heavy with paradoxes: revelation in a place of concealment, a "name" uttering absence, knowledge emerging from questions. R. Ya'akov, guided by these opening words of the *Zohar*, proceeds to explore and develop that image of an anonymous Creator, dwelling incognito in a galaxy of phenomena named and numbered, each of them wholly unique.

> The very purpose of Creation was that all would be compelled to ask, "Who created all these?"—that all would know clearly that a supreme force, in His goodness, governs the world, and none would make a claim to autonomous power. To that end, God planted in each entity some lack, a fissure in its being, making them all incomplete. But Creation soon got used to that too—it ceased to notice its own deficiency; it didn't know it needed God. There was nothing to drive it to realize the higher power over it.

The world of phenomena, congenitally insensible, prone to self-absorption, cannot hold on to that vital creature-consciousness. The world tilts toward oblivion.

> Indeed, the darkness and concealment could expand to such an extent that all would forget forever the "Who" that had engendered them. God, though, did not hide Himself completely; He gave human beings the power to penetrate that concealment. Every element He composed of two opposing forces so that, seeing both of them, people would recognize the One supreme above the duality and would set their gaze upon Him alone.

What are these dualities that comprise the world? And how, through the humbling recognition of the "two," are we led to the "One"? The dichotomies R. Ya'akov chooses to cite, as this teaching unfolds, are valences that play a central role in his teaching as a whole. He recalls them again and again, in innumerable different contexts throughout his writings, to speak of forces that profoundly influence our lives—spiritually, psychologically, and intellectually. Each symbol, to be sure, already bears a rich heritage of associations from the Bible, midrash, and Kabbalah. R. Ya'akov draws on that strength to make his own cogent message even more convincing.

"In the city, no one thinks about the wilderness; but when one is there in the wilderness, one's whole being is there. Similarly, when one is asleep, one is unconscious, unaware; but when one is awake, one has no sense at all of what it is to sleep."[2] The root cause of this partial vision, says R. Ya'akov, is that people forget. While God's vision is panoramic, encompassing all aspects of experience simultaneously, we cannot comprehend the opposing sides of anything. To understand this limitation more fully, this tendency to forget, to lose hold of the opposite, balancing possibility of any experience, R. Ya'akov recalls a series of famous paradigms. Combined and restaged, they form a complex that we must understand.

> So it was during the creation of the world—at first, "He created many worlds and destroyed them all."[3] For each world expanded so excessively that they brought themselves to ruin. After that, God created our world, saying, "*This* one pleases Me." For He saw that it was able to contain itself, to ask, finally, "Who has created all this?"

On one hand, R. Ya'akov is saying, this world we know was able to remain in existence due to the measure of contraction it had attained. This one, at last, had awakened to the possibility of an "other" outside of itself. Certain flaws remained, however, and these fatally determined the course of history. To its credit,

> This generation strove to recognize the existence of its Creator. But each entity remained so taken up with its own essence [*middah*] that it was unable to make room for the others in their own uniqueness. For each entity on its own is weak. They should illuminate one another, but instead they closed themselves off from one another.

To clarify this idea, R. Ya'akov recalls and integrates a fundamental image from the mystical teachings of R. Isaac Luria.[4] "These newly created worlds functioned as 'circles' ['*iggulim*]. A 'straight line' [*kav ha-yosher*], in contrast, interconnects one entity with another; each circle, though, expands itself as much as it is able, with no relation to the other circles." This monadic egoism, R. Ya'akov explains, characterized the Generation of the Flood. God allowed their self-absorption to augment into a deluge, finally flooding them off the face of the earth. And God promised that such a thing would never happen again; each entity would now acknowledge the others outside of itself. "After that came the Generation of the Tower of Babel. They were 'One people, sharing one language' (Gen. 11:1)—all of them encompassed fully in one another."

The absolute alienation of the previous generation is replaced, here, with absolute unification. The consequences, however, are equally disastrous. "For they said, 'The unconscious forces uniting us all are so powerful; they fuse each of our essences together so completely. Hence, we have the right to conquer whatever we desire.'"

One vital flaw characterizes these two generations: the desire to expand, unbounded and infinitely. It is portrayed as an imperialistic drive to extend one's self endlessly, to annex and possess an ever-broadening domain. In the first scenario, each separate "circle," oblivious to everything exterior to itself, would invade the territory of others to inhabit the whole world. In the second one, the separate entities become allies. They join forces, but to the same sinister end: to engulf the world in the totality they have formed. For that reason, R. Ya'akov sees their alliance as an "evil conspiracy" (*kesher resha'im*) and thus they, too, must perish.

Perhaps the most remarkable aspect of this highly original reconstruction of prehistory is R. Ya'akov's combination of kabbalistic concepts with psychological factors. The two key words here are *hitpashtut* (expansion) and *hitkallelut* (inclusion).[5] The drive to expand and the drive to incorporate are equally reprehensible, in his eyes, because each violates the other.[6]

To speak of this "other," R. Ya'akov quite often uses the term "friend" (*ḥaver*), a turn of phrase (arguably unavoidable in the Hebrew current in 19th-century Poland) that heightens the ethical aspect of the issue. In breaking up the destructive totality that the tower builders plotted, God made clear that authentic unity must be conscious.

> Each individual must recognize clearly that the friend's uniqueness shines through him as well. Their connection should be that, perceiving one's own essence, the essence of others will become equally evident. The one must see the uniqueness of the other continually before him. Each individual must contain all the others, and this will keep each one from expanding beyond bounds. Then God's glory will be magnified by each of them. Theirs is a holy alliance [*kesher tzaddikim*] that will endure and direct their minds, in full awareness, to the "Who."[7]

This plurality, founded on mutual respect and preservation of difference, opens out onto a new metaphysical dimension. Returning to the *Zohar*, R. Ya'akov quotes the next lines: "'Who' [*mi*] is there in order to be questioned … And the letters join up with one another to form the divine Name *Elohim*. Until all these [*ele*] were created, God did not reveal Himself as *Elohim*." R. Ya'akov explains: "The Name 'Who' indicates that God alone controls His world and that He is wholly invisible to all the living. All of them wonder *who* that is, but He remains completely indifferent ['*ayn lo ḥefetz*] to the efforts, the prayers, and the good deeds of human beings. The name '*Ele*,' though, indicates the opposite."

What R. Ya'akov points to here is a detail, so to speak, of the Creation story. Throughout the first chapter of Genesis the divine Name *Elohim* is used exclusively. In that chapter, the manifold phenomena of the natural world are presented, one by one, each delineated and defined in its particularity. The divine name *Elohim*, significantly, is in the plural form—it is that composite force that generates multiplicity. By engendering the revealed world in the aspect of *Elohim*, God effectively made it accessible to human understanding.[8] One "day" follows another day. The sea and land, sky and abyss, stars and crocodiles each come into being with a separate "saying" of "Let there be ...." Each of them, faced with an opposing entity, is driven to seek something beyond its own experience. The awareness of multiplicity—of the *ele*—sparks the question of *mi*. These antithetical modes combine and transpose to form the Name *Elohim*.

At this juncture, having set out the principle of the world's inherent plurality, R. Ya'akov shifts to a new plane. He proceeds to reverse some of the most widely recognized hierarchies implicit in that plurality.

> Indeed, this world is the opposite of the World to Come. It seems to everyone that Night serves no purpose—we do not labor, there are no mitzvot. A person sleeping—what glory of Heaven is there in that? In truth, though, while people are asleep, God infuses them with Torah and mitzvot, affecting their strength to the very core, and granting all that each and every individual needs for the day to come. As it says in the holy *Zohar* (1.20b), "'And she rises while it is still night, giving food to her household and instruction to her maidservants' (Prov. 31:15)—Night is governed by the Feminine [ממשלת הלילה דנוקבא] ...." In the daytime, when people are awake, that strength instilled in each of them the night before, while they were unaware, expands, empowering them to perform so many mitzvot and other good deeds.

Perhaps most striking in this passage is the interest R. Ya'akov expresses in the "other side" of human existence. Night, sleep, unconsciousness—many consider these to be secondary or discountable.[9] Daytime, full of responsibilities, deliberate actions, intellectual control are—for most of us—*real* life. Maurice Blanchot explores this attitude, which holds that "night is what day must finally dissolve: day works as its empire; it is its own conquest and elaboration .... So says reason, the triumph of enlightenment which simply banishes darkness." Or, alternately, "Night is what day wants not just to dissolve, but to appropriate .... Night must pass into day. Night becoming day makes the light richer and gives to clarity's superficial sparkle a deep inner radiance. Then day is the whole of the day and the night, the great promise of the dialectic."[10] The two possibilities Blanchot describes, interestingly, resonate with the two modes of opposition we heard R. Ya'akov describe above: engaged either in conquest or in appropriation, day would deny night its own right to exist. R. Ya'akov responds to this common mindset by reminding us here that night indeed has a life of its own.

To speak of the realm of the unconscious and the hidden forces that influence human life, R. Ya'akov recalls things said long ago. The Rabbis taught that in the stillness of night, "hordes of ministering angels sing."[11] Those songs, he adds, "cast roots deep in the hearts of Jews, by the strength their souls have." The indwelling soul (*neshamah*) receives continually—be the body dormant or alert. God Himself breathed the spirit of life into the first human being who was still inert upon the earth (Gen. 2:7). Here, R. Ya'akov reminds us of the essence of that soul. He evokes an ancient mystical saying—"The Breather breathes His Self" (מי שנופח מעצמו הוא נופח). This divine force instilled in us is what enables us to live and speak.[12] Night, then, is a time of inspiration—in darkness, night by night, the soul is renewed and reinspired in the dormant body.

The memory of an intimate connection, the grandeur of bearing a unique soul—"You alone are called 'human' [*adam*]."[13] Here, once again, one could easily be convinced, as many have been, that the soul (like the day) is superior to the obscure, material body. And thus R. Ya'akov stresses, here as well, the dialectic involved. Whether we speak of divine attributes—*ḥesed* and *gevurah*—or natural elements, "Everything that God created in His worlds, apart from Himself, all is composite."[14] R. Ya'akov elaborates:

> For every thing has a feminine and a masculine aspect, "a helpmate" and "its counterpart"—and love and affection, unity and friendship dwell between them. Who has accomplished such a thing, to join such contrary elements? There must be one divine force, mighty beyond all of them—heaven and earth, sun and moon, soul and body, masculine and feminine. And He alone makes them one so that, from each duality, the world will come to recognize the force beyond them both, uniting them.[15]

This section concludes with a lyrical vision of unity and peace. I would venture to say, though, that for most of us, most of the time, such an idyllic sense of harmony remains a distant dream. We do see the opposites, but what we live is the tension and discord between them. Who is the moon? Where is the body's grandeur? To what purity can the dust of the earth hold claim? How can darkness be as brilliant as light?

I'd like to turn now to some other teachings in which R. Ya'akov focuses on minor modalities of human existence such as these. Through them, I hope, we may come to see a way of being "otherwise." The synthesis R. Ya'akov envisions may surely come to be, but only after both sides are more fully known.

The "Other Side": A Look at Some Minor Modes

"The Lord said to Moses and Aaron in the land of Egypt: 'This month shall be for you the first of all months ...'" (Exod. 12:2). Rashi, in his first comment on the opening words of Genesis, echoes a famous challenge: By rights, the Torah should have begun, not with the epic and universal saga of the cosmos, but with this modest verse.[16] "The first of all months": here *time* begins, the cycle of months marked by the moon, the personal history of the Jewish nation. Ironically, this mitzvah to sanctify each new month—the first glimmer of meaningful connection—is given in the "heart of darkness" and exile "in the land of Egypt." R. Ya'akov presents a series of teachings on this verse. He explores the nature of this counternarrative, with its invitation to understand an alternate manner of beginning. The *Zohar* says:

> But aren't all the months, and time itself, God's alone? And yet "This month will be for *you*." Really, it is Mine, but I will entrust it to you. It is yours in the revealed sphere; the seventh month, however, remains Mine, for it is hidden and unrevealed. Your month and its letters are in [alphabetical] order—אביב [*aviv*, Spring]. My month, the seventh, begins with the last letter—תשרי [*tishrei*, the Fall of Winter], and goes in reverse.[17]

The opposition here, to be considered in depth in the following pages, is based on the two possible "beginnings" of the Jewish calendar: on Rosh Hashanah, the official "head of the year," or in the month of Pesach, when the Jewish nation is born as an autonomous entity. To explain the unusual monologue cited above from the *Zohar*, R. Ya'akov begins by reminding us that the letters of the Hebrew alphabet, like the months and seasons with their names, are far from equal. Here, once again, we find an innovative re-presentation of kabbalistic concepts combined with unexpected psychological insights in order to clarify their inner meaning.

> *Tishrei*—its letters are in reverse order—ת before ש, ש before ר, ר before יו"ד. And the Divine Name that corresponds with this month is also totally backwards.[18] In other words, the letters are not turned outward to face the world, and thus they cannot give anything [*lehashpi'a*] to others ... In a sense, they are imprisoned in themselves.[19] Indeed, every instance of stricture [*din*], all darkness—all of it comes wholly from the letters being in reverse order. Reverse order—this means that they stand facing their Source [*ha-ma'atzil*].[20]

"Like a seed that cannot sprout, so the letters are backwards." What R. Ya'akov describes here is an apparent state of immobility—with their gaze transfixed on the Creator, the letters turn their backs, so to speak, to the rest of Creation. The world waits in darkness. Tishrei, which marks the onset of autumn, the day of divine judgment on earth and, finally, a passageway into the winter months, symbolizes "God's perspective." As we will see, it is diametrically opposed to the "human perspective" symbolized in *aviv*, the Spring.[21]

R. Ya'akov probes the nature of the seventh month and its unique connection with the Creator.

> Tishrei reflects "God's side"—that is, the way each individual, at the very root, is linked to God without even being aware of it. Each year, in the month of Tishrei, at Rosh Hashanah, God gives Israel new light—illuminates them with new knowledge of Torah. Each year, He plants this new light in their hearts. And that is our whole reason for living. To be sure, God's salvation is continual, unending. During the winter, though, the forces of *gevurah* and constriction rule the world. People suffer from this, for the promised relief is still beyond their grasp. Understanding evades them—because no one can receive God's light all at once. On the contrary, the light that takes form seems, to human beings, to be the very opposite—for God's revelation begins with concealment [בבחי׳ הן הן גבורותיו].[22]

The world, in the wintertime, seems to be left to its own devices: "His supervision [*hashgaḥah*] is invisible." Those new insights, the stuff of spiritual growth that was planted in the hearts of Jews at the New Year, are left to germinate. Winter descends. The seeds of potential are forgotten, or nearly so, in the cold and rain and darkness. "In winter," R. Ya'akov observes, "our strength diminishes—we can do so much less. The days are short; all the plants wither and only the roots endure, hidden underground. All of creation slumbers, covered over with earth, too weak to break through the surface.... During the rainy months, God's influence is too immense for us. It is so overwhelming that we are forced indoors. 'A rainy day' is a 'day of isolation.'"[23] The metaphor of the seed cast almost haphazardly and abandoned, says R. Ya'akov, teaches us a profound truth. Paradoxically, "It was with tremendous kindness that God scattered His people among the nations; why does a person sow a small measure of seed if not to reap bushels?"[24] So the benefit, ultimately, was infinitely greater than had they remained free agents all those years of exile. The "kindness" implicit in such suffering, though, eludes us—caught up in the moment, our plight seems to be bad through and through. This nonunderstanding, then, is what characterizes the "winter." From Tishrei until the month of Nisan, the future takes form "backward." "Throughout the months of winter, divine light is obscured. God alone rules the world with a hidden hand."[25] The springtime heralds a new beginning.

> *Aviv*—Now the letters are in order [א, ב, י]. In Nisan, everything is different. "And they call to one another"—that is, "they *receive* from one another."[26] Now, all creatures give to one another, and they desire to connect through this mutual interchange. All of creation becomes intertwined; each of them "comes into" the other and they unite, becoming a whole. This is what it means for the letters to be in order—now they face outward toward Creation and give of themselves. And thus, in the springtime the seeds begin to sprout, the plants grow, the grasses and the trees flower and start to bear fruit; everything flourishes. Now they know their Source is with them and they no longer feel any deficiency. For at Pesach, "the harvest is blessed."[27]

It was to this time of rebirth and organic awakening that R. Isaac alluded when he declared that the Torah "should have begun" here. "'This month is yours'—yours: for your sake. In the month of spring God's involvement becomes evident—now people see clearly that His influence fills the world. 'Day' has dawned, people wake up ... They begin to grasp the meaning of events and can even come to understand what God had really given them earlier, back in Tishrei. And gradually, the promise entrusted to them can come to be realized."[28]

Such "rites of spring" celebrate the "human perspective" (*me-tzid-khem*)—here, individuality, intellectual awareness, free choice are the order of the day. The world, in springtime, suddenly seems to "make sense"; God interacts with phenomena in a comprehensible way. Now people feel "at home" (*be-nayḥa*) as they witness a progressive order that seems to be within their grasp. To illustrate this order, R. Ya'akov evokes the image of verticality. Our upright stature is perhaps the crucial factor determining our view of the world.

> People see things in terms of "head" and "foot"—the higher something is, the more honorable it is .... What God grants us in daylight, while we are awake seems *to us* to be more important than what we receive while asleep. For during the day, God focuses His plenty on our head alone, and the head passes that abundance down to the rest of our limbs, until

> it reaches even our feet .... The "head"—that is the mind, wisdom, choice; the more distant a limb is from the head, the more its intellectual power and control diminishes.

And thus, in deliberate reference to this essentially human experience,

> In Nisan, God "lowers himself" [*mashpil 'atzmo*] from one crown to the next, from one tiara to another,[29] gradually revealing Himself and all He has prepared to grow in the world, and He enables them to see it all, even what was hidden to them since Tishrei. He desires to be concealed no longer; His providence should now become evident to all. In Nisan, God says, "See, now, that I, indeed I am He; there are no other gods/powers with Me (Deut. 32:39)."[30]

The world order of springtime, then, is seen as an affirmation of the human modus vivendi. We need to make sense of the world, to discern patterns, to connect cause and effect, to understand our place in the "scheme of things." That unwearying drive to evaluate ourselves relative to others and fix hierarchies is, indeed, a basic factor of our existence. It comes to the fore in the spring, in daylight. During temporal modes such as these, we feel "at home." Our exhilaration in rediscovering sense in our lives is expressed in the Divine Name symbolizing Nisan: the initial letters of the verse **ישמחו השמים ותגל הארץ**—"Let the heavens rejoice and the earth exult" (Ps. 96:11)—spell the Divine Name in perfect order. With confidence and renewed strength the letters, and with them humankind, set about to rebuild the world.

A Counter-Story

Indeed, as R. Isaac says, *our* story "should have," by rights, begun here at the age of enlightenment. And yet in fact the Torah opens with what seems to be another story, in which the starring role, the Jewish nation, is conspicuously absent. The famous talmudic dissent between the Sages R. Eliezer and R. Joshua concerns this very constellation of possibilities. R. Ya'akov cites it in the course of his own reflections.

> This, then, is the dispute in B. *Rosh Hashanah* 11a. R. Eliezer says: The world was created in Tishrei ... the Jewish nation was redeemed in Nisan and, in Tishrei, the final Redemption will come. R. Joshua says:

> The world was created in Nisan ... the Jewish nation was redeemed in Nisan, and in Nisan the final Redemption will come. Both of them are "the words of the Living God." God, of course, could give them all His might, but human beings can receive only gradually. And that is the essence of Nisan—in Nisan, redemption is credited to the efforts made by the Jewish nation. R. Eliezer, though, believes that receiving "little by little" is the rule only in this world. In the world to come, God will give people the understanding and ability to receive Him as He is, before His self-contraction to suit human measure. This is the essence of Tishrei which, indeed, bespeaks a higher level of redemption, for it is from God's own perspective.[31]

To emphasize the connection between this dispute and the dialectic in question, R. Ya'akov offers a second, parallel opposition. It resonates clearly with many observations we have already heard.

> The Holy *Ari*, of blessed memory [R. Isaac Luria] taught of the concepts of the circle [*'iggulim*] and the line [*yosher*]. "Circles"—that is the divine order. God [so to speak] is the central point, surrounded by all the created entities; all of them draw sustenance from Him equally, and none has an advantage over any other. The entire course of their existence is a unity.[32] The human order, in contrast, is "linear"—in their waking hours people walk upright; the "head" is the focal point, and controls all the rest .... And thus even in the afterlife, "Each and every one of us will be pained by seeing what others managed to achieve in their lifetimes."[33]

The reign of lines, with their implicit hierarchy, is thus a way of staking territory, of making clear to oneself one's place on a continuum, one's relative value and importance. R. Ya'akov, fully aware of how necessary this is to our psychological well-being, stresses that it is but one perspective. True psychic wholeness is possible only when another perspective completes the second side of the picture. Significantly, the halakhic obligation daily to bind a set of tefillin—one on the left forearm and the other on the forehead—compels the Jew to ever-renewing awareness of this essential dialectic on the most personal level.

> The tefillin bound on the arm indicate God's exclusive reign; no one can "raise a hand" against it, and so it is "upon your weaker arm"—ידכה.[34] And thus it is bound upon the left arm, over which we have little control.

> Indeed, the Gemara says (B. *Berakhot* 6b), "All is written on His arm."[35] From divine perspective, everything that evolves and develops in the world is a unified whole. For Him, there is no difference between *ḥesed* and *gevurah*. The tefillin bound on the forehead indicate hierarchy [*yosher*], daytime, i.e., the stature of the Jewish nation. For these reasons, the head-tefillin comprise separate compartments for the four passages [from the Torah] they contain, to allude to the different levels each Jew can reach according to personal effort. The arm-tefillin, however, have no internal divisions—the four passages they contain are "housed" together in a single space.[36]

The tefillin, then, with their composite symbolism, enable one to bear, at least physically if not consciously, this vital dialectic: the "head" versus the "arm," intellectual clarity and control versus submission to higher powers, "our perspective" versus "His perspective."

We have seen that R. Ya'akov's interest in reaching a balanced understanding of human existence leads him to bring to the fore aspects of being that are rejected or devalorized by the diurnal mind. A case in point is his reading of the Exodus story. The descent of the Jewish nation into Egypt, their suffering, near extinction, their redemption, and the revelation at Sinai follows the paradigm of all creation: "First darkness and after that, light" [ברישא חשוכא והדר נהורא].[37] The specter of forgetting precedes all memory; slumber, deconstruction, disintegration are the sole path to wholeness. We find this essential paradox evoked in many different contexts in Izbica-Radzyn teachings. Its seeds are sown in mystical tradition:

> See, now, the secret of the matter: Had Avram not descended into Egypt, he would not have been melded [*lo nitzraf*] to begin with, and his destiny would not have become fused to God. The same is true of his descendents. When God wished to transform them into a unified people, a nation of wholeness, to bring them toward Himself, had they not gone down into Egypt first of all, had they not been welded and purified there, they would never have become His unique people.[38]

The greatness of the Jewish nation is traced, here, to the experience of having passed through the "vale of tears," of near-total loss of self. Its terrible meaning becomes clear only in retrospect.

The secret connection between suffering and revelation, R. Ya'akov reminds us, is encoded in the Torah's narrative itself. At Sinai, in a prelude to Moses' receiving the tablets, the elders of the nation "saw the Lord of Israel, and beneath His feet a paved work of sapphire stone, as pure as the very heavens" (Exod. 24:10). Stones (*livnat hasappir*), now luminously blue, reverberate in the collective consciousness of the Jewish nation.[39] Envisioning them, other stones—encrusted with blood and mortar—resurge. "What God revealed to them was that all this holiness had become possible through the extreme concealment they had endured in Egypt, when the taskmasters enslaved the Jews with clay and bricks (*levanim*). Each brick was transformed into a stone of sapphire. Truly, all that is holy comes to be only through forgetting—the deeper the oblivion into which they sank, the greater was the holiness awarded to them in the end." The truth R. Ya'akov suggests here, painful as it is, is ultimately redeeming. He continues: "The depths of the human heart, a person's real essence, come to light only via concealment. To stand transparent [*mevurar*] before God—that is a very great thing … And thus to instill that aspect of 'stones of pure marble' within one's innermost being—the only way to reach such a level is by clarifying one's self through hiddenness and forgetting. In the end, the holiness built through that process will come to light."[40]

"A paved work of sapphire stone." In a surreal reversal of events, Rashi comments that this brilliant surface "was before Him during the enslavement to recall the afflictions of Israel and their travails weighted with bricks."[41] That unsettling connection suggests an act of remembrance into the future, on the part of God, spurred by the now symbolic stone or brick (*levenah*). One midrashic tradition vivifies the association even more by moving it from the abstract level of consciousness to that of physical anguish.

> R. Akiva taught: Pharaoh's taskmasters forced the Jews with beatings to double their quota of bricks [Exod. 5:18]. Yet the Egyptians gave them no straw. They had to go out into the wilderness to gather it, and the straw they found was riddled with thorns and brambles. It pierced their feet, and the blood flowed and mingled with the clay. Rachel, a granddaughter of Methuselah, was pregnant; with her husband, they trampled the mire when suddenly her infant fell from her womb and was mixed in with the unfired brick. She screamed for her son, and her shrieks ascended to the Throne of Glory. [The Angel] Michael went down, extracted him, brought him up to the throne, made him into a brick, and placed him at the feet of the Holy One, blessed be He. Thus it is written "And beneath His feet as a paved work of sapphire stones."[42]

Dehumanizing oppression reaches a depth of cruelty. Tiny bodies become blocks, to be immured in buildings. This, says R. Ya'akov, was the Egyptians' ultimate purpose, that the nation of Israel "should be mingled/assimilated into their own midst." To say, then, that "each brick was transformed into a stone of sapphire" would mean that God drew each individual Jew out from crushing anonymity, brought each one into a luminous mosaic, restored the awareness of each self in all its integrity. The irony, suggested in Rashi's observation, is that the whole course of events was "before Him" from the beginning of the enslavement. Caught in the eye of the storm, comprehensive vision and understanding are humanly impossible. The "slaves"—the stones—each Jew—can know what he or she has earned only after the suffering has reached its end. That "end," indeed, marks a new beginning. R. Ya'akov continues:

> At the giving of the Torah, the Jewish nation saw explicitly all the greatness they had been granted through their labor with clay and bricks, that each brick was transformed into a sapphire stone. They attained this level of circumspection—"And they saw the God of Israel" [Exod. 24:10]—through the realization that, without God, they would have nothing. *And only then could the sapphire stones become "stones of pure marble ...."* In truth, one must know that one owns nothing, and that God alone can instill holiness in one permanently. Where indeed would God plant such a gift if not within the individual?[43]

The stones transmute. Sapphire becomes marble—gemmed brilliance gives way to colorless translucence. I suspect this imagery is more than a poetic evocation of two jewel images. Let's consider them more closely, in the hope of appreciating R. Ya'akov's intention more fully.

In his famous vision, the prophet Ezekiel perceives the Throne of Glory as an "appearance of sapphire stone" (Ezek. 1:26). The Sages in the *Zohar* remark on the unusual properties of that stone: whoever possesses it is protected from the fires of Gehenna and from flooding water; this hue of turquoise (*tekhelet*) terrifies the forces of evil and repels them all. The hidden strength of the "stone of sapphire" (*livnat ha-sappir*), the Sages reveal, is secreted in its composite nature. *Livnat* is a whiteness (*loven*), symbolizing divine mercy (*ra-ḥamei*), while *sappir* is a dark blueness (*ukhmo de-tekhelet*), symbolizing judgment (*dina*).[44] God manages the world in both these modes. To feel guided and encompassed by divine compassion, to be forgiven for wrongs, is to sense the attribute of *raḥamim*—white purity and affection. Adversity, hardship, loneliness—trials of many sorts, on the other hand, suggest the involvement of the attribute of *din*. It is a more somber density, suggesting forces in our lives that we tend to experience as stricture or punishment. "The paved work of sapphire stones," as we saw above, embodies this same dialectic of attributes. The throes of the Jewish nation, which were relieved in a sudden, overwhelming gesture of pity and love, are documented and converted into a monument, to be set before God eternally. The sapphire stonework recalls to all who gaze upon it the dual nature of God's interaction with the world—the potential for experience of *din* and, equally, hopefully, of *raḥamim*. And it drives home the realization that the crucial moment of transition, the turning point that marks the beginning of salvation, lies beyond human understanding. "Without God," R. Ya'akov reminds us, "they would have nothing."

"And only then could the sapphire stones become 'stones of pure marble.'" To see oneself as pavement "at the feet of the Holy One, blessed be He"—lofty as it may seem—is, in R. Ya'akov's eyes, but one stage leading to a still higher level of consciousness. Those "stones of pure marble" that R. Ya'akov evokes here originally lie deep within the *Pardes*, that orchard of mystery into which four sages venture. As the story goes (recounted in the Talmud, B. *Ḥagigah* 14a), R. Akiva cautions the four, his illustrious disciples, "When you reach the place of the pure marble stones, do not say, 'Water, water,' for it is written, 'He that tells lies shall not remain in My sight (Ps. 101:7).'" What would that fatal misperception be, so ominous in the master's eyes? The Talmud itself offers no clues toward the meaning of that cry—"Water, water!" But in the *Zohar*, the matter is investigated further.

The scholarly companions, sitting in the *beit midrash*, puzzle over the talmudic story and its message. "In the meantime, a sage of ancient years appeared among them and asked, '*Rabbanan* [Sirs], what are you discussing?' They answered, 'That R. Akiva warned his disciples about reaching the stones of marble, etc.' He said, 'Indeed, there is a sublime secret here; it has been interpreted in the Heavenly *Yeshivah*. And to guard you from erring in understanding it, I have come down to you to make its meaning manifestly clear.'"[45] He then explains that the stones of pure marble, a source from which living waters flow, signify the Torah itself—a tree of eternal life. When you reach that vision of divine wisdom, R. Akiva was saying, do not mistake those marble stones for other stones that speak of life and death, right and left, "permitted" and "forbidden." That would endanger your very souls—for the Tree of Knowledge of Good and Evil is separation, disparity (*peruda*), while the stones of pure marble are a unity, free of all schism.[46]

Here, in the ancient sage's explanation, we bear witness once again to two opposing perceptions of reality. The first view, called the "stones of pure marble," represents a primordial oneness. The image harks back, in mystical teaching, to that moment of Creation before "water was divided from water" (Gen. 1:6) and, equally, to the essence of the first Tablets of the Law. The second image, encoded in the words "Water, water," bespeaks a shattered world, fraught with boundaries and contradictions. It corresponds with the second Tablets, the mutable text of our earthly reality. That "amended" version of the Torah tells of human foibles, of crime and punishment, of exile, repentance, and reconciliation. To "become stones of pure marble," as R. Ya'akov says, or to instill that consciousness of an overarching unity in one's heart, would thus suggest transcending the dualities that govern our reality. But such a level can be reached, R. Ya'akov teaches, only by living through the darkness, by surviving oblivion. "Only then will the holiness built through that process come to light."[47]

"Ah, But to Sleep, Perchance to Dream"

We have seen one expression of the paradox "first darkness and after that—light" in the saga of the Jewish nation's suffering and redemption. Loss of self, near oblivion, disintegration, and petrifaction give way to a miraculous transformation and, finally, to eternal remembrance. The whole of that process is symbolized in the vision glimpsed by the 70 elders at Sinai. It is recognized as an unalterable law of this world. I'd like to turn now to a second context in which the same paradox plays a central role. In it, other metaphors lead us to expand our appreciation of this dialectic and its place in our lives in the world.

"I the Lord am your God, who brought you out of the Land of Egypt, the house of bondage" (Exod. 20:2). On the face of it, these, the opening words of the Ten Commandments, would seem to be the clearest possible declaration of identity and relationship. "*I* am … who brought *you* …." The Jewish nation emerges from the obscurity of exile into the light of revelation. Gathered at the foot of Mount Sinai, inspired with the awareness of having been chosen, they seem to encounter God "face-to-face." But as we know, being born is not such a simple matter. The Rabbis say that the Jewish nation in Egypt was like a fetus in its mother's womb—"He extracted His people from the midst of another people like a shepherd who plunges his hand into the animal's innards and brings out the lamb."[48] That in utero mode of being is, for R. Ya'akov, the epitome of "darkness," of hiddenness and passivity. The Jewish nation's descent into Egypt, on his reading, tells both of forgetting and of being forgotten. The image of illustrious forefathers fades into oblivion as the years pass. Abraham's "discovery" of his Creator, the binding of Isaac, Jacob and his tribes—the "glory and the dream" disappear from the collective consciousness. Loss of those memories leads to disconnection. The past is obscured, the future obliterated. In that sense, forgetting means paralysis. To despair of ever moving, changing—this is what R. Yaʿakov calls "to be in concealment and darkness, to be 'in Egypt.'" It is a human condition, a pit into which we will fall, inevitably.[49] This realization, then, alters the way we hear those first words of the Ten Commandments. As R. Yaʿakov says: "'I the Lord am your God, who brought you out of the Land of Egypt'—that is, 'It is I who helps you struggle free of that darkness, who recalls you from the abyss to your true self.'"[50] Forgetting has a frightful countenance. Perhaps that's why babies cry themselves to sleep. Thus, to assuage that terror, we "human beings need God's assurance that 'the Guardian of Israel neither slumbers nor sleeps' (Ps. 121:4). That assurance is what enables them to awaken, eventually."[51]

"Falling asleep." The Hebrew word *tardemah* suggests that, in truth, losing hold of consciousness has a second countenance as well. Izbica-Radzyn tradition evokes this word while exploring that alternative, positive aspect of existential "forgetting."

> We find this in the case of Adam, the first human—as long as he remained awake, the feminine aspect of humankind [*ha-nukba*] was indiscernible. Only after God cast him into deep sleep [Gen. 2:21] could the feminine emerge.[52]

Adam, awake, lives in solitude, in a kind of unity of being. His "ego" fills the world; his virile mastery seems absolute. Cast into sleep, his being is fissured, broken apart. Adam lets go. His self disintegrates. The result: something, someone "absolutely other," as Levinas would say, comes to be.[53]

R. Gershon Ḥanokh Henikh, son of R. Yaʿakov, evokes a second instance, and a general observation:

> Before every experience of salvation there must, necessarily, be *tardemah*—a "falling asleep." We see this in the story of Abraham. God revealed to him that the entire world was created for his sake.[54] But before such a precious light could be revealed, it had to be concealed, as the verse says, "A deep sleep fell upon Abram ..." (Gen. 15:12). And when Abraham said, "But me—You have granted me no offspring" (15:3). This, too, is a "falling asleep"—the light of salvation was obscured to such an extent that Abraham nearly lost all hope, all anticipation that it would ever shine.[55]

In essence, what R. Gershon Ḥanokh seems to be saying is that Abram's despair, like his "deep sleep," is not just a preface, a necessary precondition for God's fulfilling His promise to the still-barren "father of multitudes." Rather, doubt, questioning, and falling asleep are an intrinsic part of the process itself. In other words, in order to wake up, one must first doze off; before a new day dawns, the night must be endured. On R. Gershon Ḥanokh's reading, sleep, like despair, is recognized as a positive valence. At the same time, he understands "darkness" as concealment; "the light of salvation was obscured." In the following teaching, we will explore a more radical reading, in which the darkness is perceived as being illuminated with knowledge too brilliant for the "day" to contain. We'll begin with the biblical narrative on which it is based.

> Some time later, the word of the Lord came to Abram in a vision. He said: "Fear not, Abram. I am a shield to you; your reward shall be very great." But Abram said, "O Lord God, what can You give me, seeing I am childless, and the one in charge of my house is Dammesek Eliezer?" Abram said further, "Behold, to me you have given no seed ...." He took him outside and said, "Look toward heaven and count the stars, if you are able to count them." And He added, "So shall your offspring be." (Gen. 15:1–6)

God gestures, before Abraham's eyes, to a galaxy of "biological" descendents and assures him that they will be his heirs, and the Land of Israel will be their portion. Abraham asks for a sign—"How shall I know that I am to possess it?" (Gen 15:8). In response, the uncanny "Covenant between the Pieces" is played out:

> He answered: "Bring me a three-year-old heifer, a three-year-old goat, and a three-year-old ram, a turtledove, and a young bird." He brought Him all these and cut them in two, placing each half opposite the other; but he did not cut up the bird. Birds of prey came down upon the carcasses, and Abram drove them away. As the sun was about to set, a deep sleep fell upon Abram, and a great dark dread descended upon him. And He said to Abram, "Know well that your offspring shall be strangers in a land not theirs, and they shall be enslaved and oppressed four hundred years; but I will execute judgment on the nation they shall serve, and in the end they shall go free with great wealth."... When the sun set and it was very dark, there appeared a smoking oven, and a flaming torch which passed between those pieces. On that day the Lord

> made a covenant with Abram, saying, "To your offspring I assign this land...." (Gen. 15:9–18).

The Rabbis strive to unlock these laden images. The cloven beasts, Abraham's "horror of great darkness," the eagle, the setting sun, the furnace, point mutely, in their eyes, to the entire course of Jewish history from that moment until the end of time. Exile and submission to four alien nations, cumulative centuries of agony, the parting of the sea, giving of the Torah, the Temple in its triumph and its ruin, repentance, the ultimate defeat of all enemy peoples, the World to Come—each of those scenes flashes before Abraham during this portentous vision.[56] Could the knowledge that his children must pass through this "spacious landscape of lamentation"[57] arouse anything but dread? Indeed, R. Ya'akov says, no waking consciousness would bear the portent of such adversity. And for that reason,

> This revelation came to Abraham in a vision, in sleep [*tardemah*], in translated form [*lashon targum*] as the Holy *Ari* taught—for the *gematria* of "translation" is "sleep."[58] That is, God gave Abraham a "taste" of all the things that would happen to the Jews as individuals. What would happen to the Jewish nation as a whole—that God let Abraham experience in "real life," as we saw. Abraham actually went down to Egypt to get a foretaste of the suffering Israel would later endure there. In sleep, however, God enabled him to sense everything that would befall each and every Jew. For more can be revealed to a person while sleeping than can be revealed while awake.[59]

In this vision, then, we could say that God invests a complex, infinitely detailed history in the dark depths of Abraham's being. To be sure, it is a history with a "happy ending." R. Ya'akov does stress that "God showed him the joy and gratification that Israel will reach after all the grief they endured in this world."[60] Significantly, though, that story must remain subliminal. God "recognizes," as Henry James would say, "the danger of filling too full any ... obviously limited vessel of consciousness."[61]

And thus Abraham's outstanding characteristic, R. Ya'akov teaches, is this subconscious bank of faith and certainty in the final redemption. This "holiness found in the depths of his innermost heart" gestates, almost unheeded as the generations pass. And yet, "All the Jewish souls ever to be born emerge from [that holiness]; Abraham our forefather is the source and root of all. Even today, whatever strength a person summons to overcome the evil inclination or withstand a test—that strength is drawn from the mysterious essence of Abraham."[62] The first and everlasting covenant between God and the inchoate Jewish people is made, then, in this state of altered consciousness called *tardemah*. The vast plains of dormancy offer themselves to imagine, to enable the sowing of infinite hope. The language of hope, here, is "translation"—an alternate way of saying that marks the dreamer's psyche indelibly. The message encoded in that vision—clandestine, disguised in harrowing images—retains its power because it rests hidden beneath the threshold of consciousness. From that covert space, it emanates to all of Abraham's descendents. And thus, says R. Ya'akov, whenever a Jew discovers a spark of belief or hope in that "happy ending," we know its source is in him.

Perhaps we could say, then, that Abraham's "true self" is a composite entity, made up of all that myriad "seed" still within his loins. That self is drawn into being through the private struggles that inform each of our lives, our personal rebirths, our exodus. The ultimate promise—that such a self will actually, one day, come to be—such an event is secreted in the future. As Franz Rosenzweig said, "We never see the truth until the end."[63]

To Be Translated

Abraham, in sleep, lives the "horror of great darkness," the eagle, the furnace, the burning torch. His panoramic vision, with its immense spectrum of emotions, can be absorbed only at some level below or beyond the waking consciousness. It is an experience endurable "in translation" alone. Thus far, we've focused our attention on the necessity for "translation" in terms of human limitations. I'd like to turn now to a second aspect of "translation" in mystical and Hasidic teaching. It casts into question many of our preconceptions about the status of such altered "ways of saying."

Let's return to the story of Abraham's vision leading to the Covenant between the Pieces. The cornerstone of R. Ya'akov's teaching, we recall, was the identity (via *gematria*) between translation and sleep suggested in Lurianic teaching. Let's have a look at the reading offered by R. Isaac Luria, the "Holy *Ari*," of the same story.

> "And a deep sleep fell upon Abram." *Tardemah* is numerically equivalent to *targum*—translation. For He speaks with the prophets in *targum*. In that manner alone are they able to receive their prophecy. And thus "A deep sleep fell upon Abram." and thus [He communicated] "in a vision"

[*be-maḥaze'*]—that is, in "translated form," as the *Zohar* teaches.[64] Now, know that "translation" is the reverse side of holiness .... And so it is written "And God cast a deep sleep upon Adam": at first [the feminine and the masculine] were "back to back"—the mystical meaning of *tardemah*. God then cleaved them apart, and after that brought her back to rejoin him "face to face."[65]

God casts people into sleep, R. Isaac Luria seems to suggest, in order to derive from them some ultimate essence. The coherent "language" of the "original" (person) somehow must be altered, "translated," reexpressed in another form. Walter Benjamin makes an apt observation on this point. "It is the task of the translator to release in his own language that pure language which is under the spell of another, to liberate the language imprisoned in a work in his recreation of that work."[66] The feminine, subsumed in Adam's being, stands "back to back" with him—a presence, intimately close and yet wholly unknowable, hidden from his consciousness. Adam, in sleep, is "translated." The "new text"—Eve, or humankind—that issues from him is, in some mysterious way, strange and yet familiar. Benjamin's comments are illuminating: "Here it can be demonstrated that no translation would be possible if in its ultimate essence it strove for *likeness* to the original. For in its afterlife—which would not be called that if it were not a transformation and a renewal of something living—the original undergoes a change."[67] In this rethinking of the relationship between primary text and translation, Benjamin suggests the notion of reciprocity. Although a translation, logically speaking, must "come later" than the original, the translation actually affects the continued "life" of the original by its very existence.[68] In his words, "It is translation which catches fire in the eternal life of the words and the perpetual renewal of language."[69]

We find a fascinating illustration of this notion of metamorphosis brought about by translation in the following teaching by R. Mordecai Joseph of Izbica. He begins by citing the enigmatic lines in the Torah's narrative that precede the pronouncement of the Ten Commandments at Sinai. "The blare of the shofar sounded louder and louder; Moses speaks and God answers him by a voice" (Exod. 19:19). R. Mordecai Joseph continues:

"From here we learn that 'the translator' [*meturgeman*] should not raise his voice louder than the reader's, as it says 'and God [answers him by a voice].'"[70] This is puzzling; the *Tosefists* and the *Rif* indeed challenged what *Ḥazal* said, contending that it should be the opposite.[71] In truth, though, it was Moses who pronounced the Ten Commandments

> to Israel. But the ultimate result, that those words became engraved upon all Jewish hearts—this was the work of God. It was He who carved them in the heart of each and every individual in accordance with His own will. And thus God, as it were, is called "the Translator" [*nikra meturgeman*]. That is, after the Ten Commandments emerged from the mouth of Moses, God responded by carving them on their hearts. And thus "the translator should not raise his voice," for God surely could have engraved the commandments on their hearts with all His might, far beyond the strength of Moses. It is written, though, that "no prophet reached the status of Moses" (Deut. 34:10)—that is, there wasn't another human soul that God illuminated more than Moses. For that reason, "the Translator should not raise His voice"—beyond the level of Moses himself.[72]

In preserving the illogical, or politically incorrect, roles of Moses as "reader" and God as "translator," R. Mordecai Joseph leads us to see the tasks of each of them in a new light. Izbica-Radzyn tradition finds proof of the justice of this role-reversal in the following midrash. "It is customary for the Rav [rabbi] to speak and the student to respond. This is not so, however, in God's case—'Moses speaks and God answers with a voice'—and so 'your humility has made me great' (Ps. 18:36)."[73] With that self-effacing gesture, the Rav cedes his place as ultimate authority and source of wisdom. His silence generously enables the disciple to find his own voice. The disciple becomes the "speaker." In that manner, he can attain some measure of greatness that had remained inaccessible to him as "answerer." The midrash, of course, plays on the double meaning of the word עַנְוָתְךָ—*anvatkhah* (your humility) and *anotkhah* (your responding). God, here, forgoes the honor due to the Rav, and makes Moses *Rabbenu*—our teacher—for all generations. The benefit to the disciple here is evident. But we must ask: What essential role does the demoted "answerer" take on? What hidden power can the translation wield?

Let's return for a moment to the *Zohar*'s teaching (1.89a) that God, in the portentous Covenant between the Pieces, spoke with Abram "in translation" (*bemaḥaze'*), rather than in the Holy Tongue (*Zohar* 1. 89a). Aramaic alone, explains R. Yose there, "is sealed from the heavenly angels, and thus they did not know that God was speaking to Abraham. For he was still uncircumcised: he was *'arel*, his flesh sealed. To prevent the envy of the angels, to give them no 'opening' to intervene or object that God was addressing that impure man, He spoke in 'translation.'[74] … Really, the holy angels do know Aramaic, but they have no use for it; they take no notice of it, and detest Aramaic more than any other language."[75]

This curious notion of selective deafness demands explanation. The aspect of translation that is so reprehensible to angelic sensibilities will apparently provide the key to unlocking its importance for human beings. R. Mordecai Joseph uses the metaphor of carving or inscribing to speak of the essential cognitive process of internalization. Hearing the disembodied words of the Torah, he suggests, remains an external, even neutral event for the Jewish nation. Words acquire meaning only when they become manifest "in your heart," and when they guide and determine one's being in the world.[76] That indwelling meaning, moreover, takes a unique and induplicable form in every person; my "understanding" is my own "translation" of the original. The words voiced by Moses, as the complete expression of divine Will—that no individual can fully comprehend. And thus the Ten Commandments are truly received only when their infinite contents are splintered into a multiplicity of vessels, each vessel refracting some fragment of the whole. And thus, on R. Mordecai Joseph's reading, what I call "my" understanding is really given to me as well. It is the message entrusted to me alone, "in accordance with His own will."

This inner life, the ability to change and grow, to discover new insights, to err and to repair—those all too human dimensions are closed off to the angels. Translation, in truth, is a mutation of the divine message. In angelic eyes it is grotesque because of its very proximity and utter difference from what the Holy Scripture "really says."[77] The angels "have no need for translation." The work of incorporating Torah into the self and evolving, from it, a "teaching" is not their work. The reward God promises Abraham will never be theirs, for they can neither suffer nor choose, nor reach a level higher than where they stand, eternally.[78] Abraham's vision, in the "language of translation," thus alludes to that realm beyond the angels' ken—the Coming World meant for human beings alone.[79]

We saw one instance in which a ploy was called for to circumvent celestial opposition and assert the merit of being "human." As the guardians of purity and all absolute values, the angels would seem to have very clear ideas about right and wrong. Their "envy" generally comes to the fore (in rabbinic tradition) at such sensitive junctures when, for reasons inconceivable to them, human beings are preferred over them despite their indisputably angelic virtues. Rabbinic and mystical teaching, I would suggest, often uses the imagery of the angels to highlight the importance of reversing commonly held hierarchies. When the angels are engaged in polemics, the true limitations and error of their "Platonic" values are exposed, and contrasted with a more authentic Jewish worldview. We turn now to another instance of such a challenge, and its development in Izbica-Radzyn tradition.

The stage for one of the most famous of such debates is set as the Jewish nation gathers at the foothills of Mount Sinai. Keenly envious of that chosen people, the ministering angels clamor to receive God's favor instead. To make their superiority evident, they disparage what, in their eyes, is the most miserable of human weaknesses.

> When Moses ascended the Mount, the angels protested: What is this one born of woman doing in our midst? [God] said: He has come to receive the Torah. They retorted: That precious treasure, which You have kept hidden for 974 generations before the world's creation—*that* You will entrust to flesh and blood?! "Will humankind be able to remember You?" "Give Your glory to the heavens!" … The Holy One, blessed be He said: Moses, rebute them. [And Moses said]: Doesn't it say [in the Torah] "[I am the Lord your God] who brought you out of the Land of Egypt"? Did *you* go down to Egypt? Were *you* enslaved by Pharaoh?[80]

Moses' rebuke exposes, with a hint of irony, the dialectic concealed in this verse, the opening words of the Ten Commandments. An abyss of sensibility separates the first half of it from the second. Indeed, taught R. Mordecai Joseph, "the angels longed with all their hearts to have those first three precious words—'I am the Lord your God'—spoken to them. They knew that the rest of the Torah had no relevance for them, but those three words they wanted dearly."[81]

R. Ya'akov seeks to understand this unrequited desire. He explains: "The angels know that no earthly creature could bear the brilliance of the ineffable Name, 'I am the Lord—*Anokhi Hashem.*'" The rightful place for that "disinterested" glory truly is their celestial spheres. The full utterance, however, contains a counterforce that enables human ears to hear "I am the Lord." That is the "being together" of "*your* God—*Elohekha,* who brought you out of the Land of Egypt." And it is here that all the ambivalence of that relationship comes to the fore. R. Ya'akov continues:

> "Your God"—*Elohim* is the wellspring of suffering. From that Name, all forms of doubt emerge. When one is forced to enter a state of doubt, divine light is totally concealed. This must happen, for if the faintest glimmer of that light remained, doubt could not exist … Yet the Name *Elohim* teaches, as well, that when we strive to do God's will, we actually increase, so to speak, the might and power of the Divine.[82]

The juxtaposition of these two divine Names, then, encodes the fundamental dialectic of revelation and concealment. Each Name, in and of itself, is annihilating—the first in blinding illumination, the second in suffocating blackness. "The holy wakeful ones" (*'irin kadishin*)—the angels—R. Ya'akov reminds us, cannot sleep and never forget. Their eternally opened eyes unblinkingly hear the ineffable Name. But that superhuman strength proves to be their greatest failing. Rhetorically (in the talmudic passage cited above), Moses challenges: "Did *you* go down to Egypt?" R. Ya'akov explains: "For Egypt alludes to an entity devoid of light—as Abraham said regarding the encroaching forces of Abimelech, 'There is no fear of God in this place [Egypt]' (Gen. 20:11). Because fear [יראה] implies light [אור]."[83]

Those eyes that know no darkness could not bear the obscurity and the stricture inherent in the "Egypt" experience. Their mode is one of continuous, total awareness, of absolute and specific knowledge. And thus they were barred from going "down to Egypt";[84] they never hoped against hope and, perforce, could never unearth a spark of faith from the depths of an exiled self.[85]

Interestingly, R. Ya'akov comments that, like the angels, the Patriarchs were bound by the same limitation. Recalling the verse (Deut. 5:3), "It was not with our fathers that the Lord made this covenant, but with us," he asks:

> Why indeed was the covenant [at Ḥorev] made with us rather than with them? The task of the Patriarchs was to recognize God's glory and make it known only to the extent that God revealed it to them. Darkness, though, they knew not. They were not meant to illuminate places where the opposite seemed the truth. Their perception was in pure awareness; actually to perform some act without full control, letting God make it good—that was not theirs to do. For they could not find light within darkness. They had no part at all in such a thing .... Yes, although it does say that Abraham "went down to Egypt," the process was incomplete. He went down and came back up. The concealment was not nearly as severe as later on; he had only a hint of what would befall Israel. [The Patriarchs] were like the heavenly hosts, of whom it is said "they have no joints [in their legs]"—[*ein la-hem kefitzim*]. They perform only in accord with their own understanding, their private conviction that their acts are for the sake of Heaven.[86]

Legs that can collapse or struggle to stand, a body that sometimes folds up and retreats, eyes that may turn inward—all these movements attest to a flexibility and vulnerability that are uniquely human. Indeed we know that angels act with single-minded purpose; their sense of mission informs their very being and illuminates their path.[87] What R. Ya'akov suggests, though, is that their identity as "pure intellects" actually confines them to a one-dimensional, wholly externalized mode of being. Our most profound encounter with darkness, in contrast, happens when our "eyelids" close, when something cuts us off from outward sources of light or certainty. And then other dimensions crowd in. Secret thoughts, memories, guilt, doubts in the back of our minds make their presence felt as that inner night gathers. To sing God's praises in the bright light of "day" as the angels do, says R. Ya'akov, is very good. "But 'faith in the night'—that one can acquire only in exile, in concealment and darkness."[88]

Know My Name

And so Moses asks the angels: "Were *you* enslaved by Pharaoh?" That is: Did the "forces of primeval darkness" that reigned in the shadowy realm called Egypt nearly extinguish you?[89] Only the children of Israel can lay claim to such suffering.

> The darkness mounted as a flooding stream. The Egyptians gained control not only over their bodies, but even somewhat over their souls. Thus the Holy *Ari* taught [*Likkutei Torah, Shemot*] that the verse, "But they will ask me—What is His Name? What [shall I tell them]?" alludes to the ineffable Name itself, concealed in the last letters of those very words—[ואמרו לי מה שמו מה]. That is, they had forgotten how to recognize God. All that remained was some tiny remnant [*roshem ketzat*]—hidden in those final letters—of what they had formerly known.[90]

The Name and the illumination it affirmed are barely remembered, or nearly forgotten. Arguably, God's "four letter Name" had not been in full evidence in previous generations. In Moses' vision at the Burning Bush, God declares, "I revealed Myself to the Patriarchs as *El Shaddai* but by my Name *Hashem* I did not make myself known to them."[91] If that essential Name had never been a "known" aspect even of the enlightened experience of the forebears, how can we claim it had been "forgotten"? What R. Ya'akov seems to be saying here, however, is that although the Patriarchs did not "know" the Ineffable name fully, they were guided nonetheless by an intuitive awareness that God is "interested in the world's continued Being, and desires all of creation to realize that 'the earth is full of His glory.'"[92] This mode of awareness originates from an intimate connection with the authentic meaning of that Name, which speaks of eternal presence and a deliberate will to perpetuate the world's existence.

It seems to me that in his teachings on this *parashah*, R. Ya'akov may be implying some vital connection between forgetting, remembering, and names. That intuitive trust the forebears had in God's Name is obscured as Jacob and his sons die out. "These names," though, went down to Egypt and were infused with light. The Book of Exodus, or *Shemot*—literally, the "Book of Names"—begins like this:

> These are the names of the children of Israel who came to Egypt with Jacob, each coming with his household: Reuben, Simeon, Levi, and Judah; Issachar, Zevulun, and Benjamin; Dan and Naphtali, Gad, and Asher. The total number of persons that were of Jacob's issue came to seventy, Joseph being already in Egypt.

R. Ya'akov recalls the *Zohar*'s incisive rereading of that opening verse.

> We have learned that whenever the Jewish nation was exiled, the *Shekhinah* was exiled together with them.[93] Indeed, of the Egyptian exile, it says "These are the names of the children of Israel who came to Egypt with Jacob, each coming with his household" (Exod. 1:1). If the verse says "the children of Israel" why does it continue "with Jacob"—it should have said "with *him*."[94] Rather, "these names of the children of Israel" are the heavenly chariots and encampments that went down together with Jacob and with the *Shekhinah* into the Egyptian exile.[95]

The awkward formulation of the verse would point, then, to the possibility that "these names" are an entity demanding our attention. They apparently played some essential and independent role in the drama about to unfold. After citing the above passage from the *Zohar*, R. Ya'akov continues:

> "These names of the children of Israel went down to Egypt"—for God made their names greater; that is, He augmented the very source of holiness within them.... Until then, it hadn't been necessary. But as the darkness of exile and impurity increased, God infused them with a more permanent holiness and empowered them to withstand those trials.... In other words, "these names" bear witness to the light that accompanied each individual into Egypt. For each of them illuminates a different

> aspect of being. God gives every Jew a unique power to shine into the depths of the goodness concealed in Egypt. Each extracted the specific goodness meant for each one's own soul, and drew it into the collective [*klal Yisrael*]. Truly, just as the stars cast their light down to earth and help the plants to grow, so the Jewish nation went into Egypt. Their goal: to draw all of God's holy honor out of the exile.[96]

The "exile of the *Shekhinah*" suggested in the *Zohar* (cited above) may be manifest here in the Name that has nearly been forgotten. That bleak, blank doubt—"What is His Name, what …"—affirms that years of servitude had worn away a fundamental sense of connection with the Creator and meaning in the nation's plight. "The secret essence of the Egyptian exile," taught the Baal Shem Tov, is that "knowledge itself [*da'at*] was in exile."[97]

Knowing the faraway story of their ancestors' merits no longer sustains the Jews of Moses' generation. Estranged and alone,

> Their exile was that the illumination of former times was blocked up. All that remained was some invisible, vague sense; they could discern no real glimmer of light. How could they say "God sees" while the Egyptians tortured them mercilessly? And though they wailed their cries seemed to be unanswered. But this is the meaning of the midrash [*Tanḥuma, Shemot* 1]: "These names hint at their ultimate redemption."[98]

R. Ya'akov describes a wrenching cognitive dissonance. Contemplating their tribal names, the nation feels betrayed. If "Reuben" promises vision (*re'eh*); if "Simeon" vows hearing (*shem'a*); if "Levi" speaks of connection (*livui* and "Judah" of recognition and thanks (*hoda'ah*)—then why have we been so abandoned?[99] To repossess the certainty that God truly does know and care and will set them free, the exiles must discover that "all the names recorded [in this opening chapter of the Book of Names] are really the Names of the Holy One, blessed be He, *and* the names of Israel, *and* the names of *Moshe Rabbenu*."[100]

Winning back the assurance that God is present in their midst—"knowing His Name"—however, is conditioned on a second, introverted level of awareness. Not accidentally, Jewish tradition has it that the secret of survival in Egypt was that the exiles "did not change their names."[101] More than a symbolic refusal to assimilate into alien culture, we can understand this as a will to believe that the promise will someday come true. To change one's name in such circumstances would be to break with the past, to take on an alter-ego, even to try to exchange one's destiny.[102] In contrast, knowing, preserving, or seeking my own "name" means to find the "root of my soul and the meaning of my life. That private name marks the path to understanding the hidden point of connection one has to the Creator."[103] R. Ya'akov notes that, in this, the children of Israel are greater than the heavenly hosts—"their true names are permanent and cannot be altered. The angels, on the other hand, have no unchanging essence. Whatever mission they are charged to do—that is their name for that moment. As the midrash teaches, [the anonymous spirit wrestling with Jacob declares] 'My name now will not be my name later on.'"[104] This, then, is what the midrash means by saying that the names of the tribes "hint at their ultimate redemption." Eventually, God will declare, "I have *seen* my nation's misery" (*raiti*—Reuben) (Exod. 3:7). At last, "God *heard* their groans" (*sham'a*—Simeon) (Exod. 2:24), and assured, "I am *with them* in their suffering" (*yelave*—Levi) (Ps. 91:15). Their names become His Names. Those selves, regained through such suffering, then find the power to draw His Name and presence out of exile with them.

"The names" that the children of Israel carry with them into Egypt thus point, on R. Ya'akov's reading, toward an intimate and vital "heart's knowing" (*binat ha-lev*) that heals the wounds of doubt and forgetting. The knowledge that the heart alone can nurture is what leads to psychic wholeness. Finally, it must take form painfully, gradually, "between the straits," in darkness.[105] The saga of Exodus, as the Holy *Ari* taught, truly recounts the mystery of our gestation and our birth. The souls meant for our "houses" descend into the obscurity of this world, each one charged to seek out the shards of light it alone is meant to find.[106]

"I Write and Give My Self"

We return now to reconsider the objection that the angels voice on Sinai and the alternate evaluation that emerges. "Will humankind remember You?" Clearly, tragically, the answer is no. Giving the Torah—the ultimate revelation of God's will—to lowly mortals is, in the angels' eyes, a travesty. The discrepancy between that infinite source of light and pitiful human retainers would seem to make any real "receiving" impossible. The circuits will overload; blackout is inevitable. And, indeed, midrashic tradition testifies as much. "R. Abahu said, All forty days that Moses spent on high he learned Torah and forgot it. Moses said: Lord of the Universe, I've had forty days and still I know nothing at all! What did God do when the forty days were up? He gave him the Torah as a gift."[107]

A gift—unearned, undeserved. How can one receive, let alone retain, an entity beyond comprehension? The secret workings of this divine gesture, the Rabbis teach, are encoded in the first words of the "gift" itself. "*I* am the Lord your God, who brought you out of the Land of Egypt." (Exod. 20:2) The name of the agent "I"—*Anokhi*—the Sages tell us, attests to that unique act of transmission.

> R. Levi taught: The Holy One, blessed be He appeared to them like an icon that has faces everywhere—a thousand people look at it, and each meets a gaze. So, when God spoke, each and every Jew avowed, 'With *me* He speaks!' Thus "I am the Lord, *your* God."[108]

The suggestion here is of a composite unity. In some unimaginable way, the monolithic Word is experienced by each individual as a personal address. "*Your* God most of all."[109] R. Ya'akov expresses this notion acutely: "*Anokhi*—that is, God lowers Himself into the created world and reveals in what way each thing matters to Him [השייכות שיש לכל דבר אצלו יתברך]. And the letter *kaf* teaches that the more you direct yourself toward Me, the more I dwell within You."[110] Implicit here is a contrast between the designation of self (I) as *Anokhi* (אנכי) with the more common word *Ani* (אני). The crucial difference, of course, is in the letter *kaf*, known by grammarians as the "*kaf* of resemblance" (*kaf ha-dimayon*) or "of imagining." (In effect, *kaf* is not only a letter, but the signifier *par excellence*—the hand, *kaf ha-yad*, which points to other meanings beyond those most immediate.) Worlds of association, of correspondence open up with this gesture of "likening" two separate entities. Izbica-Radzyn teaching brings to the fore the psychological necessity of having revelation take place in this mode above all.

> Had God revealed Himself not as *Anokhi* but as *Ani*—with the totality of His light—they would have been unable, afterwards, to discover any additional, deeper levels of meaning in His words; everything would have been fully, visibly evident. The letter *kaf* signals incompleteness, an image and a hint of future understanding. As one comes to perceive more profound aspects of Torah, at every stage one realizes that until that moment one was in darkness.[111]

Face to face with God's *Ani*, Israel "should fade in the strength of his stronger existence."[112] *Ani*, as R. Ya'akov puts it, would "annul the individual and obliterate one by showing God's infinite might. No human being can perceive this aspect of the Divine." The appellation *Anokhi*, in contrast, speaks of likeness and of relationship—"of the aspect of 'self and other' [*ani ve-ho*]."[113] We could say that it suggests some potential meaning—on the horizon, but "not yet," beyond every "now." This dynamic principle of becoming revealed, explains R. Ya'akov, is the core meaning of the revelation at Sinai.

"The letter *kaf* [of *Anokhi*] tells of the source of life, out-flowing endlessly and ever-increasing."[114] Fluid as that stream of moments we call time, the true being of *Anokhi* cannot be grasped at any isolated point. Our understanding of it, rather, is continually developing and emerging. For that very reason, *Anokhi* remains wholly unknown and unappropriated. Henri Bergson speaks of the need to accept and embrace this mode of evolving understanding. Openness to change, Bergson avers, is a most profound expression of freedom:

> Intuition, bound up to a duration which is growth, perceives in it an uninterrupted continuity of unforeseeable *novelty*; it sees, it knows that the mind draws from itself more than it has, that spirituality consists of just that, and that reality, impregnated with spirit, is creation.[115]

This "uninterrupted continuity of unforeseeable novelty," I would suggest, is at the heart of the name *Anokhi*, and of the revelation it introduces. The "Giving of the Torah," most fundamentally, is considered to be the pronouncement of the Ten Commandments as a whole. Their "essence and root," as R. Ya'akov calls it, are these three words in particular—*Anokhi Hashem Elohekha*—heard from the "mouth of the Mighty One" (*mi-pi ha-gevurah*).[116] The crucial matter the Rabbis ponder is how, to use Bergson's expression, the mind "draws from itself more than it has." In other words, by what mode of transmission does this endless giving take place? Heroically, the Rabbis glimpse an answer encoded in the agent of revelation—once again, the name *Anokhi*.

Anokhi, the Rabbis teach, is an anagram (*notarikon*) of the Aramaic phrase "***a****na* ***n****afshe* ***k****etavit* ***y****ehavet*"—"I write and give My Self."[117] The traditional reading of this statement is: through studying words of the Written Torah, Jews are granted the opportunity to reach some measure of recognition of God's ways and qualities.[118] That is, understanding the writing, or Scripture, can instruct us in certain aspects of divine essence, of God's "self," so to speak.

Izbica-Radzyn Hasidic tradition adopts this basic idea, and transfers it to another plane. In doing so, the full significance of that symbolic act of writing is made clearer. "This is the meaning of 'I write and give My Self.' The [Ten] Commandments were graven into the hearts of each and every individual Jew." The human heart, in this metaphorical reading, would replace the stone tablets. The event: "The putting into me of the idea of the Infinite."[119]

Here, it seems, is a vivid image, hinting toward the impossible promise of immutable remembrance. Truly, we humans yearn to be "impressed"—to have meaningful things "make their mark" on us. And we hope, if they are really important, that they will become an unforgettable, vital part of our being.

The event most charged with meaning in the life of Israel was surely this direct encounter at Sinai. And yet the impression it left bears witness to absence rather than presence. Hannah Arendt writes eloquently of what actually occurs, in a general sense, "in writing something down"—in giving thought or speech a concrete form. "This reification and materialization, without which no thought can become a tangible thing, is always paid for, and that the price is life itself: it is always the 'dead letter' in which the 'living spirit' must survive, a deadness from which it can be resurrected only when the dead letter comes again into contact with a life willing to resurrect it, although this resurrection of the dead shares with all living things that it, too, will die again."[120] The paradox here is that the living, spoken word must eventually be recorded and petrified in written form, "because remembrance and the gift of recollection, from which all desire for imperishability springs, need tangible things to remember them, lest they perish themselves."[121] Arendt indicates some mutuality or interdependence inherent in the relationship between "letter" and "spirit"—between text and reader or, in our context, between the divine word and the human hearer. This "resurrection," it would seem, must continually be enacted. But what causes the letter to "die," to corrode, and revert to being inanimate? And what capacity empowers a "life" to make it live again?

We recall a tenet of Jewish tradition: the "Giving of the Torah" (*matan Torah*) is conceived not only as a historical event driven into the soil of memory, but as a reality continuously recurring today. The giving, in other words, is a "present-ing"—both in the sense of "making present, relevant, vital" and as an unexpected, surprising discovery—a "gift," offered to us ever anew in a flash of intuition. This, perhaps, is the emotion the Rabbis sense in the encounter with God's "face" portrayed in the *Tanḥuma* above—"To *me* He is speaking!"

And then the audible, fiery Word is seared into the hearts of the people. "'*Anokhi*'—I write and give My Self." Words, beyond speech, reach into the people's innermost being. Eternally? R. Ya'akov lays bare some of the perilous results of that act of "writing."

> Indeed, those things could become fixed in them so rigidly; one could become completely used to them, like words written and carved and decreed upon one. The source of human happiness, however, is in what we have not yet grown accustomed to—things that still seem new. Once

> they've gotten "old" they give us less satisfaction and joy. This holds true even in the realm of Torah. Habit and custom are very precious. Indeed, we even pray, "Please help us grow familiar with Your Torah."[122] But everything, even words of Torah, seem to diminish in force when they are written down. Pleasure is lost when things become habitual; people rejoice only in novelty.[123]

The allure of the "new," the offensiveness of what has gotten "old." What underlies these basic, almost instinctive attitudes? R. Mordecai Joseph evokes a moving metaphor in this regard. He points out that things we learned as children, or ideas that strike us in their originality, tend to endure as a vibrant part of our consciousness, much more so than information added on at later stages in life. The Sages, he notes, call this imbibing of novelty *girsa de-yankuta*, "the learning of one's youth."

> When a baby [*tinok*; in Aramaic, *yanuka*] nurses from its mother's breasts, it draws forth milk that had never before existed. That milk had naught a moment to "get old"; its taste is better than anything "already there." As it says of the shew-bread [*leḥem ha-pannim*], "Hot bread is placed there" [1 Sam. 21:17]—that bread never staled; it was forever fresh.[124]

R. Mordecai Joseph recalls an ongoing miracle witnessed in the days of the Temple. Although the twelve loaves of the shew-bread lay for an entire week on the table in the sanctuary "before God," they remained as warm as the moment they had been drawn from the oven.[125]

Nourishment—bread, milk—offers some intimate connection with the source of blessing and plenty. The infant "draws forth milk that had never before existed." It is meant for him alone, and is even "created" by his need. The mother enables milk to "come into the world" for her baby alone; in her arms there is no "getting old." Consider now R. Ya'akov's thoughts on the subject. He speaks of the diminishment that unavoidably occurs after things first "come into the world" and are appropriated.

> As long as something remains attached to its source, it doesn't deteriorate or spoil—like the shew-bread that stayed warm throughout the time it remained "before God." Or like the harvest—it continues to grow and flourish from day to day. From the moment it is ready and cut, though, care must be taken, for it will easily rot.... And thus "the learning of one's youth" is so good because God gives [the child] great desire

to learn. Later on, however, once knowledge is "in hand," God's presence recedes a bit.[126]

The sense of "attachment to the source" and the intense pleasure it engenders, we could say, is a first and crucial aspect of the revelation at Sinai called *Anokhi*. It means to realize, in total openness, that every aspect of Creation "matters" to God in a unique way, and that all is, ultimately, unified with Him. R. Ya'akov stresses that even now, chronologically "after" the Giving of the Torah, "whoever turns toward God will find in one's heart the encoded message of ***Anokhi***—'I write and give My Self.' For it is re-written and fixed more in the human heart each time.... Every Jewish act of loyalty and obligation—tefillin, tzitzit, Pesach, Shabbat, sukkah—renews the sense of holiness that was at the Giving of the Torah; their hearts are brightened once again as they were at Sinai."[127] The "dead letter," in Arendt's phrase, would thus be revived by the will of the spirit to *do* it, to make the exigencies of the word into a living reality in the world.

"Like words written and carved and decreed" would be the opposing aspect of the same experience. That signals the wave of the scythe. Cut off, bound, finite, the "saying" of the divine Word transmutes to a static text. In this sense, the gift of Torah, or of insight—no matter how vital—will cease to live in the fullest sense the moment it becomes a "given," an appropriated and familiar part of my understanding. Henri Bergson, in his critique of the tools of intelligence, hints at the etymological meaning of the word "understand." The French *comprendre* (or its English cognate *comprehend*) signifies to grasp, encompass, annex meaning into an existing body of ordered data. Subjugating the sense of the "absolutely new" into such a totality deprives it of life force. The joy of discovery is forgotten.

And so the Script, with the experience it commemorates, may or will always become indecipherable. And yet we can do nothing but accept this alienation and distancing from the original event. We accept, and wait hopefully for new insight, for something else to awaken us back into full consciousness, at least for a moment.

Dialectical Relationships and "The Strength to Suffer"

In the course of this chapter, we have explored some of the manifold dualities in the world of Izbica-Radzyn Hasidic teaching. We have seen that, beyond a simple definition of any fundamental opposition, the positive aspect of the "minor" mode is repeatedly brought to the fore. The hidden fertility of the bleak winter months, the night's inspiration, metamorphoses reached by sleep and translation, a forgetting that enables remembering—all these, we learn, can offer another way of coming to terms with human failings and limitations. In addition, these discussions, with their sensitivity to the underlying unity of things, guide us toward expanding our understanding of ourselves in the world. I'd like to conclude this chapter with an idea, developed by R. Ya'akov in a series of teachings that suggests a key to accomplishing that crucial and longed-for synthesis between forces that so often seem irreconcilable.

The framework in which that idea takes form is the opening and closing verses of the *sidrah Tetsavveh*:

> *And you* shall command the children of Israel to bring you pure olive oil for the light, to cause the lamp to burn always (Exod. 27:20).... *And you* shall bring forth Aaron your brother (28:1).... You shall make an altar for burning incense (30:1).... On it Aaron shall burn aromatic incense: he shall burn it every morning when he tends the lamps, and Aaron shall burn it at twilight when he lights the lamps—a perpetual incense offered before the Lord throughout the ages (30:7–8).... This is most holy to the Lord. (30:10)

"And you ..."—*Ve-'ata*. In the rhetoric of the preceding biblical chapters, God has been speaking continuously to Moses, guiding him in all the particulars of preparing offerings for the Tabernacle, constructing the altar, making the golden menorah, preparing the curtains, the veils, and the court with its pillars and sockets. Thus it is striking that in the midst of this intricate monologue, God suddenly turns to Moses, as it were, in a renewed address—"And *you* ..."—as if Moses had not been listening and receiving instructions all along. Here, it would seem, is some gesture toward particular significance.[128]

Indeed, the Rabbis taught that God "ardently desires" four things above all else from His creatures. One of them is to "cause the lamp to burn always"—to take care that this flame never die out, just as the Holy One Himself illuminates the world without cease.[129] The *ner tamid*, or "western light" of the menorah, in fact burned, the Sages said, in a continual miracle. While the other six flames of the menorah endured only "from evening to morning" and were relit daily, this undying flame, they taught, was "a testimony to all the world that God's presence dwelled with Israel."[130] The oil, replenished each evening by the High Priest, nourished the "western light" throughout the generations until the Second Temple was destroyed. We can thus sense the urgency inherent in this initial mention of the commandment "to bring oil ... to cause the lamp to burn always." Secondly, we note that, in the biblical precepts outlined here, while the lamps of the menorah are being cleaned (in the morning) and lit (at dusk) an offering of incense is burned simultaneously. Both the lamp and the incense are described as perpetual or eternal mitzvot—*ner tamid* and *ketoret tamid*. This would seem to suggest some sort of parallel or complementary importance, that both of them should be "done always" and forever.[131]

Perhaps it is no accident that in his teaching on this *parashah—Tetszavveh*—R. Ya'akov expresses a striking interest in the dialectical relationship between these two elements, the lamp and the incense. In the following pages, we will attempt to discover something about the essence of the incense and the lamp, their correspondence with aspects of human life, and, finally, the coherence they together may be able to teach us.

> "Oil and incense gladden the heart, like the sweetness of friendship by heartfelt counsel" (Prov. 27:9) שֶׁמֶן וּקְטֹרֶת יְשַׂמַּח לֵב וּמֶתֶק רֵעֵהוּ מֵעֲצַת נָפֶשׁ.
> "Oil" is light. In light, it is evident that God alone is supreme, holy, and almighty. Holy, in the sense of being visible to all. The primary role of light is to enable the recognition that God is the ultimate source and nothing is really ours. "Oil" [*shemen*] alludes to a wise and circumspect way of living, seeing the blessings in all that comes one's way, never forgetting about God. It is the aspect of Torah that is plainly discernable, revealed, explicit, and clear, what a person comprehends intellectually as God's will. But the aspect of "oil" alone is incomplete. In it, God's holiness actually remains removed and distant,[132] because the individual has no personal part in it. Yes, "oil" is the totality [*klal*] of Torah, and it is exceedingly precious. Yet our grasp of that totality is meager and shallow, and cannot go very far. The aspect of incense [*ketoret*], in contrast, is the connecting force: nothing in the world fails to bear witness to God's greatness; no place is void of His holiness. This is so despite our unawareness, even in situations sealed and concealed from the human intellect, as when we do what God has commanded with no sense of the reason for those acts.[133]

"Oil" and "incense" here mark two opposing poles of being. The lamp, fueled by pure olive oil, is the symbol of insight and clarity, that illuminated "never forgetting" or pure consciousness for which lovers of wisdom have always longed. God's very first utterance, indeed, was "Let there be light"—a divine will for transcendental perception, "unto the ends of the earth." In mystical teaching, that light [*or*] encompasses the Torah itself [*orayyta*]; it is the vital force of Torah that enables the world to exist.[134] The "incompleteness" of this total illumination, however, is in its "distance" from us. To comprehend with the intellect alone leaves one somehow alienated, indifferent. What is lacking is one's "personal part in it."

Against the obverse, "light" side of being, R. Ya'akov suggests, is another realm—the reverse, obscure mode of action with no true sense of why we must do what God has commanded. Paradoxically, though, it is those acts carried out in noncomprehension that grant us "something of our own" in the world.[135] R. Ya'akov offers an example of commandments that we carry out with no clear cognitive grasp of them: tzitzit. Seeing the blue threads they contain (Num. 15:38) can remind us of the sea; blue ocean water resembles the sky, and those blue expanses recall God's glorious throne.[136] That ultimate end of the associative chain, although inherent in the tzitzit themselves, may never be overtly evident for the Jew wearing them, and cannot, in any case, become a permanent element of consciousness.[137] A second example is tefillin.

> Tefillin, like the incense, allude to devotion to God. [In binding them on,] one joins and binds one's heart to serve God, even without feeling the depth and meaning of it all. As it says in the Talmud [B. *Berakhot* 7a], "'And you shall see My back' [Exod. 33:23]—this teaches us that the Holy One, blessed be He showed Moses the knot of His tefillin." The aspect of "back" here means that one is bound to God even without awareness of it. And the incense alludes to this, as we have seen.[138]

The knot of the tefillin, then, would testify to a subconscious or superconscious realm of devotion regardless of any intellectual efforts one might make. Notably, in evoking the mitzvah of tefillin, R. Ya'akov's focus deflects from the overtly "meaningful" component of the tefillin—the box with the four verses from the Torah it houses, which recall and recount the essence of the Jewish nation.[139] To fulfill the mitzvah of tefillin, that box must be "put [on the forehead] between the eyes" (Exod. 13:16). And so two leather thongs are threaded through slots at the base of the box, and these are interlaced to form a knot in the shape of the Hebrew letter *dalet*.[140]

Ostensibly, that knot serves a technical, functional, and secondary role. And yet, R. Ya'akov recognizes the essential aspect of the tefillin here, in the knot itself. It is placed at the back of the skull, the "opposite side" of the face. In human terms, that is the locus of being unaware, of never seeing or knowing. The "knot of the tefillin" would then embody a complex relationship. It is a nexus of absence and presence, separation and unity, shadow and light. The notion of the "knot of God's tefillin," evoked by the Rabbis in a strikingly anthropomorphic image, is traditionally read as an expression of God's ceaseless, though concealed, devotion to the well-being of the Jewish people and their final redemption.[141] The image expands in later generations. In mystical tradition, the "knot of God's tefillin" is read as teaching not only of "divine ways" but also of the hidden bonds connecting us, reciprocally, to God. The knot attests to *hester pannim*, to the suffering and uncertainty that riddle our world. "For no one can see My face and live" (Exod. 33:20). The ultimate plan, the total mercy in all of God's ways—these will never be envisioned by human eyes. All we can glimpse is the trace of the face that has turned away from us. That trace, or *reshimu*, is the "back."[142] From behind, the brilliance of the countenance cannot be seen.

Somehow, though, "what is thus withdrawn is most yours."[143] God chooses to have His glory "pass over" Moses as he stands shielded in the cleft of the rock. In this, R. Ya'akov says, a tremendous gift was bestowed. God pledged: "I will give you the strength and resilience to suffer, and I will place you so, that you will have no grievances."[144] "The strength to suffer," teaches R. Ya'akov, finds fullest expression in a Jew's resolve to serve God and fulfill His commandments *without understanding the meaning* of it all. And "with no grievances." To accept and welcome the reality of what he calls darkness and forgetting—this, R. Ya'akov says, is the secret meaning of the incense.

> The incense alludes to love and devotion between God and Israel. As the *Zohar* says (3.37b), "What is *ketoret*? Interconnection [*ketiru de-kula*]"—in other words, one must possess the certainty that one is never cut off from God, despite any unawareness or failure.[145]

R. Ya'akov stresses a truth that is fundamentally counterintuitive. Logic would infer that such lacunae should not occur: "If a person prays to God for protection from all that would distract from doing His will, from loving and adhering to Him, why, then, would misfortune befall one?" Against that intellectual, reasonable ordering of how things should be, R. Ya'akov proposes an alternate conclusion. That idea, encoded in the symbolic meaning of the incense, will be the subject of the following pages.

On one hand, we have seen that the willingness to perform the commandments "with no sense of the reason for those acts" is a basic sign of a Jew's loyalty, submission, and acceptance of God's greater wisdom. His or her actions are transformed into acts of love precisely because of that nonunderstanding. Beyond the outward "performance" of precepts, however, R. Ya'akov suggests that, in truth, the same attitude toward overt actions should (or must) permeate all aspects of one's life. R. Ya'akov recognizes how easily even the most minor factors can disturb our mental and emotional equilibrium. Worries, suspicions, aches and pains of all kinds distract us. They hinder our functioning and even have the power to distort our relationships. We tend to see such troubles as impediments set up against us, and we devote great energy to overcoming, ignoring, and, above all, regretting their interference in the grander scheme of things. What could be emptier of spiritual meaning than a blown fuse, a child's whine, a sneeze?[146] The word R. Ya'akov chooses to indicate these factors—*tirdot* (annoyances, hindrances)—highlights their effect on us. We see them as distancing us or "driving us away" (*matridim*) from God, alienating us from our lucid selves and from the lives we have so carefully sought to control. Hence our natural animosity toward them. The error of that stance, though, must be recognized: "Who would really want to be attached to God only when one's mind is clear and composed, but be cut off from God when anxious or worried? For there are times when one's mind cannot be at ease—we see this even in great people."[147] And thus R. Ya'akov's insistence that those annoying, frustrating, or threatening times when "things aren't going right" must be reevaluated. "We must believe that in such times, when one has no inner peace—then most of all one's position is infinitely more profound and superior to the [times when the] intellect [reigns]. Indeed, God wishes, through them, to teach one new and holy lessons and appreciation of His ways. And so one must accept whatever God sends, at all times, with love."[148] The "small things," insignificant, lowly, always there, beckon to us to listen and understand. Truly, "no place is void of His holiness"—or, in those places that most *seem* void of all holiness, there, most of all, we must seek Him.

R. Ya'akov evokes a striking metaphor to drive home the importance of this shift in attitude. He recalls an image evoked by the Rabbis to describe the unbearable effect of the divine light that originally flooded Creation: like a blazing torch, that light would flare up suddenly and disappear in the same moment, swallowed into its source. So blinding was its brilliance that the light itself was experienced as darkness. Light—a coherent vision of God's full plan—is never ours. Only in the darkness radiating from that flash of brightness can an authentic personal connection take form. There, candle flames—each a human soul—come into their own and learn to love.[149]

Here and in most of his teachings on the menorah and the incense, R. Ya'akov reiterates the following statement from the *Zohar*: "R. Isaac said, 'The Upper light and the Lower light, when united are called "and you" [*ve-ata*], as it is written, "*And You* give life to all."'"[150] The menorah, we learn, represents the former, "upper light" and the letter *vav* ("and"). The incense is the latter, the "lower light," a humble human "candle" called "you" (*ata*). In the *Zohar*, two contrasting attributes are superimposed on this framework: the letter *vav* represents the attribute of *yirah* (awe), while the word "you" represents *ahavah* (love). The interrelationships between each interlocking set of two are a leitmotif through the pages R. Ya'akov devotes to the subject. With each nuanced variation on the theme, a clear message takes form: it is the second element—the incense, the candle, love, "you"—that actualizes the connection. That moment of actualization, however, comes about only after a confrontation with counterforces (the first element); only then can that essential integration be achieved. As R. Ya'akov reminds us, "Light can be perceived only by means of darkness" עיקר הכרת האור הוא ע"י חושך.

"Incense"—The Helpmate Opposing Me

The following teaching illustrates that principle. After citing the opening verse of the *parashah* beginning, "And you … ," the verse from Proverbs (27:9) is quoted once again:

> "Oil and incense gladden the heart, like the sweetness of friendship by heartfelt council." "Oil" signifies light in beautiful and pleasing form. "Incense" is that which is pleasant-smelling but unattractive. What this means is that "the incense is the connecting force [*ketiru de-kula*]" as the *Zohar* teaches.[151] From the "incense" perspective, there are no gradations; everything that exists in the world was created by divine utterance and thus everything is wholly good. As the Rabbis said [B. *'Eruvin* 21b], "In the future, both [the righteous and the wicked] will be fragrant"—this is the secret of the Name *Hashem Tzeva'ot*: every worldly thing is inwardly the opposite of what it appears outwardly. And that is the essential source of aid in reaching holiness, in the sense of "a helpmate opposite him" (Gen. 2:18).[152] For those things that appear to oppose us the most, truly benefit us most of all. The incense alludes to this—its external appearance contradicts its inner essence, and hence its instrumental role in the realm of the holy.[153]

In the next lines, R. Ya'akov sets out some of the "oppositional" aspects of the incense—here, too, those parts of "being in the world" we try to "think away" as unessential and useless—and exposes their true value.[154] To make the full meaning of R. Ya'akov's teaching more accessible, let us consider some of the primary biblical and rabbinic pretexts underlying it.

In the Torah, God commands Moses to compound the incense thus:

> Take the herbs stacte, onycha, and galbanum—these herbs together with pure frankincense; let there be an equal part of each. Make them into incense, a compound expertly blended, refined, pure, sacred. Beat some of it into powder. (Exod. 30:34–36).

While the first and second Temples stood, oral tradition further specified the ingredients of the incense and their proportions. The Talmud states that eleven spices composed it: balsam, cloves, galbanum, white resin, myrrh, cassia, spikenard, saffron, costus, rind, and cinnamon.[155] The Rabbis remarked on many symbolic aspects of the incense. Its composite nature—including foul-smelling galbanum—teaches that sinners must be considered as part of the Jewish community. The vertical column of smoke formed as it burns testifies to links of mercy and forgiveness forged between earth and Heaven. The effervescence of "scent" avers that it is the quintessential offering to God.[156]

R. Ya'akov evokes God's affirmation, as it were, in the midrash *Tanḥuma*, "Of all your Temple sacrifices, I want nothing but the fragrance, and it will be as if I have eaten and drunk." In the next lines, he remarks on the paradoxical nature of this most "spiritual" or nonphysical of offerings.

> The essential source of fragrance is in the peel of the fruit, more than the fruit itself.... This indicates that we must "smell" and "sense" that God instills meaning in the peel [*kelipah*] no less than in the fruit itself; something "human" can be found even in the outer covering. For the incense alludes to those worldly things that seem most distant from our concerns. Indeed, it is made from husks, thorns, remnants of substances, such as myrrh, and from wastes discharged from plants. All these represent what is *beyond* human comprehension.[157]

At first sight, what all the components of the incense seem to have in common is a radical inferiority: tree bark (cassia), dried-up blossoms (cloves), gums, resins, balsamic secretions—all these are residual substances, presumably secondary to the "thing itself." Yet it is for that reason that the incense—a mixture of "refuse"—embodies the otherness that, through "opposing" the "me," challenges it to greatness. In reassessing the everyday things that seem extraneous, we can free them from the lowly role we have imposed on them.

In freeing them, we change ourselves. R. Ya'akov expresses the far-reaching significance of this teaching in moving terms:

> "For My thoughts are not like your thoughts" (Isa. 55:8)—what a person sees as incidental might really be essential, while what one believes is essential might be merely incidental. And so people are convinced that the time they most need an influx of holiness is during their prayers and divine service. But for God, that isn't so evident. The main thing is that even when greatly distressed, one should be filled with holiness.... Thus, regardless of all the concealment in this world, one must firmly believe that, from God's perspective, there is no separateness and division, but only wholeness. And no difference really sets the inanimate and vegetative apart from the human. Truly, from God's perspective the most precious and holy things—all illuminations and beloved souls and even the light heralding the King Messiah—all these come into being through the "lower waters" [*mayyim taḥtonim*], through whatever seems to be devoid of light/meaning. Indeed, the holiness inherent in material things is very dear to God, even though we can perceive no light in them.[158]

The prooftext R. Ya'akov chooses to illustrate his teaching is the following incident recounted in the Talmud:

> Rava saw Abaye [as he concluded his prayer] bowing first to the right and then to the left. He said [to Abaye]: Are you assuming [the precept is to bow] to *your* right? Rather, your left side is the right side of the Holy One, blessed be He.[159]

This short interchange highlights the polar opposition between "God's perspective" and ours that R. Ya'akov seeks to explain. The face-to-face relationship we hold so dear—symbolized in our standing "before God" in prayer—mandates that our relative spatial position be wholly dissimilar. As we face one another, my right is parallel to your left. The implications are profound. "Rights" and privileges, strength, justice, authority, dominance—values that inform our world—hold a different place on the "other side." From that divine perspective, so to speak, "leftness"—that "wrong side" we find sinister, gauche, erroneous, evil—is "right." The conclusion R. Ya'akov draws here does not reverse these stereotypes. Rather, it alters them fundamentally:

> We suppose that inanimate nature is devoid of light, and that God loves only those who can understand intellectually. But from God's point of view, things we hold to be worthless are precious and sacred, their value wholly beyond human perception. It is for that reason they seem to us to be inanimate: we have no tools to conceive of their sublime holiness.[160]

Such an awareness of the true nature of things can be reached only through humility. Granting dignity to what seems simple and even "worthless," trusting in the unknown meaning of things and waiting for understanding to come—these are the gestures that lead to completeness. R. Ya'akov calls that willingness to seek value and holiness in the more obscure reaches of our world "enlarging your boundaries."[161] To form my views according to the dictates of the intellect alone leave me a narrow, limited space in which to be. Letting go of them opens me to new horizons.

Who, though, can learn this other way of being? Who can pass on that understanding to others? In the opening words of our *parashah*, "And you, command the children of Israel," the humblest of God's servants, *Moshe Rabbenu,* is summoned to that mission. R. Ya'akov alludes to the qualities that merited Moses such a role. He recalls, as the Rabbis taught, that "All seven days of preparing the tabernacle [*yemei ha-milu'im*], Moses performed his duties wearing a plain white garment with an un-hemmed border [חלוק לבו שאין לו אימרא]."[162] In contrast to the splendid, ornamental priestly vestments being made ready for Aaron, that unadorned, unfinished linen garment symbolizes the temporariness of Moses' role as *kohen gadol* and, perhaps, his self-abnegation in fulfilling that role. While elaborate needlework was all around the High Priest's coat, "so that it does not tear" (Exod. 28:32), Moses' unsewn garment somehow resembles burial shrouds (*takhrikhim*), made of un-hemmed white fabric and assembled with an un-knotted thread. Such coverings surely belie any claims to permanence or invincibility. Yet in this, explains R. Ya'akov, is the secret of his greatness: Moses' unfinished robe teaches us that "no boundedness confined his being. For Moses was given majesty [*hod*] … and majesty is inwardness."[163] Here, it seems, is a key element in understanding the mission to which Moses is summoned. R. Ya'akov explains:

> "*And you* command the Children of Israel." "R. Isaac said: The Upper Light and the Lower Light, when united, are called 'And you.'" What this means is that God commanded Moses to learn the Torah with them lovingly and generously, as King Solomon said (Prov. 1:6), "Hear, my

> child, the instruction of your father, and do not abandon the teaching of your mother" שְׁמַע בְּנִי מוּסַר אָבִיךָ וְאַל תִּטֹּשׁ תּוֹרַת אִמֶּךָ. "The instruction of your father"—this is the simple aspect [*pashtut*] of words of Torah. "The teaching of your mother"—this is the inner dimension [*penimiut*] of words of Torah, which comes from the heart's depths, from the great love concealed in the human heart, like a mother's love for her child. In other words, one should never learn only the superficial level of Torah, paying it mere lip service. The words of Torah must be charged with meaning, with the Upper Light. Thus God said to Moses, "and you" are the one chosen to illuminate them, until all of them, individually, can perceive their own deficiency.[164]

In this portrait of Moses, "our rabbi and teacher," we catch sight of qualities rarely mentioned in his respect. The familiar figures of "father" and "mother," awe and love (*yirah/ahavah*), external and internal, fullness and lack seem to have shifted. To be sure, the "Torah" Moses received and passed on is traditionally understood as comprising both the Written and the Oral law—both its "masculine" and "feminine," revealed and concealed aspects.[165] R. Ya'akov's innovation here, though, is that what Moses teaches us is not only overt statutes and obligations but also something about the fundamental relationships that invest our world with meaning. Impeded by no ego clamoring for honor, in this teaching Moses embodies the "Torah of your mother." It is the reassurance, affirmation, and ultimate "knowing" entrusted to the "mother" most of all that empower her "children" to a learning fostered from within. And, perhaps we could say that the concern for material things, entrusted to "mothers" as well—a constant, endless, sometimes exhausting concern—is what empowers them, after all, to invest our world with holiness. The relationships that give meaning to one's world, it seems, can grow only through recognition of "one's own deficiency"—of a particular, vulnerable, imperfect aspect of one's being.

The Wellsprings of Salvation

Our reflections in this chapter have led us through vistas of human experience not often explored in intellectual discourse. Inherent in all the antinomies that have come to the fore is a root tension binding their conflicting elements. Izbica-Radzyn teaching speaks often and compassionately of that tension and of the pain and uncertainty it engenders. The desire to reach an authentic understanding of this dynamic and, through understanding and accepting it, ultimately to transform it—this desire is a guiding force in that worldview. We have heard, again and again, that if we wish to perceive the truth, "our way of looking at things" needs to be counterbalanced by another perspective, "from His side." To recall the absolutely other order of things, diametrically opposed to me, "opens a way out of solitude."[166] We are assured that through that opening, freedom, consolation, and hope promise themselves to us.

> The *ketoret* teaches of this: God, for His part, can "make good" [*levarer*] even the most harmful and destructive of actions. A person may feel one has done something irreparable, Heaven forbid. Or, the anguish one suffers might seem hopeless and unending. And yet the incense shows us that all is bound up with God, and God can save us in everything.

"Salvation" (*yeshu'ot*), R. Ya'akov reminds us in the next lines of this teaching, is immutably bound up with "damages" (*nezikim*).[167] Indeed, because encounters with injury and wrong so crowd our days, "everyday life is a preoccupation with salvation."[168] And that is what mandates the continual task of anticipating, of foreseeing and awaiting some kind of resolution, however distant it might be. The Rabbis put it as one of the questions each Jewish soul will be asked after its life on earth has come to an end: "Did you hope for salvation—*tzipita le-yeshu'a?*" Or, as R. Ya'akov understands it: Did you trust that God would search out and reveal an inner point of purity in every Jew, and in the Jewish nation, over and over again, ever anew, and in unimaginable ways?[169]

"Hope" for salvation wells from the earth's unknown depths. "Its horizon is the west—the place of greatest darkness and concealment, where the sun sets. And yet it is there, ultimately, that all birthing begins."[170]

Chapter 2

Selfhood

Introduction: Buried Treasure

> No one can know the originary point of vitality deep within the human heart, its meaning and its longing. For if one knew those things, one would know the Holy One, blessed be He—the source of Life in all of creation.[1]

That inner center, wholly beyond our grasp, is what we call the Self. My essence, the "soul of my soul" will forever be a mystery to me, as unknowable as God is.[2] And yet I, and you, spend our lives in search of that self. The will to grow, to realize what is uniquely ours, to discover the inborn germ of wholeness, our true identity, thrusts us on two opposing trajectories: outward and inward. Moving outward—toward others, toward things, our selves turn and return, through the world, moving inward into reflection, questioning, further becoming.

Charles Taylor, in his book *Sources of the Self: The Making of Modern Identity*, reflects on "modes of self-interpretation" that have become dominant in the modern West, the "languages of self-understanding" we use to express our "sense of self," often with little awareness of their historical contingency.[3] My lines above could, of course, be offered as a case in point. Can one responsibly use such words and concepts to unlock the meaning of writings so far removed from Western intellectual tradition as the mysteries of the *Zohar* or a Hasidic commentary written in 19th-century Poland? Does R. Ya'akov really share the concern, first voiced in modern philosophy by Decartes, with "self-awareness, the consciousness of I" as a starting point?[4] Do his teachings really give voice to the modern individualism of "self-discovery," with its aim "to identify the individual in his or her unrepeatable difference" that Montaigne originated?[5] Can we honestly discern in them that "idea, central to Herderian expressivism, that each person has his or her own original way of being"? Do the "crucial justifying concepts of the Romantic rebellion"—"the notion of an inner voice or impulse, the idea that we find the truth within us, and in particular in our feelings"[6]—resonate in Hasidic thought of the same historical period? Or do we, by using such concepts too freely, cross that unmarked border separating cultures and religious traditions, err into anachronism, and generate a creative reading that is sadly and simply wrong?

In my attempts to come to an understanding of the idea of selfhood embodied in R. Ya'akov's teachings, Taylor's study has been tremendously helpful. The breadth of his investigation of the history of ideas related to the self led me to think about parallel instances within Jewish tradition, and to question whether the historical consciousness he describes corresponds with Jewish thought in its various eras and perspectives. To compare Western philosophical tradition and the Jewish world of thought on the concept of selfhood in a comprehensive manner is a complex and difficult undertaking, and would lead us far afield.[7] And so I've chosen not to probe the conceptions of the self at work in the rabbinic, medieval, or early modern kabbalistic texts inlaid in R. Ya'akov's teachings. What matters for us here is R. Ya'akov's reading of them—the horizon of experience in which he bestows meaning to them.

The context in which his understanding takes form, we must recall, is the spiritual revival of Hasidism, beginning in the mid-18th century and, more immediately, in the branch of Polish Hasidism called the Przysucha school that emerged in the second decade of the 19th century. And so our exploration into R. Ya'akov's teachings on selfhood must begin with this broader perspective. Let's start with some of the convictions that guided the earliest Hasidic masters in the novel way of reading they vouchsafed to Jewish hermeneutical tradition.

> From the Baal Shem Tov: When one recognizes one's own faults, the sickness of the soul called "smallness"[8]—when one comes to that knowledge, one sweetens by knowing and heals oneself. The opposite happens when one experiences concealment [*sod ha-hester*], as the verse says, "Then I will hide My hiddenness" (Deut. 31:18). Here, one does not realize that one is spiritually ill, and for such a blow there is no remedy.[9]

This brief teaching, attributed to R. Israel Baal Shem Tov, renowned as the founding father of Hasidism, suggests that every individual is faced with a crucial task of coming to "know" himself/herself. The core of that knowing involves recognition of "one's heart's flaws" (*nig'ei levavo*) or imperfections. Honest self-reflection promises "sweetening"—the strength to free oneself of the "smallness" or spiritual diminution and unawareness in which one was confined. To refuse to take on the task of seeking self-knowledge imprisons one in the symbolic state called "concealment." That is a kind of isolation, even anonymity, brought on by cutting oneself off from one's inner world, a willful blindness to the need of knowing oneself with any authenticity. I think we could say that the responsibility for introspection, entrusted to every individual equally, that comes to the fore in this passage is a central element in early Hasidic teaching. Its importance is made clear in very plain terms: knowing brings healing; not-knowing destroys the self from within.

This, inarguably, is a cogent message that speaks to our most deeply rooted wishes for wholeness, honesty, connection. It voices a rare insightfulness into how the human psyche works, and empowers with the assurance that suffering is, in a sense, subjective. Understanding "sweetens" and repairs.

Disciples and followers of the Baal Shem Tov preserved his unwritten teachings in their own works and frequently evoke the perceptions the master conveyed to them within a broader context of discourse. It seems to me that here—beginning in the second generation of Hasidic tradition—a certain self-consciousness emerges. It comes to the fore in the ability and desire to describe, assess, and value the new tools of interpretation used in Hasidic readings that have begun to take form.

One of the Baal Shem Tov's most eminent and prolific students, R. Jacob Joseph of Polonnoye, transfers the seminal notion of self-interpretation we saw above from the realm of the personal-psychological to that of hermeneutics. A key phrase that often appears in R. Jacob Joseph's writings underlines his belief that one must seek and uncover that crucial connection between the verses of the Torah and the inner life of the person who studies them. "The well-known question" challenging us in understanding any given passage, he often notes, is: "The Torah is eternal. How is this [particular text] *in every individual*, who is called a microcosm [*'olam katan*] and [relevant] *in all ages and times*?"[10] R. Jacob Joseph resolves the difficulty with the following reasoning: "Now this is a great thing, [a truth] I received from my master: Every trouble a person suffers, in body or in soul—when one realizes that in that very suffering is God Himself, only in concealed form—as soon as one sees this, the concealment is taken away and the suffering ends, and with it all one's persecutions. [The Baal Shem Tov] spoke at length of this."

At the core of the hermeneutical challenge R. Jacob Joseph detects is the conviction that every word of the Torah speaks simultaneously on many levels: its descriptions and narratives, precepts and chastisements bear both evident, literal meaning and other, metaphorical meanings encoded in the minutest details of the biblical text. The "well-known question" he evokes, then, concerns that second, concealed dimension that *must* exist but at first reading evades us.

It is those verses that appear to be confined to specific time-bound circumstances or to mundane reality that most often incite this difficulty—such as the work of building the Tabernacle in the commentary cited above, with its lists of materials and tasks, or the names of 42 places enumerated in Numbers 33:6–37 that map the journey through the wilderness after the Exodus from Egypt. Passages like these don't seem to be talking about any personal truths; their relevance and immediacy "in all ages and times" is unclear. Here, then, is the question to which this early Hasidic master felt summoned to respond.

We can appreciate the particular significance Izbica-Radzyn Hasidic tradition attributes to this newly recognized hermeneutical task with the help of the following text. Its context is an unusual two-part essay entitled *Ha-hakdamah ve-ha-Petikhah,* published as a preface and an introduction to the *Beit Ya'akov.* It was penned by R. Ya'akov's son, R. Gershon Ḥanokh Henikh of Radzyn. One of the author's purposes is to map the evolution of Jewish intellectual history and esoteric tradition, with a view to distinguishing the unique contributions of key figures and schools of thought leading up to the founder of the Izbica dynasty, R. Mordecai Joseph (his grandfather). R. Gershon Ḥanokh's survey is striking in its acute nonobjectivity, despite the authoritative tone its author adopts throughout the essay. It begins with the era of biblical prophecy and ends in the author's present, the last years of the 19th century.[11]

> Then God sent us ... our master and teacher, ... R. Israel Baal Shem Tov, may his memory be for a blessing for life eternal, and opened before him the gates of wisdom, understanding and knowledge. And he began to explicate the Torah, preparing his heart to clarify its mysteries, to bring them within the reach of every individual in his times. And he brought the people to understand and realize that all the words of the Torah were given to Israel to be apprehended by each Jewish soul.... For there isn't a word of Torah that isn't needed by each and every Jew; [every word] must be reached and grasped with whatever perceptive tools one has.... He opened God's inner gate, which had been closed until his day[12]—opened it before the whole community of Jacob, for the Torah is our heritage and our betrothed; it is not way off in Heaven....[13] Thus all the events recounted in the Torah—they happen to Israel, collectively and individually, in each and every generation.[14]

The Baal Shem Tov's historical role, in this account, was to reveal that vital link between "all the words of Torah" and "each Jewish soul" and, moreover, to awaken those souls to their "need" for understanding. Note that R. Gershon Ḥanokh stresses the general as well as the particular. The meaning the Torah can potentially convey to us must matter to us "collectively and individually." It is given equally to all of Israel. But the only way each separate Jew can understand it, integrate it into his or her own life, and see how that life fits into a larger unity is by summoning "whatever perceptive tools one has."

This point brings us to an important issue we must now evaluate. The responsibility to "engage with the Torah," with which every Jew is charged, to study its laws and be loyal to its precepts, is by no means an elitist undertaking. As R. Gershon Ḥanokh makes clear some pages earlier, intellectual prowess alone wins no honor and promises no success. The Torah's mysteries are no longer the intimate ken of select kabbalists versed in secret lore as they were in the time of the *Zohar* and the days when Lurianic mystical circles flourished. Now, with Hasidism, new channels to the Torah and its meaning have been opened. They can be discovered only with an opening of the heart, every heart.

What R. Gershon Ḥanokh suggests here, I think is the conception of "individuation." Charles Taylor presents it as a milestone in the development of the modern idea of a self. "This is the idea which grows in the late nineteenth century that each individual is different and original, and that this originality determines how he or she ought to live.... [The differences between individuals] entail that each one of us has an original path which we ought to tread; they lay the obligation on each of us to live up to our originality."[15] Taylor stresses the pervasive influence this idea has had on modern culture—to the extent that "we barely notice it, and we find it hard to accept that it is such a recent idea in human history and would have been incomprehensible in earlier times."[16]

I'd like to suggest that an idea of the same nature begins to develop in the Hasidic teachings of masters who came to the fore in 19th-century Poland, beginning in its second decade. In the Introduction, we spoke of some events and forces that led to the emergence of the Izbica-Radzyn school. The figures mentioned there in effect mapped an evolution, even a revolution in Hasidic thought that we must understand better in order to appreciate the nature of R. Ya'akov's teachings as a whole, and his reflections on selfhood in particular. And so we will devote a few more words to one aspect of the evolving course Hasidic thought took, and to the turning point it reached in the early 19th century.[17]

From Lublin to Przysucha

Nearly a century after its modest beginnings in the Baal Shem Tov's small circle of disciples in the 1740s to 1750s, Hasidism had grown into a mass movement, with tens of thousands of followers living throughout Eastern and Central Europe as well as in the Land of Israel. The popularity and magnetism of the movement can be credited in part to the support, encouragement, and sense of joy Hasidism offered to "common Jews," often unlearned, with all their limitations and shortcomings. This fundamental appeal won many hearts, and succeeded in helping countless Jews to remain loyal to religious tradition.[18] And yet, in the second decade of the 19th century, groups of Hasidim began to consolidate in the study houses of Lublin with the shared sense that the way of life and connection to Torah learning that popular Hasidism taught had begun to appear simplistic and superficial. The dominant figure of the *zaddik* and the spiritual and material dependence on him expected from his followers, they felt, left little room for autonomy and personal growth among those loyal to him. Moreover, traditional, rigorous modes of learning, rooted in Talmud and codified halakhic works had, in many Hasidic communities, been pushed to the margins.[19]

R. Jacob Isaac, the "Holy Jew" of Lublin, shared these sentiments. His tremendous erudition in the "revealed Torah"—the Talmud, its commentaries, and halakhic works—and his extreme personal piety offered an alternate path that spoke to many of the discontented. The followers of the Holy Jew gained forces; parting ways with his own master, R. Jacob Isaac, known as the "Seer of Lublin," the Holy Jew left Lublin and established a Hasidic court of his own in the nearby town of Przysucha.[20]

The new path that was built under the leadership of R. Jacob Isaac and his chosen disciple and successor, R. Simḥah Bunem, entailed major and varied changes. Przysucha Hasidism shows a deliberate return to traditional modes of learning that had long been the focus for Polish Jewry—the legal discourses in the civil tractates of the Talmud and its commentaries. Interest in other realms of thought was also renewed in the Przysucha intellectual world after centuries of neglect by Eastern European Jewry, most importantly serious study of medieval rationalistic thought and the early-modern Maharal of Prague.[21] In addition, the religious elite that gathered in Przysucha felt the time had come to refocus their spiritual energy. The *zaddik*'s privileged role as intermediary and intercessor between his followers and God must be altered. R. Simḥah Bunem was the seminal figure in redirecting the objectives of Hasidic life in the new vision of Przysucha. In opposition to the trends of the two previous generations—led by figures such as R. Elimelekh of Lyzansk, R. Levi Isaac of Berdichev, R. Israel, the Maggid of Koznience, and R. Jacob Isaac, the Seer of Lublin—he advocated autonomy and a good measure of independence. R. Simḥah Bunem was famed for saying that:

> Every *avreich* [young scholar] must know that his journey to the *zaddik* and rebbe will teach him that he must seek [his] treasure not in the rebbe but in his own house. When he has traveled home again, there he must search and dig with all his strength. And, with effort, you will find it. Then you must believe [that this is the truth].[22]

This new emphasis on what lies hidden "in your own house" demands a reconsideration of many accepted values. In addition to the shift of responsibility from the rebbe or *zaddik* to the individual in search of spiritual growth, R. Simḥah Bunem addresses another necessary change of perspective. It is intimated in the biblical verse about Isaac: "And the Philistines stopped up all the wells which his father's servants had dug in the days of his father Abraham, filling them with earth" (Gen. 26:15):

> Every path one builds toward God must have inner vitality; if it has none it cannot reach Above. Indeed, the Philistines wanted to follow the path of Abraham, and they did as Abraham had done, but their actions had no inner vitality and that "stopped up" the way. Isaac wished to restore that well. Even though he had paths to God of his own, that did not keep him from digging his father's well, as the verse says. But afterwards, he dug his own. Indeed, every Jew who wants to serve the Holy One must dig a well in the self that will enable that person to draw close to the Creator, may He be blessed. For such a well does not exist, complete and whole at the very beginning.[23]

What R. Simḥah Bunem expresses, it seems to me, resonates with the new notions of "radical individuation" and "inner power" we spoke of earlier that emerged in late 18th- and early 19th-century European thought.[24] "Our modern sense of inner depths," as Taylor puts it, charges us with a new task. To "dig a well in one's self" or essence (*'atzmuto*) requires one to discover resources concealed in that dark space that belong to no one else. The path we forge, if it is rooted within, is invested with life. Treading it can draw us up to higher truths.

A formidable circle of disciples began to grow in Przysucha, coming from many and distant places. A number of them would later found Hasidic dynasties of their own: R. Menaḥem Mendel of Kotsk, R. Isaac of Warka, R. Ḥanokh of Alexandrov, R. Isaac Meir of Ger, R. Abraham of Ciachanow, and R. Mordecai Joseph of Izbica.[25] R. Simḥah Bunem's legacy, the emphasis on the individual forging a unique, personal connection to God and Torah, finds varied expression in the teachings of each school of Hasidism that branched from his root.

From Przysucha to Izbica

This brings us to the next and crucial point in R. Gershon Ḥanokh's account of how Izbica-Radzyn Hasidism came into being.

> Pre-eminent among the disciples of our master, R. Simḥah Bunem, was my honored grandfather—saintly, pious, and learned—our teacher, R. Mordecai Joseph of blessed memory ... He was the chosen one amidst his rebbe's holy flock ... And I myself heard him recount that R. Simḥah Bunem had said of him that he is like "the waters of Siloam, though they flow slowly, they penetrate to the utmost depths."[26]

Indeed, R. Mordecai Joseph's teachings compiled in the two volumes entitled (by his grandson) *Mei ha-Shiloaḥ* (the waters of Siloam) speak often and compellingly of the self and the drive to live authentically. Izbica Hasidism has been recognized as the most "radical" of all branches of Hasidic thought; the anarchism, determinism, and antinomianism it is said to preach has won the attention of many distinguished scholars.[27]

In this chapter, I would like to offer an alternate reading of R. Mordecai Joseph's teachings. It parts ways with the dominant perception of Izbica Hasidism in the academic and even broader Jewish world on a number of fundamental issues, which I hope will become clear in the course of our discussion. The guiding force in this alternate reading is the understanding voiced by R. Ya'akov of Radzyn, the son and successor of R. Mordecai Joseph. Interestingly, his teachings, recorded in the four large published volumes of the *Beit Ya'akov*, play no role whatsoever in the scholarly attempts to plumb the depths of *Mei ha-Shiloaḥ*.[28] R. Mordecai Joseph's thoughts on selfhood, individuation, truth, sin, identity, failure, despair, and transcendence are an inseparable part of the *Beit Ya'akov*. His influence, perhaps we could say, is "too often present in this book to be cited."[29] For that reason, R. Ya'akov's own teaching must be appreciated on one level as an "unpacking" of concepts that were introduced by his father, the founder of Izbica Hasidism, often in laconic and cryptic terms.[30] He explores what some of those concepts mean on a personal level and considers what they are intended to arouse in the hearts of those who hear them. With this approach, R. Ya'akov seeks to bring them "closer to home." Clearly, the stories of the Torah we will meet in the following pages are to be perceived, in a vital sense, as "our story." R. Ya'akov's reading of them can offer aid to each of us in understanding something of where we have been and who we are meant to be. This, I think, is what R. Gershon Ḥanokh suggests in the final lines that close his Introduction to the *Beit Ya'akov*:

> And now, House of Jacob, walk in the light of the Lord—**come home** [*bo'u ha-bayta*]. See and understand all the words of Torah written in this book. See and know: all its words are needed by every Jewish person, in all places and all times. All the things recounted in the Torah—they will illuminate each soul and teach one how to live, how to understand everything that happens in one's life.[31]

The Self Awakened

> "When God began to create heaven and earth—the earth being waste and void, with darkness over the surface of the deep .... And God said, 'Let there be light.' And there was light" (Gen. 1:1–3). It is written: "If You would call, I would answer You; only have a desire for the work of Your hands" (Job 14:15). "Call"—for God calls out to us. And what is this call? It is God's planting hope and anticipation in our hearts. After that, each of us makes our "calling" known so that He "may have a desire for the work of [the] hands"—so that our actions can be considered "ours." Indeed, God's calling to the inmost heart is imperceptible. All people, it would appear, are the same. If one is more active and motivated than another, it is only because that person is making God's call to him evident, and we see that person's achievements as "his own." What this shows is that the world was created with the letter *beit* and not with the letter *aleph*: to teach us that human perception is limited to what already exists. And although it is written that "the earth was waste and void," this refers only to our subjective, human view of things. In truth, the whole order of Creation recounted in the Torah is an immanent part of being, and is lived by every individual—"through my flesh, I envision the divine" [Job 19:26]. What is it, then, that brings a person to want chaos no longer? "Chaos" [or "waste and void"] represents the unruly energy [כחות שובבים]

> of childhood; when one comes to realize that one is still unbuilt, one channels that energy to serving God. But where does such an awareness originate, the recognition that until now all was chaos, and that one wants it no longer? It emerges because God planted it in one earlier. At first, though, the individual is wholly unaware of that illumination.[32]

This passage introduces a number of important concepts. I would like to set each of them out and so provide a framework for the thoughts that follow. First, a general comment regarding the way the biblical text is read. R. Ya'akov implicitly defies a linear, sequential reading of the "Creation story."[33] No reconstruction of (pre-) history, the first verses of *Bereshit*, or Genesis "start in the middle," begin *after* the beginning. That is the symbolic value of the letter *beit*, the second letter of the Hebrew alphabet. In truth, light (verse 3) preceded the primordial darkness (verse 2): the mysterious prelude to the opening verse of the Torah is shrouded in the *aleph*, the first letter, concealed from our eyes.[34]

Secondly, as R. Ya'akov himself points out, the biblical story must be read allegorically: "The whole order of Creation ... is lived by every individual." Within the microcosm that each human being is, the same developmental process unfolds. And thus introspection on the evolving self can potentially help us understand not only our own lives but also some hidden and greater truth about the cosmos.[35]

Thirdly, we note here the concept of dialogue as a formative element of the self. Fragmented, permeated with silence and oblique responses, this interchange of messages continues throughout our days on earth. Some people remain forever unaware of the Other voice. Such a life, lived out as a monologue, has little promise for growth. When the human will acts in isolation, as an autonomous ego, it can achieve nothing of real value. Such a will is bereft of an authentic self and so its attainments never become its own. Izbica-Radzyn tradition denotes that mistaken mindset with the phrase "my power and the might of my hand has won me this wealth"—כחי ועצם ידי עשה לי את החיל הזה.[36]

Against this illusory conviction of autonomy, R. Ya'akov urges his listeners to become aware of another mode of being. The dialogue between God and the human soul begins at a moment preceding consciousness. "For God calls out to us." Inaudible, undetected, that gesture inviting communication is given to the heart. Seeds of "hope and anticipation" germinate without our awareness—"God's call to the inmost heart is imperceptible." The "waste and void" or chaos of primordial Creation mirrors the early stages of human life—childhood, without self-awareness, without the ability of self-determination, emotionally volatile. When, suddenly, one begins to see that "until now, all was chaos"—then, at last, one stands on the threshold of a new phase of being. "One sees that one is still un-built." Only then can the building, the construction of a genuine, unique identity, begin. That awakening consciousness, R. Ya'akov explains, is in fact the human response to God's initial summons.

In this teaching, R. Ya'akov links the concept of dialogue to stages of maturation. Here, it is specifically the transition from the "waste and void" of childhood to nascent responsibility and self-formation through awareness of God. As we will see, though, this notion of dialogue is a paradigm that underlies multiple stages of spiritual development an individual can pass through in the course of a lifetime. Becoming aware of our ongoing dialogue with God can infuse meaning into every aspect of our experience, trials as well as joys.

The biblical figure most famed for his "face to face" dialogue with the divine as he strives to fulfill his mission is Moses. And yet in rabbinic and Hasidic readings, as we will see, the direct, intimate, perhaps enviable encounters with God so striking in the biblical narrative are counterbalanced by frightening expanses of distance and uncertainty. It is in those empty spaces, in effect, that Moses is summoned to find himself. R. Ya'akov portrays this quest for self-understanding in each subsequent stage as Moses becomes the leader of a nation and discovers his identity as most humble Jew.

Moses' Calling

We'll begin by considering one of the crucial junctures in Moses' career. R. Ya'akov, after the Sages, draws our attention to a hiatus in the biblical narrative that a simple reading would overlook. The last 15 chapters of Exodus, we recall, are devoted to the myriad tasks involved in the building of the *mishkan*, or Tabernacle. The commandment, "Let them make Me a sanctuary [*mikdash*] that I may dwell among them" (Exod. 25:8), marks a turning point in the history of the Jewish nation. In the first chapters of Exodus, the people are redeemed from Egypt; the reed sea parts before them; and subsequent chapters recount the giving of the Torah at Sinai and enumerate the guidelines it contains that will inform the legal and ethical spheres of Jewish life. The Tabernacle is to become the center of the spiritual and ritual world. It is to be "a house for God," a holy space to which each Jew can come, pray, "see and be seen," and sense that indwelling, divine presence. The structure of the Tabernacle, consisting of wood and gold, screens and curtains, linen, turquoise, and scarlet wool, is pieced together out of "contributions" or gifts offered by each and every Jew. The Tabernacle's vessels, instruments, and priestly garments are also prepared in these chapters of Exodus, and their form and function are described in rich detail. This extensive account comes to a close with a listing of the final actions needed to bring the Tabernacle to completion. The tablets are brought into the ark; then the table, the menorah, the gold altar, the curtain, the laver, and the courtyard—everything is placed as God has commanded (Exod. 40:17–33). Ironically, at this final, long-awaited moment, after months of labor and devotion on the part of all of Israel, when the work of inspired artisans' hands stands in nearly perfect composition—the story grinds to a halt. R. Ya'akov reminds us what happened.

> In the midrash *Tanḥuma*: "Having finished the construction of the Tabernacle, all sat and waited—when would the Divine Presence descend at last to dwell within it? And they wondered sorrowfully why they hadn't the power to bring it to completion." And [similarly] in *Midrash Rabba*, "Moses' heart was grieved. He said, 'Everyone has brought their contribution to the Tabernacle and I have brought nothing.'"[37]

R. Ya'akov questions how this situation came to be. Drawing a causal connection between the first midrash and the second midrash, he suggests that it was no simple oversight that Moses had "brought nothing." Moses is inherently unable to give. This apparent deficiency is rooted in his paralyzing awareness that "the earth is the Lord's and all that it holds" (Ps. 24:1)—that, in truth, no one owns anything at all. "What, then, is there to give?" All of Israel, on the other hand, for whom "God's ways are hidden, and who cannot see the light of the Lord," do harbor the illusion that they possess material wealth. They have chosen to part with something of their "own" plenty and this imbues them with the joy of giving, of fulfilling God's commandment to make "offerings" for the Tabernacle—a happiness Moses cannot share. Seeing his grief, God responds, "I will grant you something that no other being can do." When each Jew came before Moses with a contribution in hand, "Moses would look into the hearts of the children of Israel and, in measure with the love he perceived in each individual heart, he would determine where their gift should be placed"—"in the holy of holies, or by the altar, or in the courtyard."[38]

In this scenario, Moses' "lightness of being" is felt by the prophet himself to be truly unbearable. His penetrating vision of the truth about reality instills an acute sense of self-effacement and worthlessness, bringing him to a near total annulment of ego. What is particularly interesting in this description is its realistic, human evaluation of Moses' psychological state. Mystics throughout the ages have yearned and battled fiercely to attain such an exalted level of selfless devotion to God, and Moses is the archetype of success. And yet here, with "nothingness" penetrating his very being, sadness grips Moses' heart. In his eyes, the illusion under which everyone else functions has become enviable: God desires their gifts and awaits the unique contribution each of them can give. Moses, paradoxically, having shrugged off that burdensome, material concern for a "self," is left empty-handed.

But God mitigates his pain with a new directive: Moses' role will be to arrange the gifts of others, to put them in their proper places, and so to create a lasting edifice out of myriad disparate parts. R. Ya'akov combines this account with a third midrashic tradition. It, too, speaks of the unexplainable situation sketched above that occurred in the same textual gap: each separate component of the Tabernacle has been made, and yet neither all the wise men of Israel nor Moses himself are able to make it stand. Day after day, says the midrash, "Moses assembled the Tabernacle and dismantled it once again." Until finally, miraculously, on the seventh day, "Moses had finished the work" (Exod. 40:33).[39] At last, after that long process filled with joy and uncertainty, anticipation and dread, the Tabernacle comes into being. It stands. And yet once again, even more critically than before, the Rabbis point to another obstacle that bars Moses from a sense of accomplishment. "Moses could not enter the Tent of Meeting, because the cloud had settled upon it" (Exod. 40:34). Here, too, R. Ya'akov explores the moments Moses lives between these last verses of Exodus and the first verse of Leviticus.

> Like the creation of the world—the Talmud says that the grasses waited just beneath the soil, until Adam was created to pray for them. Only then did the rain fall, and they could grow (B. *Ḥullin* 60b). That is, the grasses were fearful to come out into the open, to thrust themselves into something unknown [*sefekot*], until Adam's prayers brought the rain and showed them there was nothing to fear. Thus it was at the tent of meeting—"the glory of God filled the tent"—this was the final, closing moment of the Giving of the Torah. Now, those words of Torah would enter the form of the Tabernacle under God's "signature." [Moses] was fearful to thrust himself into something new—"And Moses could not enter the tent of meeting." And so "He called to Moses" (Lev. 1:1)—only calling, not speaking directly to him, just to "moisten the world," as it was at the beginning of Creation.[40]

What R. Ya'akov describes is a transitional point along with the anxiety it provokes as one stands on the threshold, about to pass over to "something new."

Like the seeds and spores that lie still in the soil, locked in their selves until the rains come and wet the earth—so Moses is portrayed here. He stands before a momentous opening, a new beginning, but cannot enter. What impedes him, in this comparison, is not the "cloud of glory" (as a simple reading of the verses might suggest) but his own inner state: his acute, even petrifying awareness that now "something new" and utterly unknown is being asked of him.

God's "call" to Moses, recorded in the first verse of Leviticus, is those drops of rain that free the seeds from their cells and give them the power and confidence to germinate, to "thrust themselves" out of and into. That is to say, to cross a threshold demands both a parting from a familiar, often comfortable way of being and a willingness to be transformed, to become something or someone more than before. The seeds will sprout into grass, a mode of being of which they know nothing. And Moses?

R. Ya'akov reminds us that this is not the first transitional point Moses has confronted, with its challenge to "thrust himself" into the next, higher stage of being. At other significant times in his life as well, God called: "Moses, Moses!" In each of them, this doubled address served "to separate him first from the aspect of Torah he had been absorbed in until that moment, and then to prepare himself to receive new "'words of Torah.'"[41] Throughout his teachings on *parashat Vayikra*, R. Ya'akov stresses the effect this gentle manner of "calling" can have on every individual. "It infuses one with purity and desire. Purity—meaning that one turns away from everything else and faces Above, ready to receive all that God asks of one. And desire—the calling makes one's heart long to receive God's words."[42] Or, "God's calling inspires one's heart to repent and cry out in appeal."[43] Essentially, to be "called" is to be redirected. Heeding that call involves letting go of or disconnecting oneself from old ways. Only from within the void of their absence can one come to hope for, to ask for, to need "something new."

Three crucial junctures in Moses' life are marked by this manner of calling: "At the burning bush, at Sinai, and at the tent of meeting. And at all of them He called, 'Moses, Moses!'"[44] In each instance, God first calls to Moses and then speaks with him. The Rabbis in the midrash *Sifra* deliberate: What element most fundamentally is shared by these three incidents—what distinguishes them as pivotal moments in Moses' life story and, in consequence, in the history of the Jewish people? The question is a difficult one; each incident seems to be instrumental for a different reason. In his own reflections on the answers the Rabbis propose in the *Sifra*, R. Ya'akov suggests that God's revelation to Moses at the burning bush, when Moses was at the dawn of his career, marks "the beginning of speech," introducing Moses to his personal mission as redeemer of the people from enslavement. At Sinai, God addresses him as a leader and channel, with the role of communicating the Torah and God's will to all of Israel. But regarding the third instance, at the tent of meeting, the question remains. There is no fire or thunder, no clear "beginning" and no mountain peaks, only a still, small voice audible to Moses alone.[45]

On R. Ya'akov's reading, what unites these three moments is that in each "the calling alludes to something new"—to a new role Moses must take on in guiding the Jewish people along the trajectory of time as they become a nation. To facilitate this transformation, at each of these moments Moses' self-perception must be called into question once again. R. Ya'akov's comments on the first of these thresholds are particularly telling. At the burning bush, from amid the fire, God pronounces to Moses that Israel will soon be redeemed from suffering in Egypt and that he, Moses, has been chosen as His messenger (Exod. 3:4–10).

> "And Moses said, *Who am I* that I should go to Pharaoh [and free the Israelites from Egypt]?" (Exod. 3:11) That is, he asked: "Why was I chosen out of all of Israel? And, more: "Will I indeed take the children of Israel out of Egypt? ... My father, of blessed memory [R. Mordecai Joseph] taught that in "Who am I," [Moses] was asking what his unique essence [*yesoda de-garmei*] really is. Is this his portion and root? How is his very being bound up with this "taking out"? And what strength has God given him to enable him to succeed?

In other words, R. Ya'akov adds, Moses needed to know that this mission is his alone—that for some intrinsic reason he of all people has been chosen to devote his very soul to the task.[46]

Some chapters later, the Jewish nation, redeemed from Egypt, journeys through the wilderness toward Mount Sinai. In the prelude to the next crucial event in their becoming an entity united by the laws of the Torah, Moses is summoned to rise to a second challenge. The first stage of his mission is behind him. The next stage now looms, and Moses must come out to meet it. At this juncture, in R. Ya'akov's commentary we find reflections of a similar kind.

The verse reads: "Moses went up to God. The Lord *called to him* from the mountain, saying, 'Thus shall you say to the house of Jacob and declare to the children of Israel'" (Exod. 19:3). R. Ya'akov seeks to understand the meaning of this act of calling. He cites the *Zohar* (2.78b): "The Holy One said to Moses: You will be my loyal messenger—to draw Israel after Me." But why, asks R. Ya'akov, is the quality of loyalty capitalized upon at this particular moment? Indeed, we readers know full well that God recognizes Moses as "the most faithful of all My household" (Num. 12:7) in his every deed. Why is his loyalty cited now as the reason, in a sense, he has been chosen?

In explanation, R. Ya'akov begins by noting a most prosaic and general rhetorical feature of the Bible: that direct speech is presented with the formula "And X spoke, saying ..." or "And X said, saying ...". Here, in the moments before the Torah is to be given to Moses and then bestowed to the Jewish nation, that formula is weighted with significance. In effect, it points to the momentous responsibility Moses most now take on: not only to receive the infinite wisdom contained in the Torah, but to pass it on to the Jewish people of his and all generations to come. The doubled formulation in the biblical text—"spoke, saying"—alludes, in R. Ya'akov's explanation, to that two-stage process. "And God spoke" would represent the essential, divine truth encoded in pure form in the holy letters of the Torah. "Saying," on the other hand, would be the reformulation of that ineffable Will in human terms, comprehensible to "regular people"—to all those Jewish souls waiting at the foot of the mountain. Moses has been elected to teach them. In R. Ya'akov's reading, this "calling" to Moses is meant to awaken him to a vital facet of his identity that had been concealed, in a sense, from the prophet himself until this moment. Being "called," as R. Ya'akov told us earlier, stirs every heart with hope. What matters most, as it were, in God's choice of Moses as intermediary in "giving" the Torah to Israel is that "the words of Torah enter the heart of every Jew." And thus, at this moment at Sinai, what *Moshe Rabbenu*, our teacher, is actually summoned to "give over" is that vital, primary experience of hope. Any manner of learning or receiving must begin with a quickening of the heart—with the inchoate desire to hear all the Words still to come.[47]

Returning now to the third incident, which marks a final turning point in Moses' life story and in the chronicles of Jewish history, perhaps we can better understand the radically "new" reality signaled in the chapter that is about to begin.

"The midrash teaches: Before the *mishkan* was built, all of the wilderness was a place of speech; once the *mishkan* was standing, the wilderness became invalidated for speech."[48] Indeed, we know that Moses' path throughout his life has been guided by dialogues with God whose setting was many and varied expanses of unsettled "wilderness"—from the impure depths of Egypt, the hinterland of Midian, the shores of the sea, until the encounter on the rugged heights of Sinai. Now that the Tabernacle has come into existence, say the Rabbis, such barren places must cease to be the chosen sites for God's word. Another locale and a different internal state in the collective life of the Jewish people have come.

To grasp the significance of this transition, we must ask what the "wilderness," in its various forms, is meant to symbolize.

> There are certain places in the world that are alien to all humanness. These are places of desolation [*ḥaruva*]—the sea and the deserts—and Jonah the prophet even believed that "God's glory is not in the sea ..." for no one in the midst of the sea has the peace of mind to contemplate God's presence .... In such places, then, God is called "He" just like before the world was created, with no one to recognize Him. Now, even after Creation, God wishes the world to remember that aspect called "He," and so the desert, where wild animals lurk, and the tumultuous, choking seas that repulse all human presence remain. His purpose is to show us ... that He has no need of, no benefit from the world ... from our recognition of His glory.[49]

"Desolate," void of any signs of humanity or self-awareness, the desert and the seas in their very being bear witness to the hidden power that created them. The referent "He" emphasizes the separateness and autonomy of God, independent of the world He chose to bring into existence. The unseen "He"—unrecognized, unknowable—is from time eternal.

Posed against these anonymous expanses of indifference is a second, opposite mode of existence. R. Ya'akov calls it "settled places" (*yishuv*)—enclaves of civilization humankind has invented, in which we can take refuge from the chaotic forces of emptiness that reign in the wilderness. Here, people have the peace of mind to contemplate God's power and honor; they perceive themselves as free agents, empowered to fashion the best possible reality. In "settled places" God is called "You"—that is, seemingly accessible and directly present to the thinking mind.[50]

With this basic dichotomy in hand, let's return to the midrash cited above. "Before the *mishkan* was built, all of the wilderness was a place of speech; once the *mishkan* was standing, the wilderness became invalidated for speech." In a characteristic hermeneutical gesture, R. Ya'akov suggests that these two spatial dimensions (desert and Tabernacle) and these two temporal points (before and after construction) reflect two alternate psychological states.[51]

> The "places of desolation" in the human psyche are its "unruly energy" [כוחות שובבים]—the anxieties and the slumber that keep one from being there with God. And in the world—[those places are] the desert and

> seas, who "flee from their Master"—there, one is overcome with forgetting and apprehension and so cannot be there with God.[52]

What the emotions or mental states mentioned in this passage have in common is their power to absent us or, as R. Ya'akov puts it, to keep us from "being there" in the most important place of all—with the Other (*nokhaḥ Hashem*). Drowsiness, worry, un-remembering—all of them speak of an internal schism. In such states our sense of psychic wholeness splits. We are, most literally, beside ourselves. Our "selves," in this case, would be those rational, self-aware individuals we prefer to be, choosing, with total presence of mind, our actions and facing, in full responsibility, our highest values. The bothersome question R. Ya'akov addresses here is what constructive purpose the wilderness could possibly serve in an advanced world—why can't chaos just be a prehistoric stage best left to fade into oblivion? His answer strikes at the heart of our modern identity: places of desolation remind us that, in truth, "God has no need of, no benefit from the world ... from our recognition" of anything—self, history, "You," world. The wilderness outside is a vast indifference of being. The "wilderness" within is a realm of un-control that we will never conquer. And so it humbles us by reminding us, over and over again, that moments of clarity and understanding are only one aspect of our being.

From the time of the Exodus and until this moment, the children of Israel have journeyed through that place of "no water but only rock/rock and no water,"[53] with its savage disregard for the human and the divine. In all of that time, and from within that uninhabited void, Moses alone was "called." Moses alone had the strength and clarity of vision to lead the Jewish nation through that windy turmoil. The people, during all that period, are a faceless, undifferentiated mass. They grumble and they argue, they sin and plead in one voice for forgiveness. In no way does each of them face God in their singularity nor does God address them as individuals. Moses serves as their exclusive intermediary and as God's chosen and sole messenger. With the Tabernacle now standing, his elect status is about to be undermined. The intimate mode of communication in that lonely terrain Moses knows so well must now give way to a different, ramified sort of relationship. The new connection to be developed between the Jewish people and God will be public, shared, and wholly visible. It is to be enabled by Aaron and the *Kohanim*. Moreover, each and every Jew will be charged to take on an active, highly personal, and constant engagement in it.

Offerings and Selves

The first and striking manifestation of this new reality, R. Ya'akov notes, is recorded in the closing verses of the book of Exodus.

> "And God's glory filled the Tabernacle" (Exod. 40:34). As [the Tabernacle] became a completed entity, everyone saw fully that "there is none beside Him" [Deut. 4:35]; every action and every thought has its source in God alone. At that moment, "the wilderness ceased to be the place of speech." Now a new manner of serving God opened before them—the sacrifices. Through the Tabernacle, they could see transparently that "no place is devoid of His presence." Those "wild places" [*mekomot shovavim*], however, remained unaware that they were actually filled with God's light. The sea and the desert had no knowledge of that. And so the sacrifices would now serve to illuminate, spread, and expand holiness so that even such spaces would become aware of the light within them.[54]

In this teaching, R. Ya'akov suggests that a new dimension of consciousness has begun to evolve in the hearts of the Jewish people. In the first stage of their redemption from Egypt they were led passively through the wilderness, with no real understanding or cognizance of the momentous events they were living. The reality most immediate to them was one of absence, lack, and helplessness. Its extreme expression comes in the fatal moments preceding the sin of the Golden Calf—"Make us a god who shall go before us, for that man Moses ... we do not know what has happened to him" (Exod. 32:1). The wilderness itself, as we have seen, symbolizes this mental state—blind and inimical to everything, it represents a radical disconnection from the self. That is the psychological climate most conducive to sin, a mindset R. Ya'akov often describes with the Aramaic phrase "to flee from the Master."[55] The desolate places of the world are riddled with "forgetting" and unawareness. They "turn their back," hide themselves, negate the other together with their "selves." And so those forced to make their way through a psychic or real wilderness may well fall into the grip of the same alienation and estrangement.

The sense of selfhood that begins to take form in the Jewish people, now that the Tabernacle has been completed, includes an additional aspect of experience. The sacrifices (*korbanot*), with the ritual actions and materials they require, address the reality of sin and deficiency as an inescapable part of human life. Each individual must now contend with his or her own failings, must somehow summon the strength and the desire to "come back" in repentance, and, most critically, must manifest the whole of that demanding emotional and spiritual process in the physical act of bringing a sacrifice.

The offering, or *korban*, in its essence, we must recall, symbolizes a culminating point in the life of the Jew who brings it.

> To sin is to turn coarsely material. One's life forces plummet to a bestial existence; they can plunge even to mute inertness. And now, when one returned to God and brought an animal, lay one's hands upon it, and it was offered up on the altar, the offering was consumed by the fiery lion from Above, one of the holy creatures who bear the Divine Chariot. In that moment, two poles, seemingly opposing, unite.[56]

The dynamic R. Ya'akov evokes here is, in his eyes, the core importance of the sacrifices. Intrinsic to it is the conviction, voiced in many of his teachings, that every created entity actually has a "self," essence, or light that illuminate it from within. The lower the life form, the less evident that inner vitality is—both to the eye of the observer and to the entity itself. For that reason, R. Ya'akov says, inert elements, such as salt and stones, are termed (in Hebrew) "silent" (*dommemim*). Speech and vitality abide in them as well, but remain unactualized. All the orders of nature "yearn" to break out of their petrifaction and their animalism, to struggle free of their alienation from themselves and be drawn into a higher sphere of existence.[57]

This notion can help us appreciate why all the orders of nature—animal, plant, and inorganic—play such a vital role in the ritual service of the *mishkan*, and later of the Temple. The Tabernacle is comprised of wood and skins, fabrics, dyes, and metals; that in and of itself would suggest a certain inseparable, indwelling presence in the structure itself. Even more explicitly, it is the oxen and sheep, the incense and flour and hyssop who "give their whole selves." They are consumed in fire, and that is what ultimately enables the vital connection between the Jewish people and God to be realized.

But how do these physical elements have the power to engender a metaphysical connection of such dimensions? As R. Ya'akov sees it, their power lies in the intrinsic, primordial link between them and higher forms of being. He recalls the comment in the *Zohar* that sacrifices are not called *kiruv* (nearness) or *kerivut* (relationship) but *korban* (drawing close)—a gradual process that begins in distance and separation, and culminates in complete unity.

> That is, the lower a form of life is in this world, the higher its point of origin in the upper worlds—like the beast, who is drawn from the image of the ox, one of the bearers of the Divine Chariot.[58]

These "bearers of the chariot"—supernatural figures with the faces of an ox, a lion, an eagle, and a human being—like all the angelic host, R. Ya'akov notes, serve God upright, in a state of endless, unflickering brilliance that blots out any sense of their selfhood or separate existence—"they cannot remember themselves, and so they are called 'holy beasts' [*ḥayyot ha-kodesh*]." At the other extreme are the beasts of this world, "wholly unconscious, unable to stand upright. And the inanimate forms of existence in this world come from an even higher place ... For the closer one draws to the Creator, the more silent and lifeless one appears from behind."[59] In truth, both the inanimate orders of nature and the "desolate places"—the wilderness and the seas—are "charged with vitality." But, so great is the distance separating them from the Creator that they are cast into immobility, ossified and blinded to their own essence.

The sense of separateness and loneliness, to which every aspect of being must at times fall prey, is resolved through the *korbanot*. The animal and inorganic parts of the sacrifice "return" to their source, "consumed" or enveloped in fire. And the individual who offers them "returns" in repentance. When the sacrifice is accepted, when one is forgiven for all one's sins, it becomes possible once again to "be there before God, face to face, in the aspect of 'You.'"[60]

This new order in the collective life of the Jewish people, and the focus and enclosure the Tabernacle provides surely herald a transformation of great proportions. But what will become of Moses? What new insight on his own personal identity and public role is Moses now challenged to attain as he moves toward full self-realization?

Acts of *Semikhah*

> "And He called to Moses and God spoke to him" (Lev. 1:1). The midrash says: "Moses was standing off to the side. The Holy One said to him: How long will you demean yourself? Your hour has come! And thus 'He called to Moses.'" That is, after the *mishkan* was built, Moses supposed that since it would be Aaron's role [as *kohen*] to offer the sacrifices, there was no longer any need for him, and so he stood off to the side. For that reason, "God called to him and spoke with him"—[to tell Moses] that even now, all the Torah's words relating to the sacrifices will still be given to Moses alone.[61]

The midrash R. Ya'akov quotes here suggests yet another cause for Moses' hesitation to begin living the next chapter of the story: his humility, or "his fear of taking up a place that is not his."[62] In a curious combination of prophetic awareness and human ignorance, Moses foresees the role that will be given to Aaron his brother, but cannot find his own image in the scenario he knows is about to unfold. Arrested with apprehension that he might wrongly claim the portion meant for another, Moses "stood off to the side"—out of the picture, in "no place" at all. Within this emotional context, God's calling serves to draw Moses back into the story—to remind him and inform him once again who he will now be, what his place is, this time in the new reality of the Tabernacle and its ritual service. R. Ya'akov seeks to define the nascent aspects of Moses' being that he must discover at this stage.

As a first step in reaching that definition, in the next lines of the teaching cited above, R. Ya'akov sets out his view of a fundamental difference between Aaron, with his authority as *Kohen Gadol*, on one hand, and *Moshe Rabbenu*, "our rabbi and teacher," on the other. The precepts concerning the sacrifices are highly detailed and complex. Aaron represents that aspect of specificity—of direct correspondence between deeds or circumstances and the kind of sacrifice each of them calls for. Moses, on the other hand, represents the aspect of generality—the all-inclusive, undifferentiated force of the Torah as a whole as it emerges from its source in the divine.[63] On a basic level, this would mean that Aaron's portion is in the concrete realm of defined action, while Moses' portion is in the more abstract realm of contemplation, of internalizing and communicating knowledge.[64] Aaron is charged to carry out and enact the commandments voiced in theoretical form by Moses.

This clear and absolute demarcation of roles would surely neutralize any fear of treading on the other's territory. At the same time though, R. Ya'akov suggests it has a drawback and a potential danger. If Aaron were to be the sole agent aiding people in atoning for their wrongdoings, the "specificity" he symbolizes would actually bar them from ever freeing themselves totally of sin. Whatever sacrifice was prescribed would set right the particular misdeed it was meant to correct, but it could never erase the specter of all one's failings.[65] For that reason, R. Ya'akov continues, one single yet vital aspect of the sacrifices was entrusted not to Aaron but to Moses alone. To appreciate R. Ya'akov's innovation on this point, we must recall the wider context.

The first verses of Leviticus set out the fundamentals related to the animal and meal offerings that individuals are able to bring in order to atone for sins of various kinds that they have committed. The Torah delineates the manner in which these offerings are sacrificed and the wrongdoings with which they correspond. The crucial element, for our purposes now, concerns the following detail. When a Jew brings the live offering—an animal from his flock or herd, or one that has been purchased with money—to the tent of meeting, he is to "lay his hand [*ve-samakh yado*] upon the head of the burnt offering, that it may be acceptable in his behalf, in expiation for him" (Lev. 1:4). Along with this symbolic physical gesture of connection, termed *semikhah*, the "sinner" is to confess his wrongdoings verbally.[66] His words serve, in a sense, to open up conscious and unconscious dimensions of his life. As the dark recesses of his soul are exposed, his failings and errors are voiced, revealed, and exorcized. His hands, laid upon the animal "with all his might" serve to transfer "evil" to the depths of the animal.[67] R. Ya'akov now seeks to link the act of laying on the hands to the essence of Moses. Understanding this link will then clarify the new role that Moses was now to take on from this point onward.

> *Moshe Rabbenu* symbolizes totality [*ha-klal*] and so the mitzvah of *semikhah* was "his," apart from the actual offering of the sacrifice. *Semikhah*, indeed, must be done with all one's strength, as the midrash (*Sifra* 4.1) says. For, by laying one's hands upon the animal, one offered up all one's strength to God. Even though the sacrifice was brought to atone for a specific sin, [laying on one's hands] restored completeness to all that had been lacking, even those deficiencies of which one was unaware. And thus the Sages taught [B. *Menaḥot* 93b], "Whoever considers *semikhah* as an optional part of the commandment—it is as if that person has not atoned." What this means is that one cannot be forgiven and restored to completeness, because one did not connect the aspect of "Moses"—laying the hands on the sacrifice. Still, that person is forgiven for the specific deficiency—the aspect of "Aaron"—for which one's sacrifice was meant to atone.[68]

This profile of Moses as "totality" implies he represents some unifying force that can engender a sense of psychic wholeness in every individual. The most difficult part in mending a fragmented self, R. Ya'akov suggests, concerns "those deficiencies of which one was unaware" or, more literally, "the things one doesn't consciously know about." Indeed, being able to reach that sphere of "not knowing" has far-reaching significance: "*Semikhah* connects even those acts that would seem to be sins, and heals what has already been committed. It transforms even those [negative actions] to merits."[69]

"Laying on one's hands," then, summons the individual to bring all the bifurcating parts of the self to account. By bearing with all one's might on the animal's head, all of one's failings, willful as well as uncontrolled, cease at that moment to be a part of the individual. They pass, through the hands, from one's soul to the living creature that has been brought in offering. Ultimately, all that "forgetting" and slumber, all the pride and alienation is "redeemed." Transferred to the animal, all of it can ascend and be transmuted, consumed with the animal in the flames of the altar.

Within this complex of generality and specificity, the importance of "laying the hands" as a ritual action is now clear. But on what textual basis can R. Ya'akov state that "the mitzvah of *semikhah* was 'his'"—was "given" in some absolute sense to Moses as his portion in the new religious order initiated with the Tabernacle? The verses of the Torah never attribute this or any other aspect of the divine service, once the Tabernacle is inaugurated, to Moses at all. Even more puzzling, we find no statement in rabbinic or halakhic sources alluding to this connection.[70] R. Ya'akov's justification, voiced in the continuation of the teaching cited above (*Vayikra* 14), seeks to understand the "essence" of Moses on a different plane. And yet, as we will see, Moses himself attains this understanding only at the end of his life. We'll turn to this now.

After setting out the respective roles of Moses and Aaron regarding the sacrifices, R. Ya'akov writes:

> This alludes to the act of ordination [*semikhat zekainim*] that was done from generation to generation. One could be ordained only by someone who, in his turn, had been ordained, all the way back to *Moshe Rabbenu.* Being ordained empowered the individual to elevate another and repair him, to bring him to complete integration with the whole. And thus (B. *Bava Metzi'a* 86b) Rebbe said of Samuel Yarḥina, "He will be called 'wise' but he cannot be called 'rabbi.'" That is, [the master, Rebbe] had not managed to ordain him. Even so, he could be called "wise"—able to repair and elevate others, but only in the particular aspect they requested of him. "He cannot be called 'rabbi,'" for he himself had not been brought to a wholeness that includes the unconscious [*ha-she-lo me-da'at*]. He did not contain the root aspect of 'all' because he was never ordained."[71]

The axis on which this association turns is the word *semikhah.* Its second connotation, which is in effect the guiding force behind R. Ya'akov's reading, appears not in these chapters concerning the sacrifices but in a much later temporal context. Some forty years afterward, as Moses' days near their end, he learns the bitter truth that he will not enter the Promised Land. Now Moses finds himself confronting one more and perhaps the most unsettling challenge to his self-understanding. What, after Moses' life has been lived and he is gone, will remain of his "essence"? Will anything of himself, apart from memories, endure?

> Moses spoke to the Lord, saying, "May God, LORD of the spirits of all flesh, appoint someone over the community, who shall go out before them and come in before them, who shall take them out and bring them in, so that the Lord's community may not be like sheep that have no shepherd. And the Lord answered Moses, "Single out Joshua son of Nun, a man of spirit, and *lay your hand* upon him ... Invest him with some of your majesty, so that the whole Israelite community may obey .... Moses did as the Lord commanded him ... He *laid his hands* upon [Joshua] and commissioned him—as the Lord had spoken through Moses." (Num. 27:16–23)

It is in these verses that the act of *semikhah* is connected explicitly to Moses. In "laying his hands" upon Joshua, he symbolically transfers his role as leader, his authority, status, and something of his "majesty" (*hod*) to the individual God has chosen to be his successor. The Rabbis explore the meaning of this event.

> "A man of spirit"—he said, "Lord of the spirits," You recognize the spirit of each and every one of Your creations. Choose a person who will know how to deal with each and every one of them in accordance with their views. "And lean your hand upon him"—as one candle lights another; "and give some of your majesty"—as if to pour from one vessel to another.[72]

The understanding voiced in this midrash seems to resonate in R. Ya'akov's description of *semikhah* and its part in defining Moses' metahistorical identity. The indwelling spirit Joshua has empowers him to understand, on some intuitive level, each member of the community and to strike a connection with each of them. This spirit will give him the insight to lead them, both as individuals and as a people, to the Land of Israel and toward a higher sphere of wholeness. Moses' part in enabling Joshua to realize this potential is to grant him a certain aspect of illumination—to light him without diminishing his own flame, or to fill him with the brilliance that inundates Moses' own being. In other words, by being ordained, Joshua becomes more than himself. He is invested with *hod*, or majesty, whose source is somewhere far beyond him and, significantly, beyond Moses as well. R. Ya'akov reminds us that, in effect, Moses himself was *given* "rays of majesty" (*karnei hod*). In addition, the biblical verses imply that Moses himself was never fully aware that this light had become "his." The following teaching brings into sharper perspective some basic aspects of Moses' identity. It will aid us, finally, in understanding what essence, in the gesture of *semikhah*, actually passes from master to disciple and from generation to generation.[73]

Rays of Majesty

> ["When Moses descended from Mount Sinai with the two tablets of the testimony] in the hand of Moses as he descended from the mountain—Moses did not know his face was radiant" (Exod. 34:29). In the *Tanḥuma* the question is posed: Where did these rays of majesty come from? The Rabbis said it was from the cave, as it is written, "And my Presence will pass over you" (Exod. 33:22)—God placed His hand over him and hence Moses gained the rays of majesty. Others say that when God would teach him Torah, from the sparks that emerged from the mouth of the *Shekhinah* he received the rays of majesty. R. Samuel bar Naḥman said: The tablets were six handbreadths long and three handbreadths wide. Moses held two handbreadths and the Holy One held two; from the two left between them, Moses received the rays of majesty. R. Samuel said: When Moses wrote the Torah, a bit of ink remained in his quill. He brushed it over his brow and that gave him the rays of majesty.[74]

In his interpretation of the midrash, R. Ya'akov augments its images into existential and psychological terms. He reads the four possibilities offered as speaking of various levels of consciousness—that is, of preconscious, unconscious, and superconscious modes of "knowing." All four of them, in his eyes, grapple with the "impossible" relationship described in the Bible—the encounter between a mortal human, a constricted being, and the Infinite. The "rays of majesty," in that sense, suggest that while the vast brilliance of God and His Torah cannot be "contained" in anything, some trace of that "light" may remain. That trace—a luminosity or aura that radiates from the face of Moses—is "given" to him. Glowing from within, shining outward, it remains forever beyond his own comprehension. "Moses did not know his face was radiant." Thus, the moments of contact between God and Moses that the Rabbis recall are, in R. Ya'akov's reading, all moments of giving-withholding. Light, which knows no boundaries, speaks of this paradox, "the idea of infinity in us … overflowing its own idea."[75] And so R. Ya'akov writes:

> "From the cave ... God placed His hand over him"—when God impedes one from understanding, that concealment comes to illuminate one from within, for in truth His desire is to make one greater. "From the sparks"—for God wishes to explain the Torah in all its profundity, as it is "for Him." But Moses was a narrow vessel and so some sparks scattered.... The sparks are those things that can't be said explicitly, can't be spread out clearly before the mind. God desires [to say] still more, and thus He infuses the heart with understanding. The heart then glows and its light radiates outward, to emanate in the "rays of majesty." "And from the ink left in his quill"—this, too, teaches us that the "saying" cannot be said completely; the Will is too tremendous to be manifest with clarity. Just as it is impossible to describe to another how something tastes—the other can only taste for himself. Finally, "Moses held [the tablets] by two handbreadths"—when Moses would learn the Torah from God, while he was learning he was of one mind with God. Afterwards, he was left with only his own understanding, but while he learned, then his mind joined with God's. His "rays of majesty" came from this—to reveal to him that God will never abandon the Jewish people.[76]

The traces of light are a lingering presence bespeaking absence. All of these images evoke, in effect, what could *not* be given. The Hand that shadows the mouth of the cave hides God's glory from Moses' eyes; the sparks fly and scatter, cannot be caught; the Text remains incomplete; the teacher falls silent and the pupil is left to his own devices, to recollect and try to make sense of what has been shared. These things are withheld because they are too great to be recognized, absorbed, and perceived on a conscious level. Something of them, however, is entrusted to other storehouses. Perhaps the receiver himself will never be able to communicate them. Invested in him, radiating from him, the surplus of light can only be bestowed beyond himself. "For everything that has merit and holiness gives life—it sparkles and shines out from itself to others, through time, between souls, to be integrated in other entities."[77]

This, I would suggest, is the real force behind the act of *semikhah*. To "give some of your majesty upon him" means to pass on, to the generations that will live after you, the wisdom entrusted to you, wisdom that remained beyond your own mastery. We recall, once again, that during those first seven days of making the Tabernacle ready (*yemei ha-milu'im*), the Rabbis teach that Moses performed the priestly duties wearing "a white, un-hemmed garment"—a sign of all that is "incomplete, without the grasp of the intellect."[78] A fabric made to "hold on" to itself, stitched up to hide its ragged edges, would suggest a bounded, self-sufficient mode of being. Moses, in contrast, with his unhemmed garment, symbolizes what remains unfinished, unsaid, not yet written, still to be taught. The Torah he was given, that endless light, overflows his mental perception. Of this fundamental lack of correspondence between container and contents Moses is acutely aware. R. Ya'akov cites his awareness and acceptance of it, above all, as the indication of his greatness.

> As my holy master and rabbi, my father of blessed memory taught: all the other prophets, when an influx of prophecy came upon them, all their sensibilities were annihilated. They lost the sense of their own mindfulness and life force, and did not realize that it was they themselves who were pronouncing God's word. It seemed to them that the Word would last forever, would never change to take on another meaning. As the midrash says (*Tehillim* 90), "All the prophets prophesized without knowing what they were saying." This shows that they did not know themselves while they spoke. Moses, however, prophesized, saying, "'This is the thing [God has commanded you to do]' (Lev. 9:6)—'this thing' will be practiced only in this generation" (B. *Bava Batra* 120a). For Moses maintained his presence of mind while he prophesized. He realized that even a moment later the Word could change in accordance with the needs of the generation. And thus he said, "*This* is the thing God has commanded you to do"—to realize that God's words live and endure. One must never suppose that God is stamped into any single, specific form, for His words change each and every moment, as they need to be interpreted. And then, [when this is clear,] "the glory of God will appear to you" (Lev. 9:6).[79]

"Lean your hands upon him ... You shall give some of your majesty upon him." Moses' role, in the symbolic act of *semikhah,* is thus to enable Joshua and all those after him, the rabbis and teachers and learners of the Torah, to give voice and form to the rays of majesty. Here, then, is perhaps the most essential sense in which "the whole" is embodied in Moses. As R. Ya'akov reminds us, "everything that dedicated learners will ever discover is already contained in the Torah of Moses."[80] Contained, and yet hidden from the one who bears its name. The gesture of *semikhah* is Moses'. It is a mandatory act of giving over, of passing on something with which one was entrusted, and no more. And so the giving can only be done generously, with a full heart.[81]

R. Ya'akov's commentary on the Bible follows Moses to his final day in this world. In a teaching formulated in unusual circumstances, R. Ya'akov evokes a haunting image that speaks cogently of selfhood and what we can learn about it from Moses' story. His words are prefaced in *Beit Ya'akov* 4, *Va-yelekh* with the Hebrew date 5638 (1878), some weeks after R. Ya'akov's passing. A note in the lower margin of the page records, in the name of his son, R. Gershon Ḥanokh Henikh, that: "All of *Shabbos* I struggled to understand the words of the *Zohar* on this *parashah*. After the morning meal I fell asleep. My father, of blessed memory, came to me in a dream and told me, 'This is what it means.'"[82]

> "Moses went and spoke these things to all Israel. He said to them: I now am one hundred and twenty years old." (Deut. 31:1–2). The *Zohar* says: "'Moses went'—where did he go? Rather—he went as a body without arms."[83]

Our arms, R. Ya'akov explains, direct the body; when extended, they can reach higher than our head. That is, human efforts in this world—the attempt to do God's will with "the work of the hands"—can ultimately attain something of higher value than what the intellect alone can attain.

> In truth, now Moses reaches completeness. For the leader of a generation becomes complete when he can instill all his wisdom, understanding, and labors in the hearts of Israel.... And they will carry on the strength of his wisdom. With their own strength, they will direct his wisdom. For "everything that dedicated learners will ever discover is already contained in the Torah of Moses." That is what enables the Torah of Moses our rabbi, may peace be upon him, to come within the limits of the learner's perception. And thus Moses "went"—he went and delivered himself into the heart of Israel. Because in all his years of leadership, Israel was contained in his arms; authority was in his hands. Now, the leadership was placed in the hands of Israel—they will lead and his wisdom becomes a part of them. Until now, [Moses] was the "head" and Israel the "arms." Now, he gave leadership over to them.[84]

Moses' labor in this world has reached an end. The "days of his years are full" and Moses' arms have nothing more to do.[85] His wisdom, his questions, his hopes. and his striving pass from the armless body—that self that will become no more. Moses' sun sets. Slanting rays bequeath their last glow to his people Israel. In the darkness left in his wake, the moon rises. The lines from the *Zohar* R. Ya'akov cited continue: "'You are soon to lie with your forefathers and rise' (Deut. 31:16–17). The Holy One said to Moses, 'Indeed, you yourself will lie with your forefathers. But you will continue ceaselessly to illuminate the moon.'" What this means, explains R. Ya'akov's son, "is that the light of *Moshe Rabbenu* will come to be contained in all the sixty myriad souls of Israel.... Only in death is such completeness possible."[86]

Hidden Light

This is a portrait of Moses that emerges from passages scattered through R. Ya'akov's commentary on the Bible. In all honesty, the declared theme in nearly all of those passages is not specifically Moses. R. Ya'akov makes no attempt to construct a cohesive image that will exemplify certain religious or spiritual ideals. And yet an attentive reading of those teachings in which the figure of Moses appears seems to make clear that, in effect, R. Ya'akov's perception of Moses' story reflects a fundamental understanding of the human psyche and its potential for growth. This understanding finds expression in his reading of every crucial juncture in a life—in this case, the life of Moses.

The figure of Moses that emerges in R. Ya'akov's commentary truly wears a mantle of greatness. And yet, as we have seen, it is a paradoxical kind of greatness won, over and over again, by negation. No monumental figure confidently forging the future with his own heroic might, Moses—in this portrait—yearns to realize himself as an individual, a leader, and a teacher. At each successive stage of his life, God calls new aspects of Moses, unknown until that point, into being. R. Ya'akov's reading of formative events in that life detects the dialogue that seems to guide it, to make that interchange audible, and to show us ways a similar dialogue may come to summon us as well to listen and to change. A core element in his reading is the belief that the task of discovering the self—a mandatory and urgent task—will, in effect, never be completed. As we end our discussion of Moses' spiritual biography, I'd like to consider briefly some of R. Ya'akov's thoughts on why self-knowledge, for all of us, is fundamentally unattainable.

We return, once again, to the opening verse of Leviticus: "And He called to Moses." Following the *Zohar* on that verse, R. Ya'akov recognizes that the word ויקרא ("and He called") is in fact a code, a permutation of another, infinitely higher, true but secret message. The text of the *Zohar* reads as follows:

> When the sparks of the letters join together, a voice emerges from them and it is visible to all in the form אוקיר. And the voice resounds amidst them—"Humankind is more valuable than rare gold; they are more than the precious gold of Ophir" (Isa. 13:12). How fortunate is Moses

> that he was enabled to see so much. And yet his eyes did not gaze upon this word אוקיר ["(humankind is more) valuable"]. Rather, the permutation ויקרא is what he perceived, as it is written, "And He called to Moses." The other form [of the word] was not revealed to him, for one's praises cannot be made known to one's face.[87]

R. Ya'akov understands this passage as setting out a paradigm, a fundamental dualism that informs God's relationship with each of us. One aspect of that relationship is concealed, sealed; the other aspect can be known like an open book.

> The hidden things God has with a person are "sealed" and cannot be disclosed. For if one would catch a glimpse of that awesome sight, one's very life-force would be wiped out; one would have no strength left to do anything more in this world. Thus that light must be hidden and invisible [*ne'elam*] to people. And the world [*'olam*] is named after that act of concealment ... "But the revealed things are for us and for our children" (Deut. 29:28)—to give one room to define oneself ... to learn from the Torah and to live as a Jew.[88]

The word אוקיר, "humankind is more valuable," reflects that searing, unconditional, all-encompassing love God harbors for each of us but will not reveal. If one were to catch sight of this truth, one would know and be paralyzed by knowing "that free choice does not exist ... that one can do nothing aside from God's will."[89] And so the letters recombine; that brightness is sealed away. Instead, "with the drawing of this Love and the voice of this Calling," God conceals the precious truth of His affection and allows us to be separate, to seek our own selves.[90] Moses' life teaches us that the search must be undertaken with humility. To listen and realize that one is being "summoned" to become a self; to act without the conviction of one's importance; to be without clinging to what one has been given—all these values are acted out in his story.

Judah, Son of Jacob

We turn now to a second figure whose story also has much to teach. Unlike Moses, a lone individual whose unique status is undisputed, the figure that will concern us in the following pages struggles to discover himself in an atmosphere of tense oppositions. The path he travels, the trials that confront him, seemingly beyond his control, his errors and failings, and the unfolding of events raise certain vital issues. What does God really want of us? How is sin—or misjudgment, despair, regret, and sorrow—part of some larger, hidden plan, an unavoidable stage in a process? In what ways does this biblical account point beyond itself toward a vision of the historical and metahistorical destiny of the Jewish people? Finally, does the reading of it developed in Izbica-Radzyn teachings reflect some recognition of the players in this story in contemporary sociohistorical terms?

The figure in question is Judah, son of Leah and Jacob. His personal story appears in the latter chapters of Genesis beginning with brief verses about his birth, continuing with his part in the sale of Joseph his brother, the events surrounding his three sons and daughter-in-law Tamar, and finally the face-to-face confrontation with Joseph in the role of viceroy in Egypt. R. Ya'akov's commentary, as always, follows the order of the biblical text. His considerations of Judah are thus integrated into the texture of the whole narrative with all its details. Partly for that reason, his portrait of Judah takes form dialectically. That is, like each figure in the story, Judah's "essence" is defined in relation to others who act in the same sphere. These are Jacob, Joseph, and Benjamin. Judah's choices, his failings, and his ultimate triumph come to the fore in comparison with these other figures, each of whom exemplifies, in R. Ya'akov's eyes, a mode of being that stands in radical contrast to his own. The valences or belief systems each biblical personage are made to represent are, of course, founded on the symbols that are traditionally associated with each of them in rabbinic and mystical thought. And yet I hope to show that R. Ya'akov's reading not only adopts these acquired matrixes of meaning but also develops them, drawing innovative and unexpected conclusions.

Significantly, R. Ya'akov does not present these figures in discursive, analytical terms. Rather, his commentary probes the subjective, inward, evolving understanding of himself and of those around him to which each of them accedes. Unlike Moses, these players seldom engage in direct dialogue with God. Their inner world is explored and explained more often through their actions; here, midrashic traditions play a central role. The hermeneutical approach R. Ya'akov develops forgoes the privileges and manipulations of an omniscient narrator. That makes his reading into an intimate account of each hero's spiritual journey and discovery of his true identity, a story that commentator and reader somehow live along with the players themselves. Charles Taylor underlines the power of this sort of narrative in intuiting the meaning of life and the self. "In order to have a sense of who we are, we have to have a notion of how we have become, and of where we are going."[91] And "as a being who grows and becomes I can only know myself through the history of my maturations and regressions, overcomings and defeats."[92] Finally, "we want the future to 'redeem' the past, to make it part of a life story which has sense or purpose, to take it up into a meaningful unity."[93] I would like to suggest that it is for these reasons that Judah's story, seen through the prism of R. Ya'akov's commentary, is so compelling. Frankly portrayed as one who has wronged, who admits his failings, and who strives to repair the damage, his life and the stages of self-interpretation he passes through take form as a quest for meaning that, ultimately, touches on matters of the highest order. R. Ya'akov's treatment of the figures of Judah and the constellation of characters around him holds a prominent place in his teachings on the *parashot* of *Va-yeshev*, *Mikkets*, *Va-yiggash*, and *Va-yeḥi*, some 174 pages in all. This unusual volume of attention seems to attest to the importance of the issues at hand in Izbica-Radzyn tradition. We'll raise them in the course of our discussion.

The Second Day

> "Now, Israel loved Joseph best of all his sons, for he was the child of his old age; and he made him an ornamented tunic. [And when his brothers saw that their father loved him more than any of his brothers, they hated him]" (Gen. 37:3–4). This *parashah* marks the beginning of the schism that grew between Jacob's sons. Joseph envies Judah and Judah sells Joseph; the Rabbis taught (*Tanḥuma, Va-yiggash*) that this envy will endure until the Messiah comes ... This *sidrah* parallels the *sefirah* of *gevurah she-be-gevurah* and the second day of the world's creation. On the first day, light was created ... a day of light alone. On the second day, the light was partly concealed. And so it is with different souls—Joseph and Judah. Joseph is the aspect of the "perfect *zaddik*"—all of his actions are clarified in the light of reason. Judah is the aspect of the *baal teshuvah*—he thrusts himself into actions that seem to be devoid of light. And yet *his* aim is the goal that God most desires. Truly, in their inmost hearts, all Jews accept the superiority of Judah's way. For "the status that *baalei teshuvah* can attain, even perfect *zaddikim* cannot attain it" (B. *Berakhot* 34a). But in human perception bound to this world, it seems that Judah shares nothing of Joseph the *zaddik*. And thus our exile has lasted so long.[94]

The "first day" and the "second day." Creation begins with "Let there be light" (Gen. 1:3)—with the lucid, uncontested certainty of what is good and of the path paved with it. The first *parashot* of Genesis, in essence, are illuminated with that merciful light and clarity of vision. The heroes and heroines of those chapters, the forebears of the Jewish nation, are guided through moments of uncertainty, trials, and questions, toward inevitable resolution; recognition of what and who is "good" and who is not comes without long delay. And so that initial part of the book of Genesis parallels the *sefirah* of *ḥesed* (mercy, kindness) in its various permutations.[95] On the second day, "God said: Let there be an expanse in the midst of the water, that it may separate water from water" (Gen. 1:6). Separation, division now cast a shadow into that bright world of positiveness. Inequality and difference come into being; a sense of self opposed by other is born. R. Ya'akov, following the Rabbis, connects the mode that becomes a part of reality on this "second day" with the *sefirah* of *gevurah* or "might," valiançe. It is a heroic gesture of breaking up that primordial oneness and surety. Heroic, because such an act obscures the "good." Pain and suffering come in its stead. An expanse now divides the "upper waters" from the "lower waters"; with it, "hiddenness and concealment and differentiation come into the world."[96] Only a commensurate gesture of human valiance can bring one to see why the world "needs" this second day, with all the difficulty that it brings. This new state of *gevurah* informs what R. Ya'akov sees, in a sense, as the second part of the book of Genesis. The saga of Joseph and his brothers, or of Jacob and his sons, is the retelling, on an existential, psychological level, of what happened on that "second day" of Creation, a crucial turning point in the history of humankind.

Judah represents the antithesis of Joseph in the same way that separation and concealment are the dialectical opposites of endless light. The merit of Judah's mode of being stands, similarly, in stark contrast to that of Joseph. Counterintuitive, charged with darkness, uncertainty, and despair, Judah's path and the higher good to which it ultimately leads remain an enigma for many, many pages and for as many years. In his commentary, R. Ya'akov leads his readers through the saga as it unfolds, distinguished at each state between the levels of meaning concealed in the events. We'll begin our discussion of it with a consideration of some of the symbols and concepts R. Ya'akov uses to define the identity of each figure. Because Judah takes the role, in his reading, of "antithesis," we must first consider the figure of Joseph, the "thesis" and starting point, and the central role he plays in setting the stage on which the events are played out.

> "Now, Israel loved Joseph best of all his sons, for he was the child of his old age." Jacob pinned all his hopes and expectations on him; as the Rabbis taught, Joseph resembled him most of all (*Tanḥuma; Bereshit Rabba* 84.8). And Joseph strove to attain his father's qualities … to undertake no action that lacked clarity. Only if light was manifestly before his eyes … would he chose to act, and thus all his deeds were "straight" and true. And yet there is another kind of deed: it is done without clarity, and its true value becomes evident only later. This manner of acting is called *yibbum*, in which one person must aid another.[97] But Jacob had no liking for such deeds that take time to become clarified; all his actions were pure from the first moment.… Now, Joseph adopted the way of his father, seeking always to be "face to face."[98] And so his father loved him best of all.… Even though all his brothers [and the tribes they represent] have qualities more precious than those of Joseph, they all need him, for his essence is the light of reason. It illuminates human perceptions and enables everyone to understand and sense the good; without such a light, what benefit could one have from treasure houses hidden in darkness? This, then, is Joseph's role: he is the candle who casts light into all the tribes and helps them see their own essence.… In addition, Joseph the *zaddik* constricts himself to avoid getting involved in anything that is not illuminated with the light of reason. And to the human eye, it seems that no quality could be better.[99]

This passage portrays a masterful, somewhat disengaged self whose central virtues are strength of will, resolution, and control. His life is directed by the hegemony of reason over desire, and this wins him "clarity and a fullness of self-presence."[100] Such virtues, it seems, can help one be convinced that one stands "face to face" in full cognizance of reality and of what is good and true. Inarguably, this sort of instrumental control should form the basis of a successful life. Its most cogent symbol is manifest in the image of the *zaddik*, the *yesod* or foundation of the world, and the vector of *tzimtzum* or "contraction." The reified Joseph restrains and limits his every material desire; he will not be seduced to "expand" into dubious and shadowy realms. That emblematic strength of will, embodied in the "sign of the covenant"—the *brit* that is inscribed unforgettably on the body of every male Jew—is what has preserved the Jewish people through history.[101] And thus, "the tribe of Joseph guards the lineage [*yiḥus*] of Israel."[102] R. Ya'akov suggests that Jacob's affection for the "son of his old age" stems from a deep spiritual and temperamental kinship; Joseph's ways find favor in the father's eyes because they so resemble his own. The ideals they share—of truth, coherence, presence—seem to be beyond critique.

The fissures in this monolithic certainty, however, begin to draw the Rabbis' attention in the very first verse of the story. "Now Jacob settled in the land where his father had sojourned, the land of Canaan" (Gen. 37:1)—"Jacob wished to settle peacefully, but instead the trauma surrounding Joseph came upon him" (*Bereshit Rabba* 84.3). It seems that the very presumption to "settle peacefully" is marred with an element of error. In truth, the Rabbis say, "there is no peace for the righteous in this world" (*Bereshit Rabba* 84.3). On the basis of this foreboding intuition, R. Ya'akov takes a closer look at the psychological underpinnings of the situation.

> As my honored father, of blessed memory taught, Joseph's ways found favor in Jacob's eyes; Jacob wished to settle peacefully, "where his father had sojourned"—embracing Isaac's quality of awe, in "the land of Canaan"—alluding to humility and avoidance of all doubt. Only in such a manner can one "settle peacefully." But God said to him: I have greater plans for you than that. You must thrust yourself into doubts and clarification. You must draw holiness up from the depths, "and I will surely bring you back up" [Gen. 46:4], for some of your holiness must come from the world of chaos [*'olam ha-tohu*]. And so it went that Joseph was sold into Egypt. After that, Jacob and his sons descended as well, and darkness and concealment enveloped them.... Yet it was there that Israel gained their essential holiness, as the *Zohar* teaches (1. 83a).... There, they discovered [*birreru*] themselves and drew sparks of light out of the darkness; from desolation they built a settled place. That is, the unruly and wild forces in the individual—one's internal chaos and desolation—they made those forces pure by finding that they, too, contain holiness, and that we must make use of them in serving God.[103]

And so the "second day" begins. Completeness and tranquility, desirable as they may be, have not yet come; to "settle peacefully" would bury Jacob in a static, artificial nonlife. God has "greater plans for you than that." Joseph's light must be temporarily obscured; his brothers and father will ultimately follow him into the dark reign of impurity known as "Egypt." Their descendants must endure all that they endure until their efforts win them the power to rebuild—to draw a purified and more authentic self from the midst of chaos and destruction. It is a massive and exhausting plan, and will come to an end only hundreds of years later. In this teaching Jacob, as it were, is given a glimpse of it. But for the most part, on R. Ya'akov's reading, he and his sons live from verse to verse with little notion of where they are going or why.

The next stages of the story recount how it came to be that Joseph was sold, and the effect his disappearance had on his family.

> At seventeen years of age, Joseph tended the flocks with his brothers.... And Joseph brought bad reports of them to their father (Gen. 37:2). Once Joseph had a dream which he told to his brothers, and they hated him even more (37:5) ... He dreamed another dream ... And when he told it to his father and brothers, his father berated him. And his brothers envied him. (37:9–11)

R. Ya'akov speaks of these actions in no uncertain terms. The evil that Joseph himself reported about his brothers damaged the "mystery of the covenant" (*raza de-brit*), the *yesod* or foundation that he is meant to embody. In voicing his suspicions condemning his brothers, Joseph strikes not only at his own potential wholeness and the unity of his family but at cosmic harmony as well.[104] He fails to "contain himself," to restrain his tongue and his thoughts. With intentions that are less than pure, he casts aspersions on his brothers and incites his father to doubt their integrity. "And thus Joseph, the *zaddik* needed to rectify himself ... through suffering."[105] Joseph's trials in Egypt, his withstanding the seductions of the wife of Potiphar, and his mistaken appeal to the chief cupbearer (*sar ha-mashkim*) are stages in Joseph's path toward repairing the damage done to the "covenant" of the flesh and of the tongue. But that is another story. We turn now to the figure of Judah and his role in the events that followed.

Sent to seek his brothers as they pasture Jacob's flocks in Shechem, Joseph unknowingly falls into their hands. "They saw him from afar, and before he came close to them they conspired to kill him. They said to one another, 'Here comes that dreamer! Come now, let us kill him'" (Gen. 37:18–19). But Reuben intervenes; instead, they cast him alive into an empty pit. Soon afterward, "A caravan of Ishmaelites coming from Gilead" appears. "Then Judah said to his brothers, 'What do we gain by killing our brother and covering up his blood? Come, let us sell him to the Ishmaelites, but let us not do away with him ourselves. After all, he is our brother, our own flesh'" (37:25–27). The brothers agree; Joseph is sold and the Ismaelites take him with them down to Egypt. On R. Ya'akov's reading, the effects of all this are tangible at once.

> While Joseph was among them, [the brothers] saw clearly that God dwelled within them; each of them recognized his place and the preciousness

> inherent in each and every tribe. But when Joseph the *zaddik* disappeared, they began to be plagued with apprehension [*miḥushim*], and Judah more than anyone.[106]

At the root of their anxiety, R. Ya'akov explains, is a grave existential doubt: "When the aspect of Joseph, the *zaddik* seemed lost ... they lost sight of their own genealogy [*sefer yiḥusin*] as well. They feared that perhaps they, too, are not really meant to be a central part in the divine plan."[107] Perhaps, like Ishmael and like Esau, they are the chaff that will be separated out and rejected. Judah's despair is greatest of all.

Judah's Descent

"It was at that time that Judah went down, left his brothers and turned away toward a man of Adullam whose name was Hirah. There Judah saw the daughter of a certain merchant called Shua and he married her" (Gen. 38:1–2). We'll begin our discussion of this next chapter of the story with a midrash that holds an important place in Hasidic tradition. The questions it arouses, as we will see, lead its many interpreters to disparate resolutions. I would like to suggest that the viewpoints they express, in turn, may help cast new light on the beliefs that underlie the Izbica-Radzyn school of thought and its origins. The midrash, at this juncture in the story, says:

> "It was at that time that Judah went down, left his brothers" (38:1). "Judah has betrayed, and shame has been committed ... for Judah has defiled the holiness of the Lord, who loves him, [in taking in marriage the daughter of a foreign god]" (Mal. 2:11–12).[108]
>
> "It was at that time." "I will yet bring a dispossessor against you, O inhabitant of Mareshah; the glory of Israel will withdraw to Adullam" (Mic. 1:16). The king and holiness of Israel will withdraw even to Adullam, as it is written, "and he turned away to a man of Adullam" (Gen. 38:1).[109]
>
> "It was at that time." R. Samuel bar Naḥman opened with the verse, "For I know the thoughts" (Jer. 29:11). The tribes were busy selling Joseph; Joseph was busy with his sackcloth and afflictions, Reuben was busy with his sackcloth and afflictions, and Jacob was busy with his sackcloth and afflictions. Judah was busy taking a wife. And the Holy One, blessed be He was busy creating the light of the Messiah.[110]

Each of the three sections in this passage focuses on the figure of "Judah." The first, through an intertextual association, obliquely condemns his actions. Betrayal, defilement, disloyalty, and a foreign liaison corrupt Judah's name and estrange him. The second section, through a different allusion, describes a movement of retreat and diminishment. Here glory, kingship, and holiness are not violated; rather, some force "withdraws" to an extreme point called "Adullam." The third section turns full-face to treat the events at hand and the incongruities that fill them. Deeds are juxtaposed with thoughts; Judah's deeds in the context evoked are thoroughly perplexing. Are they being censured or vindicated? Is it despite them or in merit of them or for some other reason that, just now, "the Holy One, blessed be He was busy creating the light of the Messiah"?

Our understanding of R. Ya'akov's reading of this chapter in the story must start with a look at the hermeneutical traditions that took form before him, specifically with the new outlook that crystallized in the Przysucha school, noted in the first pages of this chapter. The primary figure voicing that new approach to Torah and to Jewish religious life was R. Simḥah Bunem. Vital elements of his worldview, which find expression in many of the teachings recorded in his name, are the notions of individuation, personal responsibility in attaining spiritual growth, and self-knowledge. These interests come to the fore with particular cogency in this chapter of the story of Judah. In the pages that follow, we must keep in mind just how explosive are the issues it raises on moral, theological, and psychological grounds. For Judah's symbolic stature is daunting and complex. A once and future king, he prefigures the regal "House of David" and he personally engenders the seed of the Messiah, the ultimate historical redeemer of the Jewish people. And yet at the same time Judah (*Yehudah*) is also the paradigmatic Jew (*yehudi*) whose name every member of the Jewish nation shares. With what attitude, then, are we to read the biblical narrative? Is Judah's story meant to be our story? May we identify fully with this hero, recognize his failings, question his errors, emulate his behavior? Or is he in another league altogether, beyond culpability, a chosen player carrying out a divinely determined, unfathomable plan?

A second factor contributing to the consequence of the issues is the problem of spiritual legacy. R. Simḥah Bunem, like many rebbes and religious leaders, was a charismatic presence who influenced great numbers of his Hasidim primarily through personal, immediate contact. His teachings were recorded, for the most part, in his disciples' memories alone; after his death, his children and grandchildren gathered them from various living sources and committed them to writing.[111] Two of R. Simḥah Bunem's preeminent disciples, we recall, were R. Ya'akov's father, R. Mordecai Joseph, who spent some years in Przysucha as a young man, and R. Menaḥem Mendel of Kotsk, who became R. Simḥah Bunem's successor in 1827 after the master's death. Both of them saw themselves as loyal followers. Moreover, both believed they had received the Rebbe's essential truth. And yet, as we will see, they differ radically in their understanding of R. Simḥah Bunem's teachings. The ramifications of these differences are far-reaching.

Ideologically, politically, dramatically, R. Mordecai Joseph and R. Menaḥem Mendel parted ways. What really happened to cause the break between them is a matter of intense controversy.[112] My major interest, however, is not to reexamine the outward events or disclose new information. Rather, a closer look at their readings of the story of Judah might suggest a way to understand the ideological roots of the tension between them and between their followers.

"Judah" of Przysucha

We'll begin with the following teaching, recorded in the name of R. Simḥah Bunem.

> "'For I know the thoughts . . . .' The tribes were busy selling Joseph; Joseph was busy with his sackcloth and afflictions, Reuben was busy with his sackcloth and afflictions, and Jacob was busy with his sackcloth and afflictions. Judah was busy taking a wife. And the Holy One, blessed be He was busy creating the light of the Messiah." This midrash is strange indeed. Its purpose, it seems, is to teach us a great matter. All the tribes and Jacob were intent on fasting and crying out to God—the tribes, for having sold Joseph, and Joseph himself for having been sold, and Jacob, too, mourned his son. And they prayed to God with all their heart and soul. "And Judah was busy taking a wife." To human eyes, their actions were more devoted to God, while he was intent on marrying a woman. But the midrash says that no one knows the thoughts concealed in a person's heart. The Holy One, blessed be He, preferred Judah's deed, and from it He created the light of the Messiah. Now the meaning of the midrash is clear. Examine and find and understand it.[113]

We'll do our best. R. Simḥah Bunem appears to read the midrash as a warning against misinterpretation. Motivations concealed in the heart may belie outward actions. "Human eyes" with the normative values behind them can misconstrue, judge, and condemn. But God sees things differently. "For I know the thoughts"—the purity of true intent brings forth light and realization of the truth that, in the end, will become visible to all concerned. When that happens, the merit of those actions will no longer be challenged. The warning voiced by the Rabbis certainly sounds reasonable. But what *were* Judah's thoughts? What was his intention in marrying, and why did God "prefer" his deeds?

Another teaching attributed to R. Simḥah Bunem, recorded by R. Samuel of Sieniawa, seems to address some of these questions, but in a manner that proved to be highly controversial.

> Each of them was consumed with repentance that he had been the one to cause Joseph to be driven away from their father. And Judah, as king over them—surely they would have listened to him; he could have acquitted Joseph and restored him to his father. And so he supposed that no measure of repentance would help him. But maybe, he thought, one of his seed would be able to set him right and raise him up again. Thus he occupied himself with taking a wife. Those thoughts were precious in God's eyes and so He created the light of the Messiah.[114]

Two elements in this reading draw our attention. One is the sense of despair audible in Judah's thoughts and guiding his decisions. Repentance, he feels, cannot change reality enough; something has been irretrievably lost, damaged irreparably. Secondly, we note what sounds like a certain transfer of personal responsibility. Despairing of his power to restitute matters himself, Judah seems to voice the hope that an extended aspect of himself, his progeny, will somehow have the strength to right his wrongs and restore his honor.

"Judah" of Kotsk

Hasidic tradition preserves almost no firsthand testimony of R. Menaḥem Mendel of Kotsk's teachings. His infamous seclusion for the last twenty years of his life, voluntarily cut off from his Hasidim, may well have exacerbated the situation. Even before that time, though, R. Menaḥem Mendel apparently wrote nothing of his own thoughts; alternatively, some say he wrote during the night and burned his writings in the morning.[115] Moreover, the disciples who did remain in contact with him, such as R. Isaac Meir Alter, founder of the Ger dynasty, make almost no direct mention of his ideas in their own teachings. For these reasons, it is difficult if not impossible to formulate any clear picture of his overall ideological stance, to say nothing of his reading of any particular text.[116] One important source of knowledge about what R. Menaḥem Mendel may really have said and thought is the Torah commentary penned by his grandson, R. Samuel of Sochaczow.[117] A second independent and firsthand source, also considered authentic, is R. Samuel of Sieniawa's anthology entitled *Ramatayim Tzofim*. Interestingly, both of these works contain a passage noting R. Menaḥem Mendel's reading of the story of Judah. In both versions, the passage is phrased in reaction to the teachings by R. Simḥah Bunem that we cited above. When someone recalled them in R. Menaḥem Mendel's hearing, his response was this: "Heaven forbid that the holy mouth of my master, of blessed memory, should have said such a thing!" R. Menaḥem Mendel then sets out what he believed the Rebbe had meant.

> When Judah saw what had happened and that his influence had caused it all, his heart melted within him. He grew more and more bitter until he nearly ceased to exist. Judging his own actions, he decided that he had surely lost everything he had ever gained since the day of his birth until the present. And his soul nearly perished from bitterness. But then, reconsidering it all, he strengthened his spirit and resolved to begin anew to uphold the Torah. He would prepare his heart, from that moment, to serve the Lord, his God like one reborn (having lost all that he had had). He would set out on this renewal with the Torah's very first commandment [to "be fruitful and multiply" (Gen. 1:22)]. And this thought was so precious to the Knower of all thoughts and Him who tests the hearts that from it He created the light of the Messiah.[118]

R. Samuel of Sochaczow records a similar account.

> The holy rebbe, R. Simḥah Bunem of Przysucha, of blessed memory, said that Judah thought that repentance would do no good, that nothing would restore Joseph to his father. And so he married; perhaps one of his children would raise him back up. But my grandfather of Kotsk, of blessed memory, when he was told that teaching, responded: Heaven forbid that our master would have said such a thing, that a man should depend on his children to repair him! No, surely what he said was that since [Judah] thought he had lost all that he had ever achieved, he must begin anew to serve God. And he started with the first mitzvah of the Torah.[119]

The cardinal issue raised in these two accounts concerns moral responsibility. R. Menaḥem Mendel seems to hold that the individual, as an autonomous entity, must be the sole bearer of the future, aided by no one. To suppose that a figure of such stature and nobility as Judah would shrug off that vital duty is unconscionable. And thus, says R. Menaḥem Mendel, the course of events and the motivations that lay behind them have to be explained differently. He portrays Judah's inner struggle as a tense grappling with guilt and remorse that reaches a nadir of self-assessment: "he decided that he had surely lost everything." On R. Menaḥem Mendel's reading, however, that realization does not bring him to wish for children who would "repair him." Instead, it turns to a new state of self-mastery and resolve. In a series of empowering decisions, he draws on deep, primary moral resources. Judah begins to "reconsider." He regains self-possession and wills to "prepare his heart" for that mission. Summoning his powers of rational reflection, he sees that order will surely be restored to his world if only he can grasp hold of some primary truth. The "very first commandment" to humankind mandates procreation. One's highest commitment to God, he knows, must find expression halakhically, in direct fulfillment of divine injunctions. To seek a wife, then, would be a dispassionate endeavor governed by reason, devotion, and clarity of vision.[120] The midrash would then affirm that intentions and disciplined action such as these are most "precious" to God. Judah's uncompromising, honest thought was recompensed. The outcome of it was that "He created the light of the Messiah."

This is the image of Judah and the interpretation of his story that comes to the fore in these two accounts. It is reasonable to assume that R. Menaḥem Mendel held the mode of being it portrays in high esteem. I would cautiously say that this image resonates, to a great extent, with the spiritual qualities and ethical sensibility for which Kotsk was known.[121]

"Judah" of Izbica-Radzyn

Before we begin our exploration of the very different understanding of Judah developed in Izbica-Radzyn tradition, it might be useful to recollect some biographical details. After R. Simḥah Bunem's death in 1827, the majority of his followers accepted R. Menaḥem Mendel as their rebbe. The center of Przysucha Hasidism subsequently moved with him to Kotsk. Among the young Hasidim in that circle was R. Mordecai Joseph. Neither his writings nor those of his son, R. Ya'akov, speak openly of the period he spent as R. Menaḥem Mendel's disciple in Kotsk.[122] R. Mordecai Joseph's grandson, R. Gershon Ḥanokh Henikh of Radzyn, is the first in Izbica-Radzyn tradition to evoke the memory of that time. His comments, which appear in his Introduction to the *Beit Ya'akov* (also cited at the beginning of this chapter), may contribute something to our evaluation of the issues at hand. In the course of his family chronology, R. Gershon Ḥanokh writes:

> My grandfather, of blessed memory, was the special one in the group of R. Simḥah Bunem, may he be remembered for eternal life. He served the master with dedication and "did not depart from the tent" of Torah [Exod. 33:11]. After R. Simḥah Bunem's passing, thirteen years he suffered the pain of "concealment in the cave of Adullam," for the time had not yet come for him to teach Torah publicly. His soul was among lions [after Ps. 57:5], and yet he taught Torah in secret, "and with the modest comes wisdom" [Prov. 11:2].[123]

As the devoted grandson and disciple of his venerated grandfather, R. Gershon Ḥanokh's loyalties are clear—it is R. Mordecai Joseph who held the choice place of favor. Like the biblical Joshua who "did not depart from the tent" of Moses, R. Mordecai Joseph's dedication to his rebbe won him, above all others, the right to inherit the mantle of spiritual leadership and true vision when the master left this world. This conviction serves, in R. Gershon Ḥanokh's mind, to explain the root cause of the suffering alluded to in the next lines. R. Mordecai Joseph's years as a disciple in Kotsk are described as a trying period of forced concealment. In language that echoes with persecutions remembered, R. Gershon Ḥanokh suggests that throughout that time his grandfather had to subsist "underground," and that he could speak only covertly of his beliefs to avoid drawing the attention of threatening authorities. Like R. Shimon bar Yoḥai, famed in Jewish tradition as the author of the *Zohar*'s esoteric wisdom, who fled for his life from the Roman regime, hiding in a cave for 13 long years, R. Mordecai Joseph's teaching takes form "in secret." The two biblical allusions in the passage seem to suggest one more story is also written between the lines. Psalm 57 reads: "A plea to be saved from destruction, by David … when he fled from Saul, in the cave …. My soul is among lions; I lie among men who are aflame" (verses 1 and 6). More explicitly, we know that the biblical David, oppressed and persecuted by King Saul, seeks refuge with Achish, King of Gat. When his identity is guessed, David feigns madness and resolves to flee further. "David went from there and escaped to the cave of Adullam" (1 Sam. 21:11–22:1).

As a final link in this series of associations, consider what R. Gershon Ḥanokh writes in the last paragraphs of his Introduction to the *Beit Ya'akov*. After tracing the family tree back by name through twelve consecutive generations, he adds: "The *geonim* Maharshal and Rama are my ancestors; our family lineage goes back to Rashi and back to the *tanna* R. Yoḥanan ha-Sandlar and Rabban Gamliel the Elder. Indeed, I come from the seed of David."[124]

What are we to make of all this? How much should we attribute to R. Gershon Ḥanokh's own personal agenda, with its activist, radical messianic overtones, and how much do his statements reflect a composite self-awareness that he did not originate but rather inherit from his father and grandfather out of their personal experience?[125] *Mei ha-Shiloaḥ* and *Beit Ya'akov* are both utterly devoid of overt autobiographical elements. Neither of these works contains anything explicit that could serve to reinforce, recast, or deflect the kinship R. Gershon Ḥanokh declares between his grandfather's life-story and those of King David and R. Simeon bar Yoḥai. Thus it would be unwise to assume R. Gershon Ḥanokh is reiterating convictions that were recognized and verbalized privately by his father and grandfather before him. And yet, I think we can say with some certainty, guided by R. Gershon Ḥanokh's comments, that a deep undercurrent of identification with the figure of David and of the Messiah, scion of David, along with all they represent, may well run through their teachings. The understanding that R. Mordecai Joseph and R. Ya'akov formulate of the life of Judah, as progenitor of the House of David, must be read in that light. Their commentaries reveal and conceal a dramatic battle of conflicting forces that is played out in multiple realms, in a complex pattern of overlapping layers. We'll look now at some teachings on the subject as they appear in R. Mordecai Joseph's and R. Ya'akov's works, and consider the ways that sensibility or identification finds expression in a matrix of ideas. I believe that here we have a key to recognizing and appreciating the innovative, coherent reading of the Torah and of history that Izbica-Radzyn tradition offers.

Judah's story continues. We will recall it briefly. He marries; three sons are born. Judah takes a wife for Er, his eldest son. When Er dies, Judah instructs Onan, his second son, to enter into a levirate marriage with the widow, Tamar, "to provide offspring for your brother. But Onan knew that the seed would not be his" and God caused him to die as well. "Then Judah said to Tamar, 'Stay as a widow in your father's house until my son Shelah grows up'—for he thought, 'He too might die like his brothers.'" Many days pass; Judah's wife dies. Tamar learns that her father-in-law is on his way to Timna. "So she removed her widow's garb, covered her face with a veil and wrapped herself up; she then sat by the crossroads that is on the road toward Timna, for she saw that Shelah was grown up and she had not been given to him as a wife." Judah sees her and takes her for a harlot, "for she had covered her face." She requests a pledge until Judah will send her payment—"your seal and cord and the staff in your hand." Afterward, when Judah sends a messenger to deliver the payment to the harlot and retrieve his pledge, the woman is nowhere to be found. Some time later, Judah is told that his daughter-in-law "is with child by harlotry. 'Bring her out,' said Judah, 'and let her be burned!' As she was being brought out, she sent a message to her father-in-law, 'I am with child by the man to whom these belong.' And she added, 'Recognize, if you will, whose seal and cord and staff these are.' Judah recognized them and said, 'She is more right than I, for I did not give her to my son Shelah'" (Gen. 38:1–26). Tamar gives birth to twin sons, Perez and Zeraḥ.

We'll begin with a teaching found in *Mei ha-Shiloaḥ*. R. Mordecai Joseph focuses on the same issue that concerned R. Menaḥem Mendel of Kotsk (above): Judah's mental state in the wake of the sale of Joseph and the thoughts that may have motivated his actions.

> "It was at that time that Judah went down, left his brothers . . . ." Why did Judah decide to marry at such a time? The lot had fallen to him to bring [Joseph's bloodied] tunic to their father [and so to portend the terrible news of his fate]. He saw Jacob's inconsolable distress and it disheartened him utterly. Thinking that there was no hope left for him, Judah decided to marry, reasoning: Perhaps I will have worthy sons and something eternal may grow from them. Later, though, the Holy One, blessed be He made him understand that if, heaven forbid, what you feared were true, that there's no hope for you and that your root is lifeless—if that were so, you could bear a hundred sons but they would have no more vitality than you. Because for God, the channel He uses to give life must be alive as well. If things were as you think, all your offspring would be just as transient as you.[126]

In the first lines, R. Mordecai Joseph restates the contention attributed to his teacher, R. Simḥah Bunem, that a sense of hopelessness is what brings Judah to long for children who will rebuild his future. On his reading, however (unlike that of R. Menaḥem Mendel of Kotsk), Judah does not restore his self-mastery so quickly. Rather, despair continues to propel Judah for many years; in fact, Judah's lack of hope is what causes his two sons to die childless. The dialogue that R. Mordecai Joseph "reconstructs" here suggests a kind of subconscious awakening. Only after their deaths, Judah begins to wonder if perhaps "the channel" from which new generations emerge must believe it is invested with vitality and creative power.

R. Ya'akov adopts this view of Judah's evolving psychological state. The biblical narrative, on his reading, recounts an epic search for Judah's essential self. His "life root" will ultimately be discovered, says R. Ya'akov, but this must come about "in a hidden and mysterious way." For that reason his path must first descend into a dark night of the soul. "Judah no longer believed in himself.... In his anxiety that God has abandoned him, he deteriorated severely."[127] His reaching a space called "Adullam" signals a critical state, at nearly the zero point.

> "Adullam" means that at that time, light grew so very faint until only a glimmer was left, like a candle flame about to go out. The midrash speaks of this: "unto Adullam will the king and holiness of Israel withdraw; unto Adullam recedes the glory of Israel."[128]

To express the emotional burden borne by this trajectory of diminishment, R. Ya'akov recalls an image used in the *Zohar. Malkhut* (the *sefirah* called "kingship") becomes nearly invisible, until all that remains of her is one tiny point; in the same way, the moon diminishes almost to nothing.[129] The next crucial events unfold in that gathering darkness. "Kingship" lapses into near oblivion. Judah, with all his former majesty and status, loses sight of his true self. From within what seems to be a moral and spiritual void, he is driven to act as he does; indeed, the Rabbis say that "the angel in charge of desire compelled Judah." Unknowingly, taken by passion, Judah enters into an apparent levirate relation (*yibbum*) with the wife of his deceased sons. It is a move without precedent in the Torah, and one that is even condemned as a forbidden liaison. To outward appearances, his act is "crooked" (*be-'akima*), a sowing of mixed seeds (*kilayim*), wholly dishonorable.[130]

Night reaches its blackest hour when Judah, still unaware of what he has done, commands Tamar to be put to death for what looks like shameful profligacy. As she is being brought to the pyre, she requests of him: "Recognize, if you will, whose seal and cord and staff these are." Judah realizes the truth and voices his confession publicly. Here, at last, a ray of light breaks into Judah's consciousness. "She is more right than I." This acknowledgment marks a turning point in Judah's life. A long process of reckoning will now be set in motion, of calling himself to account and trying with all the fragments of his shattered self to repair what has been damaged. Soon, we will consider R. Ya'akov's reading of those next stages. But first, let's see what Izbica-Radzyn tradition makes of this part of his story.

The Hidden Face

R. Ya'akov asks:

> Why did everything have to happen in such concealment? … Why was Judah's freedom of choice taken from him, leaving him to feel that he was darkness without light? … "Jacob was busy with his sackcloth and afflictions. Judah was busy taking a wife. And the Holy One was busy creating the light of the Messiah." That is, people think that what [Judah] did went wholly against what God wants. But that is because no human being can comprehend the tremendous value contained in what was being built. For, in truth, all the "salvations" [*yeshu'ot*] and truths from this tribe come into being through concealment. Externally, everything seems the complete opposite of the untold preciousness found within … We see the same in the image of King David.[131]

The divine plan, R. Ya'akov suggests, cannot unfold in daylight, with controlled, deliberate human actions. Instead, God's chosen players must act without freedom of choice, without any understanding of their role in any larger picture, consumed with doubt, suffering bitterly. Paradoxically, the unimaginable goodness the future will bring is what mandates its concealment. "And so these things must be built without human awareness. Thus it says of the very first moment of salvation [*yeshu'a rishonah*]—'for she covered her face.' That is, the glory of Heaven involved in that action was veiled and obscured so that, at first, it seemed the opposite of God's will."[132]

The "hidden face," in effect, is an emblem of all God's dealings in the saga of Jacob and his sons. R. Ya'akov notes that from the time their trials begin, when Joseph was cast into the pit, and through the end of the book of Genesis, the four-letter Name of God (*yud-heh-vav-heh*) no longer appears in the biblical narrative. In other words, this is a period of *hester pannim*—God's face, as it were, turns away from the world. The connection linking the Jewish nation to God seems to weaken, and trouble fills their days. The sons of Jacob/Israel are estranged from one another, and each endures a separate, spiritual exile. Joseph, who "guards the lineage of Israel," disappears into Egypt. In his absence, the "light of reason" and belief in that connection is obscured. All of his brothers, and Judah among them, forget where they came from, their worth and their integrity.[133]

On R. Ya'akov's reading, it is Tamar who symbolizes the axis on which everything will now turn. "When the Name is concealed, God comes to be called in other ways. Tamar's name alludes to this, from the word *temurah*, or exchange." Through her, Judah's actions are somehow transfigured. They take on another, infinitely higher form; through her, they will soon be read and understood in a different way. Citing the *Zohar*, R. Ya'akov explains that, in truth, Judah's liaison with Tamar was no act of *yibbum*, in which a brother is required to preserve the memory of the deceased through his own offspring. Rather, "Judah himself bore his sons' souls a second time." Er and Onan, spawned from hopelessness, bereft themselves of the power to hope, could not survive. But their deficiency, Judah knows somewhere deep within, originated in himself. And thus he will come to understand that it is he alone, ultimately, who can engender them anew, this time investing them with vitality "at their root."[134]

> And so the souls of Er and Onan transmigrated to Perez and Zeraḥ, fathered by Judah with Tamar. Her name alludes to a remnant, to offspring [*aḥarit*] and to hope in what the future will bring, as the verse says, "The righteous will flourish like a date palm [*tamar*]" (Ps. 92:13). So the Rabbis taught, "'[For I know the thoughts that I am thinking for you, says the Lord, thoughts of peace and not evil], to give you a future and a hope' (Jer. 29:11)—these are palm trees." In other words, from there God caused the light of the Messiah to begin to shine.[135]

"For I know the thoughts." R. Ya'akov does not cite this first part of the verse. But his teaching hints that perhaps we must reread and reconsider what the Rabbis meant in the midrash we've evoked so many times. The thoughts God "knows" are His own. The overarching intent of the epic tale called history is surely "peace and not evil." Its goal is an unthinkable gift: "a future and a hope" that will emerge at the end of it all. Tamar, the date palm and its fruit, is that hidden sweetness. It cannot be given outright. Rather, through Tamar, "the light of the Messiah" is conceived. Undetected, it "begins to shine" in this moment of utter darkness when Judah is nearly lost to himself.

Choice, Doubt, Compulsion

"The thoughts that I am thinking" start to become visible in the next dramatic scene of the narrative. Confronted with the evidence—"the seal and cord and staff" that symbolize him—Judah recognizes that Tamar's intentions were pure, even noble, and this in implicit contrast to his own. The Rabbis, while preserving this straightforward reading of the biblical text, thicken the plot with a second and startling reading: "When he confessed and said, 'She is more right than I' [*tzadkah mimeni*], a divine voice emerged and pronounced, 'It is I who have decreed these hidden things' [*mimeni yatzu kevushim*]."[136] Here, as it were, God reveals the force "in the wings" that guides His players on the world's stage. In effect, this insight, first voiced by the Rabbis themselves, affirms the fundamental understanding of events that is central to Izbica-Radzyn teaching.[137] We saw some signs of it above in R. Ya'akov's comments. It finds most direct expression in statements such as this one, recorded in the name of R. Mordecai Joseph:

> In these chapters [concerning the family of Jacob], God teaches us that all our actions are from God, while people's thoughts are their own.... The mitzvot, or their opposite [that is, the transgressions] that one does are in God's hand; only occasionally does He attribute them to the individual. We see this with Judah: God bore witness that "she is right—it was all from Me" (B. *Sotah* 10b). In truth, it is for this reason that Judah—and all his descendents of the tribe of Judah whose deeds resemble his—were so driven by passion that it was impossible for them to overcome it. As the midrash says, "The angel in charge of desire compelled him to do it." And thus he cannot be held guilty for being powerless to conquer his desire.[138]

The proof R. Mordecai Joseph offers here for this view is an image drawn from the *Zohar* (2.107a). David—and by inference Judah himself—willfully, knowingly agrees to live his life, even to sin as he plays the role asked of him: to be "the King's jester" [*badḥana de-malka*]. "Test me, God, and try me," says David, "so that Your words may be proved right and Your judgment faultless." With characteristic sleight of hand, the Rabbis in the *Zohar* juxtapose these two verses (Ps. 26:2 and Ps. 51:6) and draw a causal connection between them to make sense of the most troubling chapter in King David's life, the events concerning Batsheva (2 Sam. 11). As rabbinic tradition has it, David confidently asks to be put to the test, to prove to one and all his devotion and purity of heart.[139] God has a different goal in mind. He warns David that he will fail the test. Worse, David's deeds will look reprehensible; he will be severely chastised for his sins, regretfully acknowledge them, and spend the rest of his days repenting for them. R. Ya'akov integrates this idea in his own commentary on Judah's story.

> And so he is called "the King's jester"—because even in an instance when it looks as if he did not succeed in resisting temptation, that too is as God wills it to be. For he allows himself to be "defeated" by God, so that the honor of Heaven be magnified and sanctified. Thus King David, who stems from the tribe of Judah said, "So that Your words may be proved right and Your judgment faultless." And the Rabbis add that he remarked to God, "Which of us should be proven in the right—I or You?" ... Indeed, King David wished to stand firm against his desires and to constrict himself with all his might. But he himself did not have the power to overcome them because, most profoundly, *that* was God's will. And "love covers up all offenses" (Prov. 10:12).[140]

The double game R. Mordecai Joseph and R. Ya'akov describe thus demands the highest imaginable level of self-sacrifice and disregard for the ego. The "King's jester" forgoes all claim to personal dignity, moral standing, and freedom of choice. His sole wish is to give honor to his Master, "even if it may, at times, require him to do something against halakhah, as 'a time to act for the Lord [—overturn His Torah!].'"[141] The crucial challenge implicit in this role, Izbica-Radzyn tradition stresses, is this: "the King's jester" derives no personal benefit from his "sins." On the contrary, he must hold himself fully responsible for them, and endure all the remorse and sense of failure expected of people who believe they act in freedom. R. Ya'akov puts it clearly:

> The difference is that if one's real wish is to "escape from the Master," to violate God's word, and only the knowledge that "His eyes observe all the ways of humankind" [after Jer. 32:19] keeps one from deliberately going against God's will—if one waits and hopes that desire will overcome one and compel one to act without freedom of choice, if one ceases to see God before one and does one's deed without reason ... this is wholly evil. But one who has no wish to "escape from the Master" or to be driven away and forget God's presence before one—if it happens that such a person's inclination grows so strong that one has no freedom of choice to overcome that desire—this must mean that God wills it and has caused it to come about. And thus, if one sins in this manner, one should repent fully and trust in God, for He will surely turn those actions into merits.[142]

The distinction R. Ya'akov sets out here focuses on the questions of authenticity and the true motivation behind actions. In both of the instances he describes, the individual acts under compulsion, "without free choice," and, finally, transgresses. Externally, the end result and the justification for it seem identical. What separates them can be detected only emotionally and inwardly. The first individual celebrates the opportunity to be tempted irresistibly into sin; secretly, he "waits and hopes" for it. This could perhaps be called "pious heresy"—and R. Ya'akov's evaluation of it is clear.[143]

In the second instance, unavoidable sin can be transformed, but this is possible only after a painful stage of disintegration. Izbica-Radzyn tradition speaks often of this seminal point the individual must pass through on the journey toward repentance and repair. For R. Mordecai Joseph, and R. Ya'akov after him, what signals it is called *tza'akah*—a "cry" that issues from a soul nearly broken. It is a moment of truth and an overcoming. As R. Ya'akov explains, with the sale of Joseph and tragedy that came in its wake:

> Hiddenness grew so immense that no one could have broken through it, no one but Judah himself. For he has the power to shout, to call out in appeal, "Save, O Lord!" (Ps. 12:2). In the most terrible hour of concealment, he found the strength to sound and cry out with a great shout [*toke'a u-meri'a*] and to cause the walls of hiddenness to come tumbling down.[144]

The next chapters of Judah's life recount how the "power to shout" that he embodies is played out on many planes. As we will see, it is this spiritual resource that will ultimately prove—to Jacob, to Joseph, and to history—the real nature of Judah's failures and his tribe's true right to kingship. Beyond himself, Judah's story, on R. Ya'akov's reading, is meant to teach of the transforming effect of suffering and repentance and, finally, the higher merit, in an absolute sense, of the "way" Judah embodies.

Judah's Strength—The Heart of Israel

The next chapters of the biblical narrative tell of famine in the land of Canaan. At Jacob's request, Judah descends with his brothers to Egypt to seek provisions. In their first encounter with Joseph, as viceroy of the pharaoh, they are accused of being spies. Provisions are sold to them but Simeon is imprisoned as a hostage; he will be released only if their youngest brother, Benjamin, is brought back down with them to Egypt. The brothers realize all this has befallen them in divine retribution for the wrongs they committed against Joseph. They return to their father. When they tell him that the viceroy has demanded to see

Benjamin with them, Jacob refuses outright: "My son will not go down with you!" But time passes. "The famine was severe in the land." As their supplies dwindle, Jacob asks his sons once again: "Go back, bring us some food." Judah reminds him of the man's warning: "Do not see my face unless your brother is with you." Jacob's sorrow is bitter, and he blames his sons for bringing his troubles upon him. "Then Judah said to his father Israel, 'Send the boy in my care and let us be on our way … I myself will be a guarantee for him; you may hold me responsible. If I do not bring him back to you and set him before you, I shall stand guilty before you for all time.'" Israel their father then consents (Gen. 42:1–43:16).

R. Ya'akov questions why Jacob now consents to part with Benjamin, the second and only remaining son of his beloved wife Rachel. He suggests that it was Judah's determination to take responsibility for his actions, and the sense of a higher force guiding him that convinced Jacob that "salvation was soon to come."

> For he recognized Judah's strength as the heart of Israel and knew his words would not be empty. Even though, for now, concealment was so very great with no resolution to be seen—still, nothing can stand in the way of *teshuvah* [repentance]. God has the power to show that His true intent is not what it seemed to be in that time of concealment, as the verse says, "For My thoughts are not your thoughts" (Isa. 55:8). Indeed, no human being can comprehend God's final goal, for His words live and endure and they can be transformed by many devices, according to the acts people do. The strength Judah has enables him to pierce even great hiddenness, to show how God can save, and to reveal that, in truth, there never was any concealment at all.… And so, when Jacob heard Judah say, "I myself will be a guarantee for him" he knew that the spirit of God was speaking through him and his heart was strengthened that salvation was soon to come.[145]

Judah, it seems, discovers his own intrinsic strength at this time as well. R. Ya'akov continues:

> Judah was sorely angry at himself for his failure by selling Joseph and for paining his father, even causing the Holy Spirit [*ruaḥ ha-kodesh*] to depart from him. And so when he heard his father Jacob say, "Why have you caused this evil to befall me"—as if he were thinking, "my path is hidden from God" (Isa. 40:27), [Judah] understood that He who will repair Jacob's failure will repair me as well. And that encouraged his heart to step forward and offer such a guarantee.[146]

Undeniably, in this scene Judah has attained a new level of self-definition. For a second time, he offers a pledge. This time, though, the surety that promises his honest aims is given in full awareness of the risk—Judah offers himself. As the Rabbis said, he puts "his life in this world and the world to come" on the line, vowing to sacrifice all he will ever have in order to right his wrongs. The force of his will, the depth of his regret, and the sense that "the spirit of God was speaking through him" awaken Israel, Judah's father, to renewed hope that perhaps he will be saved after all from the punishments of *Gehinnom* he so greatly fears.[147] The conviction named here as a guiding force is that divine intent, though incomprehensible, can somehow be "transformed," reversed, or re-formed. Repentance and hope have the power to make things be different, to read the Text and make it mean in a different way. That is, if one can only "cry out" in truth, "God's final goal" and everything that led to it will come into sight. When the story and all its events are retold in that light, understanding of what was, resolution, and comfort come.

And so Jacob's sons return to Egypt with their youngest brother, Benjamin. Once again, provisions are sold to them; once again the money they paid is replaced in the mouth of their sacks. This time, Joseph's silver goblet is surreptitiously hidden in Benjamin's sack as well. The brothers set off for home, are overtaken and accused of stealing the master's goblet. To their horror, the goblet is found. The brothers return to the viceroy; Benjamin, he says, must become a slave forever. "Then Judah said, 'What can we say to my lord? How can we speak? And how are we to justify ourselves? God has uncovered the sin of your servants. Here we are: we are ready to become slaves to my lord'" (Gen. 44:16). Faced with the prospect of utter downfall—of losing Benjamin and causing Jacob endless agony—Judah rhetorically has no words. Despairingly, he confesses to all the wrongs he and his brothers have committed. He then throws himself into an impassioned plea on behalf of all his brothers before the Egyptian ruler—their disguised brother Joseph. These verses, which portray a final, dramatic meeting between Judah and Joseph, open the *sidrah Va-yiggash*. In the course of it, both heroes will articulate and interpret what they have lived. Izbica-Radzyn tradition offers a novel perspective on this encounter. The identities of the players and what they symbolize are named and recognized. Moreover, each figure realizes and inwardly accepts the role he and the others have been given.

R. Ya'akov depicts this emotionally charged meeting between "two kings"—Joseph and Judah—as a denouement and resolution in the saga the Bible recounts. Considering Judah's speech, he remarks that "on the face of things, none of the contentions Judah voiced were really all that convincing enough to have changed Joseph's mind and led him to release Benjamin." The effect of Judah's plea, then, can only be explained differently. In effect, a midrash on these verses already states rather cryptically that this scene must be understood as "double-talk"—as speech requiring two simultaneous planes of interpretation. What these are, though, the midrash does not explain. "'Golden apples in silver filigree, a word is spoken in many ways [*davar davur al ofanav*]' (Prov. 25:11). Like a spinning wheel [*ofan*], Judah's words turned in all directions as he spoke to Joseph."[148] Based on this midrash, R. Ya'akov's reading stages this notion of a double message. The verses Judah speaks, ostensibly to the nameless Egyptian master, are juxtaposed with other statements—Judah's meta-monologue directed to the Master of the world. While outwardly retelling an already familiar story Judah, on this reading, daringly uncovers the "plot" [*'alilah*] that, in truth, makes all sin inevitable and unavoidable.[149]

> ["Then you said to your servants, bring him down to me] and I will set my eye on him" (Gen. 44:21)—why does God draw the soul down into this world ... this place of concealment, darkness, misty obscurity and grant it no rest in the midst of it all? Doesn't God desire and always look to benefit His creations? And if He does, why did He bring the soul down from her lofty home; why wasn't her existence up in the world of souls, in peace and tranquility, enough? ... And so if it happens that one can't summon the strength to withstand a trial that confronts one, this is a powerful claim to make against God: "Why did you bring me here?—For everything is revealed and known before You; nothing is concealed. From the very beginning You knew what would happen. Why, then, did you try me?" This is what Judah meant when he cited Joseph's words, "[Bring him down to me] and I will set my eye on him" (44:21)—most profoundly, he was talking about God who draws the soul down into this world....
>
> ["We said to my lord,] 'But the lad cannot leave his father'" (Gen. 44:22)—the soul that comes into this world must abandon her Father in heaven and the clarity of divine light.... "Then our father said, 'Go, find us a bit of food'" (44:25). Here, too, Judah pleaded the case of the Jewish people before God—for who would ever want to go down into this dark and shadowy world and be nourished with coarse, bodily things? ... And so God began to hide His light from the soul, making life in the world of souls seem so limited and small that the soul would long to enter this world, just to expand and live a little bit more. But since the soul, for her own part, really had no desire to enter into doubts, she cannot be held guilty for anything she might commit in this world.

> "Now your servant has pledged himself for the boy" (Gen. 44:32)—even if he has failed, he should not be blamed for it because his sin depends on me. "I, my lord" (44:18)—it is I who am answerable as the "guarantee" of the whole Jewish nation. I am the inmost heart of Israel and there, deep within, they are clean and pure.[150]
>
> "Then Joseph could not contain himself [... And he said to his brothers, I am Joseph]" (Gen. 45:1)—that is, once the soul wins her case before God with these arguments, He can withhold in silence no longer ... Indeed, the Holy One, blessed be He rejoices and concedes, "My children have defeated me, they have defeated me" [B. *Bava Metzi'a* 59b].[151]

The alien Egyptian viceroy, whose machinations brought such turmoil to Jacob's family and cast fear and trembling in the hearts of his sons, removes his mask. In that moment of self-revelation, all of them suddenly understood "that they had never been in danger at all; it was with their own brother, who seeks their good, that they had struggled. He never wished them any evil."[152] Face to face with Joseph, the chapters and the years that have passed instantly reconfigure. Beyond the biblical narrative itself, R. Ya'akov says in the name of his father, R. Mordecai Joseph, that this story has a larger meaning: "It enables us to glimpse what will be in the ultimate time of redemption, may it come speedily. God will reveal—in a way that everyone can understand—that they were never in exile and no foreign yoke ever burdened them; they endured no suffering at all, and 'He never abandoned them' (Zech. 10:6) ... And Israel—they never abandoned God either and never sinned, not even for a moment—even though the human mind cannot imagine this is really so."[153]

This retrospective vision enables the "words of the Torah" and the lives they depict to tell a different story. R. Ya'akov stresses, however, that this miraculous possibility is long concealed. It can come to light only after the players have been "tested" and wrestled with the specter of sin and failure, until they "shout out to God" from the depths of a broken heart.

> The mysterious essence of the *baal teshuvah* is this: He cannot know, during the time of concealment, that God is with him. But when he repents with all his heart, then he sees how, from beginning to end, everything that happened to him was "the words of the living God," which endure forever [Jer. 23:36] ... And although others are forbidden to do what he did, after he has repented, his actions are healed. The words of Torah come to mean something different than they did before he repented. For now it is

> clear that he did just what God willed—and so his "sins become merits" [B. *Yoma* 86b].[154]

In light of all this, it's difficult to see what led the distinguished scholar Joseph Weiss to state that Izbica-Radzyn Hasidism seeks to present Judah as an ideal representative of "religious anarchism" and teach that "the will of God is an irrational phenomenon moving in a frequently changing, irrational and arbitrary manner."[155] Equally difficult is Weiss's contention that "since ... sin is only apparently committed and is in fact an impossibility, there is no point in penitence and it is contrary to Mordecai Joseph's teaching."[156] R. Yaʿakov, it seems, was aware that such a misinterpretation could arise. The passage just cited continues:

> However, those who dwell in darkness and do not know that the words of Torah live and endure forever, and that those words "turn and face in all directions"—such people think the Torah is solidified and changeless. If so, one cannot possibly repair what has been damaged.[157]

In other words, the "impossibility" of sin (or the pointlessness of repentance) is not a given, a priori fact that can be stated and manipulated at the will of detached thinkers. Rather, the ability to see that, in truth, one never violated God's will is granted to an individual only after the experience of sin itself has been lived personally. To suppose that Izbica-Radzyn teaching proposes a "radical antinomianism" and a romantic "freedom of the spirit" to be adopted as a universal truth, as Rivka Schatz-Uffenheimer does, is to read in a great deal more than seems to have been intended.[158] A more circumspect and attentive understanding of the symbolic valence of "Judah" in Izbica-Radzyn Hasidism, I think, might be reached by reconsidering his counterpart—the symbolic other who opposes, balances, and defines his essence. That is Joseph the *zaddik*, who personifies the "nomian" mode of being, so to speak. The comparison between the two that Izbica-Radzyn tradition develops can help us form a realistic and authentic appreciation of the "religious ideals" it offers.

Joseph and Judah—Two Modes of Being

We saw the basic paradigm in the opening pages of our discussion. We'll recall it here.

> The tribes of Joseph and Judah exemplify these two modes [*beḥinot*]. Joseph is the righteous foundation [*yesod*] and the source of all cautious apprehension [*yirot*], that no Jew should "miss the mark" and err. Judah is the *baal teshuvah*, who instills the Jewish nation with the strength never to despair.[159]

R. Ya'akov evokes various images throughout his commentary on this story to speak of the relationship these two figures share. Echoing a rabbinic adage, Joseph is the key to the outer chamber, while Judah is the key to the innermost chamber. Until the first is opened, the second remains inaccessible, and yet the final goal is surely to reach within.[160] Similarly, Joseph is the "candle" that illuminates the "treasure-house," his brother Judah. Without the light he casts, "the king's riches, silver, gold, and gems" remain shrouded in darkness, and yet the value of the treasure is infinitely greater than the candle.[161] In addition, Joseph's "light of reason" guides his brothers' paths; all of them have need of this quality, especially Judah who "has no eyes" of his own.[162] Put in practical terms:

> "Joseph" represents fulfilling the commandments. At their vital root, however, all the mitzvot serve only to clarify that God dwells within the heart of Israel. Thus the Sages said that "the mitzvot will become obsolete in the future to come [B. *Niddah* 61b]. And so the source of light is in the hands of the one who can give everything up to God—this is the power of the tribe of Judah.[163]

"To give everything up" here would mean willfully to relinquish one's subjective judgments and analytic power of evaluation. Judah's strength, which comes to the fore as his story ends, emerges from this realm of negation. The code phrases that designate it are "she has nothing of herself" (*leyt leh migarma klum*) or, alternately, the state of "having no eyes" evoked above.[164] Paradoxically, such a gesture of selflessness is both the highest expression of devotion to God and a precondition for discovering one's personal, ethical responsibility. Judah's struggle to understand himself and affirm the merit of his path culminates in the final chapters of his story. R. Ya'akov explores the new self-interpretation that Judah attains as the book of Genesis draws to a close.

Two motifs inform that image: the "heart" and the "moon." Above, we saw that Judah realizes he is "the heart of Israel"—an inner reservoir of vitality and conscience on which all figuratively depends. An additional aspect of the heart demands our attention. It concerns the dialectic that Judah represents and, in that, it is intimately connected to the metaphorical valence of the moon. Through these motifs, R. Ya'akov offers his listeners a compelling reading of those final chapters and an implicit rebuttal of Judah's opponents.

The epic tale of Jacob and his sons began with the verses describing the father's inordinate affection for the firstborn son of his beloved wife—the child who most resembled himself, who emulated his controlled presence of mind and clarity of action. It was this kinship, R. Mordecai Joseph points out, that "led Jacob to believe Joseph was the chosen one, and Joseph believed it too." But eventually, he notes, it would prove to be Joseph's gravest shortcoming and the source of Jacob's error.

> Although such qualities are good, one must trust in God as well, for human actions alone cannot establish anything eternal. Even though Joseph achieved much by guarding himself [from sin], and all the kings of Israel, of recognized greatness, were his progeny, their dominion was "not for all time" (1 Kings 11:39). An eternal edifice can never be theirs; that belongs to Judah alone.[165]

The opportunity to "trust in God," it seems, becomes real only in those unwished-for moments of un-control, when the "light of reason" is occluded. In such times of darkness, as we have seen in the events surrounding Judah, the things one may do can look faulty, unworthy, sinful. The purpose of all this, R. Ya'akov says, is to turn one inward, to start working first of all in the realm of the heart.

> The heart [*lev*] is called so because it blossoms [*melavlev*] and transmutes, altering itself in manifold ways. It cannot remain static in one single mindset. Rather, sometimes it is in expanded consciousness [*gadlut ha-moḥin*] and other times in constricted consciousness [*katnut ha-moḥin*].[166]

Most fundamentally, the heart cannot be still, certain, fixated, studied. The life force it symbolizes compels it always to become something new, turning from one state to its opposite in a systolic and diastolic rhythm. The heart can metaphorically only submit to these changing times and value them as its source of vitality.

In his teachings on this *parashah*, R. Ya'akov reminds us that Judah is both the "heart of Israel" and, as the *Zohar* teaches, symbolic of that quality inherent in the Jewish nation called "the mysterious essence of the moon" (*raza de-sihara*). To explaining the identity between the two, he notes that in an orbit of 30 days, the moon spends 15 of them waxing and 15 waning. "Had He so wished, God could have made her circuit only 15 days, forever bathed with light. But, instead, He made her full orbit encompass darkness as well. In the same manner, God created humankind in the world so that people should 'travel full circle.' This means they must pass through darkness; they will inevitably sin."[167] The *Zohar*, he recalls, records the foresight voiced on the primordial sixth day by the Torah itself: "This human You are about to create is very likely to anger You [by sinning]," and God's reassurance that He has already created *teshuvah*, to enable them to heal and repair.[168] R. Ya'akov concludes, "So, although every one must pass through darkness, each will return and shine again. *Then* they will understand they never really sinned."[169]

This, in effect, is the moment acted out in the dramatic encounter that *parashat Va-yiggash* depicts. Judah's speech vindicates his brothers before the Egyptian viceroy and the Jewish soul before her Creator. Fear, envy, accusations fade away; "their father Jacob's spirit returned to life" (Gen. 45:27). Most significantly,

> Joseph, in hearing his brother's words, realized the truth was with Judah. God had ordained all these events. Now it was clear that Judah's strength is greater than Joseph's ... Scripture alludes to this. The verse says [that Jacob] "sent Judah before him" (Gen. 46:28) in recognition that he is truly superior to Joseph.[170]

Embattled Ideologies

Drawing once again on Charles Taylor's insights, I'd like to suggest that this reading of the biblical story and the inner worlds of its characters resonates with a novel and distinctly modern aspect of selfhood. Taylor presents a certain intellectual history of ideas that passes through distinct stages. Particularly relevant to our discussion is "the notion of a radical autonomy of rational agents" as an essential dimension of the Kantian view. Human dignity, moral independence, and disengagement from sensibility mark the Enlightenment ethic.[171] This spiritual outlook changes in a fundamental way in the late 18th century. An intensified "sense of inwardness ... leads to an even more radical subjectivism and an internalization of moral sources."[172] The "subtler languages" that later take form in the post-Romantic age, Taylor says, create new ways of thinking; "self-affirmation" becomes a central issue. One influential writer in this regard is Kierkegaard, who speaks of the potential to transfigure or reverse one's life. In abandoning the aesthetic occupation with finite things, one "attains the ethical ... by choosing oneself ... in the light of the infinite." This attainment, in turn, "lifts us out of despair and allows us to affirm ourselves.... In choosing myself, I become what I really am, a self with an infinite dimension." In the still higher stage Kierkegaard later evolved, the religious, the idea of a transformation engendered through "a new stance toward oneself, overcoming despair and dread" is preserved. Now, though, "this depends on our relation to God."[173] The disparity between the religious traditions underlying Hasidism and Western streams of thought is, undeniably, significant. At the same time, the understanding we have heard voiced in Izbica-Radzyn teaching seems to resonate with the developing climate of thought Taylor sets out here, especially in the "crucial place" now given to "our inner powers of constructing or transfiguring or interpreting the world" and the self.[174]

The initial profile we saw of Jacob and his beloved son Joseph, and the mental stance they embodied, seems to share many elements of the "enlightened ethic" suggested above. In R. Ya'akov's portrayal, the "light of reason" (*or ha-da'at*) these two figures hold as the highest of values, their concern for truth, dispassion, and avoidance of doubt, audibly echo that ethic. A glance back at the profile of Judah that comes to the fore in the short statements attributed to R. Menaḥem Mendel of Kotsk makes clear that Judah, in his view, shares these identical values held by Jacob and Joseph. Notably, on R. Menaḥem Mendel's reading, Judah regains clear vision of his intrinsic moral faculties and recovers his devotion and obedience to "the law" directly after his failing in the sale of Joseph. His courage is swiftly compensated.[175]

The contrast between that view and the readings by R. Mordecai Joseph and R. Ya'akov of Judah's spiritual journey is striking. Central to their teachings on this narrative, as we have seen, is the contention that Judah and Joseph represent two distinct, opposing types, and that the spiritual ideal Judah represents is far superior. Their portrait of Judah—his path through despair, the transformations of his life engendered by seeing and living it in a new dimension, and his final self-affirmation—have much in common with the expressionist sensibility evoked above. The importance of recognizing this alternate mode, and ultimately choosing it, goes far beyond an abstract battle between equal but different ideological trends. Izbica-Radzyn tradition bases its argument of the worthiness of Judah's mode of being on metahistorical grounds. Kingship, the House of David, the messianic age—time will prove to all opponents that all this can come about only by embracing the journey through concealment that Judah embodies.

And so we see that the events of their lives compel Judah, Jacob, and Joseph to draw on their inner powers and engage in the mission to reconstruct, transfigure, and reinterpret. In the final scene of their collective story, world and self crystallize in new form for all three figures, and for their readers as well. As Jacob's life draws to an end, his sons gather around his deathbed to receive their father's prophetic blessing. Now comes the most definitive sign that Jacob sees and knows the true identity and role of each. To his fourth son, Israel says: "You, Judah—your brothers will recognize you" (*Yehuda ata yodukha aḥekha*) (Gen. 49:8). Citing the *Zohar*'s comment on this verse once again, R. Ya'akov articulates the affirmation of self Judah has achieved. "'Judah fathered the first and he fathered the second; nothing in him ever really changed.' It was he who said, 'Let us sell him' and it was he, equally, who 'pulled back the curtain' and revealed [Joseph] in Egypt."[176] These two acts, engendered and born out by the same individual, mark the starting point and endpoint of Judah's trials. The first appears reprehensible; the second is a courageous, hazardous leap of faith. As diametrically opposed in ethical value as they appear to be, these two acts are connected and joined in the "self" he represents: the "master of repentance" who can sin and who can repair. In this teaching, R. Ya'akov locates and deciphers the concept of self-awareness, or *yedi'ah* (knowing), in the key word "you." Among all his sons and their blessings, it is Judah alone that Jacob addresses in that direct form.

> This is his essence—he is called "you, Judah" because he forever seeks to be there with God. As the Targum teaches, "You admitted [your wrongs] and were not ashamed, and so your brothers will recognize you" (Gen. 49:8). And the *Zohar* says, "Thus he won the name 'You.' He proved himself through the first [Er and Onan] and through the second [Perez and Zeraḥ], he and no one else. Judah's children and all his descendents will acknowledge this when they say, 'For You are our father … [we are the clay and You are our potter and we are all Your handiwork'] (Isa. 64:7)."

The emotional charge of this statement, with the fragmentary prooftext he adds, becomes clear through the analogy R. Ya'akov then makes: "A king of flesh and blood—when he is angry with someone, the best thing to do is to hide from him; the further one can get from the king, the less able he is to harm one. But with God, the opposite is true. The closer one draws, the more protected one is. And so the verse says 'You hide me' (Ps. 32:7), for one is truly safe only with God."[177]

The essence Judah bequeaths to "his children and all his descendents," R. Ya'akov suggests, is what promises their survival in the years of desolation they will bring upon themselves with their iniquities. God, the prophet Isaiah foresees, will be enraged at them; He will hide His face and "melt them away" (Isa. 64:6). The sole measure that will restore what has been ruined and heal the breach is the "art" Judah embodies: knowing how to return once again to a stance of presence before God. To be able to say "You"—to realize that "You are our father" becomes possible only after having "come full circle." In the course of that, the long, lonely, frightening trajectory through darkness must be endured. Despair, crying out to God, "choosing oneself" are what bring one back to the light of the Countenance, to utter that address in such intimate form—"You." Judah, above all, is the archetype of such a self. With unusual adamancy, R. Ya'akov stresses this point.

> Don't ever imagine that true recognition of God belongs to Joseph. His conception of direct presence as "You" stems from the light his own mind grasps, his private understanding of what God finds worthy. Far greater is Judah's light—he possesses heroic strength even in terrible concealment, in a space where Joseph hasn't the strength to enter. And so the Sages said: "The place that 'masters of repentance' have reached—the righteous ones, despite all their wholeness, cannot reach it" (B. *Berakhot* 34a). Judah, the *baal teshuvah—his* light is called 'You.'"[178]

Judah, Son of Leah

The realization Jacob attains that he had been mistaken reverberates far into his own past and future. His new perspective on the dynamics involving his sons, and his acceptance of Judah's mode of being, here reaches a watershed. I'd like to suggest that R. Ya'akov's commentary intimates that Jacob in his last hour gains the ability, in a sense, to "redeem the past" and have it make sense as part of his own life's story. The past in question is Jacob's first painful encounter with uncertainty—his unplanned, undesired marriage with two sisters, Rachel and Leah. Now that "the trauma of Joseph" has abated, Jacob can look back at those seminal events. Through his reflections in the last years of his life, we see that Jacob has become empowered to draw together all that has happened to him into a meaningful unity. R. Ya'akov does not speak explicitly of such an emotional gesture of integration. His commentary on the earlier chapter of Jacob's life, however, makes clear just how valid and inherent it is to his reading.

We recall that Joseph, the son who long captured Jacob's affection, was his by Rachel, the beautiful wife he had so loved and lost. R. Ya'akov notes that

Jacob's journey to Lavan was really for Rachel. He found her and chose her in total clarity as his companion, and thus Rachel represents "the revealed world (*'alma de-etgalyia*)—those things one grasps consciously and does in full awareness of what one is doing." Indeed, it was for that reason, R. Ya'akov adds, that her sons, Joseph and Benjamin, found such favor in Jacob's eyes—"their actions seemed to be the height of clarity, composedness, reason, and control." But Jacob was first "given" a different wife. Leah became his in the night, without his knowledge or control, without "wanting" her. Leah represents "the concealed world (*'alma de-etcasia*)—beyond what the mind can grasp and recognize as 'good.' And thus her sons did not find favor in their father's eyes like Rachel's sons did."[179]

R. Ya'akov's critique of Jacob's shortsightedness in this chapter of his life is audible. To be sure, he says, everyone would prefer to act consciously, calculating every decision. And yet it is precisely in response to that aspiration that God causes something to happen, something beyond one's control that looks unworthy. "And a person cannot come to terms with this, and suffers greatly from it. One exhausts oneself trying to fix things up." What Jacob did unaware—taking Leah as his wife, and all that was born of that action—caused him "tremendous apprehension" (*miḥushim gedolim*) and he was unable to come to terms with all of it for many years to come.[180] The allusion here, it seems, is to the misadventure Leah's sons wrought in Jacob's world: Reuben's impropriety (Gen. 35:22); Simeon and Levi's destructive, impetuous defense of their sister Dina (Gen. 34); Judah's deeds in the sale of Joseph. For those 22 years that Joseph was lost to him, R. Ya'akov remarks, Jacob's "heart panged him with the question: 'Why is all this happening?'"[181]

The portrait of Leah herself, the embodiment of the "concealed world," that emerges in R. Ya'akov's reading here adds a new and uncommon perspective to our understanding of Judah and his father's evolving perception of that son. On the personal, psychological level, "She felt that her outward actions looked unworthy, and she suffered and strove to clarify them."[182] R. Ya'akov refers to his father's commentary. The names Leah gave her sons, R. Mordecai Joseph notes, bear witness to her efforts to alter her reality. Reuben—"for God has seen my affliction" (Gen. 29:32); Simeon—"God has heard that I am unloved" (29:33). While her first three sons were born in recompense for her suffering, R. Mordecai Joseph says that her fourth son, Judah, was given to Leah "as a gift." Judah—"'this time, I will thank [*odeh*] God' (29:35), for such a soul cannot be born as a reward for righteousness and human effort, however noble, but only as a blessing from God."[183] Leah, then, seems to reach some kind of closure with the birth of Judah. The gratitude she expresses includes her knowing that everything that happened was for the good, however painfully it all came about and, perhaps, despite the sorrow that remains.[184] Her son, Judah, will live out this truth. R. Ya'akov notes that the name Leah calls him contains all four letters of the Divine Name signifying mercy, י-ה-ו-ד-ה. The additional fifth letter of *Yehudah*, the *dalet*, "teaches that he has nothing of his own, save what God grants him—and this is his whole 'self.'"[185] Judah's mother invests her son with this aspect of her own essence: "'Leah'—for she wearied herself [*nileah*], thirsting endlessly for God's salvation."[186]

In describing Jacob's liaison with Leah, R. Ya'akov speaks of an other, darkly concealed side of his experience—the side Jacob found so difficult to value. She is the helpmate God sent to him "beyond his understanding, in the sense of 'Your Torah must be overturned, for the time has come to act for the Lord' (B. *Berakhot* 54a).... Truly, this is far superior to what one takes for oneself on the basis of one's own comprehension."[187]

The "Torah" that God Himself wills to "overturn," in this context, would represent the rational truth that a conscientious individual like Jacob has chosen and prepared to guide his life's decisions. "To act for the Lord," correspondingly, would mean to do something that seems to violate everything one believes to be good and worthy but proves, in the end, to be God's will. Leah, as Jacob's helpmate, pulls him into a tenuous space of un-control. The mode of being she opens before him, an unknown realm of fecundity, is what R. Ya'akov calls "if/mother"—אם.[188] In other words, Leah's weighty role is to draw Jacob out of his constructed, limiting vision of what is good and beautiful and true. She bears those children who do not "find favor" in the eyes of their father. Their merits, the unique qualities each of them embody, will come to light much, much later, after exile and suffering and trials of many kinds. As R. Ya'akov says, "Only afterwards does God's profound intent become clear, how great was His mercy and how precious those tribes would be."[189] Of all her children, it is Judah's strength that most resembles his mother Leah's—the ability "to thrust himself into doubt and trust in God that no harm will come to him."[190]

Presence

Explicitly or implicitly, the lives of these two biblical figures, Judah and Moses, recount a heroic quest in search of selfhood. We have seen some of the ways that Izbica-Radzyn teaching reads the verses that tell their stories and how it seeks to understand, through those figures, where each of us has been and who we, as well as they, are meant to be. One of them puts the question directly.

"And Moses said, 'Who am I?'" (Exod. 3:11). R. Ya'akov contemplates on God's oblique response: "I will be with you" (3:14). He explains: "For what a person is born with can never be blemished; it lasts forever." And remember: As a boy, the prophet Samuel's mother "made him a little cloak" (1 Sam. 2:19). A lifetime later, Samuel is brought up from the dead. He appears, "An elderly man wrapped in a cloak" (1 Sam. 28:14). And so the Sages understood: "That cloak—he grew up in it, he was buried it in, and in it he rose" (*Tanḥuma, 'Emor* 2). R. Ya'akov adds that this, the mother's gift that accompanies her child from infancy, growing with him, protecting and defining all his days, cannot be cast off or lost or exchanged. Indeed, "it will awaken first of all when the dead are resurrected. What one has accomplished on one's own will awaken after that." The inborn essence or self that "one's 'mother' instills will never be annulled. In other words, what comes from God lasts forever. 'For I will be with you.'"[191]

Chapter 3

Figures of the Feminine

Introduction: Emerging Light

> "God said, 'Let us make humankind [in our image, after our likeness]'" (Gen. 1:26). A person's form [*levush*] is the window through which God can be seen—each one according to the root of the soul ... And by serving the Creator, the window can be made larger, as the *Zohar* (3.241a) teaches, "Even one window can illuminate all the worlds."[1]

These "forms" we wear, the bodies we inhabit, says R. Ya'akov, are windows opening onto the universe. They frame our vision, circumscribing that square of something beyond ourselves that each of us can, potentially, see and understand. The "garment" or *levush* that houses my soul is given, not chosen. I carry it with me always, in all my experiencing. It encloses and separates, and yet this "garment" does not just conceal me from the world and the world from me. In truth, corporeity opens us to other horizons, and offers us a mode of transcendence as well.[2] R. Ya'akov underlines the personal, unrepeatable nature of each person's "window," shaped as it is by the "root of the soul." He adds, however, that one's horizon of vision, wherever it is focused, may expand; the beyond can become wider and closer "by serving the Creator."

In this chapter, I would like to consider teachings in which R. Ya'akov gestures toward a dynamic of this sort, a manner of "service" that summons us to think about aspects of embodiment and human experience that many of us may have overlooked. In the Hasidic tradition that R. Ya'akov perpetuates, with its kabbalistic heritage, these aspects are cogently present. They emerge in many, often unexpected places—sometimes as associations, often pointing toward deeply rooted hermeneutical codes secretly at work in the texts and in the world we strive to understand.

We'll begin with the following passage. It combines a teaching formulated in *Mei ha-Shiloaḥ* with another developed in *Beit Ya'akov*. These two commentaries set out the central motifs and some of their correspondences that will occupy us in the pages to follow. As we will see, R. Ya'akov bases many of his readings on the ideas first set out by his father. Reflecting on the famous story of how the world came into being, its mystical retelling is offered in counterpoint.[3] We recall at the outset that the word "light" appears five times in the biblical account of Creation. This repetition marks a symbolic five-stage process that is mirrored in the phenomenon of human development, physiological as well as psychological.

> The first stage is "God said, Let there be light" (Gen. 1:3)—this is the "sowing of seed" [*zeri'ah*]. For now, the individual is absolutely hidden and undetectable. The second stage: "And there was light" (1:3)—this is the time of pregnancy [*'ibbur*], when the embryo has taken form in the mother's womb; its existence can now be perceived, begins to be recognized. The third stage: "God saw that the light was good" (1:4)—this is birth [*leidah*]; the infant is fully formed, and all can see it is a "creature." The fourth stage: "God separated light from darkness (1:4)—this is nursing [*yenikah*]; at [the end of] this stage, the baby is weaned from its mother's breasts and begins to act independently. The fifth stage: "God called the light Day" (1:5)—this is consciousness [*moḥin*]; now the individual can marry, engender new life, and build a lasting edifice ... In truth, words of Torah come to life in the human heart through the same stages. Everything of value passes through these five "lights."[4]

This innovative retelling of the well-known story of Creation does seem to offer an alternative scenario. "The image of a distant, transcendental God who exists apart from his creation and the authority-based relationship established between the two"[5] gives way here to a matrix of interrelationships involving mutual presence and influence. Drawing on Lurianic teaching, which dwells much on this paradigm, R. Ya'akov often suggests that the path sketched here is not linear but cyclical or spiraling.[6] A spiritual life, lived authentically, experiences each of these stages over and over again, from the "outside" and from the "inside"—bearing and being engendered. Our ideas, beliefs, plans are always "sown" in darkness, nearly unconsciously; slowly they evolve and take on human limbs, filling us and stirring faceless within. Then they emerge, are touched by others, examined, admired, critiqued. We nourish them further, until they begin to take on a life of their own. Marked with our traits, these things come to people the world we build together, throughout our lives.

Some lines before the passage cited above, R. Ya'akov evokes, like many mystics before him, the verse "Through my flesh I may glimpse God" (Job 19:26). In awareness of the imaging used here, it seems clear that the "body of experience" who knows these "lights" the best is a feminine one. In this chapter, we will consider some of the many teachings in which R. Ya'akov contemplates the stages of the process outlined above. We will see that each of them corresponds both with an essential aspect of human creativity and with one of the Divine Names of God, along with the valences that appellation signifies. This double hermeneutical trajectory will lead us, I hope, to a new or heightened understanding of some issues at the forefront of contemporary discourse.[7]

Before we take up the successive stages and explore their meaning, I would like to consider two concepts that form the ideological foundation on which R. Ya'akov's teachings rest. Both of them are presented in Izbica-Radzyn tradition as spatial metaphors; together, they serve to clarify an essential meaning of the feminine. The first is called *yirah*; the second is *mayyin nukvin*, the "feminine waters."

Yirah: "Worlds Enough and Time"

In the genesis recounted in the opening verses of the Bible, day adds to day, light to light as reality comes into being, here to stay. But as organic and familiar as that story may sound, mystical tradition holds that, in effect, it is preceded by other, less evident things. In other words, this story has a secret counterpart. The midrash itself preserves the unsettling reminder that the biblical narrative we know so well is not the beginning at all. The Rabbis hint that the "immortal story" written in this first book of the Torah is really an afterward, the sequel to an unwritten prehistory.

> R. Abahu taught: The Holy One, blessed be He built worlds and destroyed them, built and destroyed until He built this one and said, "This one pleases Me; those did not."[8]

In this alter ego, the Creator seemingly casts "draft" after "draft" into the dustbin; the less than perfect work of His hands is sentenced, over and over again, to an ignoble end. After repeated "failures"—10 in all, according to Lurianic tradition[9]—something finally turns out right and the omnipotent artist decides to keep His latest creation. The theological challenges posed by this midrash are certainly formidable. What concerns R. Ya'akov, as he cites it, is finding the unifying principle that must be at work in this counter-story. Could anything that God brought into being really be totally devoid of worth and warrant annihilation, to be erased without a trace? Or can some intrinsic connection be found that links those lost worlds with our own, some logic that justifies their unhappy end? R. Ya'akov sets out to treat the issue by evoking an uncanny image.

> Indeed, nothing of those worlds could actively remain; they had to be destroyed. Yet their cry [*tza'akah*] endured before Him: "You made me great, and now you have rejected me!" (Ps. 102:11). And this is what aroused the divine Will to create a lasting world of repair.

Why, though, were those first worlds fated to an untimely end? And what power is contained in those disembodied, despairing cries? In seeking the meaning of the scene the midrash depicts, R. Ya'akov draws our attention to an important interplay of forces.

> Those ten worlds were destroyed because the love invested in them was so tremendously powerful; nothing shielded them from it. So close were they to their Giver that they could see their own root emerging from the undifferentiated divine Will.

The brightness and immediacy of such vision proves to be unbearable; from that excess of mercy, each of those worlds rushes back, indistinguishably, into its source. In the final moment before they cease to be, though, the worlds "cry out." The promise of greatness, that terrible intimacy—too late they understand: love must be received consciously, and must be contained and guarded in an entity that knows it is separate from the Giver. The chilling shrieks of sorrow over what has been lost reverberate and gather in primordial space. They catalyze a new reality, another beginning.

> After all that, Creation finally consented to live in "distance" [*yirah*], so that divine light would not strike it so blindingly and rivet it to the Source. Veils must come to shield it. As the *Zohar* (3.204a) says, "The primordial light was so brilliant that the worlds could not bear it. What did the Holy One do? He made light to contain the light; each one would clothe another."

The role of these luminous veils or garments, then, is to mitigate and conceal divine radiance through successive layers that take form "in between."

Diffused through them, the created world, in turn, can gradually receive some small measure of "light"—love, mercy, influx—and still endure. The central concept here is the awareness R. Ya'akov calls *yirah*. He describes it variously as a gesture of consent not to see or not to have everything, as a sense of limitation or contraction, and an essential autonomy. These together yield the opportunity to become a "vessel" (*keli kibbul*). The symbolic valence of this notion is feminine.[10] Notably, R. Ya'akov does not present it here as one pole of a binary structure—as one of two possible modes of being human (as opposed to the option of being "masculine"). Rather, every created entity, in its essence, can exist only as a containing vessel, in unending, paradoxical awareness of the wholly Other that fills its boundaries. Moreover, as we will see, the ability and willingness to receive less than everything is what enables each symbolic vessel not merely to endure but ultimately to give, in turn, something of the contents it has integrated to other spheres of being.

The Jewish nation, in R. Ya'akov's eyes, lives out this mode of awareness most fully.

> The essence of *Knesset Yisrael* [the Assembly of Israel] ... is the aspect of "mother"—a receiving vessel. This teaches us that they collectively receive the influx of God's light ... through their own free will. They take God's sovereignty and His Torah upon themselves with great awe and effort, and they add even more restrictions and precautions drawn from the facet of the "maternal." And so *Knesset Yisrael* is called "the Torah of your mother."[11]

In this instance as well, "receiving" is perceived as being contingent on "limitation." The "Torah of your mother," R. Ya'akov explains, signifies the Oral Law. With the aid of myriad hermeneutical principles, the Rabbis add "fences and boundaries" to the commandments prescribed in "God's" Written Torah. Their overt purpose, clearly, is to guard the well-being of the Jewish people, to keep them from erring by transgressing any detail or intent contained in that primary expression of divine will. More profoundly, though, it is the "Torah of your mother" or rabbinic tradition that truly engenders the relationship between God and the Jewish people. The Giver is portrayed here as dependent, in a sense, on some other entity who can receive. A "father," you must admit, cannot be called so without a "mother" accompanying him. To clarify the mutuality implicit in this connection between God and the Jewish nation, between the "masculine" and "feminine" aspects of the Torah, R. Ya'akov recalls the images we saw earlier in his account of Creation. Here, as well, he stresses the importance of autonomy. To be sure, the Almighty could compel any entity to accept divine sovereignty, and could even manipulate that entity into seeing this as a "gift of love." One grave drawback of such a show of omnipotence, however, is that it robs the subject of every shred of dignity. Echoing the phrase coined by the Rabbis, R. Ya'akov says that to receive in such a manner, no matter how precious the gift, is to "eat the bread of shame" (*nahama de-kisufa*) with one's face averted from the outstretched hand.[12] Even more crucially, any change that is effected on a passive subject voids the subject's sense of self. In other words, the "vessel" must discover its "lack" in freedom, and then must strive to reach a state of readiness to contain another. The effort to define one's self as a separate entity is an essential component of psychic well-being; forging any relationship of dignity is contingent upon it. Hypothetically,

> God could provide all the strength needed to receive a flood of His light … but what good would it do? The receivers wouldn't know themselves, wouldn't know they are the same selves they were before … it would seem to them that they have just now been created.[13]

That is, the awareness of distance and autonomy—the model of *yirah*—is what ensures the sense of continuity of self. The vessel, in receiving, is augmented, not reborn or transformed utterly. In that way alone is integrity preserved—the integrity of self and other, of giver and receiver. R. Ya'akov speaks often of the importance of patience and the difficulty usually bound up with it. A word that often appears in that context is *savlanot*. Drawn from the root ס.ב.ל., it denotes both "suffering" and "carrying, holding." To be a true vessel takes time. It is never painless. More, the process of focusing and clarifying thoughts and self, until one can receive with honor, requires the Giver to wait. This creates a moment of mutual dependence, even vulnerability. Let's turn now to the metaphor R. Ya'akov develops to speak of this moment.

Cries, Water, Rising

Earlier, we noted that in recalling the saga of the primordial worlds destroyed, R. Ya'akov seeks the inherent logic that binds that hidden part of the story with the biblical narrative we know so well. In other words, something of decisive importance must have happened between the first statement in the midrash, "those worlds did not please Me," and the second one, "this [Creation] pleases Me." It was the bitter "cry" of those lost worlds, R. Ya'akov states that "aroused the divine Will to create a lasting world of repair."[14] His suggestion seems to be that "failure" is an essential part of the creative process. That is, the flaws of rejected attempts are never really forgotten. Not only does something of them linger; they become an integral part of the work that finally pleases its creator. Citing another midrash, R. Ya'akov reminds us that God avers: "I destroy nothing, only build always."[15]

R. Ya'akov drives this idea home in his reading of the generation of the Flood. Evoking the same paradigm, he says:

> All ten generations from Adam to Noaḥ drew their vitality from the destroyed worlds. Like those worlds, they were invested with awesome force; they, too, knew no boundaries ... And so they, too, were destroyed .... All that remained of those first worlds was a cry. In the destruction of the Flood, however, Noaḥ and his sons survived. They witnessed that terrifying vista of ruin. It struck a permanent awareness [*yirah*] in their hearts—the cry of those outcast souls that perished must never be lost. The survivors knew that now they must keep their eyes set on the purpose for which they were created, and this would enable them to maintain the world's existence.[16]

The "generation after" attains, or is burdened with a new and complex consciousness of self in relation to the past. The suffering, the wrongs, and the despair of the drowned are fixed in the hearts of the saved. That memory drives them to repair. But the world that will laboriously be rebuilt can only be founded on the ruins of the one that is no more. In this sense, R. Ya'akov understands, "their cry is their remnant."[17]

It is a sound that rises, reverberating from the depths. Humans, it seems, are always lost "down under." The symbolic importance of this vector, this ascending presence, finds expression often in R. Ya'akov's commentary. We saw a hint of it earlier: "their cry ... is what aroused the divine Will to create a lasting world of repair." Another teaching considers it more explicitly. Here, R. Ya'akov reminds us that the story of the worlds destroyed and recreated is, equally, a saga of microcosmic proportions.

> For all of the Creation alludes to the human psyche. The "destroyed worlds" are lived out in the heart broken by failing. In that way alone can one ever attain understanding. So the verse says, "[Nothing had yet sprouted on earth, because the Lord God had not sent rain upon the earth and there was no one to work the soil.] A mist rose from the ground

> [and the whole surface of the earth was watered]" (Gen. 2:6–7). That is, a cry rose from the worlds that were destroyed. As it says in *Tikkunei Zohar* (52, fol. 89b–90a), "A mist [*'ed*] ... Come and see: Arousal must move from below to above [*it'aruta tzerikha mi-tata le-eila*]; only then "the earth was watered." And in the Jerusalem Talmud (*Ta'anit* 2.1): "R. Simeon ben Lakish taught: 'A mist rose from the ground'—when a cry of brokenness [*shever*] rises from below, rains will surely come."[18]

Let's distinguish the recurring pattern in this mosaic of citations. In each text R. Ya'akov quotes, the same causality is at work. The starting point in each case is a situation of hiatus. We see this most clearly in the scene drawn from the Talmud. The Rabbis are discussing times of drought and the measures the Jewish community must take in the hope of "bringing rain." R. Simeon ben Lakish suggests that crisis and the rupture of egoism it brings shatter complacency and illusions of self-sufficiency. "Need" breaks open a stony heart and causes one to cry out. If it emerges in honesty, that cry will elicit a response—here, most palpably, merciful relief for the parched earth.[19]

The mystical text from *Tikkunei Zohar*, similarly, focuses on a caesura in the biblical narrative. The scene begins in the negative: no vegetation has sprouted, no rain has been sent; no one exists to work the soil. In the midst of this stasis, unexplainably, "a mist rose from the ground." The connection to what follows, "and the whole surface of the earth was watered," reads, most simply, as a temporal juxtaposition. First mist, then rain. The author of *Tikkunei Zohar*, however, perceives an invisible catalyst at work here. "Arousal must move from below to above." Rising mist, falling rain form a circle of desire and fulfillment, an asking and an answering. The force that joins "below" and "above" in this reading and, most basically, the force that caused the first rain to fall is named in the word "arousal."

In awareness of all the overtones of that term, both to modern sensibilities and in mystical tradition, we must keep in mind that R. Ya'akov often means it in a more neutral sense, as an "awakening" of dormant or inactive potentialities. The term "arousal" describes the possibility of affecting another, of engendering the desire to respond. It is a gesture charged with affection. Arousal can only be gentle, not coercive or violent, because it appeals to the other in mutual freedom.

A troubling point in this teaching, however, must still be addressed. These reflections on the notion of "arousal," and its outcome in the joyfulness of connection, are interposed in a context of failure and brokenness. This sounds a bit miserable; how is it that things that seem so demeaning must necessarily precede that happier ending? Reading these biblical verses from within the chamber of the soul, R. Ya'akov hears them teaching a vital truth about spiritual life. To attain understanding, he suggests, one's heart must first be "broken by failing." Only after worlds were destroyed could our world come into being. The axis on which this causality turns is "arousal." It begins "below"—in the earth, in the soul, and rises like mist. Condensing "above," the heavens open and rain comes.

The composite image encoded in this process is called the interplay of "feminine waters" and "masculine waters." R. Ya'akov adopts the meaning these terms carry in mystical tradition here and in many other contexts. To understand the image more fully, we'll recall, first of all, its source in rabbinic teaching. The world came into being, the Sages teach, in a primordial watery totality—*ha-kol mayyim be-mayyim*. But then "God separated between water and water … between the waters to be above the firmament and the waters below" (Gen. 1:7). On this moment of differentiation, "R. Berekhiya taught: The 'lower waters' parted, weeping from the 'upper waters.'"[20] In kabbalistic teaching, these lower waters are referred to as *mayyin nukvin*.[21] The seas, the rivers, and the subterranean chambers in the earth, all these watery places of our world are, essentially, the feminine component of an original plurality. In the midrash, they are separated in tears. Gathered in, held between shores, banks, and within caverns, the feminine waters embody both a continual awareness of distance and an undying hope to draw closer to their source, to return to their original place above. In that sense, the feminine waters signify a dynamic principle: the vital striving to be otherwise at the root of all being. The axis of that striving is vertical. Its vector begins upward; its fulfillment is downward.

In R. Ya'akov's commentary, as in mystical teaching, this powerful image is abstracted. The feminine waters designate an emotional state that is perceived as a vital power in every facet of existence. Significantly, R. Ya'akov teaches that feminine waters rise only out of an experience of diminishment or disintegration. The paradigmatic instance in which this occurs is the history of the Jewish people. To make this point clear, R. Ya'akov compares that history to the destiny of a planted seed.

> One must thrust oneself into doubt; in that way alone can one acquire a portion of "light." As the *Zohar* teaches (1. 83a), "If Israel had not entered Egypt, they would never have been called the 'Lord's portion, His people' [Deut. 32:9]."[22]

The story is familiar; it is recorded in the first chapters of the book of Exodus. Cast like a seed in the dark soil of Egypt, the wholeness of the Jewish nation gradually decomposes over years of slavery and debasement. Somehow knowing that it is nearly lost, the decomposing seed, Jewish hearts are finally brought to cry out in despair. In that, "the seed causes 'feminine waters' to rise [*ma'alei mayyin nukvin*] and that is what enables it to sprout."[23]

By juxtaposing these two entities, the planted seed and the Jewish people in exile, R. Ya'akov hints that the same process of fragmentation, awakening, discovery of a nuclear germ of vitality, and the eventual redemption from the earth's darkness is lived out by both. In the case of the nation, it is the midwives, Shifra and Pua, who bring it to the transitional point.

> The cries of those worlds destroyed were like sparks, or "feminine waters" that aroused God's will to create a world of repair. In the same manner, these two midwives aroused "feminine waters" toward God and restored [the Jewish people to] life.[24]

The "beginning of desire" now charted, a second question confronts us. It concerns the second half of the circle described above, the moment of response that brings fulfillment, salvation, rain. At its root is a most basic theological problem: How can we speak of affecting, arousing, inciting, or engendering a change in the realm of the divine? To do so would negate the cardinal principle that God is infinite, beyond the temporality implicit in "change" and encompassing every possible future. And yet we have heard R. Ya'akov speak of "arousing the divine Will" to create and to respond. In the next lines of the teaching cited above, he turns to this question.

> In truth, God is affected by nothing. He does not need human labor. As the verse says, "If you were righteous, what have you given Him?" (Job 35:7)—it really makes absolutely no difference to Him. But nevertheless, God lowers/demeans Himself [*mashpil 'atzmo*] to people and makes it look as if they have affected Him, as if His holy honor has been made greater … God shows that He desires people's efforts; He tells them that they have "caused feminine waters to rise" and have affected Him.[25]

In a self-effacing gesture, God "leaves his eternity"[26] and offers the world an illusion called "as if" (*ke-ilu*). This willingness to allow and even encourage human beings to believe they are free to initiate a connection on their own with God is perceived as greatness. Paradoxically, that greatness is called "lowering"—God's "bending down" or willful reduction of His own supreme stature. The ultimate purpose of that gesture, in R. Ya'akov's eyes, concerns "honor" or human dignity. Feeling one has earned what one receives and moving, reciprocally, to give—both of these are essential conditions in any worthy relationship even, or especially, with the transcendent. Here, God is radically not the "existent whose impersonal neutrality" closes Him into detached indifference.[27] Rather, in a theologically risky attitude of vulnerability, God "claims to be dependent on humans, on the persons who, since they are infinitely responsible, support the universe."[28] This, in effect, is the attitude that informs the "world of repair" (*'olam ha-tikkun*)—the new era in which the "work of His hands" can endure into the future.

> Now, God cloaked and concealed His light ... so that, in this world, people can imagine they "help" God, as it were. Thus the Gemara recounts that [God reproached Moses], "You should have come to My aid," and the *Zohar* (2. 32b) says: "When people serve God in truth, they grant strength and force to the Holy One, blessed be He, as it is written, 'Ascribe might to God!' (Ps. 68:35). How? Through good deeds." Here, there are differing degrees of honor; one individual may help God, so to speak, more than another ... Each of them, by their actions and efforts to purify themselves, prepares containers to hold God's light. In that, they are called "feminine," or "receiving vessels." And then, correspondingly, God inundates the world with "salvation" [*yeshu'a*], the facet of the "masculine."[29]

In short, relatedness begins with desire and is realized with desire. Light and containers, upper and lower waters are bound together in a circle of mutual responsiveness. Still, R. Ya'akov reminds us, "For God, the main thing is the vessels."[30]

Zeri'ah: *Conceiving the Inconceivable*

We'll turn now to the first of the five stages outlined at the beginning of this chapter. In Izbica-Radzyn tradition, the key term in understanding this stage of "sowing" is called *ishah* (woman). The meaning and importance of this term come to the fore in a central biblical passage: the opening verses of *parashat Tazria'*. Some of the Rabbis' reflections on this verse will be our starting point.

> "A woman who brings forth seed and bears a male" (Lev. 12:2). "I will raise my knowledge from afar; I will ascribe righteousness to my Maker" (Job 36:32). R. Nathan said: We attribute this praise to Abraham, our forefather, who came from afar. But R. Ḥanina bar Papa said: We attribute this to the Holy One, blessed be He, for we were far from Him and He drew us closer ... Said R. Levi: Indeed, people covertly leave a moist drop in His care, while the Holy One returns it to them publicly as a handsome, fully formed living being. What praise could be greater?[31]

The subject that concerns the Rabbis in this midrash is the mystery of beginnings—the beginning of faith, of closeness, and of life itself. "Afar" signifies that invisible starting point at the very beginning. Abraham is recognized as the first "believer." In some fundamentally unimaginable way, coming from beyond the Euphrates and a culture of idolatry, he attains an unprecedented awareness of the divine power secretly directing all natural phenomena. Traditionally, Abraham is portrayed as engaging in an intellectual, cognitive process. It results in the "discovery" of his Creator.[32] While the figure of Abraham does surely represent the first Jewish "beginner," a different opinion in the midrash cited above holds that the Master of all beginnings must be given precedence. The "moist drop" in which a life is enciphered comes from even further away and is slowly brought toward human form. Its miraculous transformation from a cluster of cells into a living being is entrusted, ever anew, to God alone. In the midrashic imagination, both these instances of conceiving the inconceivable are evoked in the verse, "A woman who brings forth seed and bears."

Many of the teachings in *Mei ha-Shiloaḥ* and in *Beit Ya'akov* on this *parashah* refer to this midrash. Following the Rabbis' association, the frame of reference vacillates between the literal meaning the verses denote and a symbolic realm. Abraham, in this Hasidic reading, remains a paradigmatic figure. However, the focal point here is not his final discovery of the world's Creator but his primary wish to find and dedicate himself to serving that Creator. R. Mordecai Joseph puts it this way:

> The arousal in Abraham's heart amazes us: what caused such agitation and tumult within him to know who created the world? Countless thousands of people lived before him and it occurred to none of them to ask such a thing. This arousal itself enables us to realize that there is a Creator and Ruler; the desire [*teshukah*] that entered Abraham's heart was sent to him by God. But why, then, does the midrash attribute the praise to Abraham for it? Because his name indicates wanting [*ratzon*].[33]

The queries R. Mordecai Joseph voices in this teaching and their resolution echo his overall reading of Abraham's story; we will recall it briefly. With the weighty words *Lekh lekha* (literally, "go forth"), God adjures Abraham to "search and seek the root of his life ...'Go to yourself'... for the essence of life—you will find it within."[34] The pivotal event in the course of that journey, frequently recalled in Izbica-Radzyn teaching, is this revelatory vision recounted in the midrash:

> He saw a castle in flames and set to wonder—"Could it be that such a castle has no owner?" The master of the castle gazed upon him and said, "I am the master of the castle."[35]

R. Ya'akov reflects on the meaning of this enigmatic and crucial scene in Abraham's life.

> Those first generations [of the Flood and of the Tower builders] who had perished and been erased from the world, emptied of hope—the thought of them perplexed him. Hadn't God created the world in mercy? Doesn't He desire its existence? And if so, how did perverted thinking grow and grow until it brought itself to ruin? Who owns, who manages this "castle"? Now, "the master of the castle gazed upon him ..." What God revealed to him was: the world was created *for you*. Everything depends on you ... on your soul's willingness to be aroused to question. The world exists for the sake of that arousal.[36]

On this reading, Abraham knows profoundly that some hidden power must be actively and continually renewing the existence of the universe. His not-knowing who it is grips him and drives him to wander onward and inward. This void is filled with the answer revealed in the glance of the Master—"for you." Abraham's passionate search for understanding is what salvages the world from its flames, its egotism, and its indifference. His "wanting" to find ultimately opens into something infinitely greater than himself: to the source of life that lies beyond and, equally, within.

It is this vital sense of insufficiency, the empty space of the question still unanswered, that links the figure of Abraham to the biblical verse, "A woman who brings forth seed." R. Mordecai Joseph reflects on the essential connection between them. He notes that the word *ishah* (woman) is acutely ambivalent; many have erred in appreciating its meaning. The paradigmatic instance of such an error is recorded in the Talmud.

> R. Joshua ben Levi said: When Moses went on high, the ministering angels reproached God: "What is one born of woman doing in our midst?" [God] said, "He has come to receive the Torah." They retorted, "Your most precious possession ... how can You entrust it to flesh and blood?! ... Give Your glory to the Heavens! (Ps. 8:2)"[37]

R. Mordecai Joseph cites this interchange and explores its meaning.

> When they said "What is one born of woman doing in our midst?" the angels transgressed the commandment "Do not bear false witness" (Exod. 20:13). For them, the name "born of woman" [*yilud ishah*] expresses the height of contempt. But, in truth, it is in that merit alone that the Torah belongs to human beings.[38]
>
> The verse says, "A woman who brings forth seed ..." (Lev. 12:2). That is, one who has true desire, valiant and powerful, for God—"bears a male" (12:2)—that person will be rewarded truly and evidently. "A male" means pure, clear salvation. For all possible goodness is contained in the soul of a Jew.[39]

These teachings urge us to put aside the gender stereotypes that usually confine our thinking. "Woman" in these lines has nothing to do with "the second sex" or even (in a dreamed-of moment) with "the first sex." Rather, "woman" speaks of the incompleteness and its concomitant possibility of renewal that makes each of us human. Whoever we are, we are always and inescapably "born of woman." That given, however, is not a reductive, demeaning end but the greatest of values. Only in the "lowest" of possible worlds can anything "new" be born. Birth, R. Ya'akov reminds us, is the miracle of newness (*hitḥadshut*). It is a moment wholly alien to the angelic orders. Ageless, unchanging, angels never forget or lose or hope to find. For these reasons, the power that *ishah* contains is beyond their ken. And hence their scorn.[40] The ability to cause empty spaces to be filled, to be a channel through which a kind of "response" comes into the world, is alluded to in the word *ishah*. Abraham, as we have seen, was such a channel. His journey and his discovery of the hidden Renewer of creation, his search and its resolution, outline a potentiality open to every seeker.

R. Ya'akov, in his reflections on this issue, brings an additional dimension to the fore. The sight of the midrashic castle in flames, he suggests, compels Abraham to deal with a primary theological problem. If God's ultimate purpose is that the world should recognize His sovereignty, why is the presence of the divine so utterly concealed? Why are people left free to imagine that castles burn for no reason, and that they can do whatever they like and suppose they control their world?

> The Master's gaze said to Abraham: "I am he [*ani hu*], the castle's owner"—that is, God in His mercy left space for Creation, so that whatever it achieved would look like the fruit of its own labor .... And thus, "A woman who brings forth seed bears a male," for all of an individual's prayers and deeds are called *ishah*. And if a person prays with desire and great wanting, true salvation will surely grow out of it. We learn this from R. Ḥanina ben Dosa (B. *Berakhot* 34b), who said: "If my prayer is fluent in my mouth, I can be assured of acceptance, as it is written, 'Creator of the fruit of the lips [*niv sefatayim*], Peace, peace to the far and to the near said the Lord; I will heal him' (Isa. 57:9)."[41]

R. Ḥanina ben Dosa, the famed Tannaic master of prayer, is gifted with the certainty that words that well from the heart will never be offered to God in vain. "Bringing them forth," voicing the desire to be heard is really what bears fruit. Most of us, though, cannot hold on to this simple truth with such conviction. The effort it demands is trying and precarious. Prayer itself, R. Ya'akov reminds us, is known to mystics as *nukba*, the realm of the feminine. Inherently, what happens "is beyond human understanding, for while one prays, it doesn't look as if one's prayer is affecting anything. At that moment, God does not yet give openly. But, in truth, as we pray, 'salvation' is being emanated."[42]

R. Ya'akov often speaks of the notion of prayer as an act of "sowing" (*zeri'ah*) with all the trials of faith that gesture involves. I'd like to consider one series of teaching that focuses on this idea, in the hope of learning more about this first, vital stage in the process of becoming.

Ashes from the Altar

The opening verses of *parashat Tsav* describe some basic components of the Temple service. To understand R. Ya'akov's reflections on them and their translation "in the human soul," we must recall the essential connection in rabbinic thought and halakhic practice between the sacrificial offerings and prayer. In the wake of the Temple's destruction, the Jewish liturgy as we know it now was formally established in place of and in correspondence with the *korbanot*.[43] Referring obliquely, maybe ironically, to that premise, R. Ya'akov suggests that, in truth, "the sacrifices themselves were a place of prayer" as well.[44] Because, in his eyes, every element of the created world—from the most inert, silent forms, the vegetative, the animal, and the human—is invested with spiritual vitality, all of them "yearn" to ascend to a higher form, ultimately, to be transmuted in their return to their "source." To be offered on the altar as a sacrifice (*korban*) is one way of realizing this transformation and return.[45] In R. Ya'akov's understanding, the verses with which *parashat Tsav* begins (Lev. 6:1–6) portray this aspiration as it is lived out in a variety of ways. These, in turn, speak cogently of the act of prayer itself, with all its complexity.

Those verses set out the following details. Flames on the altar consume the burnt-offerings in the light of day. The fire lasts into the night; it never goes out. By dawn, only smoldering coals and ashes are left. Outwardly, generally, the sacrifices were consumed, and it would seem that the gesture of devotion symbolized in offering them has been consummated. The pile of whitened ashes and the smoking remains that litter the altar are called *deshen*. This refuse apparently serves no intrinsic purpose. On a superficial reading of the passage, it is simply removed—one small part placed by the *Kohen* each day at the side of the altar, and the accumulated rest to be taken periodically to a clean place outside the camp.[46]

R. Ya'akov, with his attention to minor modes, detects an important counter-story at work here. The ashes left on the altar, he suggests, are meant to teach something essential about the darker side of prayer. This waste material symbolizes those prayers beyond number that are offered up but never answered, the countless appeals that, to our minds, were ignored, met with silence, "left behind."

> Part of the sacrifice was consumed in flames and drawn above—this alludes to those human prayers that are accepted and bring benefit to the individual. What remained of the offering—the ashes—alludes to the prayers that were not "accepted" .... And that part cries out terribly. All night long it shouts to God: "Am I not pure and clean? Why wasn't I received? How is it that I was separated out from the other prayers?"[47]

Burdened with an almost unbearable self-awareness, the burned remains of the animal sacrifices protest the injustice of it all. Set apart, reduced from animal to inert form, the hope of being transmuted has turned to despair. The ashes voice their disappointment and incomprehension. Yet here as well, as we saw above, the suffering expressed in their cries (*tza'akah*) has tremendous power. "This arousal, these 'feminine waters' are what enables everything that was ruined to be rebuilt."[48] The rebuilding or possibility of repair, R. Ya'akov explains, was carried out by two symbolic actions, also part of the Temple service and described in the same biblical passage (Lev. 6:3–4). At the beginning of each new day, the *Kohen* would rake together one shovelful of whitened ashes from the center of the altar and put them on its eastern side in an act called *terumat ha-deshen.* Miraculously, those ashes were "absorbed into that place; they became part of the altar itself, illuminating the earth from within."[49] That chosen portion of ashes, in this gesture, was "remembered," noticed after all, and so raised to a state of honor and permanence, integrated into the Temple's altar. It represents, in R. Ya'akov's eyes, a second category of prayers: those requests that are indeed answered "after a while" (*le-aḥar zeman*), after nights or years of doubt and waiting.

This, admittedly, is a happy ending, albeit long in coming. But what about all the ashes that one small shovel could not contain—the rest of the *deshen* still piled on the altar and overflowing its confines? Those remains of many sacrifices, left over from the flames, must be taken away, carried outside. They embody a third category, and a state of even greater distance.

> These ashes symbolize the prayers that were never answered. But because they, too, contain goodness, they must be put in a place of purity (Lev. 6:4). In other words, those prayers too will indeed bear fruit, but only far in the future. And for that reason the ashes are called *deshen* and not *'efer* [dust] ... for they fertilize and enrich the soil.[50]

This close reading of these few verses offers a frank, realistic look at the labor called prayer. "Sowing," R. Ya'akov avers, really demands endless courage (*gevurah*). A sense of loss, failure, and decomposition are the first, negative yield of nearly every effort. The seeds one sows with toil always disappear. Then all one can do is hope. Perhaps something may sprout, sometime. But maybe nothing does. One waits and prays and slowly fades away.[51]

The human figure that lives out this trying experience most integrally is named the *saris*—literally speaking, that is an individual unable to bear children. R. Ya'akov recalls the image of the *saris*, who seems to embody barrenness, finitude, and hopelessness, to speak, paradoxically, about the inherent, unimaginable power of prayer. The image is drawn from the following prophecy, voiced by Isaiah:

> "Let not the infertile one say, 'I am a withered tree.' For thus said the Lord: 'As for the barren ones who keep My Sabbaths, who have chosen what I desire and who hold fast to My covenant—I will give them, in My

> house and within My walls, a monument and a name [*yad va-shem*] better than sons and daughters. I will give them an everlasting name which shall not perish' (Isa. 56:3–5)."

The sense of being "a withered tree," R. Ya'akov adds, depicts the despair that weighs on a soul that believes it is bereft of a future.

> Every prayer that seems to have no effect on God is called *saris*. To be infertile means to have no "opening of the womb" [*peter reḥem*], that is, to be unable to open and arouse God's mercy [*raḥmanut*] for oneself. And one cries out: Haven't I tried with all my might? Why didn't I succeed? My prayers didn't help at all![52]

God's response, R. Ya'akov continues, means these words of comfort:

> In truth, though, no prayer uttered by Israel is ever lost; God promises the individual who feels rejected that all those "unaccepted" prayers themselves have become part of His own house ... "My house" is made of those "barren" prayers.... In the end, such prayers are even greater than those that were answered right away, for they endure forever in the human heart ... in the mystery of the divine Name EHYEH.[53]

In effect, the infinite desire borne in prayers not yet answered is an indwelling presence. The words of appeal spoken by the "barren" invest the Temple with a hidden, undying, holy power. It is they that build that House out of prayer, and sustain all the hearts to offer themselves further.

The temporal framework of this aspect of the Temple service and, spiritually, of an individual's private "serving" God is highly significant. "Useless" ashes and rejected prayers, R. Ya'akov notes, are gathered up long before dawn. More precisely, the Rabbis state that the time for *terumat ha-deshen* begins "from the middle of the night."[54] In other words, the time of blackest darkness actually marks the end and, simultaneously, the beginning of the daily Temple service.[55] In that sense, mid-night is the crucial transitional point when "yesterday" ends and "tomorrow" becomes "today." In R. Ya'akov's view, we recall, night is there to remind us of everything that is beyond our control. Ultimately, the value and success of all our efforts, and the desire itself to live on into tomorrow, are determined, and not by us, in darkness—"both of them take form without our awareness."[56]

The middle of the night, as we saw above, is also the temporal locus of pain, when hope is shadowed by despair. The ashes, the "infertile ones," embody this pain. Yet here, of all places, R. Ya'akov says, is the true beginning of service. The stage called *zeri'ah* speaks of this seminal point of origin, so difficult to endure. In the teaching cited some lines above, R. Ya'akov linked the experiences of the "barren one" and of the *deshen* together in the divine Name EHYEH. Throughout his commentary, he reflects on the spiritual and emotional worlds this Name evokes. And so we'll conclude our discussion of "sowing" with some of R. Ya'akov's insights on this Name and what it teaches us about the vital first moment when "service" begins.

The Mystery of the Name EHYEH

In the midst of the Egyptian exile, in response to his request, God reveals to Moses the force that will bring redemption for the Jewish people.

> Moses said to God "When I come to the Israelites and say to them, 'The God of your fathers has sent me to you,' and they ask me, 'What is His name?' What shall I say to them?" And God said to Moses: "*EHYEH asher EHYEH* ... thus shall you say to the Israelites, EHYEH sent me to you" (Exod. 3:13–15).

This appellation speaks of a futurity and an enigmatic promise. In this Name, God literally says: "I will be who I will be." Reflecting on the compounded formulation of these verses, R. Ya'akov notes that the doubled form ("I will be ... I will be") hints that the redemption, like everything that comes to be in our world, must initially take form in absolute hiddenness, in a manner totally exceeding human comprehension. He cites the *Zohar* on this verse:

> EHYEH, in the beginning, is wholly sealed and concealed—"I am who I am" [*ana hu man de-ana*]. Later on, it is "[I am] who I will be," that is, "I am preparing to reveal Myself afterwards." As for the last EHYEH ["EHYEH has sent me to you"]: although the Mother has conceived, the Name is still concealed.[57]

R. Ya'akov reads this mystical passage as speaking of the same psychological-spiritual complex we saw above in the context of Abraham and "conceiving the unconceivable." Here, it is translated into the successive stages of awareness through which the Jewish people as a whole pass on their path from exile to redemption. The question that concerns R. Ya'akov is: Where and how did the momentous, nearly impossible reality called redemption really begin? What happened first of all to engender that moment that finally propelled the Jewish nation out of their alienation and servitude?

> God began by shining to them in the aspect of EHYEH—hinting that He wanted to save them from their oppressors. And that stirred their hearts to begin praying for it.... Until that moment they thought they would be slaves forever. But when God revealed Himself in the Name EHYEH, they began to conceive [of redemption]. And then they began to cry out to God in their distress.[58]

The first glimmer of the Name EHYEH, then, engenders an awakening, an inception of consciousness. It causes the Jews to imagine things "could be otherwise." From the impetus of this wanting, they "begin to pray." The seeds of their new awareness of pain come unimaginably "from afar," from some point beyond human awareness and choice.

Significantly, in his commentary on this biblical passage (Exod. 3:13–15), R. Ya'akov recalls that "the Holy *Ari* [R. Isaac Luria] compares the exile to a period of gestation [*yetzirat ha-valad*]." The Name EHYEH, here, symbolizes the ultimate source from which every element in our world begins, that invisible point of beginning we spoke of earlier as "sowing."

> For every thing has something of the original Will voiced in the utterance, "Let there be light." It was spoken without the arousal of any creature, as the verse says, "Remember Your compassion, O Lord, and Your kindnesses, for they are older than time" (Ps. 25:6).[59]

"Let there be," an expression of willing something that is not yet, is symbolized in the Name EHYEH. The goodness secreted in what "will be," before it is given or becomes present, is infinitely greater than all human capacities to receive. And so the promise "I will be," even after it is voiced, remains utterly beyond our understanding.[60] The first intuition of this futurity reemerges in human consciousness in the desire to pray. "A woman who brings forth seed" thus represents a crucial moment both of sowing and of "having been sown." What R. Ya'akov calls *zeri'ah*, the gesture of prayer, then, is most profoundly a response to having been aroused or affected or "shined on" by the Other. As Gabrielle D'Annuzio said, "the richest events occur in us long before the soul perceives them."[61] The light of what "will be" is planted and hidden away in me. I'm left to pray and hope to help that future come closer.

We'll turn now to the second of the five stages we outlined above: the stage called *'ibbur* or pregnancy. It is here that the "light that was planted" begins to be visible, and the future tangible.

'Ibbur: *In the Ultimate Depths of Being*

> "And the earth was *tohu* and *bohu* ..." (Gen. 1:2). From the moment of "sowing" until the fetus can be perceived—this time is called *tohu*. When the presence of the fetus becomes evident, the time is called *bohu*—that is, clearly something is there, but no one knows its identity. And the nine months are called "... and darkness was on the face of the deep" (1:2), for this is a time of expectation and hoping to know what will be at the end of it all.[62]

"Darkness on the face of the deep." The abyss (*tehom*), an unfathomable storehouse where the future waits to be born is, in R. Ya'akov's teachings, a powerful symbol of the feminine. "Hidden in it is all the goodness and the light that will ever be revealed."[63] This inner space is evoked in varied contexts in R. Ya'akov's teachings. The first one I'd like to consider offers an innovative view of the most secret regions of divine Being. Contained within that immense intimacy, human consciousness remains, paradoxically, wholly separate from it.[64]

The following reading is based on a fundamental principle in kabbalistic teaching. R. Ya'akov finds it encoded in the verse: "For a sun and a shield is the Lord God" **כי שמש ומגן ה׳ אלוקים** (Ps. 84:12). The two Names in that verse correspond with two kinds of presence.

> "Sun" is the holy Name YHVH. From this divine aspect, Creation could never come into being. Originally, all was contained in His brilliant light. But if that light were revealed, the world would see and know that there is no reality aside from God alone.... And so God made a "shield" to cover and hide His light from the world.... That is the name *Elohim*.[65]

This dialectic of impossible revelation and necessary concealment is a cogent metaphor; it appears frequently in R. Ya'akov's teachings. Through it, he addresses psychological, existential, and theological issues of great import. One context in which this metaphor is developed is the following event in the life of Moses.

To appreciate R. Ya'akov's reading, we'll first recall the biblical context in which it is placed. At a portentous juncture in Jewish history, after the sin of the Golden Calf and the breaking of the Tablets, the nation stands on the brink of destruction. Anger, despair, shame crowd in. Moses seeks to gain some understanding of a way to the future, to glimpse how what was shattered may be repaired. "And now, if I have indeed found favor in Your eyes, make Your way known to me, so that I know You, so that I may find favor in Your eyes. And see that this nation is Your people" (Exod. 33:13). Here Moses seeks, in effect, to recall and somehow relive a happier time—the memory of that primary, immediate connection between God and the Jewish people. However can that precious connection, now lost, be regained? How can that love be restored?

> He said, You cannot see My face, for no human can see My face and live. And the Lord said, See there is a place with Me. You may stand on the rock and, as my Presence passes by, I will put you in a cleft of the rock and shield you with My hand until I have passed by. Then I will take My hand away and you will see My back; but My face may not be seen (Exod. 33:20–23).

The place that is "with Me" (*hinei makom iti*) sends us back, in Lurianic thought, to that crucial moment in the act of Creation known as "the mystery of contraction [*tzimtzum*]. God, by contracting [His infinite light], made a place for the world to come into being."[66] This space willfully made empty is a matrix in which an other can originate and gestate until it finds form in the created world. The same seminal process, R. Ya'akov suggests, is reenacted in human experience. In his Hasidic reading of the verses cited above, "I will put you in a cleft of the rock" (Exod. 33:22), R. Ya'akov reflects on the meaning of this enigmatic scene.

> It says in the Talmud (B. *Megillah* 19b): "Had there remained, in the cave where Moses and Elijah stood, even a crack of light like the eye of a fine needle, they could not have endured its brilliance." The "eye of a needle" is a window of light. Through it, the crack would be healed. That is, the concealment that separates the world from God's brightness would be gone, and everyone would see that nothing new could ever come to be. For all of Creation is possible only through concealment, through the illusion that the world is separate from God … Thus

[the verse continues], "… [and I will] shield you with My hand." That way, people may imagine they are autonomous beings.[67]

Enclosed in a dark womb of not-knowing, Moses will be surrounded by the blinding brightness of God's presence. Encompassing him, infinite light—the entirety of God's goodness—will remain wholly hidden from his eyes. That concealment alone preserves him. Drawing on mystical imagery, R. Ya'akov recognizes the symbolism of this moment. "In the capacity of *nukba* [the feminine], God hides the world so that it cannot gaze on that luminosity, as the verses say, "I will shield with My hand" and "I will cover you in the shadow of My palm" (Isa. 51:16).[68] To be hidden in this way enables Moses, as the leader and symbol of the Jewish nation, to make safe passage into the new world made of sin and repentance.

That crucial transition takes place in the nearly mythical cave of rabbinic imagination.[69] The cave, "in the cleft of the rock," is thus a locus of forgiving and restoration. R. Ya'akov understands this from God's cryptic promise to Moses some verses earlier: "My face will go and I will bring you comfort" (Exod. 33:14). On a straightforward reading, the "face" that will go or pass away is the aspect of divine censure, provoked by the people's disloyalty and sin. In time, one hopes, God's fury will abate and give way, with human efforts, to reconciliation.[70] But R. Ya'akov suggests a different dynamic. It is guided by the profound conviction that God's wrath is always only superficial; most profoundly, "the Holy One, blessed be He has no anger for Israel."[71]

The Sages themselves, R. Ya'akov notes, attested to this awareness in the prayer they composed:

> "O Lord, save Your people, the remnant of Israel. In all days of trouble/pregnancy [*be-kol parashat ha-'ibbur*], may their needs be before You…." And the Rabbis explained: What are these days of *'ibbur* [trouble/pregnancy]? Even when You are filled, like a pregnant woman [*'ubarah*], with wrath [*'ervah*], their needs will be before You.[72]

"My face will go" thus alludes to an essential dynamic inherent in the laws of Creation itself. Light is alternately revealed and concealed; at times, darkness alone can enable new life to grow. Here, significantly, the unimaginable moment of being forgiven for the most grievous of sins, and of regaining wholeness, can come to be only when the brilliance of the divine countenance is totally hidden.

The unborn infant, ensconced in the womb, cannot see its mother's face. This, most basically, is an experience of *hester pannim*, "because God conceals His love for a time, and even God's abundance is wholly beyond our grasp. For now, what is needed is *yirah*, self-limitation."[73] "Even a crack of light, like the eye of a fine needle" cannot remain. Such an opening, R. Ya'akov contends, would allow one to grasp the light by threading one's cognitive powers through the crack, reaching Above, and sewing the light into one's consciousness permanently. That kind of union, clearly, is impossible for us in this world.[74]

Rather, here it is in concealment that comfort comes. Covered over, being hidden in inner space enables a connecting back once again, on a sub- or superconscious level, to the Archimedean point of one's being.

In the course of his reflections on this biblical passage, R. Ya'akov speaks of this sense of comfort using a telling image: "'Your flesh [שרך] will be healed' (Prov. 3:8). 'Healing' happens at the very root of your being [שורש שלך], at your beginning. For where does the formation of the embryo begin?—from the navel."[75] In the cave, in darkness, Moses symbolically returns to the source of life and to the secret promise of eternal life for his people. Soon, the cave will be opened, the Hand drawn away. The divine attributes that can gather up before and after sin and restore peace will be revealed to Moses and to the Jewish people. We'll return to that part later on, in the final pages of this book. Now, I'd like to consider some additional aspects of the experience called "pregnancy" as it is lived by real people.

The Child Reborn

The human emotions that accompany pregnancy—anticipation, fear, uncertainty, with danger all around—speak cogently of this vital time. *'Ibbur*, like all five stages that concern us in this chapter, designates an existential mode that each of us may pass through more than once over the course of our lives. Experiencing it in a state of awareness can bring spiritual growth and an enhanced understanding of the ways of the world. "Pregnancy," need we point out, involves two separate and radically dissimilar sensations: that of the expectant "mother" and, on the other hand, that of the expected "child" she carries. Both these entities live out the period of *'ibbur*. To appreciate this time fully, we must thus consider both unique perspectives. Let's turn now to the story of Noah, one biblical context in which the state of pregnancy can be glimpsed, through R. Ya'akov's commentary, from the rare viewpoint of the fetus.

> In Creation itself and in every individual—existence begins, and then comes the Flood. So the Holy *Ari* taught: at that time, the world entered the mystery of pregnancy [*sod ha-ʿibbur*]. And my father, of blessed memory, said this about the verse (Eccles. 4:15), "I reflected on all the living who walk under the sun with the child reborn [*ʿim ha-yeled ha-sheini*] …": the ideas a person first harbors usually don't last. Once they have been invalidated, one awakens to things of lasting value. For whatever one has been given without toil and self-awareness cannot endure. But when one wakes up and begins to seek what has been lost—then what one finds will last forever.[76]

The era represented by Noah and his sons, as we suggested above, is a generation of survivors. On the psychological reading proposed in Izbica-Radzyn tradition, the accounts of Creation followed by the Flood mirror stages of human personal development. The dialectic of destruction and renewal is an inherent part of that process: after coming into existence with no say in the matter, one longs to re-create oneself, to choose and determine a new, authentic way of being. The identity that is reconstructed is called, after the verse in Ecclesiastes, "the child reborn." In his commentary on this verse, Rashi links this image of the child reborn with Noah, who represents a new beginning in the chronology of humanity, a second stage that begins as the flood waters subside.[77]

The Rabbis speak of the profound, perhaps traumatic ordeal that led to this "rebirth": Noah, as the flood ended, "saw a new world."[78] The impression of the world's newness is tied up with Noah's own self-transformation. This takes place, R. Yaʿakov explains, in the symbolic space of the ark—the "black box" that carries his family and selected remnants of Creation from "before" to "after." Its symbolism is hinted in mystical tradition: Noah enters the ark in the "mystery of pregnancy." Safely enclosed in a metaphorical maternal womb, he waits while storms from the heavens deluge and finally annihilate the "old world." Noah's withdrawal to an in utero existence catalyzes spiritual changes. The months he spends in the ark are described, in R. Yaʿakov's commentary, as a vital time of repair, in which the errors and illusions of generations past should be replaced with other ways of thinking.

We recall the principle set out earlier in this chapter, that the initial divine impetus was to create the world out of *ḥesed*—an unconditional, one-sided, and boundless surplus of kindness. The passivity of the world itself, the object of this infinite mercy, remained an unresolved problem. As we saw, in the course of time potent social and spiritual malaises developed. The trait at the root of them, in Hasidic terms, is called "expansion" or *hitpashtut*: a childish sense of power and rightful ownership that knows no shame. This situation reaches a point of crisis in the generation of the Flood. As the Rabbis put it, the time for "rebuke" has come: now boundaries must be made, limitations accepted. This confronts the world as a difficult, painful punishment. The forces of judgment or evil accusers appear and move to constrict freedom. And yet the Rabbis note that "rebuke" (*ge'arah*) is one of the 10 means God used in the act of Creation itself.[79] In other words, the flood comes not to erase the world but to re-form and empower it to reach the next, more mature stage of existence. Noah experiences this rebuke. In Izbica-Radzyn tradition, his story teaches something essential about survival and emotional growth.

R. Ya'akov makes clear that our hero was no superman.

> Noah was saved from the flood, but only because he took refuge.... Less than pure, not perfectly righteous, he needed to be hidden away in the ark. There, in the meantime, he was safe. So the verse says, "[Go, my people, enter your rooms and close your doors behind you;] hide for a little moment until the wrath passes" (Isa. 26:20).[80]

To "hide," in R. Ya'akov's lexicon, is a painful, brave, perhaps even desperate act of contraction (*tzimtzum*). "Indeed, the tremendous constriction Noah suffered in the ark is unimaginable."[81] It is proposed here as a life-saving move. Silent, sleepless, unforgetting, Noah must negate the amoral aggression and selfish certainty of the world closed outside.

> During that year in the ark Noah annulled his very self and his life force. He was like a fetus in its mother's womb. He had no separate existence; his vitality was part of his Mother's. The sole desire of that fetus is drawn from God's will alone; and so, during that year Noah was closed up in the ark, he gave up all his life, will, and actions to God.... This is the best advice in such situations, so that the forces of stricture [*middat ha-din*] do not overcome one.[82]

The refuge Noah finds in the ark thus represents a temporary return to some primary point of stability, a return that seems to be essential in maintaining psychic wholeness. In effect, R. Ya'akov points out, being in the world is a centrifugal force that ceaselessly pulls us from that center. We expand away, "until one can forget the source of one's birth and imagine that 'my power and the might of my hand have won me this greatness' (Deut. 7:17)."

The countermovement of contraction, lived out by Noah in the ark, corresponds in R. Ya'akov's eyes with "the seventh day"—the Sabbath. Here, too, "one must contract, draw in one's active powers, and return one's strength to God. Now one makes no initiative, only trusts in God, the source of one's birth and the place from which one emerged."[83]

"Hiding oneself" means, most literally, concealing or letting go of that precious self whose endless needs we fight so hard to satisfy. A fetus, unlike us, has nothing of its own, and can pride itself on nothing. "It knows that it is not a separate entity, but remains caught up in its source."[84] Hidden from the evil eye of the accuser, in the teeming inner space of the ark/womb, Noah sets to learning the hard work of contraction. The exterior destiny of that lesson is not too rosy. When he is freed at last from the "prison of his soul," Noah immediately falls into new excesses and appetites.[85] But nonetheless, his rebirth inaugurates a new age and a new awareness of limitation and responsibility.[86] The covenant God makes with his seed—symbolized in the rainbow—ensures that "the waters of Noah" will never again destroy the world; such a wrathful "rebuke" will never be repeated.[87] Ten more generations must pass before this stage of maturation, in turn, reaches its end.

Now let's have a look at another story, and another experience of "pregnancy," this time from the other side. It, too, concerns the idea of contraction and its part in the will to survive, to leave a remnant of one's self in the world.

"Opening" Stricture

> "Now Isaac went out to meditate in the fields toward evening. Looking up, he saw camels approaching. And Rebecca raised her eyes and saw Isaac … (Gen. 24:63–64)." Isaac was the embodiment of awe [*yirot*] … Abraham, our forefather, knew Isaac's soul well, and he knew about his tremendous awe at taking any positive action. And so he sent his servant to find [Isaac's] helpmate. In truth, though, God's hand was behind it all, for the time had come for Isaac to marry. Even Isaac himself—the thought had begun to awaken in his heart that "[God] did not create [the world] for emptiness; He made it to be inhabited (Isa. 45:18)." But his great awe held him back from taking action. And so he went out the field, to appeal to God to help him find his partner.[88]

In this short teaching, R. Mordecai Joseph portrays Isaac as somehow confined in the essence he symbolizes: *yirah* or *gevurah*. His mastery over desire, his extreme spiritual devotion, his striving for clarity, and his reluctance to do anything against God's will have brought him to near immobility. As long as he remains alone and single, Isaac manages to guard himself from the specter of uncertainty. To marry would compel him—like anyone—to give up that absolute authority over his life, and consent to involve himself in the unknown, uncontrollable being of another. R. Mordecai Joseph suggests that while Abraham understands his son's dilemma well, Isaac himself must realize that his "essence" has to be mitigated. Unrelenting constriction is "emptiness." To inhabit the world demands taking on a new kind of responsibility. It is a daunting enterprise, and its final outcome is totally hidden from sight. Quite honestly, R. Mordecai Joseph points out, no one wants to enter such a space of obscurity; the thought of bringing such suffering on oneself evokes a profound sense of unease. And yet the self-contraction and "avoidance of all doubt" that Isaac has attained has brought him to a dead end: in this attribute of *yirah*, "Isaac could not bear progeny." R. Ya'akov gives voice to that mindset: "Who knows what kind of child it might be—perhaps the child will be evil, and that evil will affect him as well, for he has engendered the child and brought it into the world. Better, then, that such evil should stay held inside and un-actualized."[89]

Interestingly, Rebecca is portrayed in a similar light. "'She was barren' (Gen. 25:21). Because she was utterly pure [*mevureret*], she did not want to enter any manner of doubt and give birth to children."[90] Mystical teaching stresses that in symbolic terms, this would attest to an acme of spiritual achievement: the desire to cleave to God in uninterrupted devotion, or *devekut*.[91] Ironically, though, the life stories of Rebecca and Isaac, their marriage, and their family tells of how and why this ultimate, sterile level of devotion is to be deconstructed. R. Ya'akov cites the *Zohar* as he sets out to depict the way this deconstruction takes place.

> "R. Ḥiyya began: 'Who can tell the mighty acts of the Lord, proclaim all His praises?' (Ps. 106:2) 'Who can tell [*mi yimallel*]'—as the verse says, 'You may pick ears of corn [*melilot*] in your hand' (Deut. 23:26). 'The mighty acts [*gevurot*] of the Lord'—indeed, they are many. For all strictures and judgment [*dina*] come from those mighty acts. Who, then, has the strength to annul and cancel even one of the mighty acts God has done?"[92]

The question here, R. Ya'akov explains, is this: "'Who can tell'—who can open what God has closed?"[93] The symbolic act of picking ears of corn means that "one must sense the holiness concealed in all one's occupations, like a person who picks something up and feels it with all one's tactile senses."[94] It is

Isaac, the epitome of might, or *gevurah*, who finally summons the strength to "annul" one of God's "mighty acts"—to "open" himself and Rebecca to a new mode of vulnerability, to conceive and to bear children. The biblical verses, through the lens of the Sages, describe this dramatic reversal. R. Ya'akov cites them and explains:

> "Isaac pleaded [*vaye'etar*] with the Lord on behalf of his wife, because she was barren. And the Lord responded [*va-ye'ater*] to his plea, and his wife Rebecca conceived" (Gen. 25:21). The Talmud (B. *Sukkah* 14a) asks: "How is the prayer of the righteous like a pitchfork ['*atar*]? Just as a pitchfork throws the grains on the threshing floor from one place to another, so the prayer of the righteous turns the intent of the Holy One, blessed be He from harshness to compassion." And the *Zohar* adds: "'Isaac pleaded'—he voiced a prayer that dug a tunnel up to the highest realms and broke through to the heavenly source of fecundity [literally, the *mazal* that grants progeny], for children are given from that place. And God answered his plea.[95]

In effect, these sources reiterate the truth that, in the ultimate scheme of things, unmitigated stricture (*din*) makes human life impossible. No one can bear the aspect of uncompromising divine judgment. On the existential level, to silence and constrict desire completely would lead, in the end, to the extinction of humankind. Isaac's plea, then, serves to "change God's intent" by allowing his inborn essence of "might" to be overcome and transmuted. God responds to his plea by enabling Isaac and Rebecca to free themselves of their self-mastery and enter the equivocal realm of fecundity. Here, too, they will learn, acts of might are called for. The challenge of discovering "the glory of heaven" through bearing and raising children proves to be no less heroic. We'll consider some aspects of that challenge a bit later. First, let's take a closer look at the rabbinic metaphor and what it implies about "changing God's intent." R. Ya'akov comments:

> The pitchfork really turns the grain along with the chaff, that is, the straw and waste material surrounding it. The divine Name that dwells on the grain is YHVH. But on the chaff dwells the name EHYEH. It is the chaff that enables the fruit to develop [*yad le-peri*], for God wishes to give. And this is the meaning of the Name EHYEH, as the *Zohar* says—"EHYEH: I am ready to cause birthing [*ana zamin le-oleda*]" ... God waits, ready to give. The beginning of it all is the prayers of the righteous.[96]

The potentiality encoded in the Name EHYEH is embodied in the chaff. Here, once again, R. Ya'akov touches on that idea that is so difficult to comprehend. Dry straw, the wasted, rejected covering that surrounds and protects the "heart" of the fruit, is what holds the promise of the future. Whatever grows will draw its vitality from the chaff. The Name EHYEH speaks that promise most fully: "I am ready to cause birthing." In evoking that phrase from the *Zohar*, R. Ya'akov seeks to resolve the theological problem aroused by supposing that God's absolute will can in fact be "changed" or even reversed by another, mere human will.

> But this, in truth, is what God wills—that through the prayers of the righteous He will grant them great abundance. For God lives and endures forever; "change" is irrelevant in His regard. Indeed, even the past is in God's hands.[97]

"I am ready to cause birthing," then, signals an emergent reality—the one of an infinite number of futures that will now begin to become. This divine readiness waits for an initiative from the world. The prayers of the righteous call that readiness into actuality. Effectively, they cause a rewriting of the past by annulling what had been.

To pray, we recall, is to sow (*zeri'ah*)—that is, "to place everything in God's hands … and to believe and trust that none of it will ever be lost."[98] Isaac first casts the seeds of hope in that field at evening. Throughout his life, Isaac continues to sow the boundless future (Gen. 26:12). The next verses of the biblical narrative describe the answering of his appeal. Their focus turns to Rebecca, to her expectations and new, unaccustomed fears.

> "The children struggled in her womb, and she said, 'If it is so, why do I exist?'" (Gen. 25:22). At first, Rebecca wanted to have children so that her own root would become revealed and evident. So said my father, of blessed memory: Children are the hidden mysteries of their parents' hearts [*ta'alumot lev avotam*]. She had hoped that, through her children, God's great Name would be magnified and sanctified. But now, sensing that she would bear evil as well—if so, whatever will come of her?[99]

Rebecca's pregnancy casts her into a mode of anxiety, even confusion. R. Ya'akov speaks of the primary longing each of us has to bring the "mysteries of our hearts" into the world. Our children reveal some precious essence hidden deep within us: through them, our own identity or "root" can become "clear," evident, and cherished by ourselves and others. The implication Rebecca did not foresee in all that is the element called "evil." The twins she carries—Jacob and Esau—embody two opposite, conflicting valences. Even before birth they menace destruction of one another. Rebecca's words, "If it is so, why do I exist" (*im ken lama zeh anokhi*, literally, "why am I?") articulate her distress and sense of helplessness at this turn of events. How does the force of evil fit into the well-meant aspirations she and we wish to make real?

> Rebecca asked, "Why am I?—What good have all my prayers for children done? In the end, I will give birth to two, one righteous and one evil. What clarity will that bring? And if I am no clearer, why ever did I want to become such a self?"[100]

In effect, her reference to herself as *anokhi* rather than the more common term *ani* (I), R. Ya'akov suggests, points the way toward self-understanding and to resolution. These two terms for the self designate different stages of awareness. Passing from one to the other summons one to develop tools to deal with the ambivalence inherent in "real life."

> *Ani* refers to what is beyond human comprehension. Before Creation was the era of the worlds destroyed. For the letters of *ani* spell *ayin* [אין-אני]—nothingness, that is, God's concealed reign over an inactive world. *Anokhi*, as it says in the writings of the holy *Ari*, alludes to the "world of repair." Here, human beings act; here, the hopes and expectations people have can affect God. And that is bearing children ... for when one engenders a soul that separates from oneself, then above all one becomes clarified.[101]

While she was barren, Rebecca lived in unrelatedness, in apparent, untested purity. The self as *ani* reflects a primary state of aloneness, a lack of connection to the fullness of one's own being. This is the sense of "nothingness" that precedes a true knowing of oneself. As R. Ya'akov puts it, "Before she conceived, Rebecca was *ani*, because the mysteries of her heart were wholly concealed. Once she became pregnant she was *anokhi*." Now, "with child," the safe, static totality of so many years has suddenly been ruptured. Rebecca has been augmented into a more complex, manifold self defined by relationship.

The fetuses that struggle in her midst, though, forebode unasked-for troubles. The impending sense of multiplicity, radically beyond her control, is so foreign to her experience that Rebecca resolves "to inquire of the Lord. And the Lord answered her: 'Two nations are in your womb, two separate peoples shall issue from your body …' (Gen. 25:22–23)." R. Ya'akov seeks to explain the meaning of this response. As we noted above, he holds that the "world of repair" that succeeds the primordial worlds destroyed is founded on human action. Most basically, that mandates a striving to recognize and differentiate between opposing valences. The "two separate peoples" Rebecca contains, those twins of light and darkness, will initiate a new and portentous stage in the history of the Jewish people. R. Ya'akov considers the importance of this stage.

> "God made everything for a purpose, even the wicked for the day of retribution" (Prov. 16:4). In other words, in the "world of repair," God made light and darkness measure for measure. The *Zohar* calls this "a spark of blackness" [*botzina di-kardinuta*]. By means of darkness, light will be increased. These are the "two nations in your womb"; evil, too, will ultimately serve to increase the glory of Heaven.[102]

Contending with this dialectic of light and darkness is thus a fundamental act of clarification. The self-definition of the Jewish people and the realization of its unique and separate destiny are components in the process of "repair." The challenge this process presents is formidable. As R. Ya'akov sees it, symbolized in the complex of Jacob and Esau is "the tree of good and evil" or, as it is called in mystical tradition, "the tree of doubt" (*ilana de-safeka*). In this structure, opposing and contradictory powers are subtly intertwined. Differentiating between them is no easy matter.

Rebecca, as a body of holiness, has been chosen beyond her own wanting to give birth to this embodied conflict. The subsequent verses in the biblical narrative recount how it is played out: between brothers, among parents, through blessings. We'll return to some of the issues involved in that story in Chapter 4. What concerns us now is the transition from pregnancy to birth. Birthing is the symbolic, often traumatic introduction of something absolutely, unpredictably new into the world.

Leidah: *Crossing the Threshold*

The uncertainty and feeling of lack of control inherent in the experience of pregnancy reach an extreme point of intensity in birthing. A key concept in R. Ya'akov's understanding of this moment is called "hiddenness" or *hastarah*.

He uses this term in many and disparate contexts to speak of that threshold that must be crossed to move from potentiality to realization. Enduring hiddenness, as we have seen in the cases of Moses and Noah, is a trial of faith. Its rewards are great—but only as great as the suffering that bears them. The first and vital instance, in mystical teaching, in which the event called birthing is played out, is the metaphorical reading of the account of Creation. R. Ya'akov presents it like this:

> "And God said, Let there be light. And there was light" (Gen. 1:3). The *Zohar* (1.22b) teaches: "'Let there be light'—the aspect of 'father.' 'And there was light'—the aspect of 'mother.'" Thus in the Talmudic dispute (B. *Rosh Hashanah* 11a): R. Eliezer held that the world was created in the month of Tishrei, while R. Joshua held that it was created in Nisan ... For R. Eliezer saw the beginning of existence in God's words "Let there be"—and the world immediately was. Even though Creation was still face-to-face before its Source, R. Eliezer considered this to be the beginning. R. Joshua, though, held that Creation began to exist when it turned away in order to be for the world [*lehashpi'a la-'olam*].[103]

In juxtaposing this famous rabbinic dispute with the gender images in the *Zohar*, R. Ya'akov makes an important statement. Although both sages surely voice an aspect of truth, as Levinas puts it, "What is essential to created existence is its separation with regard to the Infinite."[104] "Father," in the kabbalistic sense evoked here, is the source of endless light, the boundless, abstract potentiality expressed in "Let there be." Our visible, tangible reality, though, really begins with "mother."[105] Light can be contained and revealed further; this will occur, however, only through a movement of turning away or separation from. It is this movement that readies the vessel for the next, essential stage of "being for"—giving what one has contained to another that has become apart from oneself. The phrase "And there was light," R. Ya'akov comments, means that:

> Some light was blocked out; hiddenness came into being as Creation became an autonomous entity. God intentionally distanced the light from its Source, so that it would want to emanate into the darkness of this world.... For if the light were not cut off from its Source, it would never consent to shine onward.[106]

"Mother," in this sense, represents a double movement of receiving and giving. The difficulty of that doubleness, it seems, lies in the transition from the first mode of being to the second. How will the "endless light" that grows within emerge into its own? R. Ya'akov speaks of this pivotal point with striking imagery.

> To engender something new—God alone can do such a thing. Human beings can only augment what already exists ... but to make something *ex nihilo*—this is God's sole domain. When the world was created, "He" became "You." This is called "the opening of the womb" [*peter reḥem*]. In the same sense, the Exodus from Egypt was an utterly new, unimagined redemption ... Beyond their knowing, God opened up compassion [*pataḥ ha-raḥmanut*]. And thus He said, "[The opening of the womb] is Mine" (Exod. 13:2); you have no power over it.[107]

In this unconventional perspective, R. Ya'akov depicts the act of Creation as a moment of birthing. The transition from the third-person, nonvisible referent "He" to the second-person immediacy of "You" reflects the dynamic we saw earlier. The mother's face, through pregnancy, is hidden from the unborn infant. She ("He") harbors the child infinitely beyond vision and thus their relationship, although intimately close, is somehow anonymous and impersonal. At birth, faces emerge. For the newborn, "she" becomes "you." The Exodus, similarly, recounts the birth of a nation. That momentous event of redemption entails an "opening" of the foreign body of Egypt, in which the Jewish people is imprisoned. Compassion, love, the desire for connection make that moment possible. Israel, "beyond their knowing" is brought out, to begin a new stage in their development. That stage of mutual responsibility is defined by the Torah and its commandments to the Jewish people. In comparing these two essentially metahistorical instances, R. Ya'akov draws attention to the metaphors that they share. These metaphors, anchored in rabbinic and kabbalistic tradition, have much to teach about the inner dynamics at hand. In the next lines of the teaching cited above, he takes a closer look at their meaning through the experience of the human agent who, not only figuratively, gives birth.

> "Woman" by nature is withholding. Her quality is containment [*tzimtzum*]; her root is the aspect of *gevurah*. And so she does not readily give in to bear. All this is called *dinin*, or stricture. In truth, if she were certain that what she will give birth to is what God wills, she would surely consent to bear. But her inherent awe causes her to think: "Who knows what will be begotten? Maybe its soul will do the opposite of what God wishes?" And she doesn't want to contend with such doubt.... Thus

God must open ... and reveal that she, too, is really filled with compassion. When this happens, all manner of abundance can flow.[108]

The hesitation and uncertainty we saw above in the figure of Rebecca appears here to speak of a general, universal condition. Thresholds of all kinds evoke fear; the unforeseeable aspect of the future seldom beckons. In other words, the womb will not willingly, easily open. Thus the birth of the new can come about only "beyond knowing" [*be-hesekh ha-da'at*], beyond human powers of choice. In that sense, "it is Mine"—in God's hands alone.

R. Ya'akov underlines the necessity—in birthing and in being born—of yielding to something bigger than oneself. The term he uses to speak of this relinquishment of power is "forgetting"—*shikheḥah.* To lose hold of what one once knew or had clearly causes a painful sense of bereavement and absence. The motif of involuntary forgetting comes to the fore, most prominently, in this familiar scenario of rabbinic invention. R. Ya'akov retells it:

The fetus in its mother's womb—a candle burns above its head; it can see to the ends of the universe. Nothing is concealed from its understanding; all the truths of Torah are revealed before it. But as it emerges into the world, an angel comes and taps its mouth, and it forgets everything.[109]

The angel's tap marks a fateful moment. In the sensibilities of the Rabbis, we must realize, the unavoidable reality of forgetting Torah wisdom is deeply unsettling. The elderly Jew who has forgotten his learning is compared to the broken Tablets of the Law; still, even those shards of memory demand respect.[110] At birth, the loss is virtually total. From infancy, the years of one's life are devoted to regaining and re-finding the encompassing vision that was gained effortlessly in those months of prenatal existence. Devastating as it sounds, R. Ya'akov seeks to explain the purpose this moment of forgetting serves in the larger scheme of things.

Although that primordial light is hidden, a trace of it remains in the human heart. When one begins to make the effort to serve God, that trace awakens and illuminates one more and more, until one attains the same measure of light one had before birth. Then, at last, one reaches completeness. So the verse says, "I have seen all the living who walk beneath the sun, with the child reborn" (Eccl. 4:15). "The child reborn" alludes to the light one acquires for oneself after birth, after the light in the mother's womb is hidden away.[111]

To be born, in other words, marks the beginning of a second, earthly existence. What informs the journey, in this world, toward completeness is the crucial task of self-construction. This is accomplished by actively seeking, choosing, and internalizing the light that will guide one's conscious life.[112] Birth comes about, then, through forgetting. The angel's tap hides away light, but sets the individual free to determine the self one wishes to be.

On the metaphorical other side of the picture, birthing too can take place only with forgetting. In mystical teaching, thought and speech mirror successive stages in engenderment. "Thought" develops and transmutes like an embryo. An unseen potentiality, as long as it remains in one's mind, thought is polysemous. When one's thoughts emerge in speech, though, they become external to the thinker. Speaking or formulating thoughts in words makes them real, finite, and limited in meaning. Moreover, once spoken, we lose our mastery over them. R. Ya'akov remarks that the same parental uncertainty and un-control over who our children will become exists in this more abstract case. "As soon as the words leave one's mouth, who knows what meaning and understandings people might draw from them?" Thus, here as well:

> Birthing [*holadah*] can come about only through forgetting. Until what is inside has been realized, until one "gives birth" to it, one can continue to clarify oneself. But as the time comes to realize that potentiality in birthing—when it is separated and goes outside of the individual—then, forgetting is inevitable. For the place where God desires to build something—there, no element of choice exists. Perhaps a precious soul will come into being. This, though, depends only on the laws God determines.[113]

"Forgetting" is a relinquishment of ownership. The "precious soul" of embodied thought—that no human being can willfully fashion, nor decide the destiny it will live out in the world.

On the Brink

In other reflections on birthing, R. Ya'akov focuses on the lived experience of drawing over the threshold from "inside" to "outside." The following teaching brings together many of the themes we have explored above, with an additional immediate, all-too-human dimension.

> "A woman brings forth seed and bears ... (Lev. 12:2)." The light that God emanates is always greater than the vessels human beings can ready. This recalls the "worlds destroyed"—light was too tremendous to be contained and the worlds shattered ... And thus the Rabbis said that a woman shrieks/groans one hundred times in the throes of childbirth. She hasn't the power to contain the light that is being emanated into her "vessel." Only after she is aroused to pray with all her being does God save her and enable her to receive that light.[114]

The surplus of light that will augment the birthing woman, R. Ya'akov suggests, is the soul of the infant about to be born. With all the trials that soul undergoes in its descent from the upper realms into this world, a climax comes in those final, terrible moments. The dissonance between the spiritual and the physical, with which we endlessly contend, leads the Sages to contemplate on human existence and the crisis called childbirth.

> "Indeed, you are made from nothing and your deeds are naught [*me'af'a* מאפע]" (Isa. 41:24). "From nothing"—full of insignificance and putrid moistness; "naught"—the one hundred shrieks [*mea pi'ot* מאה פיעות] a woman shrieks in labor, ninety-nine of them toward death and one for life.[115]

The sense of being on the brink, closer to death than life, is truly a vulnerable, lonely moment. The birthing woman's shrieks and groans thus serve a vital purpose. R. Ya'akov's father, R. Mordecai Joseph, remarks that in those intense moments of real or metaphorical birthing,

> One cannot even believe one will ever bear and be worthy of salvation. The Face seems so thoroughly concealed. God's purpose, though, is to cause the individual to cry out. In that way one can purify oneself and, finally, merit being saved.[116]

Her groans and prayers, then, are much more than a physical expression of pain or fear. Those voices the birthing woman emits enable her to merit the future; it is they that overpower the forces of evil that threaten. Her uttering them accomplishes a process of opening, both in the dimension of the human and the divine. R. Ya'akov's son, R. Gershon Ḥanokh Ḥenikh, writes:

> Those one hundred shrieks, like the one hundred blasts of the shofar [on Rosh Hashanah] annul the accusers, and arouse God to watch over us … As it says in *Tikkunei Zohar*, "'He watches through the windows' [*mashgiaḥ min ha-**ḥalon**ot*] (Songs 2:9)—that is, if you will only 'hope for the face of God'" [***ḥalu-na** penei el*] (Mal.1:9).[117]

In other words, birthing is a tense grappling with human limitations. Faced with the inherent constriction of being, it arouses one to search for ways to widen or enlarge one's capacity to receive and, ultimately, to give. "If you seek Him, He will let Himself be found by you" (1 Chron. 28:9). The birthing woman's appeal, which no words can speak, is above all a manner of seeking.[118] "Windows" open with hope; the Face, though concealed, will be just beyond sight.

Yenikah: *"Now These Calm Waters are of Milk and All Things Overflowing"*[119]

The fourth stage, which will concern us now, is called *yenikah* or nursing. The substance of "overflowing"—mother's milk—symbolizes *ḥesed* (mercy). Whiteness, the proximity of embrace, face-to-face "for the other" informs the relationship of "nursing."[120] R. Ya'akov returns often to this powerful motif to speak of important aspects of God's interaction with the world. The Divine Name that encodes the mutuality of this relationship is *Shaddai*. R. Ya'akov remarks on its meanings:

> There are holy Names that are far beyond human perception, and untouchable by human action … But in the name *Shaddai*, God bends toward His creatures, that they may reach Him through their good acts … In this way, a connection can be made between them. So the verse says, "*Shaddai*—we do not find that power to be too overwhelming" (Job 37:23). For no living being can receive all His light. And thus, in this world, God gives gradually, that His creatures may be able to bear it.[121]

The force that makes this giving possible is encoded in the name *Shaddai*. It speaks of containment "from His side" and, "from our side," of lack, desire, and their fulfillment.

> *Shaddai*—within that Name, God concealed all manner of goodness so that people would not receive everything at once … So the *Zohar* (2. 253a)

> teaches that *Shaddai* alludes to the breasts [*shaddaim*]. For they contain and limit the mother's giving, that it may come down through fine holes, without harming the infant. In the same manner, God gives all goodness in the world in the name *Shaddai*, as the verse says, "Blessings of the breast and womb" (Gen. 49:25). All this, too, comes gradually, to enable finding the strength to receive it.[122]

The connection R. Ya'akov depicts in this context, then, is a vital bridging of distance. In effect, at certain times it is the only viable mode of being. Two entities—the divine and the human—can come together in this fluctuating moment of restraint. Giving of one's fullness and receiving from another take place here in a relationship of mutual attentiveness. To be sure, the Rabbis already remarked on this connotation of the Name: "*Shaddai*—His divinity suffices [*yesh dai elohuto*] for every creature." Noting this phrase, R. Ya'akov suggests it means that God is "good enough" for each individual in his or her uniqueness. In interacting with the world, God adapts divine influence to respond to the needs of great and small.[123] Implicit in this perception of the maternal aspect of the divine, of course, is the role of the metaphorical "infant."

> "Milk" is boundless restraint. It does not flow of itself. Rather, it must be drawn out of the breast, and it will come in response to the baby's sucking and swallowing.[124]

The helplessness and total dependence of the infant on its mother resonates, on some deep level, with the mother's own situation. It is the infant's capacity to want from her that catalyzes her giving. Milk, nourishment, blessings, if no one asks for them, dry up and go away. Desire, then, is at the heart of this connection between mother and baby. To perceive God as *Shaddai* would mean to preserve experientially an element of this basic, "infantile" mode of being intimately connected to the source of all goodness. R. Mordecai Joseph suggests that recalling and reliving that connection is an essential part of a whole spiritual life.

> One must look toward God's salvation. Like a newborn who cannot exist on its own—God grants it sustenance through the mother's breasts ... So King David said, "I stilled and silenced my soul, like a suckling child at its mother's side, like the suckling child is my soul" (Ps. 131:2). Here, one hasn't the strength to fill one's lack alone.[125]

What R. Mordecai Joseph describes is not the memory of a former age of innocence, but a level of awareness that should never fade away. To be sure, babies grow up. They eat, gain strength, and struggle for independence. This natural, undeniable human drive R. Ya'akov calls *hitpashtut*. Energy, psychic and physical, must expand. But if it is unguarded, a willful escape from the center can become a self-destructive movement of rebellion. R. Ya'akov cites an extreme case in which the trajectory of "expansion" leads to moral crisis.

> In the Talmud (B. *Sanhedrin* 118a) and the midrash: The generation of the Flood said, "What is *Shaddai* that we should serve Him? What will we gain if we pray to Him" (Job 21:15)? The name *Shaddai* means containment [*tzimtzum*]. But they did not wish to conduct themselves in that aspect of *Shaddai*. And so God showed them His power—not gradually but all of a sudden. He flooded water over them in huge expansiveness, matched to their own unrestrained will to conquer.[126]

The anecdote to this drive, R. Ya'akov suggests, is a countermovement of gathering oneself in again. The primary feeling of connection lived physically by a nursing infant—"the mystery of the name *Shaddai*"—must somehow be guarded. Just beyond it, the hidden, ultimate point of origin is concealed. To preserve consciousness of *Shaddai*, ultimately, is "to know Who gave birth to one." Losing that essential consciousness is "to lose one's *yiḥus*," and to find oneself partial, cut off, and alone.[127]

What is the maternal presence expressed in the name *Shaddai*? In the following teaching, R. Ya'akov evokes the imagery we have been considering to speak of "nursing" from the side of the Giver. He notes, first of all, these elements. In the Tabernacle, and later in the Temple built by King Solomon, the Ark containing the two tablets of the Covenant was placed in the Holy of Holies. A fabric covering, the *parokhet*, hung over it, serving to separate it spatially and optically from the public arena beyond that inner chamber. Two staves (*baddim*) passed through rings at the base of the Ark. These poles were first used to transport it, like all the holy vessels, through the desert; even after this period of mobility ended, with the construction of the Temple, the staves remained affixed to the Ark. Considering some descriptions regarding the Temple, R. Ya'akov recalls these details:

> "The poles extended so that their ends were perceptible from the sanctuary, but they could not be seen outside.... There was nothing inside the

> Ark but the two tablets of stone which Moses had placed there at Horeb …" (I Kings 8:8). The Gemara (*Menaḥot* 98a) adds: "Could it be that [the poles] did not touch the curtain? The verse says, '[the ends] were perceptible.' But if they could be seen, did they pierce through the curtain? No, the verse says, 'They could not be seen outside.' How can this be? They protruded against the curtain like a woman's breasts. As it is written, 'My beloved is a bundle of myrrh, nestling between my breasts' (Songs 1:13)."[128]

After citing these sources, R. Ya'akov tries to make sense of them. He notes that unlike the other holy vessels, which were actively used in the Temple service, the Ark stood "unused" in the Holy of Holies. The staves, which extended from that inner, sacred realm and protruded into the human domain outside, thus embody a symbolic means of connection between the two.

> Indeed, the ark had no actual role that would enable its holiness to influence Israel. Resting in the Holy of Holies, it alludes to the infinite goodness God treasured away and concealed from this world … Yet it is from that place alone—from that storehouse of the future—that God "moistens" the world with a taste of that goodness. "[The ends of the staves] protruded against the curtain like a woman's breasts …"—for God desires to give and to nurse Israel, "even more than the calf desires to suckle." "But they did not pierce through the curtain"—because God's full goodness is treasured away and concealed for now. This "nursing," then, comes from God's thinking about that goodness. Just from that wanting to give, the world is moistened. And thus the ark had staves: through the staves and the curtain, the abundance of Torah could emerge from the ark and flow outside. Even though the ark remained hidden from view, God thinks and wills, in time to come, to grant all the truths of Torah to Israel.[129]

Giver and receiver, God and the world meet in the opening. It is a bordering point joining the sacred and the profane, "inside" and "outside." Endless mercy is hidden within. Yet, invisible, tangible drops of maternal kindness can be felt. They overflow outward from the unimaginable future and come to dwell now within our being.

The Place Where We Live

The presence suggested in the name *Shaddai*, with the secret fullness beyond it, continues to mark the openings of every Jewish home. In many of his teachings, R. Ya'akov cites the *Zohar* (3. 258a): "The mezuzah: *Shaddai* [is written] on the outside, YHVH on the inside." The parchment of the mezuzah, in effect, is marked on both its surfaces. The outer, visible face bears only the name *Shaddai*; written on the inner side, rolled up and concealed from sight, are the biblical verses with the most holy, four-letter Name. R. Ya'akov explores the meaning of this doubleness.

> In this age of *galut* [dispersion], the name *El Shaddai* is before us—even in such times of hiddenness, while the Jewish people is scattered among the nations, God holds them by the hand and preserves them. The name *Shaddai* tells of the enduring bond between Israel and God. Even in the deepest darkness and exile, God plants expectation and hope in Jewish hearts that they will soon be redeemed .... And so "the mezuzah: *Shaddai* on the outside; YHVH on the inside"—to hasten the coming of God's light in all its brilliance.[130]

The "light" hidden away inside the parchment scroll of the mezuzah waits for the future. The outside of the parchment is a "garment" that holds and contains it within. Marked with the name *Shaddai*, the mezuzah reminds us of the vital task of contraction (*tzimtzum*). Recalling a crucial moment in the act of Creation, the Rabbis record that God identifies Himself, so to speak, as *Shaddai*: "It is I who told My world, [you have expanded.] Enough! [***sh**-amarti le-'olami **dai***]."[131] This moment of divinely imposed limitation, R. Ya'akov suggests, must be met with its mirror image: an untiring human effort to the same gesture of self-containment.

> The name *Shaddai*, from our side, means that one must limit one's enjoyment of this world's pleasures and so draw them into holiness.... And the more one lives by the aspect of *Shaddai*, the greater one's portion will be in the endless light of YHVH.[132]

At the opening, on the threshold, the mezuzah thus marks our coming out and going in.

The fourth stage of human psychological and physical development ends with separation. As R. Mordecai Joseph put it, "the baby is weaned from its mother's breast and begins to act independently." The movement out into the world and the related image of the mezuzah convene to signal this transitional time. Now, maternal presence and influence will find expression in other ways. "Mother," R. Ya'akov notes, is the aspect of the divine that "ceaselessly endeavors for Israel."[133] Her influence becomes more abstract and, in a sense, distant as her children gain autonomy. Izbica-Radzyn tradition devotes a great deal of attention to this interrelationship as it develops and evolves. We'll turn now to consider some aspects of it.

Moḥin: *The Challenges of Creative Living*

The fifth and final stage, set out in the Lurianic teaching that underlies our discussion in this chapter, is that of consciousness or *moḥin*. The life experience that marks it, as R. Mordecai Joseph put it, is this: "Now the individual can marry, engender new life, and build a lasting edifice."[134] The possibility of "bearing something from oneself" is reached only here, after a measure of separation from parental influence has been attained.

In a variety of contexts, R. Ya'akov addresses some of the issues that come to the fore in this period of spiritual and physical growth.[135] His reflections on its challenges propose a candid and innovative understanding. Many are drawn from the perspective of the "parent" who watches as the "children" set off into a life of their own; the perspective of the "children" is juxtaposed.

Some biblical verses that speak cogently of this final stage of development are found in the first verses of *parashat Beḥukkotai*. Izbica-Radzyn teaching sees this last *parashah* in Leviticus as summarizing, in counterpoint, the content and message of the book of Leviticus as a whole. Also known as *Torat Kohanim*, the chapters of Leviticus set out the laws of the Temple service, including the *korbanot* or sacrificial offerings. This "divine service," the Rabbis say, is a prototype for the "service of the heart"—the act of prayer that comes to replace it in Jewish life after the Temple's destruction. While the majority of Leviticus discusses the overt, historically time-bound actions prescribed to the priests, the final *sidrah*, in rabbinic tradition, evokes prayer. That spiritual gesture transcends all temporal and spacial boundaries.[136] In keeping with this basic perception, R. Mordecai Joseph remarks that the formulation of the opening verse of *parashat Beḥukkotai* is strikingly nonauthoritarian. As he sees it, this verse and the passage it introduces allude to an alternative, somewhat uncustomary relationship now taking form between God and the Jewish people, a relationship phrased in tenuousness.

> "If you will follow My decrees and observe My commandments …" (Lev. 26:3). "If" is an expression of doubt, for who can know whether he/she observes the Torah as God truly wills? … Indeed, even if an individual takes care to keep to the whole *Shulḥan Arukh*, the uncertainty remains whether or not one's actions really concur with God's most profound intent. For the divine will "is elusive and so very deep; who can fathom it?" (Eccles. 7:24). In addition, the phrase "if" expresses a prayer. God, so to speak, prays: "If only [*halevai*] you will follow My decrees, and direct yourselves to My deepest will."[137]

The tenuousness or uncertainty R. Mordecai Joseph speaks of here is double. "From our side," he contends, the disparity between the human and the metaphysical can never be mitigated. While the "letter of the law," codified in practical halakhah, surely guides and obligates the Jewish people in every aspect of their lives, the infinite dimensions of God's ultimate will cannot be contained even in all its voluminous sections. Some measure of apprehension, an awareness of that disparity, cannot be rationalized away. In another teaching on this point, R. Mordecai Joseph comments that the verse means: "If you have the merit, 'follow my decrees'—try to aim toward My most profound will, to the source of life."[138]

In the second, doubled aspect of tenuousness—"from His side"—the Almighty is found in a paradoxical stance of un-control. God's words of prayer, "If only …" give voice to a pure desire along with a willful suspension of omniscience. Indeed, R. Mordecai Joseph points out, there is no explicit commandment here at all; the biblical phrases commonly used to introduce directives, such as "And God said to Moses" or "God spoke, saying …" are conspicuously absent as this *sidrah* opens.[139] The theological difficulty of the scenario, then, is evident. R. Ya'akov puts it bluntly: "What could such a prayer mean in relation to the Holy One—'is there really any doubt before God?'"[140]

R. Ya'akov's responses and reflections on the issues raised by this unassuming verse fill 28 pages of his commentary. Their volume seems to testify to its importance in his eyes. "God's prayer," the complex interrelationship signaled in that gesture, and its implications for human spiritual life are what will concern us in the following pages.

We'll begin with a look back at some of the passages from rabbinic tradition that are cited as prooftexts in Izbica-Radzyn teachings on the subject.

> "If you will follow My decrees …"—"If" is always an expression of entreaty [*ein im ele lashon taḥanunim*]. And so He said, "if only My people

> would listen to Me ..." (Ps. 81:15). Similarly, in *Sifra, Beḥukkotai* 1, "If you will follow ..."—God, so to speak, prays, "If only you will."[141]

God's unfulfilled wishes for His people, this open question cast into the future is a plea with no resolution.[142] Listening, following, loyalty, it seems, cannot be coerced. And so this divine beseeching is what remains in the end, after all the laws have been pronounced. God's people must determine, on their own, how to build a way of relating to the divine Giver of the decrees that fill the chapters of the Torah.

In a second passage, the Sages explore the theme from an additional angle.

> R. Yoḥanan said in the name of R. Yose: How do we know that God prays? From the verse, "I will bring them to My sacred mount and let them rejoice in My house of prayer ..." (Isa. 56:7). It does not say "their house" but "My house"; hence we learn that God prays. What, then, is His prayer? R. Zutra bar Tuvya said in the name of Rav: "May it be My will that My compassion subdues My anger, and that My mercy overcomes My other attributes, that I may deal compassionately with my children and meet them beyond the line of strict justice."[143]

R. Ya'akov cites these lines as a paradigm. For us, to pray is to recognize that one is un-free, and to affirm the presence and the influence of an Other in one's world. These words imply that the manner or "attribute" with which God will interact with His "children" depends on their initiative. It is their actions that will arouse His mercy or incite His anger. Their deeds can lead Him to chastise them as they deserve, or to mitigate the stern dictates of absolute justice. The precedent God metaphorically sets in this gesture of vulnerability encourages human beings to mirror His mode of appeal.

> From the force of God's prayer and the *mitzvot* He does, the people of Israel too come to fulfill His commandments and offer their prayers from below. In that manner, it is as if "they aid and increase God's strength."[144]

The mutuality described here, phrased with a generous sprinkling of qualifying "as if's" (*kivyakhol*), is fundamental.[145] Free choice, or at least the illusion of free choice, is what links entities in relationship. By praying and "hoping" for human devotion, God symbolically "makes room" for an other. R. Ya'akov sees the creation of this unfilled space of possibility as crucial. It is an essential mark of the final stage of maturation. Some insights offered by developmental psychologist D. W. Winnicott, despite their somewhat different context, seem quite relevant here. Winnicott suggests that in healthy psychic growth, the "personal continuity of existence" between mother and baby must eventually give way to separateness. It is in the "potential space" that opens up between them that "the individual experiences creative being."[146] Winnicott stresses the responsibility on the part of the mother-figure in gradually affording the child the opportunity to move from dependency to autonomy. In effect, she must allow herself to be "destroyed" as the child develops a new and personal reality, in which the subjective sense of "continuity" between self and other is replaced with "contiguity."[147]

R. Ya'akov, I'd like to suggest, seems to describe a similar willingness—on the part of the omnipotent Law-giver—to be imaginatively "destroyed" by His "children." Out of love, God recedes into the horizon of what might be, and lets them determine on their own the path they will take and who He will be for them. Will they forget about God as the intensity of those early life stages fades? Or will they find some way to preserve the experience of that primary, intimate connection as they grow into independence?

> "'If' is always an expression of entreaty," and so God prays, "If only you will follow my decrees ..." And thus the verse says, "Who could grant [*mi yiten*] that their hearts will remain theirs, to revere Me and follow all My commandments all the days, that it may go well with them ..." (Deut. 5:26). ["Go well"]—so that there will be room to bless them with all goodness.[148]

R. Ya'akov's notion of "making room," and in that effort of enabling a reality to come into being, stems from earlier sources. Rabbinic and mystical tradition use a moving image to speak of the vital importance of this potential space that opens between God and His people. R. Ya'akov integrates it in one of his teachings to expand on the emotional aspects of this new stage in the spiritual life of the Jewish people.

> "Like an eagle who rouses its nestling, hovering over its young ..." (Deut. 32:11). That is, first God shines His light into an individual and arouses that person. Then He draws the light back up and away so that one cannot see it. As the *Zohar* [1.16b] puts it, the light "touches and touches not" [*matei ve-lo matei*]. So the verse says, He "hovers"—"touching without touching" [*noge'a ve-eino noge'a*], as Rashi writes. When God "touches"

> and arouses a person, as it were, surely in that moment one desires with all one's soul and being to be drawn toward God's will. But after the light disappears, one is filled with uncertainty whether to go in the way of Torah or not. Here God, as it were, sets to pray, "If only they will follow My decrees ..." Thus in *Tikkunei Zohar* [God says], "I have revealed [the End] to My heart but not to My limbs." The "limbs" allude to the means by which the heart's intent will be carried out. All this speaks of the hiddenness God sets up for our good—to make room for us, so that whatever one accomplishes can be credited to that individual.[149]

The divine will secreted in the Heart of light, R. Ya'akov suggests, cannot be revealed to anyone, once and forever. Rather, like a blazing torch, a glimpse of it flares up and vanishes again and again, out of our grasp.[150] The Heart's deepest desire, over against the near oblivion of the "limbs"—that disjunction is there "for our good." In the space of not-knowing, a person learns to walk. There one gains strength, believing one moves in freedom toward the future God wills.

"The Teaching of Your Mother"

Parashat Beḥukkotai, then, articulates this crucial movement of separation. Direct influence—in the form of the commandments and directives that fill the book of Leviticus—ends here. In its place comes the indirect, muted presence of hope, prayer, and entreaty. These are a manner of influence as well. Their power, R. Ya'akov suggests, comes from a less evident, perhaps even undetectable sphere. In a number of passages, he voices thoughts on this alternate kind of presence. He names it "mother" or "the teaching of your mother." I'd like to consider some of these now, in the hope of reaching a clearer understanding of this idea and its meaning.

We'll note, at the outset, that in R. Ya'akov's eyes these opening verses of *parashat Beḥukkotai* are concerned with sub- or superconscious levels of human behavior. Rereading Rashi on the first verse of this *sidrah* (Lev. 26:3), he says that God's wish is that the contents of the Torah will become "kneaded into" His children's souls—"so that even the body becomes integrated, saturated and kneaded in with those words of Torah forever."[151] "Even when you are sleeping, may your dreams be filled with words of Torah."[152] And so "God prays, 'If only you will follow My decrees'—if only you will strive to do God's will, even without your own conscious awareness [*she-lo mi-da'at*]."[153]

The concern expressed here is thus for the nonrational dimensions of being, those dimensions we recognized in Chapter 1 as "feminine." This would seem to signal that a corresponding "maternal" aspect of divine influence is now coming into play. We saw a hint of this earlier in this chapter, in the identity between prayer and the realm of the feminine. R. Ya'akov draws a certain contrast between models of paternal and maternal interaction. His comparison is based on the verse in Proverbs 1:8: "Hear, my child, the discipline of your father, and do not forsake the teaching of your mother."

> "The discipline of your Father"—here, God deals strictly, meticulously with an individual. If, in response, that individual strives with all the strength he can muster to clarify himself and serve God, then all the rest is "the teaching of your Mother"—God, as it were, prays for that individual ... and God's prayer will aid and protect that person.[154]

The implication would be that the chapters of Leviticus, up to *parashat Beḥukkotai,* which define the particulars of "service" in the form of human endeavor, express a paternal presence. Authoritative, rigorous, prescribing overt action, this presence is inarguably formative. More, we recognize it as the dominant mode of relationship audible in the biblical text between God and human beings. Its defining characteristics are phrases such as: "And God spoke ... saying," or "God said." But now, in the final verses of Leviticus, this "paternal" voice gives way to something different. A few pages ago, we saw that the "maternal" presence, symbolized as "God praying," serves a no less formative role in enabling spiritual growth. In one of his last teachings on this subject, R. Ya'akov considers the image of "mother" more closely. Allusions to mystical teaching interweave in it. They point toward horizons of understanding without stating them explicitly. I'd like to consider R. Ya'akov's teaching first, and then have a look at the passage from the *Zohar* that inspired it.

> There are two aspects to words of Torah: the aspect of "father" and of "mother." As the verse says (Prov. 1:8), "Hear, my child, the discipline of your father, and do not forsake the teaching of your mother." "Mother" is the tremendous affection God will shine in the future—then it will be evident that Israel never violated His will. In effect, even in this world there is a glimmer of that light. But for now, Israel must serve in awe, and never suppose that God will some day indulgently forgive them for their laxity in serving Him. To imagine such a thing would be to "eat unripe fruit" [after B. *Sanhedrin* 107a]; "the time of that vision is not

> now" [after Hab. 2:3]. For "this world is the opposite of the world to come." Still, even now it is possible to sense something of that great love by crying out mightily to the aspect of Mother, which alludes to *binah* … Yet that aspect—strictures [*dinin*] issue from her as well, as the *Zohar* says, "She is called Mother, the feminine [*nukba*], might [*gevurah*], and a source of judgment [*dina*]." All that comes to the fore when people say, "The Holy One, blessed be He will surely forgive and forget."[155]

In this teaching, R. Ya'akov does not define "mother" in conjunction with "father." His focus is solely on "mother." His aim seems to be to resolve a certain ambivalence in the spectrum of qualities traditionally associated with that feminine aspect of the divine.[156] On the one hand, Mother is a boundless, luminous, unconditional love and capacity to forgive. On the other hand, awe (*yirah*), the stricture of judgment, and the suffering these might bring are other, less comforting sides of that same feminine valence. The key to sorting out this apparent contradiction—which is surely troubling on emotional as well as intellectual levels—is the recognition that everything in this world of ours is "backward"—"for this world is the opposite of the world to come." The "tremendous affection" of the maternal is a promised blessing. It waits and longs for the time of its full shining. In the meantime, however, opposite valences such as fear, caution, and self-limitation are what must guide human life.

Twice in this teaching, R. Ya'akov speaks about a moment of appealing to "mother's love." The first moment is presented as a distorted, self-indulgent shirking of responsibility. He invokes part of the rabbinic warning voiced in B. *Bava Batra* 50a: "Whoever says that the Holy One, blessed be He will graciously forgive all their sins [will forfeit his own life]" (*ha-'omer ha-Kadosh Barukh Hu vatran yivater be-ḥayyav*). The error of this wishful thinking is in seeking to pull the hidden future, by force, into the present. Failings and laxity, the Rabbis teach, cannot be explained away so easily; one can't just skip blithely to the happy ending and bask in forgiveness.

The second moment of appeal is wholly different. Here, R. Ya'akov introduces an additional and essential aspect of Mother. It is embodied in the *sefirah* of *binah*. His lines echo the verses in Proverbs 2:1–3, "My child, if you accept My words … if you call out to understanding [***im** la-binah tikra*] …" and the rereading in the *Zohar*: "Mother [***em***] is called *binah* [understanding]." To grasp the full burden of this appeal—as he puts it, "crying out mightily to that aspect of *binah*"—we must recall that in kabbalistic teaching, the *sefirah* of *binah* is also known as "the realm of *teshuvah*, or repentance."[157] In other words, this "crying out mightily" expresses a deep desire to return to a point of origin, to draw closer by repairing one's wrongs. Such a moment comes to be when one can recognize and take control of one's failings. Through that difficult, honest effort, one may re-find the original and powerful love that eternally wells in the maternal for her child. "If only" you can call out in truth, R. Ya'akov implies, "Mother" will surely forgive and gather you back in.

He cites some lines from the *Zohar* to set out the image of Mother that comes to the fore in these teachings. I'd like to have a look at the context in which they appear. This passage seems to serve as a subtext of sorts for the teachings just cited. The *Zohar* presents the following dialogue:

> R. Eleazar was sitting before R. Simeon, his father. He said to him: We have learned that [the Name] *Elohim* always signifies judgment. But [the Name] YHVH—in some places it is called *Elohim*, as in the verse "Adonai YHVH/*Elohim* ..." (Gen. 15:2). Why is it pronounced *Elohim*, since those letters [YHVH] always signify mercy? He said to him ... Come and see. All the plants and all the lights—all of them shine forth and receive light, moisture, and blessing from the river that wells up and flows out. All is comprised in it and it contains all. This river is called the Mother of the garden, and she is above the garden .... And so all the fountains emerge and flow with water on all sides, and they open doors in her. Mercy then flows from her .... But since they call her Mother, female, *gevurah* and judgment emerge from her. She herself is called "mercy," but judgment is aroused from her as well, and so the Name [YHVH] is written as mercy but vocalized as judgment [*Elohim*].[158]

This explanation, set out by R. Simeon bar Yoḥai, the central figure and traditional author of the *Zohar*, seems to resonate with R. Ya'akov's understanding of Mother in all its complexity. The double nature, or the apparent contradiction in that image suggested above, is traced here in the *Zohar* to references to God found in the biblical text itself. In numerous verses, the masoretic vowels attached to the ineffable Name seem to belie the letters that designate it. The four-letter Name (YHVH) is written in signs of compassion but pronounced in tones of stricture. The question of the son, R. Eleazar, addresses this incongruence. How is one to resolve the dissonance between script and vocalization? Or, alternately, how can one internalize the implicit truth that mercy and judgment are really not separate powers, but rather are bound up together in covert association?

R. Simeon offers his son a number of answers on various mystical levels. In the central one, for our purposes, he evokes the image of Mother to speak of the multiple valences R. Eleazar wishes to understand. Mother/*em* is a flowing river of light and blessing; mercy comes from her openings. And yet she is also a source of judgment. Those who receive from her may experience her influence in that mode as well.

In his own teachings, R. Ya'akov adopts this symbolism and augments it with a temporal, subjective dimension. At times, he says, the relationship between giver and receiver is lived as mutual, joyful connection. At other times, distance and stricture are much more real. "Judgment" prevails; "mercy" recedes. All that depends on the manner of relating or of appeal human beings chose. This changing dynamic is lived out in *parashat Beḥukkotai*. In many of his teachings, R. Ya'akov explores its vital role in enabling human growth. We'll consider some of them now, as we conclude the discussion of this final stage in emotional and spiritual development.

Finally, Facing the World

Until this point, our reading has focused on the opening section of *Beḥukkotai* and the blessings that grace its verses. That harmonious vision, however, lasts only 11 verses. The next section continues with the foreboding words, "But if you will not listen to Me, and will not perform all of these commandments …" What follows are 33 verses of admonition (*tokheḥah*), including frightful punishments, frustrations, even curses to be visited in retribution for disloyalty.[159] The causality involved in each of these two passages is quite clear and equally incontestable.

Faced with these verses and their unambiguous messages, the Rabbis nonetheless manage to hear them another way. R. Ya'akov cites the following midrash, which will play a pivotal role in his own interpretation.

> R. Abba, son of R. Ḥiyya said in the name of R. Jonathan: I have reckoned the blessings; I have reckoned the curses. The blessings are from *alef* to *tav*. The curses are from *vav* to *heh*, and not only that, they are backwards.[160]

A closer look at the text shows that, indeed, the passage containing the blessings begins with the first letter of the Hebrew alphabet [אם] and ends with the last [קוממיות]. Symbolically, it spans and encloses a plenitude of kindness. The second passage begins with the letter *vav* [ואם] and ends with the letter preceding it, *heh* [משה]. This, in contrast, could be seen as a symbolic negative space of existence; it ends "before" it begins. The rather technical observation of the letters comprising the text leads to the strange statement that, in an unexplained manner, the "curses" are written out of order, in reverse.

With these somewhat amorphous rabbinic reflections in mind, R. Ya'akov seeks the deeper meaning of these two sections—the blessings and the admonitions—and the interconnection between them. The image of Mother does not appear here. Nonetheless, many of the motifs we have discussed are evoked once again to speak of the fifth stage in human maturation. The following teaching begins with some phenomenological insights on the ways we interpret reality. R. Ya'akov then proceeds to examine the reasons behind our errors of perception. Finally, when these errors are righted, he suggests that a new kind of vision can come to be.

> The blessings stand facing the world, and so it is clear to people that they speak of goodness. Other verses, though, look like curses because they stand backward, facing their Source of emanation [*ha-ma'atzil*]. The world cannot see them face-to-face and for that reason they seem, Heaven forbid, to be curses. But truly, deep within they are imbued with blessing. For no evil issues from God; in the future, it will become evident that they, too, are really filled with goodness. Now, out of order, those "curses" wait and long to be straightened out. They are like a man standing on his head. He suffers terribly and hopes every moment that someone will come along and turn him right side up again, with his feet below and his head above. So this *parashah* longs and pines for God to reverse it and put it back in order, and recombine it in another way. Then everyone will see that it is really full of blessings and goodness ...
>
> Indeed, this is God's will: that the power inherent in Creation can become active only when it turns its face from the Emanator ... as it says in *Seder Raziel*: When God created His world, He turned His face away from it .... When that happens, God's influence in the world can no longer be detected.... But when the Jewish people will be repaired and able to stand face-to-face before God, the veil will be drawn away, and the profound blessings hidden inside those admonitions will be concealed no longer. They, too, will come to stand face-to-face before us and reveal all their goodness.[161]

The "curses" that secretly long to be reversed, to say other things, personify a basic hermeneutical principle. The evil or hardship they seem to threaten is but a single and finite aspect of meaning. These words of the living God, like all words of the Torah, are animated with inner vitality. As R. Ya'akov puts it, "The composition of the words and their letters will one day change, and so will their meaning ... for all of them need God to make them alive."[162] The ontology of the text implicit in rabbinic exegesis and explicit in kabbalistic readings underlies this conviction. Divine in origin, open to infinite permutations, the Torah communicates its truths to each generation according to the needs of that generation in its specific historical and spiritual constellation.[163] For now, seen "from behind," these words of the Torah read to us—beyond their will—like curses. Their reversal, the transformation of their message, is a matter of human responsibility.

In the last lines of this passage, R. Ya'akov addresses this point by alluding to some of the final verses of admonition. Amid the ruin and desolation wrought by disloyalty—the graphic description of the "curses"—a turning point is finally reached. "Then they will confess their sin and the sin of their forebears for the treachery with which they betrayed Me ... Their unfeeling heart will be humbled and then they will be forgiven ..." (Lev. 26:40–41). This unearthing of a will to right one's wrongs, to return in repentance, signals a profound spiritual change. Its power, R. Ya'akov says, is to enable the Jewish people to restore an original, immediate, and indestructible connection—"to stand face-to-face before God."

The response to that profound movement of return is the transformation of the "curses." "They too will come to stand face-to-face before us and reveal all their goodness." The specter of evil, or the premonition of suffering shadowed in those "curses," strikes fear in the hearts of listeners. In truth, though, they are a counterforce to the verses that precede them. Reading these biblical passages, living them through the text, is meant to bring those who hear to a new level of awareness. Two opposing valences must combine into a unity: distance and nearness, fear and love, *yirah* and *ahavah*. The shining face of the King, glowing with affection, radiating blessing, is but one aspect of infinity. Other aspects, other modes must be recognized there as well.[164]

R. Ya'akov traces the motif of blessings temporarily concealed in the guise of their opposite to a first cause of sorts. He names it by quoting a tract called *Seder Raziel*.[165] "When God created the world, He turned His face away from it." It is an unsettling, unexpected moment. In a gesture of seeming disregard, the benevolent Countenance is averted. God's "being there" with or for the world is no longer apparent. Creation, in response, "turns away" as well. Evil seems to rush into the void that is left. Yet R. Ya'akov suggests that this metaphor of *hester pannim* is essential.

Presence and absence, embodied in the face (*pannim*) that turns (*ponnim*) away from and back to, oscillate continually. The hidden Face makes space for human beings to find themselves. Then they can summon the strength to search for something beyond themselves. The "finding," in both its stages, involves a crucial wrestling with emptiness, with the bitter sense of being alone in one's suffering.[166] Its outcome, R. Ya'akov teaches, is a countermovement and a renewal.

> "I will come to face you once again [*u-faniti elekhem*] and make you fertile and multiple, and I will maintain My covenant with you" [Lev. 26:9]. This means that God will reveal the inward face [*penimiyut*] of it all, that it was pure goodness.... "And I will dwell in your midst" [26:11]—finally, I will be before you, face to face with that innermost point of your souls.[167]

What R. Ya'akov describes here is a decisive moment of seeing and of being seen. With the sense of proximity—the experience of the face-to-face—distance, most integrally, is still maintained. God's glance, "face-to-face with that innermost point of your souls," ultimately grants fecundity. That is the promise expressed in the next words of the verse—"I will make you fertile and multiply."[168] The "creative looking" evoked in this reading can be understood as a profoundly reassuring experience. It is an essential "getting back the self from the mother's and the father's face."[169] In R. Ya'akov's thinking, this interrelationship informs the fifth stage of development, called "consciousness" or *moḥin*. Separate yet connected, "now the individual can marry, engender new life and build a lasting edifice."[170]

The strength to engender and to build the future comes, most essentially, from the light of the Countenance, "which gazes at me and out of which I gaze."[172] R. Ya'akov alludes to this reciprocity in a provocative rereading of the biblical injunction and the longing to "see and be seen."[172] Verses that speak of it allude to the face of the Master (*et penei ha-adon*) as the destination of that longing. R. Ya'akov comments:

> "*Et penei*"—for you yourself [*et/at*(*ah*)] are the face of God. So the verse [Ps. 42:3] says, "O when will I come and show the face of the Lord [וְאֵרָאֶה פְּנֵי אלוקים]?" For I myself will be the face of the Lord. Thus it is written (Ps. 67:2), "May He illuminate His countenance with us"—not upon us, just with us.[173]

These lines speak of a collectivity of mutual presence. Now, finally, the brilliance secreted in the hidden Face radiates, refracted like a rainbow, in the human face journeying to be seen.[174]

Chapter 4

Being Otherwise

> "He gazed and there was a bush all aflame. Yet the bush was not consumed. Moses thought, 'I must draw nearer and look at this great sight, why is the bush not burned away?' (Exod. 3:3–4)." What amazed Moses was the unity of the soul with the body. After all, by nature the two are opposites. Why doesn't the divine soul compel the earthly body to do God's will? And if the body is mightier than the soul, how can the soul survive within it? ... In this vision of the burning bush, God showed Moses that whatever God wants to preserve will never be annulled.... "For My preciousness is within it." The body, God assured Moses, has tremendous worth .... But if the blinding light concealed in the body were revealed, one's life would be over that moment. "For no one can see Me and live (Exod. 33:20)."[1]

The secret brilliance of corporeity. In R. Ya'akov's readings, throughout his commentary, that difficult truth, so hard to hold onto, is continually discovered and rediscovered. Consistently, often in unexpected contexts, R. Ya'akov seeks a revisioning of the body-soul relationship. The alternate understanding he offers entails a new valorization, in which a whole group of traditional concepts must be reconsidered. Oppositional forces—containers/contents, outside/inside, peel/fruit, guilt/innocence, darkness/light, female/male—such staples of dialectical thought are rethought and cast in a new perspective. On all these planes, he insists, a different and more authentic order must come to light. In Chapter 1, we looked at some "minor modes" and tried to gain a clearer understanding of their major role in R. Ya'akov's worldview. This chapter takes up some of these themes again, to reconsider them in a more comprehensive perspective.

Now, I'd like to look at some of the teachings in which contending forces such as these are challenged, deconstructed, and finally led to tell quite a different story. That story, I believe, is an essential and innovative aspect of

R. Ya'akov's thought. In the course of our discussion, I hope to show just how far-reaching its implications are.

Introduction: Duality Reconsidered

R. Ya'akov develops his approach on the basis of rabbinic precedents. The Talmud, he notes, recounts this scenario:

> The Sages wanted to exclude [from the biblical canon] the Book of *Kohelet* [Ecclesiastes], because its words contradict one another. Why did they finally decide not to suppress it? Because its beginning and its end are true Torah.[2]

R. Ya'akov explains: "In other words, *all* of its contents are true and worthy. What seems to be the opposite is due only to our mental limitations, to our inability to understand what it really says."[3] The Book of *Kohelet*, attributed in Jewish tradition to King Solomon, meditates deeply on human existence. Its verses recount the particulars of everyday life—labor and pleasure, growth and decay, joy and travail with all their ambivalence. The compelling realism of contents like these, the Rabbis apparently felt, voices a confusing or noncohesive message. Such an inherently problematic text should surely be suppressed from the biblical canon of divine, revealed, uncontestable truth. The hesitation of the sages is resolved in a gesture that, in R. Ya'akov eyes, holds great significance. They acknowledged that the "beginning" and the "end" of that book are flashes of clarity. Its opening and closing verses resonate with commonly held values and ethical principles. The power of that message, they decided, vindicates "everything in the middle"—all the experiences, sensations, desires, and disappointments that regular people live from day to day.[4]

What R. Ya'akov seems to be suggesting is that in the normative rabbinic mind, many of the details of living become extraneous or negligible in the larger scheme of things. The gray realm of the "optional" (*divrei reshut,* as R. Ya'akov terms it) is thus relegated to secondary status in relation to the defined territory of religious obligation. Prescribed actions and spiritual responsibilities have indisputable importance. Intermediaries—hands, mouths, foods, implements—apparently serve only as a means to achieving the desired end, the fulfillment of outward obligations. Whatever sensual, subjective, individual experience goes along with such actions would surely be less essential. And in fact, rabbinic discourse wastes few words on describing things, tastes, forms, and textures, on the personal dimension bound up with overt actions. This hierarchy is clearly understandable. Yet R. Ya'akov suggests it must be augmented; horizons can be broadened.

Citing one of the 13 Principles of Faith formulated by Maimonides, he offers this subtle interpretation.

> It is said that God is un-embodied [*ayn lo guf*; literally, "has no body"]. That is, from God's perspective, "body" as we perceive it does not exist at all ... Truly, the body itself is filled with life. "Body" and "life"—the two are inseparable. Indeed, God Himself created physicality. Yet people cannot comprehend how God can dwell in the human body. In time to come, though, God will reveal that "no place is devoid of His presence," that there is really no difference between body and soul. Both, equally, are the work of His hands.[5]

In this alternate way of seeing, duality fades away. The interface between container and contents is gone. Here, finally, "the interior and the exterior gather themselves together into a single continuous space."[6] R. Ya'akov uses a number of metaphors to explore this conviction and to explain how its truth will eventually become evident.

One compelling image he evokes is the house (*bayit*). Every dwelling—from the humble body that "houses" the soul to the "Lord's Home," the Temple—is an inhabited space. In that sense, the house articulates an essential relationship of "the non-I that protects the I."[7] As a material structure, it surrounds, shelters, and encloses. All this enables a continuity of being within its walls. In the following teaching, R. Ya'akov reconsiders the primary dialectic implicit in this image.

> "A psalm of David. A song for the dedication of the House" (Ps. 30:1). The idea here is that God hid and concealed all the world's abundance of blessing in the Temple. But the "House," for its part, was extreme closedness [*godel ha-tzimtzum*]; at first, it was fearful of emanating the goodness cached in it. For the Temple was built in trepidation, with suffering and many failures. And so no human being has the strength to bear its brilliance ... Because of all that, the Temple had to be inaugurated [*ḥanukkat ha-bayit*]—to grant it strength and confidence, and assuage its fear of shining with the divine light invested in it. Now, it can become evident that God's desire is to do only good for the house of Israel ...Through its "dedication," the House will come to radiate, with a renewed will, the light concealed within it .... [Similarly], when the human soul begins to

> look for God, one realizes that God can redeem and heal all one's failings. But that flash of illumination, for a Jew, is not enough. One must try to clarify oneself more and more, until the body itself comes to glow with light.[8]

R. Ya'akov describes here a path toward enlightenment. In the two instances cited, it is the "house" (the Temple, the human body) that must, in a sense, be reeducated and guided to a new mode of self-perception.[9] What physicality knows best, it seems, is limitation, boundedness, and contingency. In this teaching the Temple itself, constructed by human labor, endures a comparable stage of uncertainty. R. Ya'akov traces this self-awareness, shared by all kinds of matter, to the ontological category of the "vessel" (*keli*). The given role of every such vessel is to contain something other than itself. In its essence, the container both conceals and gives form to the otherness within it. R. Ya'akov often reflects on the acute awareness "vessels" must have of their own difficult identity as boundedness. For instance:

> "Vessel" signifies the qualities of contraction [*tzimtzum*] and valiance [*gevurah*]. Truly, the vessel is also eminently valuable. But, due to its extreme power of contraction, it does not want to expand, to hand itself over to human understanding.[10]

The self-containment of the "vessel," then, engenders a fundamental sense of alienation, even incomprehension separating "inside" from "outside," spirit from matter. And so the value or holiness of physical objects is closed off from our sense perception. Their aura, this intrinsic worth, is concealed from us. As a result, they appear to us as mere things, shells, peels, the means to some greater end. While he recognizes the logic of this way of seeing, R. Ya'akov underlines just how short-sighted and temporary it really is. Our habitual disregard for "the things themselves" and, likewise, for our own corporeality will one day give way to a new revelation. In a strikingly (post-) modern insight, he remarks, "In the future, all the signs/signifiers [*tziyyunim*] will be filled with vitality."[11] That, he proposes, is the inner meaning of this verse speaking King David's plea to God: "In Your favor, do good for Zion, build the walls of Jerusalem" (Ps. 51:20).

> "For Zion" [*et tziyyon*]—for that place where goodness is so greatly contracted and nearly undetectable. Ultimately, though, all good will emanate from there … "Build the walls of Jerusalem"—in that time,

> even the walls will be made of the light of life. Not like now, when walls are made of inert, rejected matter.[12]

"Signs" or signifiers, in effect, fill the same role in human life as "vessels." We use them as instruments, as mediators in the enterprise of signification. Their role is to point beyond themselves, toward another, abstract dimension of being. By drawing our attention to the hidden, indwelling worth of "signs," R. Ya'akov effectively rescues them from their instrumentality, from being implicated in an arbitrary, conventional system of "mere" signifiers.

Walls, peels, all forms of externality for now must guard the "fruit" within them. The promise of the future is an end to that duality: "walls and outer skins [*kelipot*] will be needed no more—the 'wall' will be immersed within the fruit ... as the *Zohar* says, 'everything then will become whole, a complete unity.'"[13]

The passage from the *Zohar* that R. Ya'akov cites here articulates that moment of unity with this mystical idea: "Then the Name will be whole with all its aspects."[14]

Names and Naming

This notion of the "name"—referring in the *Zohar* to the Name of God—leads R. Ya'akov to ponder on the power and the meaning of names as such. I believe his comments on this subject can shed light on the matter of signification, and point toward a way in which "unity" may perhaps be regained. In the continuation of the extensive teaching cited above concerning "signs," he develops an intriguing conception of language and naming.

R. Ya'akov's conception resonates in many ways with Walter Benjamin's meditations on these themes. Both of them hold that the world, though created through God's word, becomes knowable only through human words, with the names human beings give to things. Thus, as Benjamin puts it, "the proper name is the communion of humanity with the creative word of God." And, "in naming, the mental being of man communicates itself to God."[15] The textual catalyst for their reflections is this biblical passage:

> And from the dust of the earth, the Lord God formed every beast of the field and every bird of the air, and brought them to Adam to see what he would call them. And whatever Adam called every living creature that was its name (Gen. 2:19).

R. Ya'akov reads this passage in light of the midrash *Tanḥuma, Ḥukkat* 12:

> When God decided to create humankind He consulted with the ministering angels ... He said to them, "This human that I want to create—his wisdom will be greater than yours." Then God gathered together all the beasts and wild animals and birds and had them pass before [the angels]. He challenged them, "What are the names of all of these?" The angels didn't know. After creating Adam, He brought the animals before him and asked, "What are the names of all of these?" Adam answered, "This one should be called 'ox,' this one 'lion' ..." Then the Holy One, blessed be He asked, "And Me, what is My name?" He said, "*Hashem* [ה'], for You are Master of all the creatures." Thus it is written, "I am God, that is My Name" [Isa. 42:8]—the name Adam gave Me, the name I set up conditionally between Myself and My creation."[16]

We'll begin with a consideration of the midrash itself. The Rabbis' overt concern here seems to be a moment of poetic justice. The ministering angels, they recall, fiercely opposed the creation of humankind, formed of lowly matter, riddled with forgetting.[17] In the dramatic scene staged in the midrash the angels are put to the test. Their utter failure, their inability to know the names of God's creations, is set up as a prologue to Adam's masterful success. Intuitively, gracefully, that human recognizes the still unspoken name that says the essence of each thing. Now, incontestably, God can aver, "his wisdom is greater than yours."

In his commentary, R. Ya'akov turns first to the moment of angelic blankness. He traces their inability to name to their own chronic condition: "The angels couldn't name because they have no names. What they are called changes according to each mission they are given." To back up this contention, he recalls another midrash.

> When Jacob asked [his mysterious wrestling opponent], "Please, tell me your name!" (Gen. 32.30) He answered, "['Why are you asking my name']; now I have one name, later on I will have another." And so [in Judges 13:17], "The angel of the Lord said [to Manoaḥ], 'Why are you asking my name, for it is concealed [*pila'i*]'—I never know what new name I will be given."[18]

The namelessness of the angels, R. Ya'akov explains, is an ontological state. Intensely, timelessly present before God, angels are transparent and selfless emissaries. To be designated with a single name would confine their essence and so diminish their superhuman power. And because names are alien to their own angelic being, they cannot manipulate names, cannot designate other entities with them.

In effect, however, this scene of "taking council" hints that a second, more covert intent is at work in the Rabbis' retelling of the story. What concerns them most of all is really not the angelic orders, but defining the kind of wisdom that is uniquely human. R. Ya'akov recalls the Sages' self-conscious reflection in another context: "Even though [the angels] have more expertise than we do, we are more perceptive than they. Indeed, who are truly 'angels'? Our Rabbis."[19] He questions how this human faculty of perceptiveness comes to the fore most clearly in the act of naming.

> Humanity alone, dwelling in darkness, sees things as they appear in concealment and sees their ultimate essence as well—thus humans can name. And Adam, because he could perceive the back of the ox from the Chariot, was able to understand how it emanates and becomes manifest in oxen of this world ... Then, God established the names of things in accordance with human perceptions. Indeed, from His perspective God truly has no name to circumscribe Him. All the Names He is known by correspond with human understandings of Him. Hence, "I am *Hashem*; that is My Name [Isa. 42:8]."[20]

The inspired gesture of naming, on this reading, is fundamentally creative. "Seeing things in concealment" refers to the way we contemplate our world. Some lines earlier, R. Ya'akov calls phenomena, as they appear to us, *partzufim ḥalukim*, literally, "separated aspects."[21] What is concealed is their essence—the root or "idea" from which phenomena originate, and from which they separate to reemerge in partiality, in a certain guise particular to our world. The mystical creatures that bear the divine Chariot, evoked in the famous prophetic vision of Ezekiel (Ezek. 1:4–28), here represent those primal points of origin. Adam's act of naming the creatures—"lion," "eagle," "ox"—serves to display or realize the primordial connection between the crowds of animal faces before him and the other, transcendental plane of being that corresponds with each of them. The names he gives, God then "establishes."[22] Those names now become the words, everyday words we use to speak of the things in the world.

Names and signs thus harbor the potential for wholeness. Adam named the animals in a moment of utter clarity—"he saw and understood and knew that the 'back' was just like the 'face.'" This original unity of word and being, of 'back' and 'front,' however, is exceedingly difficult, perhaps impossible, to hold onto. Words, names, signs risk becoming "mere" signifiers when subject and object split completely, when the "source" disappears from sight. Then, an empty shell or lowly beast seems to be all that remains. Then, "signs" are forced to take on a secondary, instrumental, exterior role. R. Ya'akov recognizes this diminishment as unavoidable.[23] It underlines the duality inherent in our being in the world. Drawing our attention to the "signs," however, is the first and crucial step toward their "rescue." To recognize the vitality of names themselves and their indwelling holiness is to redeem them from emptiness.

But how are we to understand the final act of naming the midrash records: Adam's naming God? R. Ya'akov's statement on this point is radical. God, he says, truly has and can have no name. "The Name"—*Hashem*—the ineffable word God invokes, as it were, to designate Himself (in the verse in Isaiah 42:8) makes sense only in relationship to human beings. It is "the name Adam gave Me," the name God "set up conditionally" for the sake of the world.

What R. Ya'akov seems to be suggesting is that each of the Names through which God reveals Himself is one part of an unthematizable whole. The "idea," God "Himself," cannot be designated in any name. All the appellations and attributes human beings invoke to speak of God are no more than shards; the essence is ungraspable. For that reason, the ultimate promise of unity finds expression in the notion we cited above: "Then the Name will be whole in all its aspects." God, as it were, will say: "See, now that I, even I am He ..." (Deut. 32:38).[24] That is, all the signifiers and referents, the many forms of relation with "Him"—all of them mutely gesture toward that "I" no eye can ever know.

"Male" and "Female"—Two Aspects of Selfhood

I'd like to return now to a figure we saw some pages earlier. R. Ya'akov presents it to speak of another vision of the future and an end to duality. "Walls and outer skins [*kelipot*] will be needed no more—the 'wall' will be immersed within the fruit ... as the *Zohar* says, 'everything then will become whole, a complete unity.'" We must take a closer look at the image of metamorphosis R. Ya'akov evokes here. Just what does this emblematic immersion of the "peel" into the flesh of the fruit mean? How would such a transformation be lived? In effect, central kabbalistic concepts seem to be the guiding force behind this image. R. Ya'akov merges certain elements from the *Zohar* and Lurianic teaching with his own sensitivity to the human condition. Decoding them may yield a unique and compelling understanding of the tension between self and other, and an intimation of its resolution.

R. Ya'akov's reflections are founded on an innovative idea developed in various places in the *Zohar*. He alludes to two passages, along with the biblical verse that inspired them. "And God created Man in His image, in the image of God He created him, male and female He created them" (Gen. 1:27).[25] On the doubled invocation of the word "image" (*tzelem*), the *Zohar* comments: "The image of God—that is, two worthy likenesses, male and female."[26] The second passage:

> Come and see. This holy image: as an individual grows, one's own likeness is formed from this countenance [*partzufa*]. Another image forms as well, and the two become joined into one; each receives from the other. When one has both these images, the individual and one's body are preserved, and the spirit dwells within.[27]

I won't attempt to decipher these heavily coded lines on my own. Most generally, though, they seem to speak of a certain doubleness intrinsic to being human. Male and female, self and body, body and spirit, holy image and one's own likeness—all these are somehow present in every living person. What seems to interest R. Ya'akov as he cites these passages is not the given fact of this duality as such, but rather the dynamic of growth, change, even transformation implicit in it. He reads these two images proposed in the *Zohar* in spatial and, by extension, psychological terms.

> When God wishes to shower goodness, it comes in abundance far beyond the capacity people have to receive. So it is with all organic growth—chaff, waste is always mixed in, for the earth hasn't the power to integrate all the goodness God plants within it. And so it is in the realm of holiness—the entirety of light is too immense to be contained. What an individual manages to internalize is called "inner light" [*or penimi*]. What one still cannot hold within is "encompassing light" [*or mekkif*]; it becomes "feminine waters." Yet, little by little, one can come to internalize that light as well. What yesterday was "encompassing light" today can be contained, and it becomes "inner light." In this manner, more "light" will forever come to encompass one ...And so it is with the light alluded to in those "two images/shadows"—they are "inner light" and "encompassing light."[28]

The dynamic R. Ya'akov charts here concerns a moment of integration, a drawing from outside to inside. The two images of the *Zohar*, on this reading, seem to speak of two aspects of selfhood. One is "my"self—the identity or sense of being I already possess in any given present. The other is an unimaginable, greater fullness of being I may attain, with effort, at future times over the course of my life. "Inner light" is "mine." The light that surrounds "me" has yet to be acquired and rendered interior. For now, it is beyond my comprehension, "too immense to be contained" in its entirety.

The joining of the two images suggested in the *Zohar* occurs, in R. Ya'akov's retelling, by a passing from the exterior inward. It is a movement without end or fulfillment. "Goodness" is overflowing; "encompassing light" augments, even as some of it is drawn inside. And so the potential of spiritual growth has no limit, because its resources are continually renewed.

Notably, R. Ya'akov employs the gender distinction hinted at in the *Zohar* to understand the spatial situation of these two images. He associates the encompassing dimension with feminine waters.[29] In locating the realm of potentiality (feminine) beyond the contained, known realm of the self, R. Ya'akov seems to be making a provocative statement. I'd like to suggest that it reflects a highly original aspect of Izbica-Radzyn teaching as a whole.

To appreciate the depth and scope of this innovation, we must take a closer look at the biblical narrative the *Zohar* alludes to. It is the Creation story that recounts how male and female were engendered, how harmony was ruptured, and how hierarchy and role stereotypes came into being. Here, cogently, R. Mordecai Joseph and R. Ya'akov after him suggest a way of understanding that differs significantly from traditional readings.

The Beginning Point: Back to Eden

Many teachings in *Mei ha-Shiloaḥ* and *Beit Ya'akov* reflect back on this seminal narrative. Often, it is recalled to speak of overarching concerns such as free choice and responsibility, good and evil, and the nature of sin.[30] Our focus here will be a different perspective in the narrative: the reading that the Izbica-Radzyn tradition constructs with its refiguring of male and female. R. Ya'akov refers frequently to his father's teachings on the subject. We'll begin, then, with two passages in *Mei ha-Shiloaḥ* that develop some of these ideas.

> ["The Lord God said, It is not good for Man to be alone;] I will make him a fitting helper ['*ezer ke-negedo*] (Gen. 2:18)." This means that God so wills

> it that an individual's aid and help should stem from things that oppose one [*ke-negedo*]. We see this in the relationship between teacher and student: R. Simeon ben Lakish would challenge his master, R. Yoḥanan, with twenty-four arguments, and the master would resolve them with twenty-four solutions, and so words of Torah flourished.... (B. *Bava Metzi'a* 84a). For when a person is challenged, one must reinforce one's view with proofs; this enables one to articulate it with utmost clarity.[31]

It sounds like a casual observation, a fact that has come to light, voiced by the Creator. Singularity is "not good." In that fatal moment, the "great dialectic" of this world is conceived of and justified. Opposition will spring instantaneously from that ideal "fitting helper," from what is other than one. Forces will clash, and the dissonance that is generated will be the source of all fruitfulness. The trick, it seems, is in recognizing the forces "against me" as helpmates and aid, as positive elements. This, as we will see, is the formidable trial the biblical text will soon recount. Before we get to that, let's look at a second teaching about the subsequent biblical scene. Here, Adam's monotonic inner consonance is effectively broken apart so that the "helpmate," another voice, can emerge.

> "Now the Lord God cast a deep sleep upon the Man and he slept" (Gen. 2:21). This is written after it says, "The Lord God formed Man from the dust of the earth. He blew into His nostrils the breath of life ..." [2:7]. And (in the book *Sefer ha-Kanah le-Ma'aseh Bereshit*), "The breather breathes of Himself. The force of the Animator is within the one who has been animated."[32] And so, for now Adam could not know he had the ability to work with his own hands. Thus, to save him from eating the "bread of shame," God in His mercy cast a deep sleep upon him. That is, God concealed the brilliant light so that he could choose and strive himself and discover his own path ... For when one enjoys the work of one's own hands—that is what brings happiness and well-being.[33]

R. Mordecai Joseph contrasts two phases in this biblical version of evolution. The apex of the first phase comes when the body of clay is inspired with the source of life. A nearly perfect creation, its sole deficiency is its very proximity to perfection. The dazzling brightness that fills Adam's world blinds him to his own self—that is, to his own creative power. Passively, he "has been animated." As long as he remains dependant, radically uninvolved in the "bread" that would nourish and sustain him, Adam faces "shame." The second phase begins, then, with a strange act of kindness. Darkness and sleep close away the "light." Human autonomy can now come into being. R. Mordecai Joseph recognizes this new phase of independence as a crucial part of psychic well-being. A sense of freedom, the ability to act and choose and believe one has earned goodness, bring with them a joy of living.

Adam is thus cast into unconsciousness to lead him toward an infinitely more challenging mode. Drawing on midrashic tradition, R. Ya'akov reaffirms the idea that, in essence, this creature called "Adam" was a composite entity. The first part of the Creation story testifies: "And God created Man in His image, in the image of God He created him, male and female He created them (Gen. 1:27)." The Rabbis learn this means that humankind was originally made with two countenances (*du-partzufin*), connected back-to-back.[34] It is this androgynous creature, then, that the verses first name as "Adam." R. Ya'akov turns to phase two.

> [While Adam was] awake, in all his splendor, the "female" was contained in the "male." As he was cast into sleep, however, that slumber separated the male from the female, split "her" from "him." Slumber took the aspect of remembering [*zakhor*] away from him.[35]

"Adam" is broken apart; the primary experience he knew until now of "standing face-to-face" before God's brilliant light is abruptly ended. R. Ya'akov suggests a hermeneutical link between this fateful moment and a second crucial instance in which an ontological unity was also shattered.

> The first Tablets of the Law were the same prototype as Adam. Originally, his being filled the whole world … Similarly, on the first Tablets, the word "and" was not written … Thus, each commandment expanded endlessly; no room was left for the next one … God's will, however, was that Israel should generate light for themselves through the strength of their own labor. And so the first Tablets were broken. Then God gave them the second Tablets.
>
> Now, "and" [the letter *vav*] is added to each of the commandments. That word connects one to the next: "You shall not kill; and you shall not comment adultery; and you shall not steal … (Deut. 5:17)."[36]

In this scenario the first Tablets, with the impossible totality of each utterance they held, had to be broken. That totality is hinted at in their writing: "You shall not kill. You shall not commit adultery. You shall not steal" (Exod. 20:13).

The dangerous absolutism that this manner of writing threatens can be abstracted: "If people would totally live by 'you shall not harm anything' [*lo tirtzaḥ*], they would have mercy even for evil. If they would totally live by 'You shall not desire' [*lo tin'af*], they would prevent themselves from giving to others, even for the good."[37]

The space between—the "and" that must be added to separate one utterance, one entity from another—serves to blunt the absolute, binding power of the divine word. Those second Tablets are written by Moses and given to Israel in the wake of the sin of the Golden Calf (Exod. 34:1). The Rabbis understand that the contents of the second Tablets are recorded in Deuteronomy. The discrepancies between this text and the "version" of the Ten Commandments that appears in Exodus thus hold great significance. On R. Ya'akov's reading, the differences between these two biblical texts reflect back on the successive stages in the creation of humankind.

"Adam," in whom the "female" was first contained in the "male," is similarly augmented by "and." He awakens to find a stranger—a distinct, gendered Other before him. Humankind, from now on, will be in doubled form—his and hers, woman and man. The "and" will now separate and perhaps at times join them together.

A second vital point linking the prototype of the Tablets to the creation story is the formulation of the Fourth Commandment. R. Ya'akov alludes to it in his comment (cited above), that as Adam was cast asleep and his rib removed (Gen. 2:21), "slumber took the aspect of remembering [*zakhor*] away from him." In effect, the first Tablets, written as it were by the finger of God, filled with endless light, read: "Remember [*zakhor*] the Sabbath day and keep it holy ... (Exod. 20:11)." The second Tablets, carved by hands of flesh, under the shadow of sin and repentance, read differently: "Safeguard [*shamor*] the Sabbath day and keep it holy ..." (Deut. 5:12).

A well-known rabbinic statement harmonizes these variants by averring that "Remember" and "Safeguard" were uttered simultaneously, a feat that is humanly impossible.[38] Kabbalistic teaching, though, hears these textual variations as referring to two distinct, opposing modes. *Zakhor/zakhar* speaks of memory and maleness; *shamor* speaks of guarding, a valence of the female, or *nukba*.[39] With these elements in hand, R. Ya'akov considers the creation story once again.

> Clearly, when the positive commandment to "love one's neighbor as oneself" is manifestly evident and fulfilled to perfection, there is no need to say, "Do not kill." So it is with memory: as long as the faculty of

> remembering [*zakhor*] exists, "safeguarding" [*shamor*] is implicit within it, and needs no explicit mention. But when *zakhor* is obscured, understanding must come in some other way. Then *shamor* is needed to help rebuild it once again.[40]

"Light" is secreted away and the "memory" of it nearly forgotten. Hope for recovering the original sense of presence and connection may be found, however, through new channels that open in-between people, toward God.

"Safeguarding" the remnants of things past, the stray fragments left over from fuller moments of being—this, R. Ya'akov suggests, is the new task to which Man awakens. Some core part of himself, "bone of my bone," absolute knowing has been taken away and then re-presented to him, transformed. R. Ya'akov evaluates the challenge and the potential of this utterly different, nascent relationship between male and female. He cites the concluding verse of this phase and comments.

> "Hence a man shall leave his father and his mother and cling to his wife, so that they become one flesh (Gen. 2:24)." In other words, he should disregard what wisdom [*hokhmah*/father] and knowledge [*binah*/mother] would teach him: that he should not enter doubtful situations, and should not go after her; that he, at least, should remain in clarity. No. Rather, he should cleave to his wife, even if he must diminish himself to reach her. And the One to whom all belongs will come and redeem them both.[41]

The closing lines of this passage parenthetically cite Lurianic writings.[42] While the kabbalistic sources are clearly the basis for his reading of the biblical story overall, R. Ya'akov does not explicate them directly. His commentary, however, uncovers his adaptation and thoroughly Hasidic re-formation of them. The contention here is quite arresting. Man—in newly gendered guise—stands before an uncharted frontier. A break must be made with parental "good sense"; here, this means the overwhelming influence of his divine origins. His rapt, secure, and ultimately static existence has to be left behind. Now Man must enter the realm of uncertainty and diminishment in order to join the Other. That adventure alone, says the verse, holds the promise of fertility and redemption. As R. Ya'akov insightfully comments, the "great countenances" (*apei ravrevei*) of Father and Mother that loom large in one's life must give way at some point to the "smaller countenances" (*apei zutrei*)—the relationships and personal understanding each of us must build on our own between "male" and "female."[43]

The next verses in the biblical narrative record that struggle with "doubtful situations" in gripping detail. Izbica-Radzyn tradition offers a provocative and highly controversial reading of this epic tale. Not all its aspects are relevant to matters at hand, and so we will cleverly avoid presenting their complexities here.[44] The following teaching recorded in *Mei ha-Shiloaḥ* sets out an idea that is fundamental to R. Ya'akov's reading. R. Mordecai Joseph evaluates a crucial verse by subtly shifting the syntax from the traditional reading.

> "Now the Lord God commanded Man, saying, 'Of every tree of the garden you are free to eat and of the tree of knowledge of good and evil you must not eat ..." (Gen. 2:16–17). In the future, when the sin of the first Man is repaired, the verses will recombine in a different way: "Of every tree of the garden you are free to eat and of the tree of good." After that, "And evil you must not eat." In other words, the good part of the tree can be eaten; only don't eat the evil part of it. God, finally, will make it clear that, in truth, Adam ate the good part alone. There was no sin. It only seemed so to Adam himself, thin as a garlic skin and no more.[45]

We'll return at the end of this chapter to R. Mordecai Joseph's conviction, phrased with striking directness, that the "sins" of humankind in Eden were illusory. The pressing issue, at the moment, is why that illusion of wrongdoing was fabricated. What intent was behind it? How does the illusion stay alive?

We saw one answer some pages ago. "God concealed His brilliant light so that Adam could choose and strive himself and discover his own path ...." As the paralyzing connection with his Source disintegrates, Adam begins his escape from solipsism. The adventure intensifies when he confronts a different, separate human face, an Other over whom he has no power. That encounter propels him, beyond his own will, into a "radical questioning of certitude," to use Levinas's phrase.[46] This questioning is engineered by the serpent. Izbica-Radzyn tradition evaluates the next, pivotal scene in a highly unconventional manner.

The appearance of the serpent and its fateful deceptions, R. Ya'akov notes, is preceded by the verse, "They were both naked, the man and his wife, yet they were not ashamed" (Gen. 2:25). That state "beyond morality" is at the root of everything that follows. Feeling no shame impedes them from fulfilling the role set out for them. Thus, these creatures have to be deconstructed still further.

> There was profound wisdom in God's design [*eitzah 'amukah be-ratzon Hashem*]. How could humility be put into the human heart, to become an integral part of them? Indeed, the world itself is founded on that

> quality [of humility and awe]. At this point Adam, the creation of God's own hands, still saw manifestly that nothing can happen without God's willing it. Profound wisdom, then, was needed to invest him with humility. That came about, by God's will, through the episode of the Tree of Knowledge.[47]

Humility (*bushah*) thus figures as a counterweight against Man's primary, intimate experience of the divine. Somehow or other, that paralyzing awareness of God's absolute power over the world must be obscured. Contingency brings with it a humbling sense of boundaries. Freedom and the burden of personal responsibility emerge. Izbica-Radzyn tradition holds that God's most profound will is to set that process in motion. The tree, the serpent, the choices and errors that unfold are all part of that divine plan. This conviction leads to a fascinating alternate understanding of the role of the serpent in the next scene.

R. Mordecai Joseph notes that from the beginning of the Creation story and until the creation of Man, God is named only as *Elohim* (Gen. 1:1–2:3). As the stage is set for the human to come on the scene, God begins to engage with the world as *Hashem Elohim*, a greater, manifest fullness (Gen. 2:4–25). The appearance of the serpent then marks a rupture of that sense of presence. When it addresses Eve, the serpent ominously refers to God as *Elohim* alone: "Did God perhaps say …" [*af ki amar Elohim*] (Gen. 3:1). By that cunning omission, "it concealed the ineffable Name … and sin came from that. God's omnipotence was effectively concealed from them."[48]

R. Ya'akov probes the psychological effect of this sudden, unexpected encounter with hiddenness.

> As long as the ineffable Name is manifestly evident, one has no desire to be an individuated [*misuyyam*], autonomous entity. For that Name means that one can see all the way to one's origin.[49] In truth, each Jewish soul is unique and individual. Nonetheless, when one lives in total clarity, one doesn't need to feel that individuality; the heart is secure in knowing one's portion will never be lost.… But when the Name is concealed from one's eyes, that security is undermined. Distance separates from one's root, and all manner of worries [*miḥushim*] are born. One starts to invent ways to protect oneself as much as possible, in the attempt to assert one's own individual, distinct identity. This, indeed, is what happened. The serpent hid the holy Name from them, and then they sought—too hard—to protect themselves with the commandment about the tree. They "made a guard to [His] guard" and that is what

> brought them to sin. Yet it is said (Ps. 30:8), "God, all is through Your favor—when You will to make me firm as a mighty mountain, You hide Your face and I am terrified." That is, when God wants to raise a person from one level to the next, higher level, one first senses a fall, and feels discouraged and anxious. Then, after that, God elevates one.[50]

The Face is hidden. In the vacant space of absence that gapes before them, humans first taste the freedom to choose. Anxiety and an unfamiliar dimension of self-consciousness quickly crowd into those moments.

The next verses testify that, indeed, distinct and separate identities have crystallized. Under questioning, Adam gives expression to a radical individuation, a novel awareness of self and other. "The woman whom you gave to be with me—she gave me of the tree and I ate (Gen. 3:12)." Against traditional readings, R. Ya'akov hears these words as a courageous statement of "being for the other." Adam declares his conscious choice to bind up his own destiny with that other, separate self opposing him now in all her strangeness.

> He answered: Once she had eaten from the tree, I had to eat; if not, she would be deficient forever, with no one to save her along with her deficiency. How could one abandon another who was first a united whole with oneself?[51]

Those words, "I had to eat" (*hayiti mukhraḥ*), are the voice of conscience. R. Ya'akov reiterates them in other teachings, with added thoughts running through Adam's mind on the meaning of it all.

> Since, at first, she had been together with him in a single body, if deficiency is in her, he realized, it must be his as well … If not, if he were wholly good, how could something bad ever emerge from him? Thus the Talmud says (B. *Yoma* 87a), "It cannot be that the rabbi is in paradise while his student is in hell." That is, the rabbi may well have been good, but if what he produced was the opposite, that is a sign that the rabbi himself was lacking, that he had not reached the full perfection God wished of him.[52]

To support his understanding of Adam's mindset, R. Ya'akov cites a midrash. In it, the sages indeed contend that Adam, at this juncture, attains a vital new plateau of ethical development. "When the first Man was asked: Who caused you to do it? He replied, I caused it myself. I myself am responsible."[53]

R. Ya'akov evaluates the significance of this moral achievement in the context of the Creation narrative as a whole.

> God's sole purpose in all of this was to teach that first generation that they must ascribe deficiency to themselves. This was exceedingly difficult for them. Their being was so intense; they were so very close to their divine Source. They knew with utter clarity that God had created them and that He conducted their existence. Thus they were incapable of taking responsibility for personal lack. God taught them now to accept incompleteness, that it is good to do so.[54]

On this retelling, God and humanity "let go" of one another. Confined no longer within a brilliant totality of being, humans are somehow set free at last. It is a profoundly disorienting moment. The distance that has opened between them makes doubt and un-control inescapably present. Man's choice to act on behalf of the Other, that estranged, deficient, "female" aspect of his own self, is God's secret hope. And thus, in Izbica-Radzyn tradition, this acceptance of personal responsibility designates the beginning of a new era.

"Mother of All Life"

The ethical event it represents is hinted in the biblical narrative. R. Mordecai Joseph sets out the paradoxical valences of humankind's cognitive state at this juncture in a highly original reading of it.

> When they realized they had sinned, the time of repair [*tikkun*] began … It was marked with Adam's naming his wife—"*Ḥavva* [Eve], for she is the mother of all life (3:20)." He recognized, after repenting, that truly, in this world a person can do nothing; all is from God. Indeed, his sin itself was God's will, only that was beyond his own comprehension. And so he called her "mother of all life" for it was she who had led to his sin. He understood that she had guided him in that matter far beyond his own understanding. Thus, in the Talmud (*Bava Metzi'a* 59a) it is said: "Honor your wives so that you may be blessed with wealth."[55]

R. Ya'akov cites this teaching and expands its core ideas with some reflections of his own.

> For Ḥavva really was given to him as a helpmate, that he should heed her words. The sin was only because hiddenness was incited by the serpent. For if it had come about through Ḥavva alone, there would have been no "sin" at all. Moreover, in truth, when the sin will be repaired fully, these events will shine with tremendous light. Once Adam understood that it was she who had brought him to this level—for he himself had been reluctant to enter doubt, only she thrust him into it—then he realized she had been given to him, not only as an aid. She elevates him in the ways of God [*menaset oto be-darkei ha-Hashem*], in matters that are higher than what his own mind can comprehend. Life in its essence flows to him through her. And so he called her "mother of all life"—for all comes from her [*ki mi-mena ha-kol*].[56]

On this reading, Adam's final act of naming thus articulates and sums up the weighty changes he has endured. The feminine first faced him as an oppositional force and, finally, brought on his downfall. The apparently negative draw of that influence strikes with full force in the moments after the deed is done. As R. Mordecai Joseph poignantly puts it, "Adam was terribly aggrieved [*hitmarmer me'od*]—'Why did such an error happen to me?'"[57] But as Adam comes to the realization that "his sin itself was God's will," he understands that it was the power of the feminine that had enabled him to actualize that divine will. With that realization, humankind crosses an unknown threshold, into Life—life in "this world." Ḥavva in some profound sense represents that transitional, life-giving force.

To appreciate the full significance of Adam's naming of her and the essence of the feminine implicit in that act of naming, we must consider some of the kabbalistic ideas that underlie this aspect of Izbica-Radzyn tradition. R. Mordecai Joseph states:

> Creation came into this world through the sin. As the *Zohar* says, "The First Man had nothing at all of this world." And in the writings of the Holy *Ari*, before the sin, "he was barely anchored in this world." After the sin, he became firmly placed into this world. That was God's will, so that goodness could be attributed to the work of human hands.[58]

"This world," reiterated so many times in this teaching, refers to the order we know, to our limited, mortal, all-too-human existence. The most cogent symbol of the boundedness that informs it is embodiment. Humans, in their new stance of "being in the world," are now "clothed" in bodies.

R. Mordecai Joseph sees this rite of passage as the crucial means of repairing the sin.[59]

The hope of "repair," he teaches, is granted to humankind in a moment of illumination: Adam, at last, sees "that she had guided him far beyond his own understanding ... that life in its essence flows to him through her." He "honors" Ḥavva, calls her "mother of all life." With that gesture, Adam's bitter grief gives way—"so God saved him and granted them, as a gift, garments of light."[60] Now, R. Mordecai Joseph notes, the next verse thus reads: "And the Lord God made garments of skin for Adam and his wife, and clothed them (3:21)."

The double reading that R. Mordecai Joseph offers here—garments of light/garments of skin [אור/עור]—asserts a fundamental belief.[61] The flesh, or the luminous casing that will now contain human inwardness, should be recognized as a precious gift. Humankind is "blessed with wealth," is granted that body as Adam realizes that the feminine, with her influence, has brought them to greatness. Greatness, having a body, is what enables them to fulfill "God's essential will," to take on the challenge of living in this world. Plowing and sowing, bearing fruit "in our image, after our likeness," nourishment and growth—these are the reasons for human existence.[62]

Divine intent in creating the human is thus fully realized here, with embodiment. Corporeity anchors humankind in the world. It will mandate a continual, painful struggle with matter, appetite, decay, and failure. R. Ya'akov stresses that the other aspect of corporeity must always be remembered as well.

> When God said, "Let us make humankind" (Gen. 1:26), He "wrapped in a robe of light" (Psalms 104:2). As it were, He made a garment of His light, to enable His influence to flow to the lower realms. And he clothed the first humans ... making them a garment, raiments of skin in which to cover them.[63]

That "garment of skin," R. Ya'akov adds, is the layer of "encompassing light" we humans can, potentially, sense most clearly. Sense, yet easily misunderstand. He remarks, "People think the soul is most important, and the body secondary ... But for God ... it is the opposite—"encompassing light" is the main thing, and "inner light" comes second ... Indeed, holiness in its essence is in "encompassing light."[64]

The body, then, becomes an interface between the human and the divine. That is the secret meaning of the feminine here. In many passages, R. Ya'akov recalls an opaque kabbalistic teaching, found in *Tikkunei Zohar* and re-found in Lurianic writings: The name Ḥavva corresponds with a mystical writing of God's ineffable Name.[65] Her name bears testimony to the humbling human reality after sin—a reality in which the full brilliance of God's presence is no longer visible. What remains is an "interpretation," the letters that recall the trace of that absence. Ḥavva and the corporeity that the feminine brings into the world are thus another way of saying. In humility, embodiment gestures beyond itself to an enduring, concealed presence.

And so R. Yaʿakov evaluates the outcome of all this and distinguishes a paradigm to aid in understanding.

> "Shall I bring to breaking/birthing [*ashbir*] and not enable to bear, says God?" (Isa. 66:9). That is, at times the word of God seems to destroy human actions. But that is only to enable new birth—to augment and to gain. So it was with the breaking of the Tablets. They were shattered, but that was only for Israel's good. For if they hadn't been broken, words of Torah would have been implanted in the heart of each individual. There would have been no need to labor, and no way to gain reward. People, though—as the midrash says (*Kohelet Rabba* 4.6), "Every person wants to be called 'one who works for a living.'" And so, whenever an individual discovers a new understanding of Torah, one mends the broken Tablets [*me-aḥe luḥot nishbarim*] and shows that really they are whole.[66]

To draw together the shards of a lost unity, to bear new ways of meaning—this, finally, is a laboring "for the good." Body and soul, female and male can be mended with the notion of "and." That is the Hebrew letter *vav*. The human form, the *Zohar* teaches, is symbolized with that letter.[67] "And" comes into being through the experience of sin. It will join one thought to another, past to future, despair with hope. Now, together, the two may set out on the way to all the possibilities of life.

Endpoint: The Spark at the Body's Core

Clearly, Izbica-Radzyn tradition offers an important reassessment of physicality and its essential role in human life. "The body," R. Yaʿakov avers, "has tremendous worth."[68] Its full brilliance will become evident, though, only far into the future. This conviction emerges from the innovative reading of Genesis we saw above. I'd like to turn now to that opposite, endpoint dimension. Here as well, we can detect an implicit and powerful challenge to traditional views. Izbica-Radzyn teachings on the role of corporeity in metahistory offer an important and moving message.

We'll begin with the following teaching. In it, R. Ya'akov introduces some essential concepts.[69]

He begins by recalling the symbol of the seed and the process of decay and regeneration it represents. At its center, the seed has an indestructible germ of life. R. Ya'akov calls it "a point of divine will." This point is a nuclear, imperceptible force "inherent in every thing ... and in each and every individual Jew."[70] All organic growth germinates from that originary point. In all the nights of our lives, in sleep and finally at death, we "plant" ourselves—that is, we entrust our souls, deliver them into God's hands.[71] R. Ya'akov notes that in the *Zohar*, the point of vitality at the core of the seed/soul is called *kusta de-ḥiyyuta*—a "corner of life."[72] All awakenings—from morning to morning, from "night" to eternal life—begin from that undying "corner" of vitality. But beyond the personal plane of experience, he suggests that the same dynamic is at the center of Jewish history as a whole. One narrative in which it finds expression is the saga of Joseph. Within the matrix of these ideas, he proposes this innovative perspective.

R. Ya'akov recalls the moving denouement in which Jacob/Israel is reunited with the firstborn son of his wife Rachel at last in Egypt.

> "And Israel said to Joseph, 'I never expected to see you again, and here God has let me see your children as well'" (Gen. 48:11). [Israel/Jacob] realized now that in the midst of all the darkness and concealment he had suffered, the light of this salvation had been taking form.

That concealment began when Joseph was sold by his brothers, cast into a pit in the earth, and lost away. The years of his absence, with the specter of his alleged violent end, were a tortured time in his father Jacob's life. Now, with his son and grandsons alive and whole before him, Joseph seems to have been resurrected from the dead. Metaphorically, Joseph is that "corner of life." His strength has been proven invincible to the powers of evil. He is the seed from which "salvation" has sprouted. Through Joseph, the patriarch's family and their offspring, the germinal nation of Israel are given a new life and hope of surviving the famine. This primary association offers a link to a second, central figure. Interestingly, his identity, much like Joseph's, also begins in question. R. Ya'akov cites a midrash:

> Once, our Rabbis and other wise men were in dispute: What are Elijah the prophet's origins? Some said he is a descendent of Rachel. Others

> said a descendent of Leah. In the midst of their dispute, I appeared to them. I stood before them and said: Gentlemen [*Rabbotai*], I am from none other than the seed of Rachel. They answered, Give us a sign … [Elijah recalls the time he revived the son of a widow from the dead (1 Kings 17:10–24).] And I told them: That boy was a descendant of Joseph.[73]

Thus, R. Ya'akov concludes, the "corner of life," which never disappears, from which God will revitalize each aspect of being, stems ultimately from Rachel. Both these figures, Joseph and Elijah, are Rachel's "seed" (*zar'ah shel Raḥel*). In recompense for her trials and her humility, R. Ya'akov says, "Every moment of redemption will begin, will be awakened by Rachel's sons … Indeed, Elijah is the "corner of life" for the Jewish nation … It is Elijah who will revive all the dead; it is he who will be the harbinger of the Messiah, son of David.[74]

These reflections lead R. Ya'akov to this surprising declaration.

> Every moment of salvation is aroused solely by that "corner of life," and it is called *nukba* [the feminine]. For God chose to contain it in the body, of all places [*davka ba-guf*]. And the relationship between body and soul is like that between female and male, as the *Zohar* teaches.[75]

The authority of mystical tradition is undeniably the foundation on which R. Ya'akov develops his view on this issue. However, as we will see, closer inspection makes evident that he parts ways significantly from the accepted hierarchy espoused in the *Zohar*.[76]

To appreciate the dialectical challenge R. Ya'akov presents here, we must realize that the opponent whose ideology he addresses explicitly is a figure of no less monumental authority: Maimonides. We saw a hint of R. Ya'akov's Hasidic, perhaps ironic rereading of Maimonides in the first pages of this chapter. Now, in greater detail:

> *Rambam*, of blessed memory, wrote (in his commentary on the Mishnah, *Sanhedrin*, chapter 11), "[God] has no body or bodily form [*ayn lo guf ve-ayn lo demut ha-guf*]." Does it really need to be pointed out that God has no body? People, though, assume that the mind [*de'ah*] is honorable in God's eyes but the body has no such honor. Thus he stated that God is not like humans of flesh and blood. For people live in subjectivity and limitation. God, in contrast, is bounded by no physicality or form. He guides everything; from God's perspective, all material things have vitality and inwardness and honor.… In truth, they contain even more life than the

> mind does … Anyone who contemplates God's brilliance will see that the body is full of life as well, for God is her guide.[77]

In these comments, Maimonides is effectively turned against himself. Rationalism—claiming the superiority of the intellect and concomitant denigration of corporeity—is, in effect, a human error. The negative view of physicality it expounds is wholly absent from the divine lexicon. God harbors no concept of "body" in that derogatory sense. Indeed, from "God's perspective," the opposite is the truth.

This brings R. Ya'akov to his next crucial argument. The cardinal belief in resurrection of the dead (*teḥiyyat ha-metim*) proves the inherent holiness and value of corporeity. It seems to me that on this point as well, R. Ya'akov's unnamed interlocutor may well be Maimonides. To estimate his ideas on this issue in a wider context, we must recall that "the Maimonidean description of the incorporeity of the eternal life in the world to come and his alleged failure to reformulate in the *Mishneh Torah* the belief in bodily resurrection triggered an acrimonious dispute, peaking in the accusation that Maimonides really denied this religious belief because it is incompatible with philosophical principles."[78]

R. Ya'akov's conviction of the body's essential part in resurrection comes to the fore in a wide variety of teachings. The arguments he presents in support of it draw on many of the themes we have considered. One important nexus in the biblical narrative for reflections on this subject is the death of Sarah. The *parashah Ḥayyei Sarah* opens with an extensive description of Abraham's efforts to acquire a proper place for Sarah's burial. These actions, and the whole of Abraham's relationship with his wife, are heavy with mystical symbolism. In R. Ya'akov's commentary, the first verses of the *sidrah* thus spark the following intuitive association.

> "For this let every faithful man [*ḥasid*] pray to You at times of finding [*le-'et metzo*]. Only that the rushing mighty waters not overtake him" (Ps. 92:6).[79] In the Talmud (B. *Berakhot* 8a): "'At times of finding': one [sage] said [this refers to finding] a wife; one said—Torah; one said—death; one said—burial." These "times of finding" speak of situations in which a person must deal with concealment. In such times, no one has the strength to reach clarity through one's own efforts; the imagination, like the intellect, run out. For a person's struggle to win clarity cannot possibly succeed everywhere, in every instance. After all, what power does one have against the unknown?[80]

Doubt, R. Ya'akov explains, casts its heavy cloud over just about every aspect of human existence. Sometimes, people can summon the resources to navigate through them. But at certain junctures, the path leading to the next moment seems totally obscured. R. Ya'akov recalls the hesitation voiced even by the illustrious sage, R. Yoḥanan ben Zakai, on his deathbed: "I do not know where they will lead me [to Heaven or to *Geihinnom*]."[81] The only encouragement that can be mustered, then, is in knowing that "finding always occurs unthinkingly."[82] In R. Ya'akov's eyes, this means that thought (*da'at*), intellectual effort, and conscious choice cannot penetrate the nebulous night of "the unknown." More acutely, all a person's major challenges are truly in that domain where the mind cannot reach. And so prayer alone can help. The appeal: "'Only that rushing mighty waters not overtake one'—that every bit of clarity one has should not be extinguished."[83] The fear of being "extinguished" grips with greatest intensity in contemplating one's own burial. So R. Ya'akov reflects:

> This is totally hidden from human comprehension. For what enters the grave? The most deficient aspect of the body, all that one didn't manage to clarify and illuminate in life. For a person is invested with a spirit [*nefesh*] in order to give light to the body; whatever one can illuminate becomes "soul" [*neshamah*] ... Everything else that still remains as "body" goes into the grave, to be hidden in dust. But like seeds planted in the soil—the time will come and God will clarify them as well; then they will emerge from the earth. All that, though, is in God's hands alone ... whomever God finds worthy to revive and enable to grow, embodied ... that individual will rise and live again.[84]

The task of "giving light to the body," in R. Ya'akov's inherited worldview, is a responsibility of the highest order. Physicality, need, desire are insatiable forces at the root of all human actions. The Hasidic ethos teaches a way to elevate bodily needs by responding to them in holiness. Caring for others, building a community, fulfilling the commandments, "the work of the hands"—such outward projects gain merit for the body's "owner." And yet, at the end of it all, some aspect of physicality, still not transmuted to spirit, stays behind. That remnant of a lived life is covered over by earth. In this teaching, and in many others, R. Ya'akov reiterates the vital importance of the "left over," lifeless body in the larger scheme of things.

To appreciate it fully, we must note that he speaks often and with great poignancy of the pain inherent in human life, in the very fact of being embodied. It is with that sensibility that he hears God's promise to Abraham:

> "I will give to you and to your offspring after you the land of your sojourns [*eretz megurekhah*]" (Gen. 17:8). That is, in that place where you were in fear [*magor*] and anxiety, in suffering and constriction in this world—there, in measure with all that, God will grant goodness for all one's labor.[85]

This correspondence between the "place of suffering" and its final healing in "goodness" is vital on an emotional level. In touching that point, R. Ya'akov offers a paradoxical vision of resolution.

> Even in the future, the memory of what one suffered in this world will remain. That will enable people to sense the goodness they will receive at last in all its intensity. For if goodness were given without suffering before it, no one would be able to taste it in total awareness. That manner of giving is called "so" [כה], as the verse says, "So shall you bless ..." (Num. 6:22). In other words, anything new must be given in accordance with the understanding a person already has. One's grasp of things should only become clearer through it; whatever perceptions a person has already attained must never be annulled. For that understanding came from personal toil, and such efforts are very dear to God .... Thus the most essential aspect of the resurrection of the dead is that the body itself will live again, that it will recognize it is the same one as before and not a new creature.[86]

We need to discuss the logic that links all these elements together. The locus of "suffering," R. Ya'akov suggests here, is the body. That vulnerable flesh of being represents the fundamentally subjective nature of experience. As Charles Taylor puts it, "The world as I know it is there for me, is experienced by me, or thought about by me, or has meaning for me."[87] Thus notions like "pure thinking," the unencumbered flight of the spirit, concerning things in terms of their essence—all these, in the end, are humanly impossible.[88]

This sense of "myself," in R. Ya'akov's teaching, is inextricably tied up with corporeity, with living in a body. The unique and wholly personal "grasp of things" I have is the product of a lifetime of gathering together my thoughts and experiences from their myriad dispersions.[89] That internal order called "my understanding" thus incorporates and reflects, in some basic way, my personal situation.

But "body," in R. Ya'akov's eyes, is not an indifferent, neutral symbol. As we saw above, "body" is tightly linked to the notion of "deficiency." Here, paradoxically, is the most authentic locus of the personal. What distinguishes me, my understanding, and my experience from that of others is the peculiar defects that, above all, mark me as an individual. On this point, R. Ya'akov draws on a perhaps unsettling insight voiced by the Rabbis. They relate to this prophecy of salvation:

> Then the eyes of the blind shall be opened, and the ears of the deaf shall be unstopped. Then the lame shall leap like a deer, and the tongue of the dumb shall shout aloud. (Isa. 35:5–6)
>
> The dead, when they rise again, will rise together with all their defects [*be-mumam ye'amdu*]. So no one will be able to say, The ones He resurrected are not the same ones who died.[90]

R. Gershon Ḥanokh Ḥenikh records his father's comments on this statement:

> "Their defects"—that is the deficiency planted in every individual at birth. And one suffers from it all the days of one's life, and recalls it continually. When, at last, God will heal that deficiency, one will be able to see how very good it is, for the memory of one's suffering in this world will still remain. But if the dead were to arise in perfect form, they would not recognize themselves.[91]

The contention here sounds more than a bit disquieting. Even after a lifelong struggle with lack and imperfection, after death has freed one at last from the burden of physicality, personal identity will be defined, not by the glorious achievements of the spirit, but by those same inescapable flaws. The humbling truth, however, is that my deficiencies, above all, are most closely "mine." The conscious awareness of the continuity of identity is rooted, first of all, in deficiency. Thus the chance to "recognize oneself" is granted in a gesture of mercy. Bodily resurrection enables the dead to recall "all the vagaries of fortune that passed over them" in life, and to see the mark of all that on "themselves."[92] After that, healing comes.

In another context, R. Ya'akov expands this imagery.

Citing the verse "Remember that you were slaves in Egypt," he offers a penetrating understanding of its meaning. "Egypt" figuratively evokes the narrow straits, the worries and distractions that take up our lives in this world. Thus the injunction woven into the Ten Commandments (Deut. 5:15) to recall that primary situation of "bondage" has a deeper, urgent meaning.

> [When He said, "Remember …"], God revealed that you will eventually leave that place. From that day onward, a "corner of life" is inside you. Prepare yourself. Be ready, for God may summon you at any moment … But why, after all, is that "corner of life" necessary? Surely God could awaken even a stone, invest it with a living spirit, and it would live. Yet it is all for a person's own benefit. If no "corner of life" remained within, one wouldn't recognize oneself upon awakening. One would seem to be transformed into a different person, a new creature. No trace of all one's past efforts would remain. Thus, at the resurrection of the dead, each individual must recognize and know that he/she is the same self who lived before in this very same, material garb [*levush*].[93]

The "trace of all one's efforts" is marked, imperceptibly, in the depths of the body. That garb of corporeity that masks the soul—in life it is a burdensome site of private, incommunicable suffering. After death, in the "world of truth," at the End, "all the garments will be filled with life."[94]

The Dead Will Live Again

In the paragraphs above, we explored some of the emotional valences of resurrection from the rare perspective of the dead themselves. Throughout the chapters of this book, we have seen R. Ya'akov's extraordinary ability to uncover the underlying layers of life experiences. That penetrating, creative way of reading finds especially remarkable expression in his moving understanding of death "lived from the inside." In effect, it may be seen as an emblem of the most profound conviction that informs Izbica-Radzyn teaching as a whole.

The framework for his reflections on this subject is the story of Abraham and Sarah that takes form over long years of barrenness. The inner world of these two figures can be glimpsed in these verses, appearing at a crucial juncture in their lives.

> And Sarah laughed to herself, saying, "Now that I am withered, am I to be restored to youth—with my husband so old?" Then the Lord said to Abraham, "Why did Sarah laugh, saying, 'Shall I in truth bear a child, old as I am?' Is anything too wondrous for the Lord?" (Gen. 18:12–14)

Against the mainstream, R. Ya'akov holds that, in fact, both Abraham and Sarah perceived themselves as "old." Despite their unshakable belief in divine miracles, by this time they had given up hope that their prayers for a child would be answered. Both had concluded, intellectually, that according to the laws of nature, bearing progeny was physically impossible.[95] But why, he wonders, did these righteous people have to endure such extreme "concealment" before their son Isaac was born at last? Why did they first have to be "reduced to complete despair, with no conceivable hope at all for salvation?"[96] The answer he discovers begins with the private struggle the biblical narrative depicts. It then reaches far beyond them into other, symbolic realms.

One missing hermeneutical link that will help us appreciate that answer concerns the figure of Isaac. Traditionally, Isaac embodies the *sefirah* of *gevurah* (might) and the attribute of *yirah* (awe or fear). The second of the 19 blessings forming the *Amidah* speaks of ways that essence finds expression. The resurrection of the dead, evoked in that blessing, is described as a supreme gesture of divine omnipotence. Encoded in Isaac's birth and the process that led to it is thus a profound truth about the dynamics of resurrection and how it will ultimately come about.[97]

From thoughts about Sarah's and Abraham's inner life, R. Ya'akov turns to contemplate a second, surreal plane. A comparable drama is played out here, but translated to new proportions.

> "Death" speaks of absence. The dead themselves harbor no more hope of being alive. For if they could sense the "breath of the bones" [*hevla degarmei*] that, in truth, always remains, they wouldn't be called "dead." But because they feel hopeless and utterly despairing—in that subjective sense [*metzido*] they are "dead." "Death" means a degradation to a lower state [*hashpalah*], as the *Zohar* (3.138b) says ... The dead are humbled—that is, one can't comprehend the hope of returning to live again. Truly, though, the "breath of the bones" never dies. Indeed, that is what enables resurrection to life, as the *Zohar* (3.169a) teaches. And when the dead come back to life, God will make clear to all that no one, not even for a moment, every really lost hope in God. All those days when it looked as if one was dead and gone—like a person who sleeps for a while and, upon wakening, recognizes oneself—so in the future, when the dead live again, all of them will know themselves. They will recall all the experiences of their lives and the days they rested/died. Now they will see that it is they themselves who have risen to live again.[98]

In a bold stroke, "death" here is transmuted into a wholly psychological state. In it, an oppressive sense of distance and diminishment seems to cut the threads of hope stretching invisibly into the future.[99] Despair, on this reading, is a "living death." It is a mode of enduring on the margins of consciousness, without the strength to imagine being otherwise. In this teaching, R. Ya'akov names the agent of awakening in different terms. The "breath of the bones"—an uncanny turn of phrase the *Zohar* evokes—respires without ceasing. Like the "corner of life," this undying spark of vitality is planted at the body's core, deep within the bony essence of the self.[100] Now, as he begins to decipher the significance of all this, R. Ya'akov cites Ezekiel's stirring prophetic vision.

> The hand of the Lord came upon me. He took me out by the spirit of the Lord and set me down in the valley. It was full of bones. He led me all around them; there were very many of them spread over the valley, and they were very, very dry. He said to me, "O mortal, can these bones live again?" I replied, "O Lord God, only You know." And He said to me, "Prophesy over these bones and say to them: O dry bones, hear the word of the Lord! Thus said the Lord God to these bones: I will cause breath to enter you and you shall live again …" I prophesied as I had been commanded … And He said to me, "O mortal, these bones are the whole House of Israel. They say, 'Our bones are dried up, our hope is gone; we are doomed.' Prophecy, and say to them: Thus said the Lord God … I am going to open your graves and lift you out of the graves … I will put My breath into you and you shall live again." (Ezekiel 37:1–14)

R. Ya'akov comments:

> Ezekiel answered God, "Only You know." If You will say that they never lost hope, that their bones never dried out, *then* they will live. But those bones—they themselves despaired totally. Yet all this, in the end, is for the individual's good … For God, there is no difference at all between resurrecting the dead and preserving the living. God grants vitality to all without cease. So it is said (*Sifre, Pinḥas*, citing Job 12:10), "'In His hand is the spirit of all life'—these are the living—'and the breath of all humankind'—these are the souls waiting in the treasury." People think that what is "in hand" is guarded best of all … While for God, the souls of the dead are really no more distant from Him than the souls of the living. Truly, the human mind cannot comprehend how such salvation could ever come about. After resurrection, though, God will illuminate everything. Then all will realize that their vitality was never really lost. The "breath of the bones," that "corner of life" was in them always. No

> Jewish soul ever died. None of them stopped hoping and praying and shouting for God's salvation, not even for a moment.... All this is the "mystery of Isaac."[101]

Coming full circle, R. Ya'akov returns once again to the figures of Abraham and Sarah and their personal encounter, in life, with such a powerful revival. Isaac is born into the world; the boundless power concealed in prayer comes to life. At last, "God revealed to Abraham and Sarah their own secret hearts: that, in truth, they never did despair of salvation, but only hoped without cease." In that sense, R. Ya'akov notes, their story is a kind of paradigm, a model after which the whole of history takes form. The prophet Isaiah gives name to it.

> Listen to Me, you who pursue justice, you who seek the Lord: Look to the rock you were hewn from, to the hollow you were dug from. Look back to Abraham your father, and to Sarah who brought you forth. For he was only one when I called him, but I blessed him and made him many. Truly the Lord has comforted Zion, comforted all her ruins. (Isa. 51:1–3)

R. Ya'akov explains the underlying, immediate meaning of these words:

> Just as the future was concealed from Abraham and Sarah, and they couldn't imagine how salvation would ever come about, just as they despaired completely and hadn't the strength to pray any more—yet God saved them, all the same .... So we must believe in total faith that the last part will also come to be. You, too, will be saved. God will comfort Zion and all her ruins ... All this, though, and the coming of the Messiah, will occur "unthinkably"—when "the mind is suspended" [*be-heseḥ ha-da'at*], in some inconceivable way.[102]

When darkness gathers in the western sky, hope's last rays seem to die away. Yet turning, returning, the eastern sky will find the morning, with light and consolation and new life in its wings.[103]

Many promises have filled the pages of this book. The last and greatest one contains them all. R. Ya'akov begins to speak of it by recalling a humble story.

> A simple man asked R. Oshaya, "If I share a good word with you, will you relate it to the congregation in my name?" He answered, "What is it?" "All those gifts our forefather Jacob gave to Esau—the nations of the world will return them one day to the King Messiah! How is that? For it is written [Ps. 72:9], 'The kings of Tarshish and the isles will return gifts'—it doesn't say they will bring them, but return them."[104]

Here is a "good word" to reassure an unsophisticated soul. Jacob worked long and difficult years for those "gifts"; threatened with danger, he had to give them up. The thought, the proof that the fruit of his labors was never really lost, that one day everything will be restored, and by the Messiah no less—surely that is good news everyone must know about. With all his simplicity, the simple man knows that R. Oshaya will value the honest humanness of his insight. On the face of it, this story comes in response to an odd formulation in the biblical narrative. Jacob says to Esau, "Please accept my gift which was brought to you [*asher huvat lakh*]" (Gen. 33:11).[105] Deeper down, R. Ya'akov hears the worry and the consolation the verses of the Bible awaken in a "simple man." Audible as well is the honor the Rabbis pay to those feelings by recording them in the midrash. Now, in his commentary, the concerns they speak come to resonate in an additional register. The "gifts" that were brought, R. Ya'akov suggests, symbolize the losses beyond number that the Jewish people have borne throughout the generations. The "good word" concealed in the second verse is a nearly unimaginable moment of restoration.

> In time to come, everyone will see that all the concealment and the exiles that Israel endured—all of it only seemed to be so. In truth, they never suffered. So it says, "They will be as if I never rejected them" [Zech. 10:6]. And as for all the sins of Israel—the same is true. In the inmost heart of Israel, nothing ever separated them from God's will. It only looked as if they sinned ... like a person who "misses the mark." But soon, when God will redeem Israel, He will "put His signature to it" and aver that none of the sins of Israel came from the depths of their hearts.[106]

In one bold stroke, ages of suffering and mountains of sin would become an unreality. Now, rhetorically, R. Ya'akov must let the just protest of historical consciousness be heard: "But if Israel never really sinned, why, then, have they been so driven by suffering? Why have they been forced, over and over, to give up so much?" R. Ya'akov prefaces his own response with an impassioned rejection of one prevalent, debilitating misconception.

> One must never, ever imagine that all the suffering Israel has endured in this world was to atone for their sins, and that after they have suffered enough they will be forgiven and rewarded for their loyalty to God's commandments. No, that cannot be. For such a thing would be no comfort to the Jewish people. Rather, the thought itself that perhaps they had sinned—only the suspicion, the doubt in their minds that it might be so—that is what caused them to suffer, and to strive to better themselves and return to wholeness. Indeed, at the coming of the great and awesome day of the Lord [Mal. 3:23], God will clarify Israel for the good, for always. Then He will reveal the depths of their hearts. And all will see and know that Israel never sinned, and never transgressed God's will, not even by a hairsbreadth.[107]

What grants R. Ya'akov such vision into the hearts' depths, such unshakable certainty of knowing God's most secret will? A hint of an answer might be found in these words, spoken in his commentary by the biblical Jacob/Ya'akov. With his flocks and his children and their mothers crowded around him, Jacob says, "'I will make my way slowly …' (Gen. 33:14). I must attune myself to each and every one who is with me; I cannot ignore even one lamb for even a moment."[108]

Perhaps it is this attentiveness and respect and love for all that is human that enabled R. Ya'akov to understand so much. By caring about "everything in the middle," he seems to have caught a glimpse of some truth about the "beginning" and the "end." Guided by his profound belief that "no soul, no matter how distant from God will ever be rejected,"[109] R. Ya'akov points a way that can lead us home.

Endnotes

Introduction

1. Citation appears in *Dor Yesharim*, Lublin, 1925, 6. On the significance of some of the differences between the first and second editions of this book, see Rachel Elior, *"Temurot"* 403, n. 32.
2. In Polish, the family name is spelled "Lajner." It was anglicized variously to "Lainer" and "Leiner." The name often appears in family records as Leiner—e.g., the printing press in Warsaw managed in the early 20th century by some of R. Ya'akov's descendents, called Drukarnia Leinera. The branch of the family that settled in New York adopted the spelling "Lainer."
3. The title of this chapter is borrowed from Catherine Chalier's pioneering work, *Figures du feminin: Lecture d'Emmanuel Levinas*. Chalier's approach to and engagement with traditional Jewish sources in all her works has been inspiring and encouraging to me in many ways.
4. R. Gershon Ḥanokh Henikh, Introduction to *Beit Ya'akov* (1998), 16. The full title of this two-part essay is *Ha-Hakdamah ve-ha-Petiḥah le-Beit Ya'akov*. It was originally published at the beginning of the first volume of *Beit Ya'akov al-ha-Torah, Sefer Bereshit*. A new edition of the same essay was retitled as *Sha'ar ha-'Emunah ve-Yesod ha-Ḥasidut: Hakdamah u-fetaḥ ha-sha'ar le-Beit Ya'akov*, edited and annotated by R. Elḥanan Reuven Goldhaber and R. Judah Joseph Spiegelman (Bene-Berak, 1996), with parallel Hebrew translation of passages in Aramaic from the *Zohar*. I will refer to both parts of this text as Introduction. Page citations refer to the Jerusalem 1998 photocopy edition and note the Bene-Berak 1996 edition as well.
5. Introduction to *Beit Ya'akov*, 17; (1996) 57–58. These words (based on Isaiah 8:6) would become the title of the published volumes containing R. Mordecai Joseph's teaching, *Mei ha-Shiloaḥ*. The meanings of this title are discussed in more detail in Chapter 2.
6. The significance of these events is treated in Chapter 2. A great deal of scholarly attention has been devoted to this enigmatic episode in Hasidic history. Most extensive is Morris Faierstein, "The Friday Night Incident in Kotsk: The History of a Legend,"

re-published most recently in *All Is in the Hands of Heaven* (Piscataway, New Jersey: Gorgias Press, 2005), 111–125.

7 Most prominently, Faierstein, Elior *"Temurot,"* and Magid. Primary sources documenting the controversy are cited in the research of these scholars.

8 Yoetz Kim Kadish Rakatz, *Siaḥ Sarfei Kodesh* (Lodz, 1928–1931). See, for instance, 1: par. 298; 5: par. 8. Other works that have been widely used by academic scholars in search of bibliographical information should be handled with caution. One such work is *Ha-Admorim mi-Izbica* by Judah Leib Levin, a Gerer Hasid. Levin borrowed extensively from *Dor Yesharim* and other Izbica-Radzyn sources without citation and with a good measure of editorial license; he altered names, dates, and other important details. Shlomo Zalman Shragai, a great admirer of Izbica-Radzyn teaching, devoted a number of publications to its central figures. His generous appreciation, unfortunately, was not always matched with scholarly precision. Shragai, too, borrowed freely without reference to his primary or secondary sources, and erred frequently in the information he offered. His relevant works are cited in the bibliography.

9 Many speculations relate to the unusual circumstances of the publication of the first volume of *Mei ha-Shiloaḥ*. Printed in Vienna by a press owned by the non-Jewish Anton della Torre, with no approbations, or *haskamot,* like traditional Jewish religious works, the work was the first written record of R. Mordecai Joseph's controversial teachings. Another hint of the tension surrounding this tradition is audible in the Introduction that R. Gershon Ḥanokh Henikh included in this first edition of *Mei ha-Shiloaḥ*. Shragai testifies that soon after publication, copies of *Mei ha-Shiloaḥ* were burned by opponents to Izbica. Cf. *"Ḥasidut ha-Baal Shem Tov be-tefisat Izbica-Radzyn,"* 166.

10 *Dor Yesharim* (1925), 44.

11 *Dor Yesharim* (1925), 83. R. Abraham Joshua Heschel voiced this explanation on his deathbed, as he reflected on his own life and his desire, unfulfilled, to move in the 13th year of his leadership in the community of Chelm. Another descendent notes that R. Gershon Ḥanokh also passed away in his 13th year as rebbe. Cf. Preface by R. Mordecai Joseph Lainer to Beit *Ya'akov* 4 (Brooklyn, 1976; Jerusalem, 1997). See Chapter 2 for more on the symbolic 13-year period.

12 Izbica-Radzyn accounts speak of "thousands" of Hasidim in R. Mordecai Joseph's court; this following remained, for the most part, in the years of his successor, R. Ya'akov. See *Ma'amar Zikaron la-Rishonim* (1997), 10.

13 The high visibility of these comments has created the mistaken impression that R. Gershon Ḥanokh Henikh was the scribe or even the closet "author" of R. Ya'akov's teachings. The details that follow make clear, though, that many hands were involved in the process of recording, redacting, and arranging the teachings contained in the volumes of *Beit Ya'akov.*

14 R. Abraham Joshua Heschel's son by his second wife was R. Yeruḥam. R. Yeruḥam left Poland in the early 1930s. After a time in England, he immigrated to the United States and founded the Radzyn community in Brooklyn. R. Yeruḥam's son was R. Mordecai Joseph Lainer. A first edition of *Beit Ya'akov al ha-Torah, Sefer Bereshit* (Warsaw, 1891) in his possession contained marginal comments and corrections written by his grandfather, R. Abraham Joshua Heschel, and his father, R. Yeruḥam. This particular volume was reprinted in a photocopy edition in Jerusalem 1978 and again in Jerusalem 1998, preserving these marginal notes.

15 *Beit Ya'akov 'al ha-Torah* (Lublin, 1906). This collection of teachings is often referred to as *Beit Ya'akov ha-Kollel.* It was republished by R. Mordecai Joseph Lainer, together with another short work entitled *Sefer ha-Zemanim* on Shavuot (first published in 1976). It appeared most recently in a photocopy edition in Jerusalem 1997. For the sake of convenience, I will refer to that composite volume as *Beit Ya'akov* 4.

16 On the date of her death, see *Dor Yesharim* (1925), 85. On the second marriage, see *Dor Yesharim* (1925), 56.

17 See the introduction to *Mei ha-Shiloaḥ* 2. R. Ya'akov's daughters from this marriage were Ḥayya Sheindel (Tannenbaum) and Tobe (Epstein).

18 Introduction to *Beit Ya'akov* (1998), 21; (1996), 72. Compare *Dorot Rishonim* (1925), 28; *Zikaron la-Rishonim* (1997), 36–37. Additional works are listed in *Zikaron la-Rishonim.*

19 R. Ḥayyim Simḥah, on the basis of biographical data, sketches the course of controversy surrounding him from 1860, with the publication of *Mei ha-Shiloaḥ,* vol. 1, through the 1870s, his arrest in 1883, and his ongoing battle against the rabbinic community throughout his life. A second, less controversial aspect of R. Gershon Ḥanokh's activities was his extensive commentary on the Torah (two volumes, Brooklyn 1971, 1982) and the Festivals (Warsaw 1902–1908), both entitled *Sod Yesharim.* Like the commentaries of his father and grandfather, these volumes were not written by R. Gershon Ḥanokh himself; rather, they are based on his disciples' handwritten records of the teachings he delivered orally. (See title pages of *Sod Yesharim,* Brooklyn editions.) Shaul Magid devotes his book *Hasidism on the Margin: Reconciliation, Antinomianism and Messianism in Izbica-Radzin Hasidism* to R. Gershon Ḥanokh's ideology, with special attention to his important Introduction to *Beit Ya'akov.*

20 His first controversial work was *Sidrei Taharot* (Piotrokov, 1902), in which R. Gershon Ḥanokh gathered all the material from a wide range of Talmudic and midrashic sources applying to the mishnaic tractates *Kelim* and *'Ohalot* (for which there is no Talmudic commentary) and arranged it in the form of a traditional Talmudic tractate. Concerning his rediscovery of the *ḥilazon:* the means of identifying this species of snail had been lost centuries earlier, probably in the Gaonic period. After a long search, on the basis of rabbinic descriptions, R. Gershon Ḥanokh believed he had found the *ḥilazon* in an aquarium in Naples. He engineered the reproduction of the dye and

reinstituted the *petil tekhelet,* or blue thread prescribed in the Bible (Num. 15:38) among the Radzyn community. R. Gershon Ḥanokh wrote three works on the subject of the *tekhelet* as well as numerous responsa defending his views. For more on this subject in English, see Shaul Magid, "'A Thread of Blue': Rabbi Gershon Henoch Leiner of Radzyn and His Search for Continuity in Response to Modernity," 31–52. Another innovative aspect of R. Gershon Ḥanokh's thought is his attempt to reformulate the relationship between Maimonides and Kabbalah. Magid discusses this issue extensively in *Hasidism on the Margin.* See also Roland Goetschel, "*Sha'ar ha-Emunah we-Yesod ha-Hasidut* and Maimonides," *Daat* 64–66 (2009) xxvii-xxxv.

21 Published in Jerusalem, 1961. R. Mordecai Joseph Elazar is credited with reaching a peace with Kotsk in 1900, at a meeting in Marienbad with R. Israel Pilov, a grandson of R. Menaḥem Mendel. See Z. Glicksman, *Der Kotzker Rebbe* (Lodz, 1938), 48; Faierstein, *All Is in the Hands of Heaven* (1989), 19.

22 The Yiddish poet Itzhak Katzenelson wrote a monumental poem (some 1,200 lines) in memory of R. Samuel Solomon's valiant resistance to the Nazis. After the war, it was found buried in the ruins of the Warsaw ghetto, and published (in Hebrew translation by Menaḥem Zalman Volfovsky) as *"Ha-Shir 'al ha-Rebbi mi-Radzyn"* by *Beit Loḥamei ha-Ghetta'ot,* Ha-Kibbutz ha-Me'uḥad, 1972. A second account was written by Leyb Rochman, "The Golden Chain," *Radzyn Memorial Book* (Poland), a translation of *Sefer Radzyn,* edited by Itzhak Zigelman (Tel Aviv, 1957). Rochman writes that R. Samuel Solomon ordered his Hasidim to flee to the forests and to join the partisan resistance. Hearing that the Gestapo was looking for him, he left Radzyn and sought refuge in the ghetto of Wlodawa, near the Bug River dividing Poland from Russia. This is corroborated in a recent publication by Radzyn Hasidim, *Va-Yizraḥ ha-Shemesh u-Va ha-Shemesh* 2 (Bene-Berak, 2008).

23 A small community of Radzyn Hasidim existed in Tel Aviv before World War II. R. Yeruḥam, son of R. Abraham Joshua Heschel, migrated to the United States in the 1930s and founded the Radzyn community there.

24 R. Abraham Issakhar of Sosnowiec was a central figure in the management of the Radzyn yeshivah, called *Sod Yesharim,* founded by his brother-in-law, R. Samuel Solomon. After R. Samuel Solomon, the last rebbe of Izbica-Radzyn Hasidism, was murdered, he hid for more than two years in the forests of Poland and survived the Holocaust. His wife and daughter perished. As the war ended, R. Abraham Issakhar returned first to the destroyed community of Radzyn and then to Sosnowiec, in southern Poland, where his father, R. Isaiah Englard, had served as rebbe. He reestablished a rabbinic court (*beit-din*) there and took on the halakhic responsibility of restoring Jewish life for the survivors who passed through Sosnowiec. In 1948 he left Poland and resettled in the United States. See a recent Radzyn publication for additional biographical information: *Va-Yizraḥ ha-Shemesh u-Va ha-Shemesh,* vol. 2 (Bene-Berak, 2008).

25 *All Is In the Hands of Heaven,* 87. The two examples he offers as excellent illustrations are "Adam's sin and the Zimri episode." It should be noted, though, that R. Ya'akov's teachings on the latter are, for the most part, not extant. They were destroyed in the Holocaust along with the rest of his commentary on Numbers. The only extant teaching referring to the subject appears in the fourth volume of *Beit Ya'akov.* These passages are all quite abbreviated in comparison to those in the first three volumes. Taken alone, they cannot be held to represent any subject definitively. It thus seems un-circumspect to drawn such far-reaching conclusions on the basis of such meager evidence. The former example, "Adam's sin," is discussed in Chapter 4. My reading there suggests a different view.

26 "A Late Jewish Utopia of Religious Freedom," 245, n. 3. This essay, published 27 years after Weiss's death and translated from German is based on his earlier study in Hebrew: *"Torat ha-Determinism ha-Dati le-R. Joseph Mordecai Lerner [sic] mi-Izbica."* Regrettably, Weiss doesn't seem to have gotten far beyond the "endless quotations." He offers no evidence to prove his contentions. This, unfortunately, did not discourage subsequent scholars from citing them as authoritative.

27 *Hasidism on the Margin,* Introduction, xii.

28 "The Denial of Free Will in Hasidic Thought," 120.

29 Citing a personal conversation (in Hebrew) in January 2008. R. Elḥanan Goldhaber is a Radzyner Hasid and descendent of R. Ya'akov's daughter, Gittel Rayzel (Sochaczevski). He and R. Judah Joseph Spiegelman republished, edited, and annotated a number of Izbica-Radzyn works, including *Sifrei ha-Tekhelet; Mei ha-Shiloaḥ,* vols. 1 and 2; *Sha'ar ha-Emunah ve-Yesod ha-Hasidut = Hakdamah ... le-Beit Ya'akov;* and *Beit Ya'akov 'al Sefer Bereshit,* 2 vols. R. Elḥanan used the phrase "captured the headlines" in relation to R. Gershon Ḥanokh Henikh. He dismissed the prevalent scholarly view out of hand.

30 This method of transcription presents evident textual problems to the critical reader. Nonetheless, I've chosen (in awareness of the measure of naivety involved) to relate to the published teachings, with all their linguistic details, as an authoritative text representing R. Ya'akov's thought and intent.

31 These additions are marked in square brackets, to indicate they are not cited in the text of the *Beit Ya'akov* itself.

32 This library would include the writings of medieval thinkers such as Maimonides and Nahmanides, R. Judah Loew ben Bezalel, or Maharal of Prague; early kabbalistic tracts; the *Zohar* literature; works in the Lurianic mystical tradition; and classics of Hasidic thought.

33 In many instances, this translation is juxtaposed in a note with the JPS version.

34 This is mostly for personal reasons. My encounter with the spiritual world contained in the *Beit Ya'akov* has been in Hebrew. I've tried my best to translate into Western idiom the experiences and the understanding that fill its volumes, but have found it

emotionally difficult to refer to R. Ya'akov in anglicized form. My editors have kindly consented to bend Jewish Publication Society policy in this case.

35 *Beit Ya'akov* 2 (Lublin, 1904; Jerusalem, 1998), Hosafot, 504.

Chapter 1

1 *Beit Ya'akov* 2, *Bo*, 9. My translation of the verses from Isaiah reflects R. Ya'akov's reading. Long after the beginning of this chapter was written, I realized just how central this verse from Isaiah was in the thinking of R. Simḥah Bunem of Przysucha, a spiritual forebear of Izbica-Radzyn Hasidism. R. Pinḥas Menaḥem Elazar of Piltz recounts the following (*Siftei Tzaddik, Bereshit*): "R. Isaac Meir of Ger would say that every Jew has one verse that arouses that individual's heart in serving God. And thus the Holy Jew once asked R. Simḥah Bunem what that verse was for him. R. Simḥah Bunem replied, "Lift your eyes on high and behold: Who has created these things …." (Isa. 40:26). This anecdote is cited in two collections of teachings attributed to R. Simḥah Bunem: *Ḥedvat Simḥah* with the commentary *Simḥat Yehonatan, Bereshit,* 6, n. 3; *Kol Mevaser, He'azinu* 1.

2 *Beit Ya'akov* 2, Bo 9.

3 *Bereshit Rabba* 3.7; *Kohelet Rabba* 3.14.

4 *Etz Ḥayyim,* 1.4, 3.1, etc. For a discussion of these seminal concepts in Lurianic thought, see Mordecai Pachter, *"Iggulim ve-Yosher: Le-Toldote'a shel Idea (Mi-Kabbalat ha-Ari 'ad ha-Rav Kook)."*

5 Terms often used by R. Moses Cordovero (commentary on *Sefer Yetzirah,* chapters 1 and 2; *Pardes Rimmonim*) and in Lurianic teaching.

6 My understanding of these concepts, so central to this Hasidic worldview, is closely bound up with the thought of Emmanuel Levinas. Indeed, the kinship between the two systems is striking, although Levinas most likely had no intellectual contact with this school of Hasidism, and very little with Hasidic teaching in general. I have, nonetheless, adopted and adapted many of Levinas's terms and categories here. I hope that readers familiar with Levinas's writings will tolerate the shifts in the philosopher's meaning that may have taken place. And, equally, I hope those unfamiliar with Levinas's works will soon grow comfortable with categories and terms that may seem, at first glance, to be foreign or uncustomary to Hasidic discourse. I have found the combination of the two thinkers to be inspiring and very fruitful.

7 *Beit Ya'akov* 2, *Bo* 9, 93. Subsequent citations, until noted otherwise, refer to the continuation of this teaching.

8 R. Moses Ḥayyim Luzzatto, in his mystical work *Da'at Tevunot* (s. 40), sets this idea out in clear terms. He weighs the hypothetical possibility of Creation in a single divine utterance, a brilliant show of omnipotence. "Had God done so, He would have sealed the mouths of all His creatures.… It would have been absolutely impossible for

us to understand anything of His ways; His power wholly surpasses our limited minds. The Supreme Will, however, wanted human beings to comprehend something of His actions—even to strive ardently for a bit of understanding. And thus He chose to interact with the world 'on its terms' [*le-fi 'erekh ha-nivraim*] rather than on His."

9 The notions of *nukba* (the "feminine") and its nighttime reign will be considered in depth later in our discussion. R. Ya'akov does not develop them further in this particular teaching.

10 Maurice Blanchot, *The Space of Literature*, 167.

11 R. Ya'akov cites B. *Ḥagigah* 12b, where this reasoning appears: The celestial purity of the angels' song would make inaudible the feeble praises human beings can offer. And so God decreed to silence the angels during the day in honor of the Jewish people, so that their voices, too, may be heard.

12 This enigmatic phrase appears in an early kabbalistic work. R. Ya'akov cites *Sefer Kanah le-Ma'aseh Bereshit* 8. For a comprehensive discussion of this idea and its sources in mystical thought, see Moshe Hallamish, *"Le-Mekoro shel Pitgam be-Sifrut ha-Kabbalah: 'Kol ha-Nofe'aḥ—mi-Tokho Hu Nofe'aḥ.'"*

13 B. *Yevamot* 61a.

14 In Hebrew, הכל בשיתוף. Citing *Zohar* 1. 136b. See also *Batei Midrashot* 2, *Midrash temorat ha-shalem* 4 (94b).

15 *Beit Ya'akov* 2, *Bo* 9.

16 Rashi on Genesis 1:1. He quotes R. Isaac in *Yalkut Shimoni, Bo* 187.

17 *Zohar* 2. 186a. R. Ya'akov cites this passage a number of times in the teachings we will now discuss.

18 R. Ya'akov alludes to the complex of 12 verses that correspond, in Lurianic tradition, with the inner essence of each of the 12 months. Each verse is signaled in four words. The first letters or the last letters of these four words form one of the permutations of God's four-letter Name. The verse corresponding with Tishrei is ויראו אותה שרי פרעה "The princes of Pharaoh saw her" (Gen. 12:15). R. Ya'akov does not explore the significance of this particular verse, but I think the connection with his portrayal of Tishrei is quite clear. Avram and Sarai find themselves in Egypt, driven there by famine. The evil eyes of foreign princes fall upon Sarai, and she is stolen away and nearly violated. The blessed meaning of these fateful events and the "happy ending" come to light only much later. The verse corresponding with Nisan will be discussed presently.

19 R. Ya'akov cites *Zohar* 3. 86b with its play on the word *kilayim* (mixed seeds) as being inherently impeded from organic growth, based on the root כ.ל.א.—prison.

20 *Beit Ya'akov, Bo* 35. This notion of the letters' dimensionality does appear already in rabbinic thought. In B. *Shabbat* 104a, for instance, we find the comment that the letter *gimmel* turns mercifully to the *dalet*, anxious to ease its poverty (*gomel dalim*), while the *dalet* averts its face in shame.

21 These two perspectives, termed *me-tzido* (literally, "from His side") and *me-tzidenu* ("from our side") are widely used in basic kabbalistic works such as *Derekh Emunah* by R. Meir ibn Gabbay and *Shenei Luḥot ha-Brit* by R. Isaiah Horowitz.

22 *Beit Ya'akov* 2, *Bo* 34, 107. This telling phrase, *hen hen gevurotav*—"That, indeed, is His true might"—appears in B. *Yoma* 69b. It is the Rabbis' heroic response to the despair voiced by the prophets Jeremiah and Daniel at the sight of the Temple's destruction and the suffering of the Jewish people. How, the prophets protested, can we still speak of God's might (*gevurot*) when the forces of evil seem to have overpowered Him, ravaged His sanctuary, and enslaved His children? The Rabbis counter: God's silence, His willful noninvolvement, are indeed far greater acts of might—*hen hen gevurotav.* The suffering inflicted by human agents may, potentially, bring Jews to reassess, to repent. This paves the way for a greater good, for a reward that has been earned.

23 *Beit Ya'akov* 2, *Bo* 35, 108. "A day of isolation" alludes to Prov. 27:15, *yom sagrir* to Prov. 27:15.

24 Citing B. *Pesaḥim* 87b.

25 *Beit Ya'akov* 2, *Bo* 35.

26 Ibid. R. Ya'akov cites the Aramaic *targum* of Isaiah 1:6. The angels' joyous shouts "translate" into an actual exchange, a mutual giving.

27 Citing B. *Rosh Hashanah* 16b.

28 *Beit Ya'akov* 2, *Bo* 35, 108.

29 Citing *Zohar* 2. 37a, מנזרא לנזרא מכתרא לכתרא.

30 *Beit Ya'akov* 2, *Bo* 36, 110. As a sign of favor, notes R. Ya'akov, the *mishkan* was erected in Nisan. Here, as well, the image is of verticality: that Tabernacle is an opening, an avenue for all prayers to "rise," gathering together to ascend, to be drawn in to the Eternal One (*ḥei ha-'olamim*).

31 *Beit Ya'akov* 2, *Bo* 35. R. Ya'akov recalls this dispute without quoting it verbatim.

32 "The entire course of their existence is a unity" reads וכל השתלשלות הברואים הוא אחד.

33 The phrase R. Ya'akov uses to evoke this "painful experience" originates in B. *Bava Batra* 75a: literally, "each one is burned by his friend's *ḥuppah*"—כל אחד ואחד נכווה מחופתו של חברו. My translation tries to reflect the meaning of the metaphor the Rabbis use, of each Jew feeling "burned" by the aura of merit that seems to surround everyone but oneself. The irony is clear: in this conceivable future, envy, dissatisfaction, mourning over loss live on in the human heart.

34 R. Ya'akov refers here to the unusual possessive form of "your" hand in Exod. 13:16—rather than the normative final letter *khaf,* the Torah uses the grammatical "feminine" ending: the vowel *kamatz* and the letter *heh.* The Rabbis learn from this abnormality that the arm in question is the left, fainter, darker side, evoking the experience of vulnerability and uncontrol. Cf. B. *Menaḥot* 37a and Rashi there.

35 The statement alludes to the Rabbis' contention that God, too, binds tefillin, linking Him in similar bonds of affection with His chosen people.

36 *Beit Ya'akov* 2, *Bo* 35, 109. This teaching ends here.

37 B. *Shabbat* 77b. *Zohar* 1. 32a, and others.

38 *Zohar* 1. 83a.

39 In effect, the translucent crystals called "sapphire" may, as the commentators attest, be of various hues. The "work of sapphire stones," says Ibn Ezra, was a whiteness; Naḥmanides saw it as an "icy gleam" [כעין הקרח]; Ḥizkuni suggests it may be black. Rabbeinu Baḥya, in saying that the blue sapphire stone has healing powers, hints toward a mystical understanding of that "color of sea and sky" called *tekhelet*. More on this below.

40 *Beit Ya'akov* 2, *Mishpatim* 11, 288.

41 Cf. Rashi, Exod. 20:2, citing B. *Sotah* 12a.

42 Ḥizkuni cites this midrash in his commentary on Exod. 24:10. A similar version appears in *Pirkei de-Rabbi Eliezer*, s. 48.

43 *Beit Ya'akov* 2, *Mishpatim* 11, 289.

44 *Zohar* 3. 226b–227a (*Raya Mehemna*).

45 *Zohar* 1. 26b.

46 *Zohar* 1. 26b. See also *Tikkunei Zohar* 40, cited by R. Ya'akov in *Beit Ya'akov* 2, *Tetzave* 2, 359: "Their sin was in saying that these were two disparate kinds of water when, in truth, their source is one." Interpretations of this talmudic passage are numerous and complex. The brief synopsis here is meant to evoke some of the aspects relevant to R. Ya'akov's reading.

47 *Beit Ya'akov* 2, *Mishpatim* 11. Compare this passage from *Akeidat Yitzḥak* by R. Isaac Arama, *sha'ar* 3, which suggests a very similar schema. "'When you reach the place of stones of pure marble'—to the precious reality above the firmament, more pure than that called '*beneath* His feet, a paved work of sapphire stones.'"

48 *Yalkut Shimoni, Va-etḥannan*, s. 826.

49 *Beit Ya'akov* 2, *Yitro* 101. The notion that "exile" and "redemption" should be understood as existential as well as historical events is a basic tenet of Hasidic teaching. R. Jacob Joseph of Polonnoye, for examples, cites the Baal Shem Tov: "Just as the Egyptian exile and redemption were experienced by the Israelite nation as a whole, so is it experienced by every individual." *Toledot Ya'akov Yosef*, *Shemini* 88a. For more on this principle, see Chapter 2.

50 *Beit Ya'akov* 2, *Yitro* 103.

51 *Beit Ya'akov* 2, *Yitro* 101.

52 *Beit Ya'akov* 2, *Yitro* 98. R. Ya'akov alludes here to a famous innovation of Lurianic teaching, which we will discuss soon below.

53 Levinas, interestingly, also calls this "the feminine," although his context is somewhat different. See, for instance, *Time and the Other*, 85. This "event" and its meaning in Hasidic teaching are considered further in Chapters 3 and 4.

54 R. Gershon Ḥanokh Henikh refers to the midrashic teaching that the summary pronouncement, "These are the generations of the heaven and of the earth when they were

created [בהבראם]" (Gen. 2:4) alludes to the metahistorical role played by Abraham [אברהם]—in a transposition of the same letters. Cf. *Bereshit Rabba* 12.9.

55 *Sod Yesharim, Rosh Hashanah* 67.

56 See *Bereshit Rabba* 44.17–22.

57 Cf. Rainer Maria Rilke, *Duino Elegies*, 10.

58 The numerical value of *targum* and *tardemah* is equivalent: 650. We'll see the Lurianic teaching cited here in greater detail below.

59 *Beit Ya'akov* 1, *Lekh Lekha* 41. "Real life" seems to be R. Ya'akov's intent in the word *be-haketz*—in wakefulness, as opposed to *be-sheinah,* in a dream state or reverie. Throughout this passage, R. Ya'akov uses the expression *"le-hat'im lo"* [להטעים לו], with all its levels of connotation: literally "to taste," more figuratively "to sense," and in abstract terms, "to drive home the true meaning" or *ta 'am.*

60 *Beit Ya'akov* 1, *Lekh Lekha* 40. R. Ya'akov learns this from the verse "And behold, a smoking furnace and flaming torch *passed* between the pieces"—"It doesn't read 'pass' but 'passed' … in the past tense, for God showed him what will surely pass away, and what will ultimately be." A similar message appears in the midrash, based on other verses phrased in the past tense. See *Bereshit Rabba* 44. 22.

61 The recognizing James speaks of here is his own as author. See "Centers of Consciousness," Preface to *The Princess Casamassima* (Charles Scribner's Sons, 1908).

62 *Beit Ya'akov* 1, *Lekh Lekha* 21.

63 Franz Rosenzweig, *The Star of Redemption,* 398.

64 *Zohar* 1. 89a. The contention is based on the Hebrew word *maḥaze'* (Gen. 15:1) used in introducing the Covenant between the Pieces. The Sages of the *Zohar* consider *maḥaze'* to be an alternative form of vision, which they call *targum,* the primary form of "vision" being *mareh* (identified with the Holy Tongue). The nuance of inferiority that *maḥaze'* suggests stems from its place in the impure prophecy of the heathen prophet Bilaam (Num. 24:4). See discussion of this text from the *Zohar* below.

65 *Likkutei Torah, Lekh lekha,* d.h. *ve-tardemah.*

66 Benjamin, "The Task of the Translator," in *Illuminations,* 80.

67 Ibid., 73.

68 Ibid., 71.

69 Ibid., 74.

70 This practical statement is cited from B. *Berakhot* 45a. The Rabbis there speak of the practice current in synagogues during the Talmudic period. At the public reading of the weekly Torah portion, each verse was read from the scroll in Hebrew and reiterated by the appointed "translator" from the Aramaic rendering composed by Onkelos, know as the *Targum.* The "language of translation," in rabbinic terms, is thus Aramaic. See *Tosefot Berakhot* 8a and J. *Megillah* 4.1, fol. 74d.

71 Both the *Tosefists* (B. *Berakhot* 45a) and R. Isaac Alfasi (i.e., *Rif*) (B. *Megillah* 14b) find

it necessary to offer a less "simple" reading of the biblical verse to make the rabbinic statement more consistent with traditional theology. As the *Rif* puts it: "When it says 'he answered him' don't I know that means by a voice? But whose voice? It says 'a voice'—with the voice of Moses." אלא אמר ר׳ שמעון בן פזי מנין למתרגם שלא יגביה קולו יותר מן הקורא שנ׳ משה ידבר והאלקים יעננו בקול ממשמע שנאמר יעננו איני יודע שבקול מה תלמוד לומר בקול בקולו של משה.

In other words, as the *Rif* sees it, the speaker/reader (voicing the original message) must be God; the "answerer/translator" (human, secondary in status) cannot be but Moses. R. Mordecai Joseph resists this perceived need to shift the Rabbis' meaning. His comments seek, instead, to explain the profound necessity of understanding the words of the Talmud literally.

72 *Mei ha-Shiloaḥ* 1, *Yitro*, 79–80. Elsewhere, R. Mordecai Joseph adds another comment on the same point: "This is because the translator clarifies and interprets the words of the reader to make them understandable. Thus he should not raise his voice louder than the reader's. For he cannot make things more explicit than the text pronounced by the reader's own voice. Cf. *Mei ha-Shiloaḥ* 2, *Berakhot* 45, 183.

73 "Your humility ..."—וְעַנְוַתְךָ תַרְבֵּנִי. This prooftext (*Midrash Tehillim* 18.29) is cited in note *gimmel* in *Mei ha-Shiloaḥ* 1, 80; an unpublished manuscript (*gilion*) is noted as the source for the association.

74 The Aramaic word here is *patra* פטרא. The equivalent Hebrew idiom would be *pitḥon pe*, an aperture or "opening of the mouth." See commentary by R. Yehudah Halevi Ashlag, *Perush Ha-Sulam*, on *Zohar* 1. 89a. The play between sealed and opened, I think, needs no elaboration.

75 *Zohar* 1.89a. What the angels' attitude toward Aramaic actually is has been widely debated. See *Tosefot* and *Tosefot Ha-Rosh*, *Berakhot* 3a, d.h. "ve-onim"; *Tur*, *Oraḥ Ḥayyim*, par. 56; *Sefer Eliyahu Rabba*, *Oraḥ Ḥayyim*, par. 101. We will not distinguish here between "good" and "bad" angels. For our purposes, both share the same basic characteristics.

76 Deut. 6:6.

77 *Sefer Eliyahu Rabba*, *Oraḥ Ḥayyim* 101.9 brings this suggestion in the name of *Ma-'adenei Melekh*.

78 Cf. *Midrash Tehillim* 1, citing Zech. 3:7, where the angels are called "these standing ones." More on angelic anatomy below.

79 R. Judah Loew ben Bezalel of Prague (Maharal) presents this view forcefully. He cites the talmudic injunction (B. *Berakhot* 8b) to read the current Torah portion three times in the course of the week: twice in Hebrew and once in Aramaic—שנים מקרא ואחד תרגום. Maharal rejects the possibility that *targum* represents the lowest, most evident level of understanding (the "vernacular," the "language everyone knows"). Instead, he contends, the "translation" represents the *highest* level, that of the World to Come, while the two readings in the Holy Tongue symbolize the "lower world" and the "intermediary world."

For that reason, the famous injunction "Turn [the Torah] over and over, for everything is within it" (*Mishnah Avot* 5.22)—the endless task of interpretation—is phrased in Aramaic הפוך בה והפוך בה דכולה בה. See *Derekh Ḥayyim* 5.22 and *Tiferet Yisrael,* chapter 13. I would cautiously suggest that Maharal's reflections here might be directly relevant to R. Ya'akov's understanding. His writings were rediscovered in the "third generation" of Hasidism; publication of many volumes was initiated by R. Levi Isaac of Berditchev and R. Israel, the Maggid of Koznicez, with their approbations. Cf. Ze'ev Gries, "The Hasidic Managing Editor as an Agent of Culture," 149–150. R. Simḥah Bunem of Przysucha was a noted admirer of Maharal's works.

80 B. *Shabbat* 88b. The angels cite the biblical verses from Psalms 8, but out of order—8:5, then 8:2. Their eventual defeat by Moses is documented, as the Rabbis see it, in the conclusion of the Psalm itself: "O Lord, our Master, how majestic is Your Name in the [lower] world" (8:10).

81 This teaching is mentioned a number of times in the *Beit Ya'akov*, prefaced with the phrase "So said my saintly father, may his holy memory be for a blessing." Cf. *Beit Ya'akov* 2, *Yitro* 99, 100, 101, etc.

82 *Beit Ya'akov* 2, *Yitro* 100. Based on an exposition of Num. 14:17 in *Pesikta de-Rav Kahana* 25.1

83 It's unclear whether R. Ya'akov alludes here to a specific source or a general association. See R. Eliezer Azkiri's *Sefer Haredim,* chapter 3: שם אור זה יראה. A permutation of the letters that both words have in common אורה—יראה may well suggest the connection. But see discussion below.

84 Cf. *Beit Ya'akov.* 2, *Shemot* 9: "The Land of Egypt was a place of such impurity that the angels could not go there, as it says in the *Zohar* 1.117a."

85 Compare R. Zaddok Ha-Kohen of Lublin's comment on this point. "As it says in the *Mekhilta* (*Be-shallaḥ* 6), '[The children of Israel] were redeemed only by virtue of their faith.' Because faith in God plays a role only regarding what we do not know intellectually." *Divrei Sofrim, Likkutei 'Amarim* 5. We recall that Maimonides calls the angels *seḥalim nivdalim,* "pure intellects" (*Guide for the Perplexed* 1.49). Trials of faith are alien to their being.

86 *Beit Ya'akov* 2, *Yitro* 104. On the notion that the angels have no joints in their legs, see J. *Berakhot* 4a; *Yalkut Shimoni* 15.588; *Zohar* 2, 170a. Compare R. Ya'akov's portrayal of Jacob, discussed in Chapter 2.

87 Cf. *Bereshit Rabba* 50.2, Maharal, *Gur Arye,* Gen. 18:2.

88 *Beit Ya'akov* 2, *Shemot* 1, based on the verse in Ps. 92:3.

89 *Beit Ya'akov* 2, *Bo* 1: כי הוא היה אחוז בחושך קדמון. This is R. Ya'akov's description of Pharaoh's primeval strength.

90 *Beit Ya'akov* 2, *Shemot* 7. The verse cited is Exod. 3:13. We saw above (in the verses associated with the various months) another instance of this exegetical method of gleaning

meaning from the first or last letters of a series of words from a biblical verse. In general, *roshei teivot,* the first letters gathered together, proclaim some overt meaning. *Sofei teivot,* on the other hand, often suggest a less evident or subverted truth. (See *Sefer Peliah,* d.h. *u-re'e ve-haven be'avur hagezerah.*) This, in effect, is exactly R. Ya'akov's point here. See also *Beit Ya'akov* 2, *Shemot* 3, for another teaching on the subject.

91 See Exod. 6:3 and Rashi there.

92 *Beit Ya'akov* 2, *Shemot* 3, citing Isa. 6:3.

93 See *Bamidbar Rabba* 7.1. The provocative idea of "the exile of the *Shekhinah*" has been considered extensively by many scholars; its details lie beyond the scope of our discussion here.

94 The dissonance the Rabbis hear in the verse, of course, stems from the term "the children of Israel" which, historically, comes to mean the Israelite nation. More literally, and more relevant at this stage, it refers to the direct progeny of Jacob himself, otherwise known as *Yisrael Saba.* Compare *Bereshit Rabba* 73.2; 1 Chron. 29:10 and Rashi there.

95 *Zohar* 2, 2b.

96 *Beit Ya'akov, Shemot* 7–8. Two prooftexts seem to be in the background here. The first is evoked by Rashi, following the midrash, in his commentary on Exod. 1:1. The tribes and their descendents, like the stars, are brought out and in by name and number. The second appears in *Bereshit Rabba* 10, "Every single plant is able to sprout only grace of its angel/star that strikes it, urging, 'Grow!'" Cf. *Beit Ya'akov* 2, *Shemot* 2, where R. Ya'akov cites this source.

97 This is a basic tenet of the Hasidic reading of the Exodus story. See R. Jacob Joseph of Polonnoye, *Toledot Ya'akov Yosef, Metsora,* 95a. Compare *Beit Ya'akov* 2, *Yitro* 103.

98 *Beit Ya'akov* 2, *Shemot* 8. The conviction that blocks of the biblical text are "the Names of the Holy One, blessed be He" is frequently expressed in mystical teaching. For a classic explanation, see Naḥmanides, Introduction to his commentary on Genesis.

99 These meanings of all the names are made explicit as the sons of Jacob are born and named. (Gen. 29:32–30:24). (They come to the fore more clearly, of course, in their Hebrew form.) As we will see, their promise on the human level—between the mothers Leah or Rachel and their husband Jacob—come to speak of God's own relationship with the Jewish people.

100 *Beit Ya'akov* 2, *Shemot* 8.

101 *Shemot Rabba* 1.5. Three other heroic gestures are mentioned there as well.

102 This possibility is voiced by R. Ephraim Solomon ben Ḥayyim of Luntshitz (*Keli Yakar*) in his commentary on Exod. 1:1.

103 *Beit Ya'akov* 2, *Shemot* 5. I've translated the term *ha-adam* that R. Ya'akov uses with "me," an admittedly modern and less literal way of putting it, because he communicates this teaching as a direct and compelling address to his readers.

104 *Beit Ya'akov* 2, *Shemot* 6, citing *Bereshit Rabba* 78.4 on the verse from Gen. 32:30 and Judg. 13:18.

105 R. Ya‘akov reminds us that Egypt (*mitzrayim*), in Lurianic teaching, is symbolized by the narrow passageway of the throat (*metzarei ha-garon*). The throat, or neck, connects the "head," the mind or intellect, with the "heart," and its emotions and intuitions. When the throat constricts, head and heart are alienated from one another; the integrated self becomes a schism. This condition is at the root of existential "exile."

106 Cf. *Likkutei Torah, Shemot*, and *Beit Ya‘akov* 2, *Shemot* 21.

107 *Tanḥuma, Ki tissa* 12.

108 *Tanḥuma, Yitro* 17.

109 *Mekhilta, Mishpatim* 20. Cited by R. Ya‘akov in *Yitro* 90.

110 *Beit Ya‘akov* 2, *Yitro* 90.

111 *Mei ha-Shiloaḥ* 1, *Yitro*, 80.

112 Citing Rilke, *Duino Elegies*, 1.

113 *Beit Ya‘akov* 2, *Yitro* 90. Many interpretations of this "aspect of 'self and other'" [אני וה״ו] have been made. Cf. B. *Sukkah* 45a, and Rashi there. My translation follows the understanding voice by R. Eliezer Azikri, *Sefer Haredim*, chapter 66, with some overtones from Levinas. I have not found a source that links *ani ve-ho* specifically with the name *Anokhi* as R. Ya‘akov does.

114 *Beit Ya‘akov* 2, *Yitro* 89. He cites *Tikkunei Zohar* 19a—*kaf* alludes to the highest *sefirah* of *keter*, the "crown" and source of all emanated being.

115 Henri Bergson, *The Creative Mind*, 35.

116 B. *Makkot* 24b.

117 B. *Shabbat* 105a. A more literal translation would be "I Myself write and give." Indeed, this is the usual interpretation. Cf. *Dikdukei Sofrim*, B. *Shabbat* 105a. As we will see, though, Hasidic teaching prefers the less "neat" rendering, with its more profound existential message. We find a number of other encoded messages perceived in the same word. See *Tanḥuma, Yitro* 15; *Midrash ‘Aseret Hadibrot*, 1.94.3.

118 See, for instance, R. Barukh Halevi Epstein, *Torah Temimah* on Exod. 20:2, n. *gimmel*.

119 Levinas, "The Old and the New," 138.

120 Hannah Arendt, *The Human Condition*, 169.

121 Ibid., 170.

122 Siddur, *Birkot ha-shaḥar* ותרגילנו בתורתך.

123 *Beit Ya‘akov* 2, *Yitro* 92.

124 *Mei ha-Shiloaḥ* 1, 239 (on *B. Shabbat* 21b). There seems to be an unwritten, emotional association here between the shew-bread (literally, "the bread of the countenance") לחם הפנים and its place "before His face" לפניו תמיד (Exod. 25:30)—held, as it were, in God's reassuring gaze.

125 These loaves were held up before the pilgrims who came to Jerusalem, with the exclamation: "See the Lord's affection for his people! Those removed and those replacing them

are equally fresh." Each Sabbath the *Kohanim* replaced them with newly baked loaves, and the bread removed was eaten in purity. Cf. B. *Hagigah* 26b.

126 *Beit Ya'akov* 2, *Be-shallah* 103. Compare *Beit Ya'akov* 2, *Terumah* 2. See B. *Betza* 37a on the connection between the stage of becoming "ready" and impurity.

127 *Beit Ya'akov* 2, *Yitro* 90–92.

128 This form of address—ואתה—is reiterated three times in close succession: Exod. 27:20; 28:1; 28:3. R. Ya'akov devotes many teachings to the entities called "you," "and you," "I," "he," etc. Some of them are discussed in later chapters. As we will see, these pronouns signify fundamental concepts in kabbalistic thought as a whole.

129 *Shemot Rabba* 36.4. Compare *Tanḥuma, Tetsavveh* 2, and see *Mei ha-Shiloaḥ* 1, *Tetsavveh*, 88 d.h. *ve-ata*.

130 Cf. commentaries by R. Ephraim Solomon ben Ḥayyim of Luntshitz (*Keli Yakar*) and R. Ḥayyim ben Attar (*Or ha-Ḥayyim*) on Exod. 27:20.

131 See commentary by Rabbenu Baḥye (Exod. 28:20). He interprets the notion of *ner tamid* as a promise: while the Temple lies in ruins and the Jewish people in alienation, that illumination seems to be gone. But the *Shekhinah* will return and the Third Temple built. And then all will see that the lamp never ceased to burn, and that it will continue evermore. For a similar idea regarding the eternal role of the incense, see *Tanḥuma, Tetsavveh* 15.

132 In allusion to the verse "He appeared to me from afar" (Jer. 31:2) מרחוק ה׳ נראה לי.

133 *Beit Ya'akov* 2, *Tetsavvah* 5. The key phrase, "the connecting force" [*ketiru de-kula*] will be discussed below.

134 Cf. *Beit Ya'akov* 2, *Tetzave* 10, citing *Zohar* 1.134a.

135 Levinas describes this "inside" surface as the "reverse of the sleeves of a lady's gown" which supports "the essence of the thing ... where the threads are invisible.... In [the notion of facade] is constituted the beautiful, whose essence is indifference, cold splendor, and silence." *Totality and Infinity*, 192–193. R. Ya'akov speaks of this aesthetic aspect as well in *Beit Ya'akov* 2, *Tetsavveh* 4.

136 *B. Menaḥot* 43b.

137 *Beit Ya'akov* 2, *Tetsavveh* 5, 361. Cf. *Zohar* 3. 263a in which the words "And you shall see it/Him" (Num. 15:38) [וראיתם אותו] are understood as alluding to God Himself. Perhaps for that reason the Rabbis teach that the mitzvah of tzitzit counterbalances all the rest of the *mitzvot* together. Cf. B. *Shavuot* 29a.

138 *Beit Ya'akov* 2, *Tetsavvah* 5, 363. The event in question here occurs after the sin of the Golden Calf. Moses pleads for forgiveness on behalf of the Jewish people: "If I have truly gained Your favor, pray let me know Your ways." God's response: "you cannot see My face, for no one can see Me and live ... I will put you in a cleft of the rock and shield you with My hand until I have passed by. Then I will take My hand away and you will see My back" (Exod. 33:20–23). It is this verse that leads the Rabbis to teach that Moses merited seeing—not God's countenance and the tefillin themselves, but "His back"—the knot on the

"other side." Unlike our earlier discussion of tefillin and the essential symbolic differences between the arm-tefillin and head-tefillin, here R. Ya'akov draws his imagery exclusively from the head-tefillin. The reason will hopefully become clear in the following pages.

139 Cf. Maimonides, *Mishneh Torah, Hilkhot tefillin* 3. 2–11.

140 Cf. B. *Menaḥot* 34a–35b and Rashi there; Maimonides, *Mishneh Torah, Hilkhot tefillin* 3.1

141 This is in keeping with the overall understanding of "God's tefillin," said to contain the verse, "Who is like Your nation, Israel, unique in all the world (1 Chron. 17:21)." Cf. B. *Berakhot* 6a.

142 The motifs of "face" and "back" (*aḥorayim*) play a major role in Lurianic teaching. My comments are based on the understanding of these themes voiced by R. Moses Ḥayyim Luzzatto (Ramḥal). Cf. *Kelaḥ Pitḥei Ḥokhmah,* s. 27 and s. 76. R. Ya'akov's reading has echoes in the teachings of R. Zaddok Ha-Kohen of Lublin. See, for example, *Poked 'Akarim* 12a; *Yisrael Kedoshim* 52a; *Takkanat ha-Shavim* 80a.

143 Rilke, *Sonnets to Orpheus,* 2.23.

144 His formulation is: שאתן לך כוח ותקופות לסבול ואתן אותך במקום שלא יהי׳ לך שום תרעומת.

145 *Beit Ya'akov* 2, *Tetsavveh* 6. The central point of association, noted in many of R. Ya'akov's teachings on the subject, is the word *kesher,* denoting a knot or relationship—with its proximity, both homiletic and homonymic, with *ketor,* the root form of *ketoret* (incense).

146 Cf. R. Ya'akov's innovative comment (on a passage in Job 41 ostensibly describing the legendary leviathan): "'And his sneezes radiate light' עטישתיו תהל אור—one should never pause in serving God, but must encourage oneself continually to strive onward. And that service will merit one to see the right path illuminated before one...." *Beit Ya'akov* 2, *Tetzavveh* 6, 364.

147 Ibid.

148 Ibid.

149 *Beit Ya'akov* 2, *Tetsavveh* 7, 365. The images here allude to B. *Pesaḥim* 8a: "The righteous, before the *Shekhinah,* are like candles before a torch" and to the verse (Prov. 20:27) "The Lord's candle—a human soul."

150 *Zohar* 2. 179b. The verse cited is Neh. 9:6. The following lines condense statements made and elaborated throughout the series of teachings on the subject.

151 *Zohar* 3, 37a.

152 That formulation is voiced by God to describe, on the literal level, the role foreseen for Eve in relation to Adam. R. Ya'akov, of course, understands this relationship not in a social sense of gender differentiation, but in more abstract, psychological terms. His perception of the feminine will be considered in depth in Chapters 3 and 4. R. Mordecai Joseph comments along similar lines. See *Mei ha-Shiloaḥ* 1, *Bereshit,* 15.

153 *Beit Ya'akov* 2, *Tetsavveh* 4. The divine Name *Hashem Tzeva'ot,* translatable as "Lord of the Hosts," evoked here seems to indicate the concept of multiplicity, in the sense that "the hosts" speaks of created entities in the heavens and on earth.

154 Jan Patochka describes this attitude in *Body, Community, Language, World,* 58–69.

155 B. *Keritot* 6a; J. *Yoma* 4, 41d. The four ingredients named in the Torah were the major components; the other seven the Rabbis list were included in much smaller quantities and served to enhance the fragrance of the incense. Commentators differ on the identity of the various ingredients and the correspondence between those listed in the written and oral traditions. For a review of these, see, e.g., R. Jacob Tzvi Mecklenberg, *Ha-Ketav ve-ha-Kabbalah* on Exod. 30:34.

156 Cf. B. *Keritot* 6b, *Tanḥuma Tetsavveh* 14.

157 *Beit Ya'akov* 2, *Tetsavveh* 4. The use of the word *kelippah* doubtless alludes to kabbalistic connotations. R. Ya'akov touches on these in *Beit Ya'akov* 2, *Pekudei* 55, citing *Zohar* 2. 108b.

158 *Beit Ya'akov* 2, *Pekudei* 56. These themes are treated in depth in Chapter 2. On the "lower waters," also known as "feminine waters" or *mayyim nukbin,* see Chapter 3.

159 Against the accepted practice current already in the Amoritic period of concluding the *Shemonah Esrei* with three steps backward, and then bowing to the left and to the right. In this action, one "takes leave from the Master"; the appropriate gestures are prescribed in recognition of "God's right side" first of all. Cf. B. *Yoma* 53b and *Shulḥan 'Arukh, Oraḥ Ḥayyim* 123.1.

160 *Beit Ya'akov* 2, *Pikudei* 56.

161 After the promise voiced in Deut. 12:20, כי ירחיב ה׳ את גבולך.

162 *B. Ta'anit* 11b. The following lines are based on various commentators seeking its meaning. Cf. Rashi and Maharsha on B. *Ta'anit* 11b, and R. Meir Judah Leibush, *Ḥiddushei Malbim, 'Avodah zarah* 34a.

163 *Beit Ya'akov* 4, *Tetsavveh.* The allusion is to the "rays of majesty" (*karnei hod*) that emanated from Moses' face upon his descent from Mount Sinai (Exod. 34:29). See Chapter 2.

164 *Beit Ya'akov* 2, *Tetsavveh* 27. To come to terms with one's own incompleteness is a necessary stage, in R. Ya'akov's eyes, in the formation of a community: ultimately, an "emissary" is needed to unite their incompleteness. And thus the next injunction voiced is, "And you shall bring forth your brother Aaron"—for he, concludes R. Ya'akov, will be your delegate (*shaliaḥ tzibbur*). We saw another expression of this idea in the opening pages of this chapter.

165 Cf. R. Naphtali Tzvi Judah Berlin's commentary on Prov. 1:8; also see Chapter 3.

166 Levinas, *Time and the Other,* 77.

167 Cf. B. *Shabbat* 31a. In a hermeneutic tour de force, the Rabbis link the six sections, or "orders," of the Mishnah—that is, the rabbinic reconstruction of the Torah's message called "the Oral Teachings"—with the following prophetic vision (Isa. 33:6): "And He shall be the faith of your times, a wealth of salvation, wisdom, and knowledge; the fear of the Lord is His treasure." Resh Lakish said: "Faith" is the order of *Zera'im;* "times" is the order of *Mo'ed;* "wealth" is the order of *Nashim;* "salvation" is the order of *Nezikim;* "wisdom" is the order of *Kedoshim;* "knowledge" is the order of *Taharot.* In explanation:

Zera'im deals with agricultural laws (to sow one's hope into indifferent soil is a noble act of faith). *Mo'ed* concerns the festivals and other time-bound entities. *Nashim* sets out marital law; *Nezikim* treats issues of torts, wrongs, and injuries. *Kedoshim* deals with laws related to the sacrifices. *Taharot* centers on questions of ritual impurity and purification.

168 Levinas, *Time and the Other*, 79.

169 *Beit Ya'akov* 2, *Ki Tissa* 31, 418.

170 *Beit Ya'akov* 2, *Ki Tissa* 31, 418 משם הולכים כל ההולדות.

Chapter 2

1 *Beit Ya'akov* 2, *Mishpatim* 4, 272.

2 "Soul of my soul" is the expression in *Zohar* 1. 103b, *nishmatin de-nishmatin*. R. Ya'akov cites it in *Beit Ya'akov* 2, *Mishpatim* 4, 272.

3 Charles Taylor, *Sources of the Self: The Making of the Modern Identity*, 111.

4 Jan Patochka, *Body, Communication, Language, World*, 10.

5 Taylor, *Sources of the Self*, 182.

6 Ibid., 184; 368–369.

7 Alexander Altman examines some relevant topics in his pioneering essay, "The Delphic Maxim in Medieval Islam and Judaism," 1–40. He considers Homeric psychology, with its notion of psyche (cf. Taylor, *Sources of the Self*, 118) and the ways biblical verses speak of the soul; Platonic philosophy of the soul's elements, reason, and moral theory (ibid., 115–126) up against the Rabbis' world of thought; Augustinian inwardness, search for self-knowledge, the soul's finding God (ibid., 127–142) and the medieval Jewish ethical and kabbalistic thought systems, to name only a few.

8 A reference to the mystical *sod ha-katnut*, a notion developed in Lurianic thought to speak of a state of spiritual/emotional immaturity or limitation, in contrast to the possibility of "greatness" or *gadlut*, a temporary state of expanded vision and being. For an extensive treatment of these subjects in Lurianic Kabbalah, see Mordecai Pachter, "*Katnut ve-Gadlut be Kabbalat ha-Ari*," 171–210.

9 *Keter Shem Tov*, s. 25. The New JPS translation of the verse cited here is "Yet I will keep my countenance hidden"—reading the doubled form of the verb ס.ת.ר. as expressing an emphatic statement.

10 For example, *Toledot Ya'akov Yosef*, *Va-yak'hel*, s. 3.

11 For general comments on this text and author, see my Introduction. For more information, see Shaul Magid, *Hasidism on the Margin: Reconciliation, Antinomianism, and Messianism in Izbica/Radzin Hasidism*, esp. 3–39.

12 An allusion to Ezek. 46:1.

13 Cf. Deut. 30:12.

14 Introduction, 15 (1996), 53.

15 Taylor, *Sources of the Self,* 375.

16 Ibid., 376.

17 An important study on this subject is Rachel Elior's essay *"Temurot be-Maḥshavah ha-Datit be-Ḥasidut Polin—Bein 'yirah' ve-'ahavah' le-"omek' ve-'gavan'"* ("The Innovations of Polish Hasidism—From Love and Fear to Depth and Variety."

18 Much recent scholarship on Hasidism has been devoted to revising the widely held but mistaken belief that Hasidism was founded as a largely "popular" movement. See, most prominently, Moshe Rosman, *Founder of Hasidism: A Quest for the Historical Baal Shem Tov.* My point here is not to revert to outdated convictions, but to bring to the fore a different and important aspect of Hasidism as it evolved in the early 19th century. More extensive treatment of the period and the issues in question may be found in Glynn Dynner, *Men of Silk,* 3–53; Rosen, *The Quest for Authenticity,* 123–134; Faierstein (2005), 1–8.

19 R. Ḥayyim of Volozhin, disciple of the Vilna Gaon and an opponent to Hasidism, laments the neglect of traditional modes of learning in the Hasidic world. On his return from a journey through Eastern Europe in the first years of the 19th century, he wrote, "In many of their study halls there is not even a whole *shas* [the Babylonian Talmud]!" *Nefesh ha-Hayyim* 4.1. Mordecai Wilensky documents this situation in his work *Ḥasidim u-mitnagdim* (Jerusalem, 1990) as a major factor in the vociferous opposition to Hasidism voiced by Lituanian Jewry.

20 This move is documented in Hasidic sources as a painful break, fraught with ideological and personal conflict among the two Hasidic leaders and those loyal to each. See, e.g., *Tiferet ha-Yehudi* (Piotrkow, 1912), 26, s. 83. Tzvi Meir Rabinowitz discusses the issue in *R. Ya'akov Yitzhak mi-Przysucha, Ha-yehudi ha-kadosh* (1932; Tel Aviv 1960). See also Michael Rosen's extensive study, *The Quest for Authenticity.*

21 For a general discussion of these subjects, see Alan Brill, "Grandeur and Humility in the Writings of R. Simhah Bunim of Przysucha," 419–448. On the influence of Maharal on one Hasidic thinker, see Bezalel Safran, "Maharal and Early Hasidism."

22 The last phrase is an allusion to the rabbinic saying in B. *Megillah* 6b. These lines conclude a well-known tale extant in many versions and attributed to many authors. As Przysucha Hasidic tradition has it, R. Simḥah Bunem would tell this tale to each young man when he first arrived in Przysucha: A certain Reb Isaac of Cracow, a poor Jew, had a dream night after night that he must travel to Prague and there, underneath a bridge near the king's palace, he would find a buried treasure. Heeding the dream, he makes the long journey to Prague. But, ashamed to dig before the king's guards, he hesitates. Days pass, until at last one guard asks why he is there. With Reb Isaac's account of the dream, the guard laughs in scorn: "I, too, had a dream—that in the city of Cracow there's a Jew named Isaac, and if I'll dig under the oven in his house I, too, will find a treasure.... But what's a dream worth?" R. Isaac understands he came to Prague to hear those words. He returns to Cracow, digs, finds the treasure and with his new riches

builds a synagogue in gratitude to God. This version of the story originally appeared in *Ma'amarei Simḥah,* recorded by R. Israel Berger (Piotrkov, 1911), 49, s. 30.

23 *Kol Simḥah, Toledot* (Breslau, 1859), 32, s. 7.

24 Taylor, *Sources of the Self,* 375–376.

25 For a detailed discussion of the Przysucha school and its roots and branches, with an emphasis on R. Mordecai Joseph, see Morris Faierstein in "Personal Redemption in Hasidism," 214–224. See also Michael Rosen, *The Quest for Authenticity: The Thought of Reb Simhah Bunim.*

26 *Hakdamah,* 16; (1996), 57–58, quoting Isa. 8.6. According to the *Targum,* the waters of Siloam are a veiled reference to the House of David. R. Gershon Hanokh's statement here, of course, is highly subjective and could be disputed by nearly everyone outside the Izbica-Radzyn camp. For more on the politics involved, see below.

27 See my Introduction and discussion in the second part of this chapter.

28 Some reasons for this are considered in the Introduction.

29 As Emmanuel Levinas admits in his preface to *Totality and Infinity* in reference to the debt owed his own teacher and mentor, Franz Rosensweig and his *The Star of Redemption,* R. Ya'akov does in fact attribute central ideas to his father on numerous occasions. In many other instances, though, the same ideas and others are presented with no explicit attribution.

30 This opacity is due, in large part, to the textual history of *Mei ha-Shiloaḥ*: the teachings it contains—transmitted orally—were gathered by two of Mordecai Joseph's descendents from the writings and recollections of his students, redacted and reordered in the two volumes bearing that title. The first volume of *Mei ha-Shiloaḥ* was assembled and published by R. Gershon Ḥanokh in 1860, six years after his grandfather's death. The second volume, assembled by another grandson and namesake, R. Mordecai Joseph of Lublin (son of R. Ya'akov), from additional material, at times with variations on the earlier published passages, was published in Lublin in 1922.

31 Introduction *(Petiḥah),* 46, (1996), 157. (Emphasis added.)

32 *Beit Ya'akov* 1, *Bereshit* 7.

33 Following Rashi, of course, and consistent with rabbinic tradition. See Rashi on Genesis 1:1.

34 This idea is found in ancient mystical tradition. See, for example, *Sefer Peliah,* d.h. *meraḥefet.*

35 Allegorical interpretations of this nature have solid precedents in rabbinic and kabbalistic thought. Cf. *Tanḥuma, Pekudei* 3; R. Moses Cordovero, Commentary on *Sefer Yetzirah,* ch. 3; *Zohar* 1.24b.

36 After Deut. 8:17. In the biblical context, this verse warns against harboring the illusion that what we have gained is the fruit of our labors. In truth, all plenty and prosperity is God's gift: "Remember that it is the Lord your God who gives you the power to get

wealth" (Deut. 8:18). This phrase appears frequently in the teachings of R. Mordecai Joseph and his followers, including his grandson, R. Gershon Ḥanokh, R. Zaddok Ha-Kohen, and R. Ya'akov.

37 *Beit Ya'akov* 2, *Pekudei* 53. Citing the midrash *Vayikra Rabba* 1.6.

38 *Beit Ya'akov* 2, *Pekudei* 53. Apparently based on *Tanḥuma, Pikudei* 8. In another teaching, R. Ya'akov notes that the Temple later will share this intrinsic quality: "The Shekhinah will dwell in this house, and each person who comes here will be given what they seek from God." *Beit Ya'akov* 3, *Vayikra* 4.

39 *Ba-midbar Rabba* 12.9.

40 *Beit Ya'akov* 3, *Vayikra* 7. The allusion made in the phrase "moisten the world" (למרטב עלמא) is to B. *Succah* 53b. For more on this phrase, see Chapter 3.

41 These are the next lines in the teaching cited above, *Beit Ya'akov* 3, *Vayikra* 7. In effect, in only one of the three instances in question does the biblical text actually read "Moses, Moses!" (Exod. 3:4). However, the Rabbis (*Sifra, Vayikra* 1) extrapolate from that story that the same occurred at Sinai (Exod. 19:3) and in our case here (Lev. 1:1).

42 *Beit Ya'akov* 3, *Vayikra* 3.

43 *Beit Ya'akov* 3, *Vayikra* 5.

44 *Beit Ya'akov* 3, *Vayikra* 17, citing *Sifra, Vayikra* 1 and *Ba-midbar Rabba* 14.21.

45 R. Ya'akov's reflections in this passage from the *Sifra* appear in *Beit Ya'akov* 3, *Vayikra* 10 and 17. In *Beit Ya'akov* 3, *Vaykira* 5, R. Ya'akov cites the resolution the Rabbis reach: all three instances document a direct communication from God, *mi-pi hagevurah*. The explanation he offers is somewhat different.

46 *Beit Ya'akov* 2, *Shemot* 39.

47 *Beit Ya'akov* 2, *Yitro* 45. Compare the midrash *Mekhilta, Be-shallaḥ* 1 on the formulation "And He said, saying …": "R. Simeon bar Yoḥai taught: "This ['said'] refers to [the message of] the moment; that ['saying'] refers to [the message given to all] the generations."

48 R. Ya'akov cites this midrash in a number of teachings, sometimes in the name of his father, R. Mordecai Joseph, and othertimes without mention of him. Cf. *Beit Ya'akov* 2, *Pikudei* 56; 3, *Vayikra* 28. The source noted is usually *Mekhilta, Bo* or B. *Zevaḥim* 46a. I have been unable to find a rabbinic source with the formulation R. Ya'akov uses— משהוקם המשכן נפסלה המדבר מ/לדיבור.

49 *Beit Ya'akov* 2, *Bo* 1. The division of the world R. Ya'akov presents here (*ḥaruva-yishuv*) is based on *Zohar* 2. 157a. The citation of Jonah refers to *Tanḥuma, Vayikra* 8.

50 Ibid. The evaluation of "settled places" and the psychological state of self-collection termed *yishuv ha-da'at* that comes to the fore in these teachings is, I think, more complex and ambivalent than the reading Don Seeman offers in "Martyrdom, Emotion and the Work of Ritual in R. Mordecai Joseph Leiner's *Mei ha-Shiloaḥ*," 253–280.

51 This "gesture" adopts a classic Hasidic technique of interpretation that appears in teachings attributed to the Baal Shem Tov. On the basis of a concept formulated by

R. Abraham ibn Daud (Raavad) in his medieval commentary on the kabbalistic text *Sefer Yezirah*, R. Jacob Joseph of Polonnoye developed the idea of *'olam-shanah-nefesh* or עש״ן. The Hasidic version of the concept as R. Jacob Joseph presents it designates three dimensions in which people can grasp reality: the spatial (*'olam*, or "world"), the temporal (*shanah*, or "year"), and the spiritual (*nefesh*, or "soul"). The concept is applied often in Hasidic commentaries as a hermeneutical technique, particularly with the aim of clarifying the relevance of every verse of the Torah "in all places and times, for every Jew." Cf. R. Jacob Joseph's work, *Toledot Ya'akov Yosef, Lekh lekha* 4; *Terumah* 2.

52 *Beit Ya'akov* 3, *Vayikra* 27. In other teachings, R. Ya'akov identifies the corresponding temporal dimension with night and sleep, as we saw in Chapter 1. I've chosen to translate R. Ya'akov's term להתיצב נוכח השי״ת with the accepted English translation of Heidegger's *Dasein*—"being there." My intent is not, however, to include all of the philosopher's implications of the term.

53 T. S. Eliot, "The Wasteland," IV in *Collected Poems, 1909–1962* (London: Faber and Faber, 1980).

54 *Beit Ya'akov* 2, *Pikudei* 56.

55 Cf. *Zohar* 1.48a.

56 *Beit Ya'akov* 3, *Vayikra* 2. The reference here is to the famous vision seen by the prophet Ezekiel (Ezek. 1) of four winged creatures, each of them with four faces, glittering with the color of burnished copper, with human hands under their wings. The Rabbis (B. *Ḥagigah* 13a, etc.) refer to what is described in this vision as *ma'aseh merkavah*, "the account of the Chariot."

57 See, for example, *Beit Ya'akov* 3, *Vayikra* 1 and 2. The most straightforward way this can occur is by being consumed by a human being in an appropriate manner.

58 *Beit Ya'akov* 3, *Vayikra* 18.

59 *Beit Ya'akov* 3, *Vayikra* 18.

60 *Beit Ya'akov* 3, *Vayikra* 9.

61 *Beit Ya'akov* 3, *Vayikra* 14, citing the midrash *Vayikra Rabba* 1. In the preceding lines of the midrash, the same gesture of hesitation "stood off to the side" is attributed to Moses at the same three instances in which God "called" to Moses and one more—at the burning bush, the reed sea, Sinai, and here, at the tent of meeting.

62 *Beit Ya'akov* 3, *Vayikra* 12.

63 *Beit Ya'akov* 3, *Vayikra* 14. The terms he uses are פרט וכלל.

64 To adopt, with some limitations, the dialectic suggested by Hannah Arendt, *The Human Condition*, esp. 289–294.

65 *Beit Ya'akov* 3, *Vayikra* 14.

66 Although the verse reads "hand," the Rabbis taught (*Sifra* 4; B. *Bava Metzi'a* 86b) that both hands are to be used in *semikhah*, based on Lev. 16:21. From this context, Maimonides learns that confession must accompany *semikhah*. It is this action, in effect, that is

translated into the halakhic guidelines for repentance, or *teshuvah,* following the destruction of the Temple, when sacrifices cannot be offered. See *Mishneh Torah, Hilkhot teshuvah* 1.1–3.

67 *Beit Ya'akov* 3, *Vayikra* 36.

68 *Beit Ya'akov* 3, *Vayikra* 14.

69 *Beit Ya'akov* 3, *Vayikra* 36. The term in question is *she-lo mi-da'at.*

70 An indirect consideration of the issue does appear in the commentary by R. Ephraim Solomon ben Ḥayyim of Luntshitz (*Keli Yakar*) on Lev. 1:4.

71 *Beit Ya'akov* 3, *Vayikra* 14. The Talmud suggests that difficult historical or political circumstances impeded Rebbe from ordaining Samuel even though, in the master's eyes, his disciple Samuel was worthy. And yet external circumstances were apparently not the real cause. The Sages note that "Rebbe saw written in the Book of Adam [*sefer adam ha-rishon*] that Samuel was not destined to be ordained." Indeed, the many teachings and halakhic views of the figure named *Shmuel* are recorded in the Talmud without the honorary title "Rabbi." The historical chain of *semikhah,* beginning with Moses, was broken at some point during the time of the Second Temple. Attempts were made in various periods, amid controversy, to renew the full traditional form of rabbinic ordination, but they were ultimately not successful. The contemporary practice of rabbinic ordination thus has symbolic value, but lacks the absolute transfer of authority, stemming from Moses himself. See *Encyclopedia Judaica* 14, 1140–1147.

72 *Ba-midbar Rabba* 21.16.

73 In the following teaching, R. Ya'akov cites the midrash *Tanḥuma.* The Solomon Buber edition of the *Tanḥuma* reads somewhat differently than his citation of it. I've chosen to present R. Ya'akov's version of it here, because it contains some elements of interpretation relevant to our interests. Parallel midrashic sources are *Shemot Rabba* 47.6 and *Yalkut Shimoni, Shemot* 34.405–407.

74 *Beit Ya'akov* 2, *Ki Tissa* 69 in reference to *Tanḥuma, Ki Tissa.*

75 Levinas, *Totality and Infinity,* 77 and 79.

76 *Beit Ya'akov* 2, *Ki Tissa* 69.

77 *Beit Ya'akov* 2, *Ki Tissa* 70.

78 *Beit Ya'akov* 3, *Shemini* 6, citing B. *Ta'anit* 11b. And see Chapter 1.

79 *Beit Ya'akov* 3, *Shemini* 8. The convincing prooftext the midrash offers to bear witness to this typical loss of selfhood is the prophecy voiced by Samuel (1 Sam. 12:11), "And the Lord sent Jerubbaal and Bedan and Jephthah and Samuel …." Referring to himself in the third person, the prophet's words attest to a fundamental schism of subject and object.

80 *Vayikra Rabba* 22.61. This midrash is cited in the passage below.

81 See Rashi and Naḥmanides on Num. 27:12. The concept of *semikhah* holds an important place in the self-definition expressed by R. Ya'akov's grandson, R. Ḥayyim Simḥah, in his record of Izbica-Radzyn tradition. See *Dor Yesharim* (1925), 10–11.

82 The editor of this volume, R. Ya'akov's son R. Yeruḥam, adds that his brother (R. Gershon Ḥanokh Henikh) recorded this testimony on the manuscript along with the date (5638/1878). This, in fact, is the only teaching in the four published volumes of the *Beit Ya'akov* that is dated, and in which the circumstances surrounding the teaching are recorded. See also *Ḥiddush ha-Tekhelet* in *Sifrei ha-tekhelet,* 4 in reference to this event. Moving testimony of R. Ya'akov's awareness the previous autumn of his own impending death (the following summer) may be found in his grandson's memoirs. R. Ḥayyim Simḥah Leiner, *Dor Yesharim* (1925), 61.

83 *Beit Ya'akov* 4, *Va-yelekh,* 118.

84 Ibid., 118, citing *Zohar* 3. 284a. The teachings recorded in volume 4 of the *Beit Ya'akov* generally differ in style from those in volumes 1–3. They are much shorter and their language is more abstruse; translating them, as a result, demands a greater measure of interpretation and uncertainty remains. See also *Beit Ya'akov* 3, *Beḥukkotai* 102. For parallel sources on this *parashah* in Izbica-Radzyn tradition, see *Mei ha-Shiloaḥ* 1, *Va-yelekh,* 197–198; 2, *Vay-yelekh,* 129–130; *Sod Yesharim 'al ha-Torah* 2:390–391.

85 *Mei ha-Shiloaḥ* 2, *Va-yelekh,* 129 citing B. *Rosh Hashanah* 11a.

86 R. Gershon Ḥanokh Henikh, *Sod Yesharim, Simḥat Torah,* s. 18. The identification of the sun with Moses and the moon with Joshua, or with the Jewish people, is found already in rabbinic literature. See B. *Bava Batra* 75a. We might note that the *Zohar*'s reading (3.284a) of the verse is based on a radical rearrangement of the syntax of the verse. In the masoretic text, the word "rise" connects not with "You will lie with your fathers" but with the continuation of the verse, "… and this people will rise up and stray …." Cf. *Mekhilta de-Rabbi Yishm'ael, Beshallaḥ* 1 where this rereading is first proposed.

87 *Zohar* 3. 3a. Cited in *Beit Ya'akov* 3, *Vayikra* 16. A more literal and not gender-neutral translation of the verse would read: "I will value man [*adam*] more than rare gold and a person [*enosh*] more than the precious gold of Ophir." Although the verb appears in the first-person future tense, I've chosen to translate it in the third-person present to reflect R. Ya'akov's belief that, in effect, the verse speaks of an eternally present reality, and not a state to be realized only in the future.

88 *Beit Ya'akov* 3, *Vayikra* 16. The translation of these verses is my own.

89 Ibid. The issue of free choice will be treated extensively in the next section of this chapter.

90 These words, interpolated in T. S. Eliot's *Four Quartets,* Little Gidding V are from a 14th-century mystical work entitled "The Cloud of Unknowing." Cf. *The Norton Anthology of English Literature.* 2:2292, 4th ed., ed. M. H. Abrams (New York and London: W. W. Norton, 1979).

91 Taylor, *Sources of the Self,* 47.

92 Ibid., 50.

93 Ibid., 50–51.

94 *Beit Ya'akov* 1, *Va-yeshev* 17.

95 This parallel is based on the 49 permutations of the seven lower *sefirot* (*ḥesed, gevurah, tiferet, netzaḥ, hod, yesod, malkhut*) as they take form, for example, in the Counting of the Omer. In the first seven permutations, *ḥesed* is dominant; in the eighth, *ḥesed* is combined with *gevurah.* And thus the ninth permutation, *gevurah she-be-gevurah,* represents a distinct transition to another mode of being, in opposition to the mode of *ḥesed.* Comparisons between these 49 permutations and the portions of the Torah may be found in other parts of R. Ya'akov's commentary as well.

96 *Beit Ya'akov* 1, *Va-yeshev* 17. The rabbinic source of this idea is B. *Rosh Hashanah* 31a—"On the second day He divided what He had made and reigned over them all."

97 The concept of *yibbum* will be discussed below.

98 An allusion to the Lurianic concept of *pannim be-pannim.* The contrasting stance, represented by Judah, is "face to back" (*pannim be-aḥor*). We'll consider this symbolic stance in the course of this chapter.

99 *Beit Ya'akov* 1, *Va-yeshev* 16. Beginning in rabbinic literature, the term "tribes" refers both to the 12 sons of Jacob and to the 12 family groups descended from them. R. Ya'akov often uses this terminology; I've reflected it in my translations.

100 Perhaps not accidentally, this figure corresponds in many ways with the portrait of Decartes's "disengaged reason" that Charles Taylor presents. See *Sources of the Self,* 143–158. The citation appears on p. 157.

101 All these are also symbols traditionally associated with Joseph. Cf. B. *Yoma* 35b, etc.

102 *Beit Ya'akov* 1, *Va-yeshev* 1.

103 *Beit Ya'akov* 1, *Va-yeshev* 2, 306.

104 In *Mei ha-Shiloaḥ* 1, *Va-yeshev,* 49, R. Mordecai Joseph underlines the severity of his actions in the metaphysical realm: "It seemed to his brothers that Joseph sought to fracture the unity between the Holy One, blessed be He and *Knesset Yisrael*" represented by Jacob, on one hand, and the tribes on the other. See also *Mei ha-Shiloaḥ* 1, *Va-yeshev,* 38 and 45.

105 *Beit Ya'akov* 1, *Va-yeshev,* 10. The correspondence between "the covenant of the flesh" (*brit ha-ma'or*) and "the covenant of the tongue" (*brit ha-lashon*) is found in early kabbalistic texts such as *Sefer Peliah* and *Sefer Kanah,* and developed extensively in the *Zohar* and Lurianic thought. In *Bereshit Rabba* 84.7, the Rabbis suggest that Joseph sowed the seeds of contention in accusing his brothers of three specific sins. My portrait of Joseph in this chapter is incomplete; it does not present the full complexity and implications of all he symbolizes in Izbica-Radzyn teaching. One important aspect I have not discussed appears in R. Ya'akov's commentary on the *haftarah* of *parashat Va-yiggash,* the prophecy of Ezekiel, especially verses 37:17–20 concerning the reunion of the tribes in the future to come. Cf. *Beit Ya'akov* 1, *Va-yiggash* 35.

106 *Beit Ya'akov* 1, *Va-yeshev* 16, 326.

107 *Beit Ya'akov* 1, *Va-yeshev* 17, 327. On the importance of *yiḥus* in later Izbica-Radzyn tradition (and its connection to *semikhah*), see *Dor Yesharim* (1925), 10–11.

108 These verses are spoken by the prophet Malachi. They refer to the Jewish population around him living in the territory that belonged to the tribe of Judah. Malachi condemns their disloyalty to their nation in betraying their wives by taking heathen women. But the Rabbis transfer and in a sense trace the source of the prophet's accusations to the individual Judah whose name they bear as a collective.

109 On the geographical and emotional valences attached to Adullam, see below.

110 *Bereshit Rabbah* 85.1.

111 The most important and reliable collections of R. Simḥah Bunem's teachings are *Kol Simḥah,* first recorded by R. Simḥah Bunem's disciple, R. Alexander Zusha of Plozk (Breslau, 1859); and *Ramatayim Tzofim* by R. Samuel of Sieniawa (Shinav) (Warsaw, 1882). For a modern biography, see Michael Rosen, *The Quest for Authenticity: The Thought of Reb Simhah Bunim.*

112 One account attributes it to messianic expectations. Cf. R. Pinḥas Zelig Glicksman, *Tiferet Adam,* 12–17. Faierstein offers an extensive treatment of this controversial subject in *All Is in the Hands of Heaven* (1989), 89–98. Elior suggests that in addition to personal and ideological differences, R. Mordecai Joseph's intense interest in learning and teaching Kabbalah stood in sharp contrast to R. Menaḥem Mendel's distancing himself from mystical literature and concentration on *halakhah.* Cf. *Temurot* 404, and on the event in general, 407–409. The Izbica-Radzyn camp, unlike followers from Kotsk and Ger, is reticent on this issue. The second edition of the family history written by R. Mordecai Joseph's great-grandson, R. Ḥayyim Simḥah, *Dor Yesharim* (1925), does not speak of a "break" between R. Mordecai Joseph and R. Menaḥem Mendel. The first edition (1909), 17–18 describes their parting as amiable. S. Z. Shragai combines primary sources (largely without direct citation), speculations, and memories in his account in *Benetivei Hasidut Izbica-Radzyn.* Its historical authenticity, though, is questionable.

113 The last phrase is the rabbinic expression דוק ותשכח ותבין. *Ramatayim Tzofim, Eliyahu Rabba* (2003) 5, s. 56*, 76. The marginal note in which this text appears is prefaced with the phrase, "The editor notes … " *Ramatayim Tzofim,* originally written by R. Samuel of Sieniawa (Shinav), a disciple of R. Simḥah Bunem, was republished and annotated by R. Aaron Walden (a follower of R. Menaḥem Mendel and R. Isaac Meir of Ger) in 1903. It was published in a new edition most recently in Jerusalem, 2003. A similar version of the teaching appears in *Kol Simḥah, Va-yeshev.*

114 *Ramatayim Tzofim, Eliyahu Rabba* (2003) 5, s. 56, 75–76. The Rabbis state that Judah's status as "king over them" was recognized by his brothers before Joseph was sold. Cf. *Bereshit Rabba* 64.17.

115 Jerome Gellman states this (without mentioning a primary source) in *The Fear, the Trembling, and the Fire: Kierkegaard and Hasidic Masters on the Binding of Isaac,* xvi. Accounts (often imaginative and literary) of R. Menaḥem Mendel's life and times abound. The most extensive in English is Abraham Joshua Heschel, *A Passion for Truth.* For a brief summary

of what Kotsk represents, see Arthur Green, *The Language of Truth,* xx–xxv. Two important primary Hasidic sources are A. Walden, *Shem Ha-gedolim ha-ḥadash,* under the heading "R. Menaḥem Mendel"; and R. Abraham Issakhar Benjamin Alter, *Me'ir 'Eynei ha-Golah.*

116 The historical authenticity of the thousands of anecdotes and witticisms attributed to "the Kotsker" is dubious, and so they contribute little to reconstructing the worldview of this enigmatic figure. On this problem, see Ya'akov Levinger's research in Hebrew: "*'Imrot Authentiot she ha-Rebbi mi-Kotsk*" ("Authentic Sayings of R. Menaḥem Mendel of Kotsk,") 109–135; and *"Torato she ha-Rebbi mi-Kotsk le-Or ha-'Imrot ha-Meyuḥasot Lo 'al yedei Nekhdo R. Shmuel mi-Sochaczow"* "The Teachings of the Kotsker Rebbe according to His Grandson R. Samuel Bornstein of Sochaczow," 413–431.

117 R. Samuel's mother was R. Menaḥem Mendel's daughter. His father, R. Abraham of Sochaczow, a noted Torah scholar, is famed for his responsa *Avnei Nezer* and *Eglei Tal.* R. Abraham was one of the privileged few who maintained personal contact with R. Menaḥem Mendel during his seclusion. He became the Rebbe's son-in-law some seven years before his passing. R. Samuel was only four years old when his grandfather died in 1858, and thus the teachings he records in the name of R. Menaḥem Mendel were most likely reformulated for him by his father, R. Abraham. Levinger, cited above, discusses this issue.

118 *Ramatayim Tzofim, Eliyahu Rabba* (2003) 5, s. 56, 76. The editor of this edition, R. Aaron Walden, inserts his own reservations in this note: "Even the greatest of men have wearied themselves in the struggle to fathom the mysteries of his words.... But here is a brief summary of his holy message."

119 *Shem mi-Shmuel, Va-yeshev* 5672, 73–74.

120 The portrait sketched here draws on Taylor's evaluation of Plato's moral doctrine. See *Sources of the Self,* 115–126.

121 See Rabinovitz, *Bein Przysucha le-Lublin,* 463–513; Green, xx–xxiv; Rosen, 260–274.

122 Rachel Elior identifies certain passages in *Mei ha-Shiloaḥ* as covert references to the ideological and personal tension between R. Mordecai Joseph and R. Menaḥem Mendel of Kotsk. See *"Temurot,"* 402–427.

123 Introduction, 16; (1996), 68.

124 This concludes the first part of the Introduction (*Hakdamah*) 22; (1996), 74. His references are to R. Solomon Luria, a distinguished 16th-century Talmudist; R. Moses Isserles (16th century); R. Solomon Yitzhaki, the classic Torah commentator (11th century); and two illustrious rabbinic figures of the 1st century, known for their lineage from the House of David. In effect, a number of hasidic dynasties trace a similar genealogy back to King David, most notably *Ḥabad.*

125 These messianic overtones are particularly audible in the lines of his Introduction (22) immediately following the citation above. On R. Gershon Ḥanokh's political and religious

activism see Shaul Magid, "'A Thread of Blue': Rabbi Gershon Henoch Leiner of Radzyn and his Search for Continuity in Response to Modernity," 31–52. See also Magid's discussion of the subject in *Hasidism on the Margin.*

126 *Mei ha-Shiloaḥ* 1, *Va-yeshev,* 49. Although R. Simḥah Bunem's name is not mentioned here, his teaching is clearly the basis for these comments. Note 14 in the 1995 edition of *Mei ha-Shiloaḥ* refers the reader to *Kol Simḥah, Va-yeshev.* I've reordered the first three clauses of this teaching to make the causality involved here more readable. In effect, the biblical text suggests (with the plural form of the verb) that the brothers together brought the tunic to Jacob. But the midrash (*Bereshit Rabba* 85) says the act fell by lot to Judah alone.

127 *Beit Ya'akov* 1, *Va-yeshev* 16, 326.

128 *Beit Ya'akov* 1, *Va-yeshev* 39. This interpretation of "Adullam" appears in many of his teachings. R. Ya'akov rephrases the midrash cited above, *Bereshit Rabba* 85.1.

129 *Beit Ya'akov* 1, *Va-yeshev* 39, in reference to *Zohar* 3.191a and *Zohar Hadash, Shir ha-Shirim* 69d. R. Ya'akov reminds us of the symbolic connection between the tribe of Judah and the moon, originating in the *Zohar.* See *Beit Ya'akov* 2, *Va-yeshev* 40. We'll discuss this moon imagery more extensively below and in Chapter 3.

130 *Beit Ya'akov* 1, *Va-yeshev* 39, citing *Bereshit Rabba* 85.9. The notion R. Ya'akov suggests of *yibbum* as "crookedness" comes from *Tikkunei Zohar* 21, fol. 60b; the matter of *kilayim* is found in *Zohar* 3.86b. Torah law forbids marriage between a father and daughter-in-law in Lev. 20:12.

131 *Beit Ya'akov* 1, *Va-yeshev* 39. Cf. *Mei ha-Shiloaḥ* 1, *Va-yeshev,* 51. In *Va-yeshev* 7, R. Ya'akov cites a passage from the *Zohar* 2.103b, noting that the family tree from which King David eventually emerged branched through figures (Perez, Boaz, Oved), all of whose actions or circumstances seemed, at first sight, less than honorable.

132 *Beit Ya'akov* 1, *Va-yeshev* 7. The reference is to Tamar, who concealed her identity as she waited for Judah at the crossroads (Gen. 38:15).

133 *Beit Ya'akov* 1, *Va-yeshev* 13. R. Ya'akov notes that the link between the four-letter Name and the "lineage of Israel" comes to the fore in *Kiddushin* 71a. He points out that, in effect, the Name does appear once more during that period, in Gen. 49:18, but it is Jacob who utters it in a moment of horror, foreseeing that, in generations to come, the lineage of Israel will nearly be blotted out. This period of hiddenness comes to an end in the opening verses of the book of Exodus (*Shemot*). The Torah recalls the names (*shemot*) of the tribes and this, in R. Ya'akov's reading, signals the beginning of the redemption. For more on names, self-awareness, and redemption see Chapter 1.

134 Ibid. Naḥmanides (Gen. 46:2) suggests the soul identity between Er and Onan / Perez and Zeraḥ. The idea is developed in Lurianic teaching. Cf. *Likkutei Torah, Va-yeshev.*

135 *Beit Ya'akov* 1, *Va-yeshev* 18, citing B. *Ta'anit* 29b. See also *Beit Ya'akov* 1, *Mikkets* 39.

136 B. *Sotah* 10b. ממני יצאו כבושים. My translation follows Rashi's explanation. For an extensive consideration of this subject, see Uziel Fuchs, *"Mi-meni Yatzu Kevushim—'Al Ma'amar Talmudi she-Huga,"* 521–531.

137 It is cited a number of times. See, for example, *Mei ha-Shiloaḥ* 1, 51; *Beit Ya'akov* 1, *Va-yeshev* 13, 18, 39; *Va-yiggash* 22, and others.

138 *Mei ha-Shiloaḥ* 1, *Va-yeshev*, 51.

139 B. *Sanhedrin* 107a–b. The *Zohar* embellishes that theme. The phrase that appears in the *Zohar* is actually *badiḥa de-malka* but it is cited consistently in Izbica-Radzyn teaching as *badḥana*.

140 *Beit Ya'akov* 1, *Va-yeshev* 16. The expression he cites from *Mei ha-Shiloaḥ* 1, *Va-yeshev*, 47 is: למי נאה ליצדק אני או אתה. I've been unable to trace a source for it.

141 *Mei ha-Shiloaḥ* 1, *Va-yeshev*, 48, citing the Rabbis' exposition of Psalm 119:126 in B. *Berachot* 63a, with allusion to Rashi's comment there. This verse is usually translated (e.g., JPS) as stating something rather opposite: "It is a time to act for the Lord, for they [an inimical force] have violated Your teaching."

142 *Beit Ya'akov* 1, *Va-yeshev* 39. The transformation of sin to merit follows the conception voiced by Resh Lakish in B. *Yoma* 86b.

143 Compare Shaul Magid's view on the subject: "What I mean to say is that ... the masters of the Izbica and Radzyn traditions and other masters in mid- to late-19th century Polish Hasidism more generally, are heretics ... they created the religious critique inside tradition, sufficient for those who followed them to read (or misread) them and implement that critique in a more overt fashion." *Hasidism on the Margin*, 253. The term "pious heresy" is used by Allan Nadler in his review of Magid's book in *The Jewish Quarterly Review*, 282.

144 *Beit Ya'akov* 1, *Va-yeshev* 10, in allusion to Joshua 6:20 and the collapse of the walls of Jericho. This idea appears in *Mei ha-Shiloaḥ* 2, *Va-yeshev* 29. The connection between *tza'akah* and the effort to repent is central in rabbinic thought. Cf. B. *Shabbat* 16a, 17a.

145 *Beit Ya'akov* 1, *Mikkets* 39. R. Ya'akov points out that this offer could be considered "criminal" (*'avon pelili*)—for how could Judah promise something beyond his control? His certainty, R. Ya'akov concludes, could only stem from Above, and that is the reason Jacob knows that "God was speaking through him." This idea appears in *Beit Ya'akov* 1, *Va-yiggash* 1, 3, and 13. Maimonides recognizes Judah as "the heart of Israel" in *Mishneh Torah, Hilkhot melakhim* 3.

146 *Beit Ya'akov* 1, *Mikkets* 39. The expression R. Ya'akov uses for "he was sorely angry" is הרעים נפשו מאוד. The "failure" Judah refers to seems to be Jacob's feeling that God was indifferent to his suffering.

147 R. Ya'akov cites *Tanḥuma, Va-yiggash* 4: "Judah had been given the sign that if one of his sons would die in his lifetime, Gehinnom would open before him." In that midrash the Rabbis also learn that Judah pledges "his life in this world and in the world to

come." As R. Ya'akov explains in other teachings (based on *Tur, Oraḥ Ḥayyim* 417), each of the 12 tribes symbolizes a different, essential aspect of reality. Like the 12 hours of the day and night, the 12 signs of the zodiac and months of the year, they form a cosmic unity. Harm to any one of them would destroy the crucial balance on which the world's continued existence depends. Cf. *Beit Ya'akov* 1, *Va-yeshev* 3, 8, 12, etc.

148 *Bereshit Rabba*, 93.3. The simplest explanation, as another midrashic passage states, is that his stance was multivalent. Were these words of combat or pacification, expressing anger or love? Cf. *Bereshit Rabba*, 93.6–7.

149 The reference to these events as a plot (*'alilah*) appears in *Beit Ya'akov* 1, *Va-yiggash* 16. This idea is suggested in midrash *Tanḥuma, Va-yeshev* 4. The notion of a divine plot in connection to sin is found in rabbinic thought, foremost regarding the first sin in the Garden of Eden (based on Ps. 66:5). See, for example, *Batei midrashot* 1, *Midrash yelamdeinu, Bereshit* 10. The following allegorical reading involving the soul's descent into the world is common in the *Zohar* literature. See Tishby, *The Wisdom of the Zohar*, 2: 749–754.

150 *Beit Ya'akov* 1, *Va-yiggash* 15.

151 *Beit Ya'akov* 1 *Va-yiggash* 12, 15, 16. These three teachings set out, in various formulations, the double reading suggested above. In the passages above, I've taken the liberty to reorganize their contents and combine elements from all three to express the ideas in them as cogently as possible.

152 *Beit Ya'akov* 1, *Va-yiggash* 10.

153 *Beit Ya'akov* 1, *Va-yiggash* 3, 10 and 12. Compare *Mei ha-Shiloḥ* 1, *Ḥukkat*, 158–9. For more on this point, see the end of Chapter 4.

154 *Beit Ya'akov* 1, *Va-yiggash* 11. This is R. Ya'akov's formulation: שנשתנה פרוש הד"ת [דברי תורה] מכפי שהיו מתפרשין קודם תשובתו.

155 Weiss, "Utopia," 218, 222.

156 Ibid., 237. Rachel Elior echoes or summarizes this judgment: "Further, since the omnipotent divine will is concealed within the illusions of reality, all human deed is inconsequential." *The Oxford Dictionary of the Jewish Religion*, "Izbica," 363.

157 *Beit Ya'akov* 1, *Va-yiggash* 11.

158 Schatz, "Autonomia," 554–558.

159 *Beit Ya'akov* 1, *Va-yiggash* 10. The expression "to miss the mark/target" parallels the Hebrew להחטיא את המטרה. "To miss" shares the same root as "to sin."

160 *Beit Ya'akov* 1, *Va-yiggash* 12 and 31. The rabbinic source is B. *Shabbat* 31b.

161 *Beit Ya'akov* 1, *Va-yeshev* 16, *Va-yiggash* 29.

162 *Beit Ya'akov* 1, *Va-yiggash* 29, in reference to the famous parable of the maiden without eyes in *Zohar* 2.94b–95a, 99a. For a general discussion and review of the literature on this image in the *Zohar* see Daniel Abrams, "Knowing the Maiden without Eyes." However, R. Ya'akov's allusion to this image means something quite different from all the readings Abrams reviews. R. Ya'akov quotes the verse, "Who is blind if not My

servant ... ?" (Isa. 42:19). The "blind devotion" evoked here is closely linked to the notion of the "concealed world" that no human gaze can penetrate. Judah, then, represents the most profound awareness of this inherent state of "eyeless-ness." More on this below and in Chapter 3.

163 *Beit Ya'akov* 1, *Va-yiggash* 11.

164 Both these phrases originate in the *Zohar.* Both are feminine images—the moon (*levanah*) "has no light of her own," illuminated as "she" is by the sun.

165 *Mei ha-Shiloaḥ* 1, *Va-yeshev,* 48.

166 *Beit Ya'akov* 1, *Va-yeshev* 3. The terms are borrowed from Lurianic thought and widely integrated in Hasidic teaching. Compare their use in the first pages of this chapter.

167 *Beit Ya'akov* 1, *Va-yiggash* 13. Similar motifs appear in *Va-yiggash* 7.

168 *Zohar* 1, 205b.

169 *Beit Ya'akov* 1, *Va-yiggash* 13.

170 *Beit Ya'akov* 1, *Va-yiggash* 12.

171 Taylor, *Sources of the Self,* 383.

172 Ibid., 390.

173 Ibid., 449–451. In his note 71 (583), Taylor attributes "a great deal in [his] description of Kierkegaard" to Jane Rubin's discussion in *Too Much of Nothing: Modern Culture and Self in Kierkegaard's Thought* (publication information is not cited).

174 Taylor, *Sources of the Self,* 455. An extensive study on the relation between Kierkegaardian existentialism and R. Mordecai Joseph Leiner of Izbica's thought can be found in Jerome Gellman's book, *The Fear, the Trembling, and the Fire.* His discussion focuses on the Binding of Isaac and considers other Hasidic masters and thinkers as well. Heschel compares Kierkegaard and R. Menaḥem Mendel's thought in *A Passion for Truth.*

175 Compare Don Seeman's suggestion of a similar kinship between R. Menachem Mendel and R. Mordecai Joseph on the issue of *yishuv ha-da'at* in "Martyrdom," 276.

176 *Beit Ya'akov* 1, *Va-yeḥi,* 64. Literally, the statement in the *Zohar* (2.94a) reads: "Judah is the first father and the second father ..."—יהודה אבא קמאה ואבא תניינא ולא הוה ביה חלופא לעלמין. The phrase I translated as "pulled back the curtain" could be put in a different metaphor as "pierced the barrier" [בקע את המסך]. However, the central role of disguises and play-acting in this scene suggests that a revelation of what is going on "backstage" is equally relevant (the word *masakh* having both meanings of curtain and barrier).

177 *Beit Ya'akov* 1, *Va-yeḥi* 66.

178 *Beit Ya'akov* 1, *Va-yeshev* 10.

179 *Beit Ya'akov* 1, *Va-yetse'* 63 (in the standard edition, this teaching is misnumbered 43). The concept of revealed and concealed worlds in connection with Rachel and Leah originates in Lurianic teaching, as R. Ya'akov indirectly notes in this passage. Cf. *Etz Ḥayyim, Sha'ar* 23, chap. 4.

180 *Beit Ya'akov* 1, *Va-yetse'* 66.

181 *Beit Ya'akov* 1, *Va-yeshev* 12. והיה לבו נוקפו מה זה ועל מה זה.

182 *Beit Ya'akov* 1, *Va-yetse'* 66.

183 *Mei ha-Shiloaḥ* 1, *Va-yetse'*, 42.

184 R. Mordecai Joseph suggests this in his observation in that teaching of the differences in the Torah cantillation of the words "and she bore …" regarding Leah's first three sons, on one hand, and Judah, on the other. *Mei ha-Shiloaḥ* 1, *Va-yetse'*, 42.

185 *Beit Ya'akov* 1, *Va-yetse'* 65. The cognate of the letter called *dalet* is *dalut*, or poverty. Cf. B. *Shabbat* 104a.

186 *Mei ha-Shiloaḥ* 1, *Va-yetse'*, 40. A source for this idea may be R. Menaḥem Naḥum of Chernobyl, *Meor Einayim, Likkutim* (Jerusalem, 1999), 294.

187 *Beit Ya'akov* 1, *Va-yetse'* 63. My translation of this important verse attempts to follow the intent implicit each time it is used. For more on this aspect of relationship, see Chapter 4.

188 *Beit Ya'akov* 1, *Va-yetze'* 63. Without vocalization, this word holds both readings: *im* (if) and *em* (mother). The connection between motherhood and contingency—"if …"—is discussed in Chapters 3 and 4.

189 *Beit Ya'akov* 1, *Va-yetze'* 63.

190 *Beit Ya'akov* 1, *Va-yiggash* 13.

191 *Beit Ya'akov* 2, *Shemot* 39. This allusive and opaque teaching reads in Hebrew: וזה כי אהיה עמך... ובמה שהאדם נולד בו אינו נוגע שום פגם וזה עומד לעולם וכמ״ש (שמואל א׳ ב׳) ומעיל קטן תעשה לו אמו. וכתיב (שם כ״ח) איש זקן עולה והוא עוטה מעיל ואיתא במדרש (תנחומא אמור) תנא הוא המעיל אשר בו גדל בו נקבר בו עלה ... והיינו שזאת נתעורר תחילה בתחית המתים. ומה שמצד אדם נתעורר אח״כ. שהבירור שיש לו מצד לידת אמו אינו נתבטל היינו שמה שהוא מצד השי״ת אינו נתבטל וזה כי אהיה עמך.

Chapter 3

1 *Beit Ya'akov* 1, *Bereshit* 41.

2 Jan Patochka's thought has contributed much to these paragraphs. See his work, *Body, Community, Language, World*.

3 In the passage below, I've interpolated R. Mordecai Joseph's comments with R. Ya'akov's. The five stages and explanations of them in terms of human development are set out by R. Mordecai Joseph on the basis of motifs originating in Lurianic teaching. Cf. *Etz Ḥayyim, Sha'ar ha-'ibburim*, 1–2. These concepts, in turn, are based on *Zohar* 1, 3b, and 16b. R. Ya'akov specifies the biblical verses, with the mention of light that corresponds with each. Three additional levels of correspondence are indicated in the teachings cited below (the five periods from Adam to Jacob; the five "Makers" named in the midrash *Bereshit Rabba* 1.1; and the five corresponding *sefirot*). For the sake of coherence, I have not included them here.

4 *Mei ha-Shiloaḥ* 1, *Bereshit*, 10–11; *Beit Ya'akov* 1, *Bereshit* 7. Three of these stages are set out by R. Isaac Luria. R. Mordecai Joseph augments the process by discussing two more substages: *zeri'ah* (before *'ibbur*) and *yenikah* (after *leidah*), as R. Ya'akov notes.

5 Citing Tamar Ross, *Expanding the Palace of Torah: Orthodoxy and Feminism*, 190. Ross cites this as "one of the broader issues raised by feminist readings of the [biblical] text."

6 An extensive treatment of the three stages developed in Lurianic teaching (*'ibbur, leidah*, and *moḥin*), and some consideration of their presence in Hasidic thought, may be found in Mordecai Pachter's discussion, "*'Iggulim ve-Yosher,*" 59–90.

7 Among the authors who have addressed the theological questions at play here are Tamar Ross, Rachel Adler, Mary Ellen Ross, and Marcia Falk. My discussion seeks to address some of the issues they and others raise.

8 *Bereshit Rabba* 3.7; *Kohelet Rabba* 3.14. Cited in *Beit Ya'akov* 1, *Noaḥ* 2. My translation of the midrash follows Rashi. The following citations, until noted otherwise, are from this teaching.

9 In effect, this teaching as a whole reads the midrash as reflecting the basic Lurianic concept of "the breaking of the vessels." In the course of it, R. Ya'akov cites *Etz Ḥayyim, Sha'ar shevirat ha-kelim* as a source.

10 The work *yirah* is usually translated as "fear" or "awe." It is most often evoked in the context of sin (*yirat ḥet*), punishment (*yirat ha-'onesh*), and reverence before the divine (*yirat-shamayim* or *yirat ha-romemut*). The connection between *yirah* and the feminine is drawn already in rabbinic teaching. See, for example, B. *Berakhot* 33b and 61a on the verse (Isa. 33:6): "The fear of God is a storehouse/ granary."

11 *Beit Ya'akov* 2, *Beshallaḥ* 7. The allusion is to the verse (Prov. 1:8), "Hear, my child, the instruction *[mussar]* of your father, and do not abandon the teaching [torah] of your mother."

12 R. Ya'akov cites this phrase from J. *'Orlah*, 3 here and in many other teachings.

13 The rather innovative way R. Ya'akov puts it in Hebrew: אך מה הנאה יגיע להם מזה שהרי יכירו א״ע [את עצמם] שהם אותם עצמם ... שהרי הם כבריאה חדשה.

14 The "bitter" sense of betrayal audible in this cry comes to the fore in *Beit Ya'akov* 1, *Noaḥ* 1.

15 *Beit Ya'akov* 1, *Noaḥ* 2. Cf. *Midrash Tehillim* 75. In speaking of this idea, R. Ya'akov often recalls the Talmudic saying (B. *Gittin* 43a): "One cannot learn anything without failing first"—literally: "No one can 'stand' with words of Torah until one has 'stumbled' [*nikhshal*] from them."

16 *Beit Ya'akov* 1, *Noaḥ* 2.

17 In his words, *za'akatam hi hasharatam. Beit Ya'akov* 1, *Noaḥ* 2.

18 *Beit Ya'akov* 1, *Bereshit* 15.

19 It is R. Berekhiya, in the next line of this passage, who speaks of the "heart of stone" that must be reformed in times of national crisis, such as prolonged drought. R. David ben Naphtali Hirsch Frankel, author of the Talmudic commentary *Korban ha-'eidah*,

points out here that R. Simeon ben Lakish's statement pivots on the double meaning of the word *'ed*; in our verse it means "mist" yet it also signifies "catastrophe," as in the verse (Prov. 17:5), "One who rejoices in [another's] catastrophe will not go unpunished" שמח לאיד לא ינקה.

20 *Bereshit Rabba* 5.4. Perhaps these tears are what identify the "lower waters" with salt, the material distilled out of them and offered on the altar. Cf. Rabbeinu Baḥye on Lev. 2:13.

21 Note, though, that the gender differentiation appears already in the midrash. Cf. *Bereshit Rabba* 13.13: "R. Levi taught: The upper waters are masculine; the lower waters are feminine." But it is the kabbalistic term in Aramaic, *mayyin nukvin,* denoted with the letters מ"נ, that is most often used in Hasidic teaching.

22 *Beit Ya'akov* 2, *Yitro* 99.

23 Ibid. The imagery of the seed in reference to the Jewish experience in exile is first developed in R. Judah Halevi's *Kuzari,* 4.

24 *Beit Ya'akov* 2, *Shemot* 21, in reference to Exod. 1:15–20.

25 *Beit Ya'akov* 2, *Yitro* 99.

26 Levinas notes that such a gesture "embarrasses the traditional theology which treats of creation in terms of ontology" (*Totality and Infinity,* 293).

27 This is Levinas's description of Heideggerian Being from which, he insists, the "I" must be liberated (*Totality and Infinity,* 298).

28 Richard Cohen cites this as Levinas's homage to R. Ḥayyim of Volozhin, author of *Nefesh Ha-hayyim.* Cf. Introduction to *Time and the Other,* 24.

29 *Beit Ya'akov* 2, *Beshallaḥ* 5 (132, 135). The Talmudic reference concerning God's "reproach" to Moses records a telling moment: On high, Moses watches silently as God affixes "crownlets" to the letters of the Torah, semiotic signs loaded with hermeneutical and religious significance. Moses hesitates to offer words of encouragement, and this is what evokes God's reproach. By initiating a greeting—"Shalom"—Moshe would have "aided" God, as it were, in accomplishing the task. Cf. B. *Shabbat* 89a and Rashi there. In Lurianic teaching, this Talmudic passage is connected explicitly to the concept of "feminine waters." Cf. *Likkutei shas, Shabbat.*

30 *Beit Ya'akov* 2, *Shemot* 2: בהשי"ת העיקר הוא הכלים. In a kabbalistic tradition voiced by R. Isaiah Horowitz (*"Shlah"*), the crownlets are recognized as a symbol of the responsibility invested in the "lower" worlds to actualize their essential connection with the "letters"—their divine source. Cf. *Shnei Luḥot ha-Berit, Toledot Adam, Sha'ar ha-gadol* 13, citing *'Avodat ha-Kodesh* by R. Meir ibn Gabbay.

31 *Vayikra Rabba* 14.2. R. Ḥanina bar Papa refers to the possibility of *teshuvah*—repentance, or "return."

32 Cf. *Bereshit Rabba* 30.8. Maimonides develops this approach in *Mishneh Torah, Hilkhot 'avodat kokhavim* 1.3.

33 *Mei ha-Shiloaḥ* 1, *Tazria',* 109.

34 *Mei ha-Shiloaḥ* 1, *Lekh lekha,* 21. The reflexive is suggested in the phrase *lekh lekha*—the "going" is somehow connected with the self. Classical commentary does take note of it but in a more external sense, e.g., Rashi: "Go—for your good, for your own benefit." R. Mordecai Joseph's reading clearly reflects the principal innovation of the Przysucha school outlined in Chapter 2.

35 *Bereshit Rabba* 39.1.

36 *Beit Ya'akov* 1, *Lekh lekha* 2. The figure of Abraham as the first father of Jewish faith and the ultimate purpose of creation is a pillar of rabbinic teaching. See, for instance, *Bereshit Rabba* 12.9 on Gen. 2:4.

37 B. *Shabbat* 88b. We discussed other aspects of this passage in Chapter 1, with an eye to the nature and role of angels in Izbica-Radzyn teaching.

38 *Mei ha-Shiloaḥ* 1, 242–243.

39 *Mei ha-Shiloaḥ* 1, *Tazria',* 99. In the last line of this teaching, R. Mordecai Joseph alludes to the strange truth (supported by nature and *halakhah*) that a Jewish woman can bear children both like and radically unlike herself—female and male, "all possible goodness." The legal status of those children as Jews is determined according to the mother; and thus the very existence and survival of the Jewish nation depends on the capacity called the "feminine"—*ishah* or *nekevah.* See *Beit Ya'akov* 2, *Shemot* 22.

40 *Beit Ya'akov* 3, *Tazria'* 9.

41 *Beit Ya'akov* 3, *Tazria'* 5. The counterpoint of revelation and concealment that R. Ya'akov hears in the midrashic dialogue seems to be signaled in the formulation "I am he"—"I" is presence, while "he" is the stance of a hidden referent.

42 *Beit Ya'akov* 3, *Tazria'* 8. The identity between prayer, *nukba,* and the *sefirah* of *malkhut* is made in Lurianic teaching. Cf. *'Etz Ḥayyim* 1.8.

43 *Keneged* or *bimkom.* Cf. B. *Berakhot* 26a.

44 *Beit Ya'akov* 3, *Tsav* 6: *ki ha-korbanot be-makom tefillah.*

45 This subject was discussed extensively in Chapter 2.

46 These actions are prescribed in Lev. 6:3–4. Relevant rabbinic sources concerning the removal of the ashes from the altar (*dishun ha-mizbeaḥ*) are: B. *Yoma* 21–24; B. *Temurah* 34a; J. *Yoma* 2.4–5.

47 *Beit Ya'akov* 3, *Tsav* 12.

48 *Beit Ya'akov* 3, *Tsav* 11.

49 *Beit Ya'akov* 3, *Tsav* 14. R. Ya'akov cites Rashi, B. *Pesaḥim* 26a and *Pesikta zutrata, Tsav* as his sources. Rashi notes this as one of the miracles that regularly occurred in the Temple. The word *terumah* or *haramah* stems from the root meaning "to raise" or separate out as an offering.

50 *Beit Ya'akov* 3, *Tsav* 9. The three kinds of prayer outlined above are set out in this teaching. *Deshen* signifies fertility, "fatness." Its cognate is *shemen*; together these words allude to satiety.

51 In a number of teachings, R. Ya'akov speaks of the exhaustion and diminishment that come from this struggle. See, for instance, *Beit Ya'akov* 3, *Tsav* 14: בכל יום ויום מתגדל צעקתם כי הולכים ודלים. The intrinsic connection between *zeri'ah* and courage come to the fore, as R. Ya'akov sees it, in the structure of the *Amidah* prayer itself. The second of the 18 blessings, called *gevurot*, uses these very metaphors: God "sows" justice and "causes salvation to sprout"—*zore'a tzedakot, matzmiaḥ yesu'ot*.

52 *Beit Ya'akov* 3, Tsav 9.

53 *Beit Ya'akov* 3, Tsav 14. This motif and "response" appear, in varied formulations, in this teaching and in *Beit Ya'akov* 3, Tsav 9. In the last teaching in *Beit Ya'akov* on this subject, R. Ya'akov notes that the role of the *Kohen* in gathering up the ashes is symbolically fulfilled by God Himself in "gathering up" all those prayers left behind. Cf. *Beit Ya'akov* 3, *Tsav* 19. On the Name EHYEH see below.

54 B. *Yoma* 20a, cited in *Beit Ya'akov* 3, *Tsav* 9.

55 Cf. *Beit Ya'akov* 3, *Tsav* 15, citing B. *Yoma* 22a: *Terumat ha-deshen* is: סוף עבודה דימָמא דאתמול ותחילת עבודה דיום מחר.

56 *Beit Ya'akov* 3, *Tsav* 16. On the concept of night, see Chapter 1.

57 *Zohar* 3. 11a. In kabbalistic teaching, this Divine Name designates the first and highest *sefirah* called *keter 'elyon*, often called "the unknowable place"—*'atar de-lo etyad'a*. Cf. R. Joseph Gilatilla, *Sha'arei Orah, sha'ar* 10. This passage, on R. Ya'akov's reading, with its three mentions of this Name, sets out three successive stages of revelation. They are introduced in the phrases "in the beginning," "later on," and "as for the last."

58 *Beit Ya'akov* 3, *Tazria'* 3. Many of the ideas in the following pages first found expression in my essay, "Exodus and the Feminine in the Teachings of R. Yaakov of Izbica," 447–470.

59 *Beit Ya'akov* 2, *Shemot* 21.

60 R. Ya'akov discusses this paradox in *Beit Ya'akov* 2, *Shemot* 45.

61 Cited in English translation of Gaston Bachelard, *On Poetic Imagination and Reverie*, 16.

62 *Mei ha-Shiloaḥ* 1, *Bereshit*, 12. R. Mordecai Joseph's explanation of *bohu* is drawn from the reading in *Sefer ha-Bahir* 17, cited also in *Hashmatot le-Zohar* 1.263: *bo-hu* literally means "he [some unknown entity] is in there" בוהו—בו הוא.

63 *Beit Ya'akov* 1, *Bereshit* 5. On "the deep" as a storehouse of the future, see, for example, *Beit Ya'akov* 1, *Bereshit* 23.

64 Compare the discussion of imagery made by Gaston Bachelard, *The Poetics of Space*, 183–210. There he uses the phrases "most secret regions" and "immense intimacy."

65 *Beit Ya'akov* 1, *Bereshit* 6.

66 *Likkutei Torah, Ki Tissa, d.h. hinei*. The concept first appears in *'Etz Ḥayyim* 1.2. The interpretation of *makom* developed here seems to be based on the rabbinic idea: *hu mekomomo shel 'olam* … Cf. *Bereshit Rabba* 68.9.

67 *Beit Ya'akov* 1, *Bereshit* 6.

68 Ibid., *Lekh lekha* 44.

69 The "cleft in the rock" in the passage in Exodus merges with a second and similar account involving the prophet Elijah in 1 Kings 19. There the cave is mentioned explicitly; the rabbis draw the two incidents together in B. *Megillah* 19b, cited by R. Ya'akov in the teaching above. An explicit reference to the cave as symbolizing "the mystery of pregnancy" or *sod ha-'ibbur* is made by R. Zaddok Ha-Kohen of Lublin, *Kedushat Shabbat* 7, 59. R. Ya'akov does not use this term, but the imagery is clearly there; this will become more evident below.

70 Cf. B. *Berakhot* 7a.

71 *Mei ha-Shiloaḥ* 1, *Ki tissa,* 96; *Beit Ya'akov* 4, *Ki tissa,* 52. The counterreading in these teachings reflects the *Targum Yerushalmi* on this verse.

72 B. *Berakhot* 28–29b, cited in *Beit Ya'akov* 2, *Mishpatim* 33.

73 *Beit Ya'akov* 2, *Ki tissa* 53. *Hester pannim,* literally a "hiddenness of the face," describes a subjective sense of abandonment when God's "countenance of favor" is figuratively concealed.

74 These reflections on the rabbinic needlework metaphor and its implications appear in *Beit Ya'akov* 1, *Lekh lekha* 44.

75 *Beit Ya'akov* 2, *Ki tissa* 55. Citing B. *Sotah* 45b. Based on *Mei ha-Shiloaḥ* 1, *Va-yetse',* 41. See also *Mei ha-Shiloaḥ* 1, *Mishlei,* 221.

76 *Beit Ya'akov* 2, *Bo* 5. R. Mordecai Joseph's comments on this verse appear in *Mei ha-Shiloaḥ* 2, *Kohelet* 136.

77 R. Ya'akov cites Rashi in *Beit Ya'akov* 1, *Noaḥ* 1. A literal translation of the whole verse would render *ha-yeled ha-sheini* as "the second child," the successor of a "first child" who came before him. Clearly, though, in Izbica-Radzyn teaching, the verse speaks of one single individual. Cf. *Beit Ya'akov* 1, *Bereshit* 27.

78 *Bereshit Rabba* 30.8. The midrash names four other figures who also experienced dramatic trials of fortune—Moses, Joseph, Mordecai, and Job. The "new world" they saw similarly reflects a basic evolution in each one's sense of self.

79 B. *Hagigah* 12a, cited in *Beit Ya'akov* 1, *Noaḥ* 4.

80 *Beit Ya'akov* 1, *Noaḥ* 19. The verse cited resonates with the description of Noah's retreat into the ark. In effect, Noah's righteousness or lack thereof is a disputed point in rabbinic tradition and classical commentary.

81 *Beit Ya'akov* 4, *Noaḥ* 6.

82 *Beit Ya'akov* 1, *Noaḥ* 19. The Rabbis speak of Noah's sleeplessness and silence in *Tanḥuma, Bereshit* 9. R. Ya'akov offers this unusual feminine imagery without elaboration. The Lurianic mystical teaching of *sod ha-'ibbur* in relation to Noaḥ is set out in detail by R. Yitzḥak Isaac Ḥaver, *Pitḥei She'arim, Netiv partzuf nukva de-ze'ir anpin, petaḥ* 5.

83 *Beit Ya'akov* 1, *Noaḥ* 1.

84 Ibid., *Noaḥ* 19.

85 Cf. Gen. 9:20–27. The midrash *Tanḥuma, Bereshit* 11 cites this verse, "Free me from the prison of my soul" (Ps. 142:8) as Noaḥ's prayer.

86 *Beit Ya'akov* 1, *Noaḥ* 45.

87 Ibid., *Noaḥ* 40, after Isa. 54:9.

88 *Mei ha-Shiloaḥ* 1, *Hayyei Sarah,* 31. The verse from Isaiah is cited in the Talmud B. *Pesaḥim* 88b as the ultimate mandate for procreation.

89 *Beit Ya'akov* 1, *Toledot* 3. Compare *Toledot* 18 and 19. We might note that the phrase R. Ya'akov uses, "avoid all doubt," was in fact coined by the Rabbis as good advice. See *Mishnah Avot* 1.16.

90 *Beit Ya'akov* 1, *Toledot* 20. R. Ya'akov does point out here that underlying this similarity was a certain opposition. In kabbalistic terms, Isaac is "strict judgment," *dina kashya,* while Rebecca is "mild judgment," *dina rafya.* Cf. *Zohar* 1. 137a.

91 *Beit Ya'akov* 4, *Toledot,* 14, citing *Zohar* 2. 123b. An important pretext that plays this kabbalistic ideal against the evolving Hasidic ethos is R. Elimelekh of Lyzansk's reading of these verses. See *Noam Elimelekh, Toledot.* This early and classic Hasidic commentary doubtless guides R. Ya'akov's reading.

92 *Zohar* 1. 134a and 1. 249a. R. Ya'akov cites these two passages together in *Beit Ya'akov* 1, *Toledot* 2, 3, 4, 5, 6, and 7.

93 *Beit Ya'akov* 1, *Toledot* 3.

94 Ibid., *Toledot* 6.

95 R. Ya'akov cites the passage from the Talmud in *Beit Ya'akov* 1, *Toledot* 17, 18, 20, and 21. He cites the passage from the *Zohar* (1. 137a) in *Toledot* 19.

96 *Beit Ya'akov* 1, *Toledot* 21.

97 Ibid.

98 Ibid., *Toledot* 8.

99 Ibid., *Toledot* 22. The Aramaic phrase R. Ya'akov uses, *mai nafka mina,* literally, "what will come of it," frequently appears in Talmudic parlance to question the logical "outcome" of a given contention. In the context of this teaching, the phrase becomes immediate and literal.

100 Ibid., *Toledot* 22.

101 Ibid.

102 Ibid., citing *Zohar* 1.15a.

103 Ibid., *Bereshit* 6. A more literal translation of "to be for the world" would be "to affect or give abundance to the world." The reasons for the phrase I chose will, I hope, soon become clear.

104 *Totality and Infinity,* 105.

105 *Beit Ya'akov* 1, *Bereshit* 23.

106 Ibid., *Bereshit* 6.

107 *Beit Ya'akov* 2, *Bo* 59. The plain reading of the verse is clearly that "the firstborn [*peter reḥem*] ... is Mine"—the possessive referring not to the "opening of the womb" but to its issue, the newborn male.

108 *Beit Ya'akov* 2, *Bo* 59. The connection between these qualities and the feminine is a standard element of mystical teaching.

109 B. Niddah 30b, cited in *Beit Ya'akov* 1, *Bereshit* 27.

110 B. *Berakhot* 8b.

111 *Beit Ya'akov* 1, *Bereshit* 27.

112 This interpretation appears in the note handwritten on the page this teaching appears (*Beit Ya'akov* 1, Jerusalem, 1998), 19.

113 *Beit Ya'akov* 3, *Beḥukkotai* 13.

114 Ibid., *Tazria'*, 1.

115 *Vayikra Rabba* 27.7. In labor, in Rabbinic Hebrew, a woman "sits on the birthstool" *al ha-mashber;* in modern Hebrew the word *mashber* designates a crisis situation.

116 *Mei ha-Shiloaḥ* 1, *Tazria'*, 110.

117 *Sod Yesharim, Rosh Hashanah* 95, citing *Tikkunei Zohar* 22a.

118 See *Mei ha-Shiloaḥ* 1, *Tazria'*, 110.

119 St. John Perse, *Elogés and Other Poems,* translated by Louise Varese (New York: W. W. Norton, 1944), 62. Cited by Bachelard, *On Poetic Imagination and Reverie,* 61.

120 Cf. B. *Bekhorot* 6b; On the connections between milk, whiteness, and *ḥesed,* see, for example, R. Moses Ḥayyim Luzzatto on Lamentations 2:19.

121 *Beit Ya'akov* 1, *Lekh lekha* 47. This teaching seems to be inspired by Rashi's commentary on Deut. 32:11.

122 Ibid., *Vayeḥi* 1; see also *Beit Ya'akov* 2, *Yitro* 41. In another teaching, R. Ya'akov uses the metaphor to speak of the understanding of Torah that God grants to scholars. See *Beit Ya'akov* 3, *Beḥukkotai* 28.

123 *Beit Ya'akov* 1, *Lekh lekha* 45, citing Rashi on Gen. 17:1. D. W. Winnicott develops his concept of the "good-enough mother" and her continuous, active adaptation to the infant's needs in *Playing and Reality,* 10–11, etc.

124 *Beit Ya'akov* 1, *Vayeḥi* 72. See also *Beit Ya'akov* 2, *Vaera* 1.

125 *Mei ha-Shiloaḥ* 1, *Vayeshev* 29.

126 *Beit Ya'akov* 1, *Noaḥ* 4.

127 *Beit Ya'akov* 1, *Lekh lekha* 47.

128 *Beit Ya'akov* 2, *Pekudei* 50.

129 *Beit Ya'akov* 2, *Pekudei* 50. The allusion in this passage to the fundamentally asymmetrical relationship between mother/teacher and child/student is from B. *Pesaḥim* 112a: "More than the calf desires to suckle, the cow desires to give." R. Ya'akov seems to allude here to what every nursing mother knows: the mere thought of her baby can cause milk to come.

130 *Beit Ya'akov* 1, *Toledot* 50.

131 B. *Ḥagigah* 12a.

132 *Beit Ya'akov* 2, *Vayera* 3 (pp. 48, 50).

133 *Beit Ya'akov* 2, *Ki tissa'* 33: דאָם הוא המידה שמשתדלת תמיד בשביל ישראל.

134 *Mei ha-Shiloaḥ* 1, pp. 10–11. See n. 4 above.

135 R. Ya'akov recalls this fifth stage in an innovative re-reading of *Bereshit Rabba* 1.1. See *Beit Ya'akov* 1, *Bereshit* 1.

136 Cf. *Sifra, Beḥukkotai* 1 on Lev. 26:3.

137 *Mei ha-Shiloaḥ* 2, *Beḥukkotai*, 87–88. The prooftexts alluded to in this teaching will be considered below.

138 *Mei ha-Shiloaḥ* 2, *Beḥukkotai*, 87, based on *Vayikra Rabba* 25. Contentions such as this about the relativity inherent in halakhic practice are considered one of the "radical" aspects of Izbica teaching. On antinomianism and related issues in that regard, see Chapter 2.

139 *Mei ha-Shiloaḥ* 2, *Beḥukkotai*, 87.

140 *Beit Ya'akov* 3, *Beḥukkotai* 24, citing *Berakhot* 3b and the wonder voiced by the Rabbis themselves.

141 *Beit Ya'akov* 3, *Beḥukkotai* 2. He quotes B. *'Avodah zarah* 5a.

142 Cf. Franz Rosenzweig's description of the soul's prayer as "the cry of an open question." *Star of Redemption*, 185.

143 B. *Berakhot* 7a.

144 *Beit Ya'akov* 3, *Beḥukkotai* 21, after B. *Shabbat* 89b.

145 Cf. Michael Fishbane's explanation: "... the word *kivyakhol* ... this term introduces a blatant anthropopathism into the midrash and signals an implicit *al tiqre* [*do not read* this *but* that] hermeneutic." "Extra-Biblical Exegesis: The Sense of Not Reading in Rabbinic Midrash," 29.

146 D. W. Winnicott, *Playing and Reality*, 97–108. My gratitude to Avivah Gottlieb Zornberg who first introduced me to Winnicott's thought and to this concept in particular.

147 Winnicott, pp. 89, 97.

148 *Beit Ya'akov* 3, *Beḥukkotai* 18.

149 *Beit Ya'akov* 3, *Beḥukkotai* 24. The reference is to *Tikkunei Zohar* 66b, after B. Sanhedrin 99b.

150 R. Ya'akov borrows the image of the torch from B. *Pesaḥim* 8a in the teaching just cited.

151 In his commentary on this verse, Rashi speaks of "laboring [*'amelim*] in Torah learning." On the connection to "well-kneaded dough" [*pat 'amelah*], see B. *Pesaḥim* 37a. R. Ya'akov mentions this association in *Beit Ya'akov* 3, *Beḥukkotai* 18 and 24.

152 *Beit Ya'akov* 3, *Beḥukkotai* 21.

153 *Beit Ya'akov* 3, *Beḥukkotai* 4, 5.

154 *Beit Ya'akov* 3, *Beḥukkotai* 12. In this and many other teachings, R. Ya'akov draws on certain kabbalistic concepts to construct his understanding of this *sidrah*. *Parashat Beḥukkotai* is the thirty-third *sidrah* of the Torah. This corresponds, within the model of the 50 permutations of the seven *sefirot* from *ḥesed* to *malkhut*, with the permutation

hod she-be-hod. The role of the feminine in this context is alluded to in the *Zohar* 3. 280a which R. Ya'akov cites.

155 *Beit Ya'akov* 3, *Beḥukkotai* 81. The notion of what people might say appears in B. *Bava Kama* 50a.

156 The qualities he names belong to the lexicon of kabbalistic symbolism. The "masculine" and the "feminine" are commonly juxtaposed in fundament dialectical relationships, such as *ḥesed/gevurah, raḥamim/din, ahavah/yirah.* Compare the passage from *Zohar* 3, 65a below.

157 See, for example, R. Joseph Gikatilla, *Sha'arei Orah, sha'ar* 8.

158 *Zohar* 3, 65a-b. My translation is based on David Goldstein's translation of the *Zohar* passage in Tishby, *The Wisdom of the Zohar* 1:344–345, with some changes.

159 On the division of the text into these two sections, see the passage from *Vaykira Rabba* cited below.

160 *Vayikra Rabba* 35.1.

161 *Beit Ya'akov* 3, *Beḥukkotai* 88. The text that longs to be re-ordered seems to allude to Deut. 23:6. "The Lord your God turned the curse into a blessing." Compare *Beit Ya'akov* 4, *Ḥukkat,* 87.

162 *Beit Ya'akov* 3, *Beḥukkotai* 97.

163 *Beit Ya'akov* 3, *Beḥukkotai* 15.

164 *Beit Ya'akov* 3, *Beḥukkotai* 91. This inherent multiplicity of aspects is hinted in the Hebrew word for face, *pannim*—the plural form of *pan,* or "aspect."

165 Compare *Beit Ya'akov* 1, *Bereshit* 11. Here, the same statement is cited, but its source is noted as *Sefer Raziel, Sitrei otiot.* The reference seems to be to *Sefer Raziel ha-Malakh* (first published from earlier manuscripts in Amsterdam in the late 17th or early 18th century). The introduction of that ancient mystical text, identified with *heikhalot* or *merkavah* mystical traditions, states that Adam was give *Sefer Raziel* as he was expelled from the Garden of Eden.

166 For that reason, R. Ya'akove explains, "If one swallows the *maror* (bitter herbs) of the Pesaḥ seder without chewing it, one has not fulfilled the mitzvah related to that symbolic action (B. *Pesaḥim* 115b). Bitterness must be felt, confronted, and crushed. Only then can it be "sweetened," i.e., transformed into a positive, constructive part of human experience. Cf. *Beit Ya'akov* 3, *Beḥukkotai* 90; *Beit Ya'akov* 4, *Pesaḥ,* 122, citing Lurianic teaching.

167 *Beit Ya'akov* 3, *Beḥukkotai* 74. Compare *Mei ha-Shiloaḥ* 2, *Naso,* 91 on the verse "May God shine His countenance"—"May God reveal His hidden secrets/side [*sitro*], 'that He speaks only peace for His people'" [Ps. 85:9].

168 Compare Levinas, *Totality and Infinity,* 94. His words shed much light on R. Ya'akov's teaching.

169 Winnicott, *Playing and Reality,* 118. This expression appears in the context of Winnicott's reinterpretation of Lacan's mirror stage in ego development.

170 Cited in note 4 above.

171 Thus Franz Rosenzweig concludes his work: "The Star of Redemption is become countenance, which gazes at me and out of which I gaze." *Star of Redemption*, 423.

172 Cf. B. *Ḥagigah* 2a: כדרך שבא לראות כך בא ליראות.

173 *Beit Ya'akov* 2, *Ki tissa* 66. את פני היינו שאתה בעצמך הוא פני ה׳ כשה״כ (תהילים מ״ב) מתי אבוא ואראה פני אלקים שאני בעצמו אהיה פני אלוקים כמו נאמר (שם ס״ז) יאר פניו אתנו ולא כתוב אלינו רק אתנו.

174 The connection between the rainbow and a human face is suggested in B. *Ketubot* 77b. The link between the face of R. Simeon bar Yoḥai, the rainbow, and "the face of the Master" is explicit in *Zohar* 2. 38a.

Chapter 4

1 *Beit Ya'akov* 2, *Shemot* 36. "For My preciousness …" is a phrase from the midrash *Pirkei de-Rabbi Eliezer* 40. מאי יקרא אית בגוה.

2 B. *Shabbat* 30b.

3 *Beit Ya'akov* 2, *Ki tissa* 26.

4 Rashi, in contrast, neutralizes the opposition between "middle" and "beginning/end": if the latter are true, all the more so are the contents as a whole (*lo kol she-ken*). B. *Shabbat* 30a.

5 *Beit Ya'akov* 2, *Ki tissa* 26. Cf. Maimonides, *Perush ha-Mishnayot*, ch. 10–11. Maimonides' formulation of this principle, more precisely, is *ayno guf*. In *Beit Ya'akov* 2, *Terumah* 48 R. Ya'akov addresses Maimonides' classical view of the (inferior) body and (superior) intellect directly. As we will see, he seeks to dismantle this traditional hierarchy.

6 Maurice Blanchot, *The Space of Literature*, 138, quoting Rilke.

7 Gaston Bachelard, *The Poetics of Space*, 5.

8 *Beit Ya'akov* 3, *Shemini* 53.

9 R. Ya'akov points out here this double meaning of the word *ḥanukkah*—inauguration—and education, or *ḥinukh*: "Just as we educate the young … to teach them a new order of things …." *Beit Ya'akov* 3, *Shemini* 53.

10 *Beit Ya'akov* 2, *Ve-yak'hel* 22. Compare Chapter 3, where this experience is discussed in relation to pregnancy and birthing.

11 That is, כי כל הציונים יתמלאו לעתיד עם חיים.

12 *Beit Ya'akov* 3, *Tsav* 1, citing *Zohar* 2, 108a as a prooftext. The intrinsic linguistic connection here is between Zion (*tziyyon*) and "sign" (*tziyyun*).

13 *Beit Ya'akov* 3, *Tsav* 1, citing *Zohar* 2, 108a–b: יתחבר כלא בחיבורא חדא.

14 ויהא שמא שלים בכל תקוניה.

15 Walter Benjamin, "On Language as Such and the Language of Man," 324 and 318. This is Benjamin's seminal essay on these subjects, first published in 1919. Susan Handelman's

discussion of signs and naming in the thought of Benjamin, Gershon Scholem, and Emmanuel Levinas in *Fragments of Redemption* is enlightening on many of these issues.

16 I've quoted the midrash with the ellipses that appear in this teaching. In the *Tanḥuma* (S. Buber edition), as in R. Ya'akov's citation of it, the Name of God that Adam pronounces is designated with the Hebrew letter *heh*. Another version of the midrash (*Bereshit Rabba* 17.4) records the Name that Adam pronounces as Adonai, literally, "My absolute master." The traditional reading of the sign ה׳, however, is *Hashem*, literally, "the Name." In the course of his teaching, R. Ya'akov favors this reading over that of *Bereshit Rabba*. Many thinkers have pondered the latter puzzling act of naming. See, for instance, R. Moses Alsheikh on Gen. 2:19–20; Rabbeinu Baḥya, Gen. 2:19; Malbim on Isa. 42:8.

17 Some lines earlier, the verse the Rabbis place in the mouths of the protesting angels is "What is humankind, that You should be mindful of them…." Cf. B. *Shabbat* 88b, and discussion in Chapter 1.

18 *Bereshit Rabba* 17.4.

19 B. *Nedarim* 20b.

20 *Beit Ya'akov* 3, *Tsav* 1.

21 The term is borrowed from Lurianic mysticism (cf. *Etz Ḥayyim* 13.1.49), although R. Ya'akov's use of it is somewhat different.

22 As Susan Handelman comments regarding Benjamin's theory, "So Adam the name-giver and not Plato is the real father of philosophy." *Fragments*, 138.

23 Benjamin links this deterioration to "the Fall": after Adam sinned in the Garden of Eden, the pure language of names and language itself become instrument, "mere" signs. R. Ya'akov does not recognize the same causality.

24 *Zohar* 2. 108b. Cited by R. Ya'akov in *Beit Ya'akov* 3, *Tsav* 1.

25 This and subsequent verses adamantly resist attempts toward a gender-neutral translation. "Man" here is *ha-adam;* that word should perhaps be rendered "humankind." The continuation would then be "in the image of God He created **it**." In the following pages, I've chosen, in general, to cede to the non-gender-neutral JPS translation. Considerations are stylistic and, to an extent, ideological: my goal here as always is to offer translations that reflect R. Ya'akov's reading most coherently.

26 "Two worthy likenesses"—*tarin dioknin tavin. Zohar* 3. 122b.

27 *Zohar* 1. 120a. For a scholarly analysis of the theory of the tzelem developed in the *Zohar*, see Tishby and Lachower, *The Wisdom of the Zohar* 2: 770–773; G. Scholem, *Levush ha-Neshamot ve-Ḥaluka de-Rabbanan* (Tarbiz, 1955). It appears that R. Ya'akov adopts and alters the view of the *Zohar* considerably in accordance with his own agenda.

28 *Beit Ya'akov* 3, *Tsav* 3. "Images/shadows"—here R. Ya'akov uses the word *tzelalim* (shadows) rather than the plural form of *tzelem*. In effect, the *Zohar* does sometimes identify the image with the shadow. His intent, however, does not seem to be to speak of shadows specifically, but rather to avoid using the word *tzelamim* with its connotations of idolatry.

29 In Chapter 3 we considered some of the emotional valences of that term, drawn from rabbinic and kabbalistic thought.

30 See Chapter 2 for some consideration of these important themes in Izbica-Radzyn teaching. As we noted there, most scholars who have studied the Izbica-Radzyn school have channeled their energies to analyzing these issues.

31 *Mei ha-Shiloaḥ* 1, *Bereshit*, 15.

32 The vastly more elegant and succinct original reads: מאן דנפח מעצמו נופח וכח הפועל בנפעל. *Sefer ha-Kanah* is an early kabbalistic work. R. Ya'akov cites this statement in a number of teachings. For more on this idea in mystical tradition, see Moshe Hallamish's essay, "*Le-Mekoro shel Pitgam be-Sifrut ha-Kabbalah: 'Kol ha-Nofe'aḥ—mi-Tokho Hu Nofe'aḥ*.'"

33 *Mei ha-Shiloaḥ* 2, *Bereshit*, 15.

34 The notion of two countenances is mentioned in the Talmud, B. *Berakhot* 61a; *'Eruvin* 18a and is developed extensively in kabbalistic teaching. R. Ya'akov's son, R. Gershon Ḥanokh Henikh, devotes a great deal of attention to this motif in his teachings in *Sod Yesharim* on Rosh Hashanah.

35 *Beit Ya'akov* 1, *Bereshit* 61. On this gender distinction, see below.

36 *Beit Ya'akov* 1, *Bereshit* 60 and *Beit Ya'akov* 4, *Va-etḥanan*, 106. R. Ya'akov alludes here to three rabbinic teachings. B. *Ḥagigah* 12a on Adam's panoramic being; B. *Shabbat* 87a—each commandment filled the world with scent, and God summoned the wind to drive it away so that the next commandment could have "room"; B. *Pesaḥim* 5a on the additional letter *vav* in the second Tablets.

37 *Beit Ya'akov* 2, *Yitro* 86. What R. Ya'akov indicates here, I think, is the psychological dimension of the actions each of these commandments names. Their intent is to rein in natural human tendencies, not to vitiate them entirely. As he says in another teaching, "Do not kill" in the absolute sense means to feel no anger, ever. This, clearly, is beyond the power of any human being. *Beit Ya'akov* 4, *Va-etḥanan*, 106.

38 B. *Rosh Hashanah* 27a, cited in *Beit Ya'akov* 1, *Bereshit* 67, 68.

39 *Zohar* 3.92b. Cited in *Beit Ya'akov* 1, *Bereshit* 68.

40 *Beit Ya'akov* 1, *Bereshit* 68. To understand (*lehavin*) seems to imply a rebuilding as well, as in the phrase *va-yiven et ha-tzel'a*—God's reconstructing Adam's rib in the form of Eve (Gen. 2:22).

41 *Beit Ya'akov* 1, *Bereshit* 61. The parallel between the *sefirah* of *hokhmah*/"father," and *binah*/"mother" is standard kabbalistic terminology. The syntax of this sentence, modeled on the syntax of the verse, is surely deliberate.

42 "As it says in *Peri 'Etz Ḥayyim, Rosh Hashanah,* 3 ..." (The passage appears in some editions at the end of chapter 2.)

43 *Beit Ya'akov* 1, *Bereshit* 60. His allusion here as well is to an important kabbalistic concept. Its roots are in the Talmud. Cf. B. *Hagigah* 13b. Compare R. Moses Ḥayyim Luzzatto, *Sefer Kin'at Hashem Tzeva'ot*, 123, *inyan ha-keruvim*.

44 The issues of sin and free will in Izbica-Radzyn teaching have been discussed extensively, most recently by Maggid, *Hasidism on the Margin*, chap. 4, and Faierstein, *All Is in the Hands of Heaven.*

45 *Mei ha-Shiloaḥ* 1, *Bereshit,* 15. R. Ya'akov cites this teaching in *Beit Ya'akov* 1, *Bereshit* 60.

46 *Totality and Infinity,* 304.

47 *Beit Ya'akov* 4, *Bereshit,* 4.

48 *Mei ha-Shiloaḥ* 2, *Bereshit,* 14.

49 R. Ya'akov refers to B. *Kiddushin* 71a: the four-letter Name, termed in Hebrew "the explicit Name" (*ha-shem ha-meforash*), was revealed or pronounced weekly in the Temple service. Its revelation testified to familial lineage (*yiḥus*)—that is, to personal, genealogical roots. On the vital importance in R. Ya'akov's teaching of guarding this sense of lineage, see Chapter 2.

50 *Beit Ya'akov* 1, *Bereshit* 64. In his reference to the verse from Psalms, R. Ya'akov reverses the sequence of events apparent on the usual reading. Cf. JPS translation: "For You, O Lord, when you were pleased, made [me] firm as a mighty mountain. When You hid Your face, I was terrified." The phrase "make a guard to [His] guard" refers to the interdiction Eve "adds" to the commandment (Gen. 3:3): "It is only about the fruit of the tree in the middle of the Garden that God said, "You shall not eat of it *or touch it,* lest you die." In rabbinic usage, the expression "make a guard to [His] guard" usually refers to the constructive role of rabbinic law to enact measures to prevent the transgression of biblical laws. See, for instance, Lev. 18:30 as it is cited in B. *Yevamot* 21a. R. Ya'akov clearly alters this plain sense.

51 *Beit Ya'akov* 1, *Bereshit* 66. R. Ya'akov refers once again to the Lurianic teaching cited above, *Peri 'Etz Ḥayyim, Rosh Hashanah* 3.

52 *Beit Ya'akov* 1, *Bereshit* 61. The same expression "I had to eat" appears in *Bereshit* 70.

53 *Midrash Tehillim* 92, cited in *Bereshit* 61. In this teaching, however, R. Ya'akov shifts the plain sense of the midrash. In the midrash, Adam refers to death. He recognizes that he is responsible, by incurring the punishment for eating of the tree, for making mortality a human reality.

54 *Beit Ya'akov* 1, *Bereshit* 66. The "first generation" he speaks of is apparently not only the human players Adam and Eve. We saw similar reflections regarding the "worlds created and destroyed" before this, our world, came into existence. See Chapter 1 and Chapter 3.

55 *Mei ha-Shiloaḥ* 2, *Bereshit,* 14. The talmudic phrase אוקירו לנשייכו echoes the notion of "preciousness" or *yekar* considered below.

56 *Beit Ya'akov* 1, *Bereshit* 67. A similar teaching appears in *Beit Ya'akov* 4, *Bereshit* pp. 4–5.

57 *Mei ha-Shiloaḥ* 2, *Bereshit,* 12.

58 Ibid., 15–16. He cites *Zohar* 3.83a and *Etz Ḥayyim* (היכל ו, שער מ״ן ומ״ד, דרוש א).

59 *Mei ha-Shiloaḥ* 2, *Mishpatim,* 54–55: והיינו שבבואו לעה״ז בלבוש הזה היה לתקן חטאו.

60 *Mei ha-Shiloaḥ* 2, *Bereshit,* 12–13.

61 Two sources suggest that reading: Onkelos translates "garments of skin" with the Aramaic phrase *levushin di-yekar—yekar* meaning honor or preciousness. The midrash (*Bereshit Rabba* 9.5) records that "in the (personal) Torah scroll owned by R. Meir it was found to be written "garments of light."

62 *Mei ha-Shiloaḥ* 2, *Bereshit*, 13, and *Beit Ya'akov* 1, *Bereshit* 68. This view of the body's instrumental role is articulated already by R. Sa'adia Gaon. *Sefer Emunot ve-De 'ot* 6.4.

63 *Beit Ya'akov* 2, *Tetsavve* 37.

64 *Beit Ya'akov* 2, *Tetsavve* 32.

65 He refers to the esoteric ways of writing out YHVH in expanded form, known as *miliu*. The name of each of the four Hebrew letters that composes that appellation is written out as the letter is pronounced. One of these permutations is known as "the forty-five letter Name" [שם מ"ה]. The numerical value (*gematria*) of *Ḥavva*, 19, equals the sum of those "filling in" vowels. Absent from this sum are the first letters themselves—YHVH = 26. YHVH, as we saw above, is the aspect of divine presence that became concealed with the sin. Thus, the *miliu* is all that remains. Cf. *Beit Ya'akov* 1, *Bereshit* 61, 67, 68, etc., citing *Likkutei Torah, Bereshit,* and the source of this theme in *Tikkunei Zohar* 65, fol. 96b.

66 *Beit Ya'akov* 2, *Ki tissa* 72.

67 *Zohar* 3, 66b, cited in *Beit Ya'akov* 4, 106.

68 See note 1 of this chapter.

69 *Beit Ya'akov* 1, *Va-yeḥi* 38. In the standard edition, this teaching is misnumbered 35. References in the next few pages unless noted otherwise refer to this teaching.

70 This concept comes to the fore in the writings of other Hasidic thinkers as well, most notably R. Judah Leib Alter of Ger, known as *Sefat Emet*. In the wake of his grandfather, R. Isaac Meir (*Ḥiddushei ha-Rim*), the *Sefat Emet* stresses the uniquely Jewish aspect of this "inner point." Mendel Piekarz traces the historical evolution of this important subject in *Ha-nekudah ha-penimit ezel Admorei Gur ve-Alexander,*" 617–660. Arthur Green touches on it in *The Language of Truth,* xxvii–xxix; lvi; and notes 50, 54, and 55.

71 R. Ya'akov cites Ps. 31:6.

72 *Zohar* 1, 83a. קוסטא דחיותא. The midrashic version of this concept is the *luz*—an indestructible bony element in the spine. Cf. *Bereshit Rabba* 69.8. R. Ya'akov mentions it in *Beit Ya'akov* 1, *Vayetse'* 57, 58.

73 *Tanna de-Vei Eliyahu Rabba* 18.

74 In the course of this teaching (*Beit Ya'akov* 1, *Vayeḥi* 38), R. Ya'akov cites sources from the Talmud attesting to all these qualities. Cf. B. *Sotah* 49b, B. *Bava Batra* 123a. Cf. *Beit Ya'akov* 1, *Noaḥ* 24, where the same motifs appear.

75 R. Ya'akov cites *Zohar* 1.85b; 2.146b; 2.259b. The same view is basic to Jewish medieval thinkers such as R. Sa'adia Gaon and Maimonides. For a general discussion of the body-soul relationship in Jewish tradition, see Moshe Hallamish, *An Introduction to Kabbalah,* chap. 13.

76 As Tishby (*Wisdom of the Zohar*) writes: "The Zohar stresses the fact that the divine soul is the essence of man, and that his body is but an outer garment that has no relevance at all to his fundamental human nature" (2: 680). "The duality of soul and body, as two elements hostile to one another, is frequently mentioned in the Zohar, and the soul is therefore depicted as an exile or fugitive in this world" (2: 683). "Even though the Zohar's idea of the nature of the body from the point of view of good and evil is not absolutely clear, there is no doubt that the body is see as the abode and the foundation of man's evil inclinations" (2: 767).

77 *Beit Ya'akov* 2, *Terumah* 48. R. Ya'akov's grammatically incorrect reference here to the body (*guf*) in the feminine (*hu ha-mashgiaḥ shelah*) seems to indicate the gender issues implicit in the mind-body relationship he describes.

78 Isadore Twersky, *Introduction to the Code of Maimonides* (*Mishneh Torah*), 43. Cf. *Mishneh Torah, Hilkhot Teshuvah* 8.2 and critique by R. Abraham ben David of Posquieres (*Rabad*). Maimonides' famed self-defense is formulated in his *Treatise on Resurrection* (*Ma'amar Teḥiyyat ha-Metim*), written in 1191.

79 A literal reading of this verse understands these times of "finding" in a passive sense. Seforno, for instance, explains that at the first signs that misfortune has "found" one, prayer is required to prevent a flood of suffering from striking. On the Rabbis' reading, though, the person of faith must be a "finder." Circumstances can challenge one to set out in search; prayer is needed to navigate one toward success.

80 *Beit Ya'akov* 1, *Ḥayyei Sarah* 2. These textual associations appear in *Mei ha-Shiloaḥ* 1, 30. R. Ya'akov expands on the themes set out there.

81 B. *Berakhot* 28b, cited in *Beit Ya'akov* 1, *Ḥayyei Sarah* 2.

82 That is, *metzia ba-a be-heseḥ ha-da'at*. B. *Sanhedrin* 97a.

83 *Beit Ya'akov* 1, *Ḥayyei Sarah* 4.

84 *Beit Ya'akov* 1, *Ḥayyei Sarah* 2.

85 *Beit Ya'akov* 1, *Ḥayyei Sarah* 31. The experience of "sojourning" for a fleeting lifetime in this world is hinted, on this reading, in the word ***megur****ekhah*. It evokes the association of fear, uncertainty, and resulting anxiety, or **magor.**

86 *Beit Ya'akov* 1, *Toledot* 13. His unusual formulation of the last sentence in this passage reads in Hebrew: **שזה עיקר תחיית המתים שהגוף עצמו יהיה ויכיר את עצמו שהוא הוא שהיה כבר ולא יהיה כבריה חדשה.**

87 Taylor, *Sources of the Self*, 130.

88 Using very similar reasoning, Jan Patochka, in his conception of the body as "personal situation," contests Cartesian "pure thinking" and, similarly, the "objectifying understanding" proposed by Kant as well as Husserl. Cf. *Body, Language, Communication, World*, editor's note by James Dodd, xv–xxviii.

89 Taylor points out that Augustine himself stressed the etymological link between cognition and the notion of "gathering" in *Confessions* X.xi.18. Cf. Taylor, *Sources of the Self*, 539, n. 4.

90 B. *Sanhedrin* 91a. A similar statement appears in B. *Ketubot* 111a: "The righteous will rise in their garments (*be-levusheihem*)."

91 *Sod Yesharim al ha-Torah,* vol. 2, *Va-etḥanan,* 346. On the more conventional reading of this rabbinic statement, it is not the deceased themselves, but others who must recognize them. See, for example, Naḥmanides, *Sha'ar Ha-gemul;* R. Moses of Trani (*Hamabit*), *Beit Elohim, Sha'ar ha-yesodot,* chap. 59.

92 R. Ya'akov frequently makes idiosyncratic use of the rabbinic expression כמה הרפתקי דעדו עלייהו (B. Kiddushin 33a) in this psychological sense. I hope the notion of "vagaries of fortune" captures it well enough.

93 *Beit Ya'akov* 2, *Yitro* 122.

94 *Beit Ya'akov* 2, *Shemot* 42. "World of truth" is a rabbinic formulation posed in contrast to our "lower world of phenomenon" know as "the world of falsehood," *'alma de-shikra.*

95 Most commentators distinguish between Abraham's complete faith and Sarah's inferior ability to trust in God, hence God's "anger" directed to Sarah (Gen. 18:15). Contrast R. Ya'akov's twofold defense of Sarah in this teaching (*Beit Ya'akov* 1, *Va-yera'* 21, p. 145): he equates her inner state with that of Abraham, and identifies her "error" only in claiming to know the hidden reaches of her husband's heart. (That is, her intuition was correct but presumptuous.)

96 *Beit Ya'akov* 1, *Va-yera'* 21. A second important issue is raised in this context, on the basis of R. Mordecai Joseph's teaching in *Mei ha-Shiloaḥ* 1, *Va-yera',* 27. It concerns the conviction for which Izbica-Radzyn Hasidism is perhaps most (in)famous. "All is in the hands of heaven, even the fear of heaven"—that is, free choice truly does not exist. This formulation is in oblique reference to the rabbinic statement (B. *Berakhot* 33b): "All is in the hands of heaven except the fear of heaven." On the antinomian aspects of this issue, see Faierstein's insights in *All Is in the Hands of Heaven;* Magid, *Hasidism on the Margin,* 142, n.12; and references in Chapter 2 above.

97 R. Ya'akov mentions these elements in the course of the same teaching, *Beit Ya'akov* 1, *Va-yera'* 21. He recalls, in addition, the motif of "sowing" (*zeri'ah*) in connection with Isaac (see Chapter 3) and with resurrection, as we saw some pages earlier in this chapter.

98 *Beit Ya'akov* 1, *Va-yera'* 21. Throughout this teaching R. Ya'akov refers to the dead in the singular (*ha-met*). The English language seems to have no one-word equivalent for this singular form and so I preferred the (less personal but more convenient) plural.

99 In *Beit Ya'akov* 2, *Mishpatim* 46, R. Ya'akov suggests the connection between hope (*tikvah*) and line (*kav*). The image may be inspired by the expression *tikvat ḥut ha-shani,* "cord of crimson thread," in Joshua 2:18. R. Moses Ḥayyim Luzzatto offers a beautiful discussion of this motif in *Derush be-inyan ha-kivui.* Many of R. Ya'akov's insights resonate with Ramḥal's conception of hope.

100 It seems to be more than a coincidence that the Aramaic word *garmei* [גרמי], like its Hebrew equivalent *etzem,* means both bone and essence.

101 *Beit Ya'akov* 1, *Va-yera'* 21.

102 *Beit Ya'akov* 1, *Va-yera'* 40. R. Ya'akov cites B. *Sanhedrin* 97: Three things will come "when the mind is suspended"; the Messiah is one of them. The tone of this teaching is unusually emotional; it ends with a prayer [אכי"ר]. I've combined some of the expressions he uses in stressing these ideas to condense his message into a coherent whole.

103 *Beit Ya'akov* 1, *Va-yera'* 43. R. Ya'akov borrows this imagery of west and east from B. *Shabbat* 156a, on the basis of Isa. 41:2.

104 *Bereshit Rabba* 78.12. A "simple man"—*'ama de'ar'a*. The encounter between Jacob and Esau he refers to is told in Gen. 33:1–11.

105 The passive formulation "was brought" sounds awkward; more natural would be "I have brought."

106 *Beit Ya'akov* 1, *Va-yishlaḥ* 36. The notion of "missing the mark" [מחטיא] refigures "sin" [חטא] itself. A reference is offered in this teaching to another teaching by R. Ya'akov in *parashat Re'eh,* one of the volumes of *Beit Ya'akov* lost in the Holocaust. Compare the reading of the reconciliation between Joseph and his brothers developed in Izbica-Radzyn tradition discussed in Chapter 2. See especially *Mei ha-Shiloaḥ* 1, *Va-yiggash,* 55–56.

107 *Beit Ya'akov* 1, *Va-yishlaḥ* 37. This conviction comes to the fore in other contexts as well, most notably after the incident of the Golden Calf. Cf. *Beit Ya'akov* 2, *Ki tissa* 52: "Deep down, Israel did not sin.... Even as they did that deed ... their intent and desire was for the glory of Heaven." R. Ya'akov cites *Mei ha-Shiloaḥ* 1, *Ki tissa*, 95.

108 *Beit Ya'akov* 1, Va-yishlaḥ 39. אני מוכרח להתנהג עם הדעת של כל אחד ואחד ואין ביכולתי למנוע השגחתי מקניני אף משה אחד רגע אחד. I've interpolated the handwritten comment in the margin of this teaching (Jerusalem, 1998) 297.

109 *Beit Ya'akov* 1, *Hayyei Sarah* 4, after 2 Sam. 14:14 and a rich mystical tradition on that verse.

Bibliography

Note: The works listed below are works cited in this volume. Primary sources, such as the Talmud, midrashim, kabbalistic works, Bible commentaries, and works of medieval Jewish thought are not listed here. Publishing information refers to editions used in preparation of this volume. First editions are provided only for Izbica-Radzyn works. This list is not meant to represent a comprehensive bibliography of Hasidic or scholarly works.

Hasidic Sources

Aaron ben R. Tzvi Hirsch of Opatow, ed. *Keter Shem Tov* (The teachings of R. Israel Baal Shem Tov). Brooklyn: Kehot, 1987.

Alexander Zusha of Plozk. *Kol Simḥah*. Breslau, 1859.

Alter, R. Abraham Issakhar Benjamin. *Me'ir 'Eynei ha-Golah*. Piotrokov, 1928–1932.

Berger, R. Israel. *Ma'amarei Simḥah*. Piotrokov, 1911.

Borenstein, R. Samuel of Sochaczow. *Shem mi-Shmuel*. 8 vols. Jerusalem, 1992.

Goldhaber, R. Elḥanan Reuven Goldhaber, and R. Judah Joseph Spiegelman, eds. and annotators. *Beit Ya'akov al ha-Torah, Sefer Bereshit*. Bene-Berak: Machon le-Hotza'at Sifrei Raboteinu ha-Kedoshim mi-Izbica-Radzyn, 2006.

Jacob Joseph of Polonnye. *Toledot Ya'akov Yosef*. Jerusalem, 1973.

Lainer, R. Yeruḥam of Radzyn. *Ma'amar Zikaron la-Rishonim*. New York: Y. Lainer, 1950; Jerusalem: Y. Lainer, 1997.

Leiner, R. Gershon Ḥanokh Henikh. *Ha-Hakdamah ve-ha-Petikhah le-Beit Ya'akov* ("Introduction to *Beit Ya'akov*"). In *Beit Ya'akov al-ha-Torah, Sefer Bereshit*. Jerusalem, 1998.

———. *Sha'ar ha-'Emunah ve-Yesod ha-Ḥasidut: Hakdomah u-Fetaḥ ha-Sha'ar le-Beit Ya'akov* ("Introduction to *Beit Ya'akov*"). Ed. and annotated by

R. Elḥanan Reuven Goldhaber and R. Judah Joseph Spiegelman. Bene-Berak: Machon le-Hotza'at Sifrei Raboteinu ha-Kedoshim mi-Izbica-Radzyn Hasidei Radzyn, Torat Avraham, 1996.

———. *Sifrei ha-Tekhelet.* Ed. R. Elḥanan Reuven Goldhaber and R. Judah Joseph Spiegelman. Bene-Berak: Machon le-Hotza'at Sifrei Raboteinu ha-Kedoshim mi-Izbica-Radzyn, Torat Avraham, 1999.

———. *Sod Yesharim al ha-Torah.* Vol. 1. Brooklyn: M.Y. Lainer, 1971; Vol. 2, *Sod Yesharim al ha-Torah* (*Tinyana*). Brooklyn: M.Y. Lainer, 1982.

———. *Sod Yesharim: Rosh Hashanah, Yom Kippur, Sukkot.* Warsaw: M.Y. Halter, 1902; Brooklyn: M.Y. Lainer, 1992.

———. *Sod Yesharim: Purim, Pesaḥ.* Piotrokov: Zederbaum, 1905; Brooklyn: M.Y. Lainer, 1992.

Leiner, R. Ḥayyim Simḥah. *Dor Yesharim.* Lublin: N. Nershenhern et. al., 1909; Lublin: Druk Ressemedjanzs, 1925; Jerusalem: Y. Lainer, 1997.

Leiner, R. Mordecai Joseph. *Mei ha-Shiloaḥ.* 2 vols. Vol. 1, ed. R. Gershon Ḥanokh Henikh, Vienna, 1866. Vol. 2, ed. R. Mordecai Joseph of Lublin, Lublin, 1922. Republished by R. Elḥanan Reuven Goldhaber and Judah Joseph Spiegelman. Bene-Berak: Machon le-Hotza'at Sifrei Raboteinu ha-Kedoshim mi-Izbica-Radzyn, Torat Avraham, 1991.

Leiner, R. Mordecai Joseph Elazar. *Tiferet Yosef.* Brooklyn: Y. Lainer, 1992.

Leiner, R. Ya'akov. *Beit Ya'akov al ha-Torah.* 4 vols. *Beit Ya'akov 'al ha-Torah, Sefer Bereshit* [Genesis]. Warsaw, 1891; Jerusalem: M.Y. Lainer, 1998. *Beit Ya'akov 'al ha-Torah, Sefer Shemot* [Exodus]. Lublin: n.p., 1904; Jerusalem: M.Y. Lainer, 1998. *Beit Ya'akov 'al ha-Torah, Sefer Vayikri* [Leviticus]. Lublin: n.p. 1937; Jerusalem: M.Y. Lainer, 1998. *Beit Ya'akov 'al ha-Torah 'im Sefer ha-Zemanim 'al Ḥag ha-Shavu'ot.* Jerusalem, 1976; Jerusalem, 1997.

———. *Sefer ha-Zemanim 'al Haggadah shel Pesaḥ.* Lublin, 1903.

———. *Sefer ha-Zemanim 'al Ḥag ha-Shavu'ot.* Lublin, 1906.

Lipman, R. Elimelekh of Lyzansk. *No'am Elimelekh.* Jerusalem, 1987.

Rabinowitz, R. Zaddok Ha-Kohen of Lublin. *Divrei Sofrim.* Bene-Berak, 1973.

———. *Likkutei 'Amarim.* Bene-Berak, 1973.

———. *Poked 'Akarim.* Bene-Berak, 1973.

———. *Takkanat ha-Shavim.* Bene-Berak, 1973.

———. *Yisrael Kedoshim.* Bene-Berak, 1973.

Rakatz, Yoetz Kim Kadish. *Siaḥ Sarfei Kodesh.* Lodz, 1928–1931.

———. *Tiferet ha-Yehudi.* Piotrokow, 1912.

Samuel of Sieniawa (Shinav). *Ramatayim Tzofim* in *Tanna de-Vei Eliyahu Rabba.* Jerusalem, 2003.

Twerski, R. Menaḥem Naḥum of Chernobyl. *Meor Einayim*. Jerusalem, 1999.
Walden, Aaron. Editor with notes and commentary. *Kol Simḥah*. Ra'anana, 1998.
———. Editor with notes and commentary. *Ramatayim Tzofim* in *Tanna de-Vei Eliyahu Rabba*. Jerusalem, 2003.
———. *Shem ha-Gedolim he-Ḥadash*. Warsaw, 1864; Jerusalem, 1990.
Yustman, R. Pinḥas Menaḥem Elazar of Piltz. *Siftei Tzaddik*. Jerusalem, 1957–1964.

Secondary works

Abrams, Daniel. "Knowing the Maiden without Eyes." *Daat* 50–52 (2003): lix–lxxxiii.
Altman, Alexander. "The Delphic Maxim in Medieval Islam and Judaism." In *Studies in Religious Philosophy and Mysticism*, 1–40. Ithaca, N.Y.: Cornell University Press, 1969.
Arendt, Hannah. *The Human Condition*. Chicago: University of Chicago Press, 1998.
Bachelard, Gaston. *On Poetic Imagination and Reverie*. Trans. Colette Gaudin. Dallas: Spring Press, 1971.
———. *The Poetics of Space*. Trans. Maria Jolas. Boston: Beacon Press, 1969.
Benjamin, Walter. "On Language as Such and the Language of Man." In *Reflections: Essays, Aphorisms, Autobiographical Writings*, ed. Peter Demetz and trans. Edmund Jephcott. New York: Shocken, 1978.
———. "The Task of the Translator." In *Illuminations*, ed. Hannah Arendt and trans. Harry Zohn, 69–82. New York: Shocken, 1969.
Bergson, Henri. *The Creative Mind*. Trans. M. Andison. New York: Philosophical Library, 1945.
Blanchot, Maurice. *The Space of Literature*. Trans. Ann Smock. Lincoln: University of Nebraska Press, 1982.
Brill, Alan. "Grandeur and Humility in the Writings of R. Simhah Bunim of Przysucha." In *Hazon Nahum: Studies in Jewish Law, Thought, and History*, ed. Yaakov Elman and Jeffrey Gurock, 419–448. New York: Yeshiva University Press, 1997.
Chalier, Catherine. *Figures du feminin: Lecture d'Emmanuel Levinas*. Paris: La Nuit Surveillee, 1982.
Cohen, Richard. Translator's Introduction to *Time and the Other*, 1–27. Pittsburgh: Duquesne University Press, 1995.

Dynner, Glynn. *Men of Silk: The Hasidic Conquest of Polish Jewish Society.* Oxford: Oxford University Press, 2006.

Elior, Rachel. "Izbica." In *The Oxford Dictionary of the Jewish Religion,* ed. Zvi Weblowsky and Geoffrey Wigoder. New York: Oxford University Press, 1997.

———. "*Temurot be-Maḥshavah ha-Datit be-Ḥasidut Polin—Bein 'yirah' ve-'ahavah' le-"omek' ve-'gavan'*" ("The Innovations of Polish Hasidism—From Love and Fear to Depth and Variety"). In *Tarbiz* 62 (1993): 381–432.

Faierstein, Morris. *All Is in the Hands of Heaven: The Teachings of Rabbi Mordecai Joseph Leiner.* Hoboken: Ktav, 1989. 2d ed., Piscataway, New Jersey: Gorgias Press, 2005.

———. "Personal Redemption in Hasidism." In *Hasidism Reappraised,* ed. Ada Rapoport-Albert, 214–224. London: Littman Library, 1996.

Fishbane, Michael. "Extra-Biblical Exegesis: The Sense of Not Reading in Rabbinic Midrash." In *The Garments of Torah: Essays in Biblical Hermeneutics,* 19–32. Bloomington and Indianapolis: Indiana University Press, 1989.

Fuchs, Uziel. *Mi-meni Yatzu Kevushim—'Al Ma'amar Talmudi she-Huga.*" In *Teshurah le-'Amos,* ed. Moshe Bar Asher, Noaḥ Ḥakham, and Yosef 'Ofer, 521–531. Alon Shvut: Tevunot, 2007.

Gellman, Jerome. "The Denial of Free Will in Hasidic Thought." In *Freedom and Moral Responsibility: General and Jewish Perspectives,* ed. C. H. Manekin, 111–131. Bethesda: University Press of Maryland, 1997.

———. *The Fear, the Trembling, and the Fire: Kierkegaard and Hasidic Masters on the Binding of Isaac.* Lanham, Maryland and London: University Press of America, 1994.

Goetschel, Roland. "Sha'ar ha-Emunah we-Yesod ha-Hasidut and Maimonides." In *Daat* 64–66 (2009) xxvii-xxxv.

Green, Arthur. *The Language of Truth.* Philadelphia: The Jewish Publication Society, 1998.

Gries, Ze'ev Gries. "The Hasidic Managing Editor as an Agent of Culture." In *Hasidism Reappraised,* ed. Ada Rapoport-Albert, 141–155. London: Littman Library, 1996.

Hallamish, Moshe. *An Introduction to Kabbalah.* Trans. Ruth Bar-Ilan and Ora Wiskind-Elper. Albany: Southern University of New York Press, 1999.

———. "*Le-Mekoro shel Pitgam be-Sifrut ha-Kabbalah: 'Kol ha-Nofe'aḥ—mi-Tokho Hu Nofe'aḥ.'*" Bar Ilan 13 (1976): 211–223.

Handelman, Susan. *Fragments of Redemption.* Bloomington: Indiana University Press, 1991.

Heschel, Abraham Joshua. *A Passion for Truth*. New York: Farrar, Straus and Giroux, 1973.

Levin, Judah Leib. *Ha-Admorim mi-Izbica*. Jerusalem, n.p., n.d.

Levinas, Emmanuel. "The Old and the New." In *Time and the Other (and Other Essays)*, 121–138. Trans. Richard A. Cohen. Pittsburgh: Duquense University Press, 1995.

———. *Time and the Other (and Other Essays)*. Trans. Richard A. Cohen. Pittsburgh: Duquesne University Press, 1995.

———. *Totality and Infinity: An Essay on Exteriority*. (1961) Trans. Alphonso Lingis. Pittsburgh: Duquesne University Press, 1969.

Levinger, Ya'akov. "*'Imrot Authentiot she ha-Rebbi mi-Kotsk*" ("Authentic Sayings of R. Menaḥem Mendel of Kotsk"). *Tarbiz* 55, no. 1 (1985): 109–135.

———. "*Torato she ha-Rebbi mi-Kotsk le-Or ha-'Imrot ha-Meyuḥasot Lo 'al yedei Nekhdo R. Shmuel mi-Sochaczow*" ("The Teachings of the Kotsker Rebbe according to His Grandson R. Samuel Bornstein of Sochaczow"). *Tarbiz* 55, no. 3 (1986): 413–431.

Magid, Shaul. *Hasidism on the Margin: Reconciliation, Antinomianism, and Messianism in Izbica/Radzin Hasidism*. Madison: University of Wisconsin Press, 2003.

———. "'A Thread of Blue': Rabbi Gershon Henoch Leiner of Radzyn and His Search for Continuity in Response to Modernity." *Polin* 11 (1998): 31–52

Nadler, Allan. Book review of *Hasidism on the Margin: Reconciliation, Antinomianism, and Messianism in Izbica/Radzin Hasidism* (by Shaul Magid). *The Jewish Quarterly Review*, 96, no. 2 (Spring 2006): 276–282.

Pachter, Mordecai. "*Iggulim ve-Yosher: Le-Toldote'a shel Idea (Mi-Kabbalat ha-Ari 'ad ha-Rav Kook).*" *Daat* 18 (1987): 55–90.

———. "'*Katnut' ve-'Gadlut' be Kabbalat ha-Ari.*" In *Lurianic Kabbalah*, ed. Rachel Elior and Yehudah Liebes, 171–210. Vol. 10, *Meḥkarei Yerushalayim be-Maḥshevet Yisrael*. Jerusalem: Hebrew University n.p., 1992.

Patochka, Jan. *Body, Community, Language, World*. Ed. James Dodd. Trans. Erazim Kohak. Chicago: Open Court, 1998.

Piekarz, Mendel. "*Ha-nekudah ha-penimit ezel Admorei Gur ve-Alexander …*" In *Meḥkarim be-kabbalah, be-philosophia yehudit uve-sifrut ha-mussar ve-hehagut*, ed. Joseph Dan and Joseph Hacker 617–660. Jerusalem: Magnes, 1987.

Rilke, Rainer Maria. *Duino Elegies*. Trans. J. B. Leishman and Stephen Spender. New York: W. W. Norton and Company, 1939.

———. *Sonnets to Orpheus*. Trans. M. D. Herten Norton. New York: W. W. Norton, 1942.

Rabinowitz, Tzvi Meir. *R. Ya'akov Yitzhak mi-Przysucha, Ha-yehudi ha-kadosh*. Tel Aviv: Zioni, 1960.
Rosen, Michael. *The Quest for Authenticity: The Thought of Reb Simhah Bunim*. Jerusalem and New York: Urim, 2008.
Rosenzweig, Franz. *The Star of Redemption*. (1930) Trans. William W. Hallo. Notre Dame, Ind. and London: University of Notre Dame, 1970.
Rosman, Moshe. *Founder of Hasidism: A Quest for the Historical Baal Shem Tov*. Berkeley: University of California Press, 1996.
Ross, Tamar. *Expanding the Palace of Torah: Orthodoxy and Feminism*. Hanover, N.H.: Brandeis University Press, 2004.
Safran, Bezalel. "Maharal and Early Hasidism." In *Hasidism—Continuity or Innovation?* Cambridge, Mass.: Harvard University Press, 1988.
Schatz-Uffenheimer, Rivka. "*Autonomia shel ha-Ru'aḥ ve-Torat Moshe*" ("Autonomy of the Spirit and the Torah of Moses"). *Molad* 4 (1964) 554–561.
Seeman, Don. "Martyrdom, Emotion and the Work of Ritual in R. Mordecai Joseph Leiner's Mei Ha-Shiloah." *AJS Review* 27, no. 2 (2003): 253–280.
Shragai, S. Z. *Be-Heikhal Izbica-Lublin*. Jerusalem, 1977.
———. *Be-Netivei Ḥasidut Izbica-Radzyn*. 2 vols. Jerusalem, 1972.
———. *Be-Ma'ayanei Ḥasidut Izbica-Radzyn*. Jerusalem, 1980.
———. "*Ḥasidut ha-Ba'al Shem Tov be-Tefisat Izbica-Radzyn*." In *Sefer Baal Shem Tov*, 153–201. Jerusalem: Mosad Harav Kook, 1960.
Taylor, Charles. *Sources of the Self: The Making of the Modern Identity*. Cambridge, Mass.: Harvard University Press, 1989.
Tishby, Isaiah, and Fischel Lachower. *The Wisdom of the Zohar*. 3 vols. Trans. David Goldstein. Oxford and London: Oxford University Press, 1991.
Twersky, Isadore. *Introduction to the Code of Maimonides (Mishneh Torah)*. New Haven, Conn.: Yale University Press, 1980.
Weiss, Joseph. "A Late Jewish Utopia of Religious Freedom." (original German, 1964). In *Studies in Eastern European Jewish Mysticism*, ed. David Goldstein . London and Portland: Littman Library, 1997.
———. "*Torat ha-determinism ha-dati le-R. Joseph Mordecai Lerner (!) mi-Izbica.*" In *Sefer Yovel le-Yitzhak Baer*. 447–453. Jerusalem: Ha-ḥevra ha-historit ha-Israelit, 1960.
Wilensky, Mordecai. *Hasidim u-Mitnagdim*. Jerusalem: Bialik, 1970.
Winnicott, D. W. *Playing and Reality*. London and New York: Routledge, 1989.
Wiskind-Elper, Ora. "Exodus and the Feminine in the Teachings of R. Yaakov of Izbica." In *Torah of the Mothers*, 447–470. Ed. Ora Wiskind-Elper and Susan Handelman. Jerusalem: Urim Publications, 2000.

Index